Cities and states developed in South Asia between c. BC 800 and AD 250, as Hinduism and Buddhism arose and spread. Drawing on archaeological studies and also on texts and inscriptions, this book explores the character of the early Indian cities, paying particular attention to their art and architecture and analysing the political ideas that shaped the state systems. The authors chart the development of the settlement pattern in the Ganges valley through the rise of cities and the formation of the Mauryan empire and its successor states. They also trace the spread of cities and states throughout South Asia to the opening centuries of the Christian era, offering an Indian perspective on the contacts with the Greek and Roman worlds that followed the invasion of Alexander the Great.

THE ARCHAEOLOGY OF EARLY HISTORIC SOUTH ASIA

THE ARCHAEOLOGY OF EARLY HISTORIC SOUTH ASIA

THE EMERGENCE OF CITIES AND STATES

F. R. ALLCHIN

Emeritus Reader in Indian Studies, University of Cambridge

With contributions from George Erdosy, R. A. E. Coningham,
D. K. Chakrabarti and Bridget Allchin

CAMBRIDGE
UNIVERSITY PRESS

Published by the Press Syndicate of the University of Cambridge
The Pitt Building, Trumpington Street, Cambridge CB2 1RP
40 West 20th Street, New York, NY 10011–4211, USA
10 Stamford Road, Oakleigh, Melbourne 3166, Australia

First Published 1995

Printed in Great Britain at the University Press, Cambridge

A catalogue record for this book is available from the British Library

Library of Congress cataloguing in publication data

Allchin, F. Raymond (Frank Raymond), 1923–
The archaeology of early historic South Asia: the emergence of cities and states /
F. R. Allchin; with contributions from G. Erdosy ... [*et al.*]
    p.   cm.
Includes bibliographical references and index.
ISBN 0 521 37547 9. – ISBN 0 521 37695 5 (pbk.)
1. South Asia – Antiquities.
2. Excavations (Archaeology) – South Asia.
I. Erdosy, George.   II. Title.
DS338.A45   1995
934–dc20   94–23181   CIP

ISBN 0 521 37547 9 hardback
ISBN 0 521 37695 5 paperback

CONTENTS

FIGURES

PREFACE

The emergence of cities and their distinctive culture in early historic South Asia offers a subject of peculiar interest for the archaeologist. This is not least because it presents us with a view of the antecedents of a living civilization which still confronts us. A vague but distinct awareness of this struck me on my first visit to India fifty years ago, and gradually took root as familiarity grew and knowledge developed. In due course the idea of this book arose as a natural consequence. As time went by I became increasingly conscious of the difficulty and complexity of the task, partly because of the unevenness of so much of the available evidence, and partly because of the diversity of the source materials.

The first concrete plan for the book was drawn up in the mid-eighties. Around that time several of my research students had taken up topics relating to early historic urbanism; and several younger colleagues visited Cambridge, some of whom were to become involved in the work. Among them was Dr George Erdosy whose PhD research from 1982–86 was on the early cities of the Ganges valley; in 1986 Dr Makkhan Lal, whose monograph on the settlement history and rise of civilization in the Ganga-Yamuna Doab had been published in 1984, visited Cambridge as an Ancient India and Iran Trust–Wallace India Trust Visiting Fellow; so too in the following year did Dr Dilip Chakrabarti. Research interests in Sri Lanka during the late eighties provided a further stimulus, and led to my offering a paper on the rise of cities in South Asia for a Cultural Triangle conference at Habarana in 1988.

A firm proposal for the book was put before the Cambridge University Press in 1986. As by then only three years remained before my retirement, I thought it sensible to speed the work by involving several younger people. Sadly, good schemes are apt to go awry, and what was conceived as a means of speeding the work turned out to be a cause of protracted delay! In the end I found myself writing twice as many chapters as I had originally intended and bringing in a further contributor. The manuscript was completed by the end of 1993.

Certain features may be noted. The book is primarily intended as a synthesis: as such its focus shifts between significant early observations, sometimes from very early reports, for example by Colin Mackenzie or Cunningham, and research which is still very much in progress. We have tried to integrate narrowly archaeological data with the wider aspects of historical archaeology, including textual, epigraphic, numismatic and art-historical evidence. In our view all these subjects are components of an early historic civilization; and their associated techniques have been regarded in Indian archaeology as elements of the methodology of early historic archaeology; just as they have in Greek or Roman archaeology. How far we have succeeded is for the reader to judge.

Multiple authorship

The resulting book is a composite work, in which rather more than two thirds are my own and the remaining third is the work of four other authors. The main task of editing has been to try and make an integrated volume. One aspect of composite authorship is that individuals remain just that! It has been my aim to allow as much freedom as possible to the other authors. At times this results in different views on a subject being expressed in different places, for example, by myself and Erdosy in chapters 3 and 4 on the one hand, and 6 on the other. Such differences are most often of interpretation rather than of substance. As such they constitute a necessary and useful part of the dialectic of archaeological interpretation; and serve a constructive role in giving perspective to the ongoing debate. For instance, it seems perfectly reasonable that there should be different views on the way in which the Indo-Aryan languages gained dominance and spread throughout so large a part of South Asia, or on the use of the term ethnicity. In any event, such differences seem small by comparison with the broad agreement which attends the main thrust of our book. Another aspect of composite authorship is that inevitably there are some overlaps between chapters. These arise for a number of reasons: the imprecision of the dating of some of the archaeological and even more of the historical sources; because the same topics may be used or approached by different authors from different points of view, and so on.

A quite unforeseen consequence of multiple authorship was that, while the manuscript was actually in press, Dr George Erdosy requested us to adopt his recently changed name (Dr Muhammad Usman Erdosy). After much thought and consultation we decided that we should retain his original name throughout this book, believing that what was begun under one name should be finished under it, and that this would be helpful to readers wishing to consult his other writings.

Transliteration

Our aim throughout has been, as far as possible, to standardize the transliteration of Indian words, names and terms. The principle I have used is to follow the accepted transliteration, as agreed by the International Congress of

Orientalists at Athens in 1912, but wherever possible to exclude all diacritical marks: thus we generally write the Sanskrit and Prakrit *rājā* as *raja* or raja, *Pāṇini* as Panini, and *Aṣṭādhyāyī* as Astadhyayi. Such words are given in the index with their proper transliteration and full diacritical marks. Some sections are exceptions to this convention. In parts of chapters 6 and 7 involving the discussion of matters relating to the Late Vedic literature we have retained the diacritical marks.

A special note is called for concerning the spelling of the word Kharosthi (*Kharoṣṭhī*), in view of there being no consensus on its usage. In early sources *Kharostī*, *Kharoṣṭī*, *Kharoṣṭhī* and *Kharostrī* are found, but it is not clearly established which form is the earliest or historically the best. Recently Professor B. N. Mukherjee has argued in favor of *Kharoṣṭī*, against the more general acceptance (*Kharoshṭī and Kharoshṭi-Brāhmī Inscriptions in West Bengal*, India Museum: Calcutta, 1990). For guidance I sought the views of Professor Sir Harold Bailey, who drew my attention to a short discussion in his *Indo-Scythian Studies*, vol. VII, (Cambridge: Cambridge University Press, 1985, 46–49). Although I do not follow the form he suggests (*Kharostrī*), the upshot of the discussion seems to be that the choice remains an arbitrary one, and thus I decided to follow what appears to be the more commonly used form.

ACKNOWLEDGEMENTS

I am grateful to a number of persons and institutions for their advice and support and for giving permission to use illustrations. Professor Romila Thapar gave me very positive advice, pointing out some pitfalls to be avoided in connection with Chapter 4, and discussing a number of other things; Dr Janet Ambers of the British Museum Radiocarbon Laboratory gave assistance and advice on questions of calibration of radiocarbon dates; Dr Ranabir Chakravarti kindly read through the draft of Chapter 13 and offered a number of helpful suggestions and comments; Dr M. C. Joshi offered encouragement and advice while he was Director General of Archaeology in India; Dr S. P. Gupta gave a speedy and generous response to my plea for assistance in obtaining photographs; and others helped in various ways: Dr B. M. Pande; Dr K. N. Dikshit; Dr J. C. Harle; Mr J. R. Knox; Mr John Guy; Dr Andrew Topsfield; Dr Gustav Roth and Shri Rajendra Prasad helped me to obtain photographs from the Patna Museum; my grandson Benjamin Zeitlyn helped with a number of the drawings.

The following have been kind enough to permit the use of copyright illustrative materials, as acknowledged in the figure captions: Mr L. N. Rangarajan for a number of the illustrations from his translation of the Arthasastra; Dr George Michell; Dr Javed Husain; the Archaeological Survey of India; the Faculty of Oriental Studies, Cambridge for permission to use materials from the Wheeler Archive; the Curator of the Patna Museum; the Curator of the Mathura Museum; Prithivi Prakashan, Varanasi; the Director of the National Museum, New Delhi; the Trustees of the British Museum; the Director of the Victoria and Albert Museum; the Director of the Ashmolean Museum, Oxford.

I would like to thank my fellow authors, Bridget Allchin, Dilip Chakrabarti, George Erdosy and Robin Coningham, not only for their contributions but for the extent to which they have offered criticism and advice. I also wish to acknowledge the excellent work of Sal Garfy who drew all the principle maps.

I gratefully acknowledge a grant from the Fellows Research Fund of Churchill College Cambridge towards travel expenses of a visit to Delhi when postal means appeared unlikely to produce required photographs.

Finally let me make a very special mention of Bridget Allchin who gave me extraordinary help and support, tolerating and even making good my protracted neglect of other work and putting up with my absorption in the final stages of the book. Without her support it would have been difficult to reach completion.

PART I

THE BACKGROUND

CHAPTER 1

THE ARCHAEOLOGY OF EARLY HISTORIC SOUTH ASIA

F. R. ALLCHIN

The aim of this book is to review the broad developments leading up to and attending the emergence of cities and states in South Asia, and to the formation of what we may call an Indian urban style of life and culture. Our approach will be primarily archaeological, but we shall also take into account such textual, inscriptional or other evidence as available and relevant to our aim. We shall use a definition of archaeology that is rather wider than is common today, but one which has emerged over the past two centuries of research on early India. This definition accepts as ancillary party of early historic archaeology such subjects as: domestic architecture, city planning and the construction of secular and religious monuments; the development of various branches of art including sculpture and painting; epigraphy and the early use of writing in South Asia; the standardization of weights and measures and the use of coinage. We accept all these as relevant to our subject and as contributing to building up a balanced picture of early historic Indian civilization. We consider them to be as much fit subjects of archaeological investigation as are the more fashionable aspects of the subject. Another feature of our study is that it seeks to adopt an international approach, treating South Asia as a whole (i.e. India, Pakistan, Bangladesh, Sri Lanka and Nepal), rather than restricting our scope to a single country or region. This is probably the first time that such a broad overview has been attempted. In this context we should remark that Afghanistan is for the most part treated as peripheral to South Asia. We shall on occasion refer to such cities as Kandahar, Begram or Ai Khanum, but rather as comparisons for South Asian cities than as integral parts of South Asia.

At the outset we must make another point regarding this book. Although our subject deals centrally with the emergence of cities and states in South Asia, it is not our aim to offer definitions of these and other such terms, nor to become involved in lengthy discussions of matters of archaeological theory. Rather it offers a primarily descriptive account of the emergence of South Asian cities and states, attempting to integrate the several categories of evidence mentioned above.

The subject of this book, *Early historic South Asia, the emergence of cities and states*, is one which has been hitherto largely neglected. The late A. Ghosh, the first Director General of Archaeology in independent India, was the first archaeologist to produce a monograph on *The City in Early India* (1973). To date there are few comparable works: T. N. Roy's *The Ganges Civilization* (1983) is an invaluable and detailed study of the material culture of 'the painted grey ware and northern black polished ware periods in the Ganga plains', but its somewhat restricted geographical horizon, its focus on specifically archaeological data, and its limited concern with many questions of wider interpretation, make it less helpful for our purpose than it might otherwise have been. Two other recent studies, using settlement archaeology as their base, deserve mention: they are Makkhan Lal's *Settlement History and the Rise of Civilization in the Ganga-Jamuna Doab* (1984) and G. Erdosy's *Urbanisation in Early Historic India* (1988). The scope of both these works is mainly limited to the Ganges valley, and they report the results of field surveys of sites in Kanpur and Allahabad districts respectively. Romila Thapar's *From Lineage to State* (1984) offers a far broader focus on social formations in the Ganges valley in the mid-first millennium BC, and provides many insights into the central questions of the rise of cities and states; but its approach is essentially that of the ancient historian. In some respects similarly oriented is another important contribution, also the work of an ancient historian, Ram Sharan Sharma, whose *Material Culture and Social Formations in Ancient India* (1983) offers a thoughtful and detailed study, although with a somewhat more restricted scope. Its timescale concludes around BC 300, thus leaving aside the Mauryan and post-Mauryan periods which we regard as integral to our subject.

In this situation there appears to be a prima facie case for a book of this kind. It is clear that our aims differ from those of most of the earlier writers, both with regard to the breadth of the geographical and chronological horizons we have set, and in terms of the breadth of our definition of archaeology. The task is not made easier by the paucity and restricted nature of much of the available evidence, and one may well wonder why this should be the case. In seeking to find an answer to this question, it may be helpful to enquire into the history of early historic archaeological research in the countries of South Asia, and into its current position. Therefore, before embarking on our subject itself, we shall briefly review this question, if only to offer some explanation of why there should have been such a neglect of early historic archaeology.

The archaeological background

Archaeology was first introduced to South Asia by European merchants, colonial adventurers and travellers. These were followed from the late eighteenth century onwards by British officers serving with the East India Company or in the army. The inception and early growth of archaeology were the work of a series of brilliant scholars, among whom Sir William Jones stands first. Under his inspiration and that of the Asiatic Society of Bengal which he founded in 1784, a small band of scholars was formed, and the serious business of data collection began. Only thereafter did archaeology take root. Among the achievements of the first half of the nineteenth century were the decipherment of the earliest datable Indian inscriptions, many until that time unreadable even by indigenous scholars, and the discovery of coins of the Indo-Greek and Bactrian Greek rulers of Afghanistan and northwest India. With a few notable exceptions excavation, if resorted to, was crudely done and amounted to little short of plunder.

A notable step forward occurred in 1861 when Major General Alexander Cunningham retired from the army and was appointed as the first Surveyor, later Director General, of the newly created Archaeological Survey of India. Cunningham was no newcomer to the subject: he had already made a study of early coins, and in 1854 published a monograph on the Buddhist remains at Sanchi, *The Bhilsa Topes*, besides numerous other pieces of research. He now embarked upon an epic series of archaeological tours which took him to many parts of northern India, ranging from Bengal to the Northwest Frontier, published year by year in the twenty three volumes of his *Archaeological Survey Reports*. One of his central goals was the rediscovery and identification of the great cities of early Indian literature, that is to say of the early historic period. During his remaining years he published a series of other important works. Although Cunningham contributed little to the development of archaeological research techniques, particularly excavation, his contribution in terms of the rediscovery of ancient India was enormous.

By the end of the nineteenth century certain characteristic features of archaeology in South Asia had become well established. In its protohistoric and early historic phases archaeology had become recognized as an aid to the rediscovery of an emerging and later fully formed civilization, and had accepted its scope as including evidence deriving from inscriptions and textual sources, as well as from coins. It had from the time of Sir William Jones onwards been generally accepted that the study of the monumental remains and ancient arts of Indian civilization were integral parts of the subject.

In 1902, as a result of the direct enthusiasm of the Viceroy, Lord Curzon, John Marshall, a young archaeologist whose early experience had been in Greece, was appointed as the new Director General of Archaeology. His appointment marked the beginning of an altogether new stage of archaeological discovery which lasted, till Marshall's retirement in 1928 and beyond, until the outbreak of the Second World War. During this period almost every aspect of the subject was advanced: excavation, architectural conservation, epigraphy, publication and the creation of museums. Although Mortimer Wheeler was later to criticize Marshall's methods of excavation, the fact remains that they were the basis of his momentous discoveries of the Indus civilization, and the excavation of a whole series of important early Buddhist sites and monuments. Among the early historic cities of South Asia several of Marshall's excavations remain to this day without parallel and as such will be frequently referred to in later chapters of this book. This positive assessment does not however mean that progress in archaeology in India during this period was uniformly excellent: by the thirties there were already many signs of stagnation and a lack of fresh thinking, and these were highlighted in the critical report produced for the Government by Sir Leonard Woolley in 1939.

Sir Mortimer Wheeler's brief spells as Director General of Archaeology in India and later as Archaeological Adviser in Pakistan, between 1944 and 1947, witnessed his tempestuous impact on what had by then become the sleepy and quietly inefficient Archaeological Survey of India; and on its successor in the newly created Pakistan. Many things demanded revitalization and many needed drastic change. Particularly in the field of excavation techniques Wheeler set out to train a body of young scholars as field archaeologists. The success of this programme has left a lasting record in the great spate of published excavations of the following two decades, and undoubtedly marked the start of a major turning point in South Asian archaeology. Wheeler, however, was from the outset clearly aware of his limited occupancy of both these posts, and perhaps for this reason he set clearly defined objectives for what could be achieved. He realized that there was not time to develop equally all aspects of archaeology or archaeological training; something which in different circumstances he might well have done. As it was many departments were scarcely touched by his reforming zeal. Among the topics which did not receive the attention they deserved were consideration of the wider aims of the excavation of early historic cities, and the practical demonstration of how much might be achieved by more extensive excavation. Apart from the limited training dig carried out under his direction at Taxila (Sirkap), his only other excavation of an early historic city was a second training dig at Taxila, on the Bhir mound. This excavation, which photographs show to have been on a considerable scale, has so far not been published.

Early historic archaeology in South Asia since Independence

It is not our intention to follow the history of South Asian archaeology through the past five decades. Rather, we shall touch briefly on certain aspects of recent archaeological research in South Asia, particularly insofar as they relate to the early historic period. Our aim is to indicate some areas of research which in our view need enhancement, and to point to some instances which deserve further stimulus.

There has been a tendency to neglect the use of archaeology to augment the limited information available for the early historic period, from other sources. This has arisen partly because much greater interest has been generated by the later prehistoric and protohistoric periods; partly because the research programme inaugurated by Sir Mortimer Wheeler concentrated primarily upon establishing basic culture sequences at selected sites; and partly also because of the enigmatic character of the Indus civilization, with its undeciphered script and sudden demise, which tended to hold archaeologists' attention. Little attention has so far been given to the great potential of the excavation of early historic settlements as a means of learning more about almost every aspect of life and society, and of augmenting the information derived from texts. For example, few complete house plans have been excavated at any early historic site. To find published examples of such plans we have to return to the excavations of Marshall in the early decades of this century! With only a few exceptions, for example at Sonkh (Hartel 1976; 1993a), early historic excavations in the second half of the twentieth century have been confined to cutting tiny sections through city ramparts or occupation deposits with a view to obtaining pottery sequences and chronological data. There are many topics within the field which require properly designed research programmes. For example, archaeologists have scarcely attempted to find ways of throwing light on such longstanding historical debates as those concerned with establishing or confirming the dates of the Buddha or of the era founded by Kaniska.

It is not an exaggeration to say that early historic archaeological research in South Asia has suffered from a number of major lacunae. Undoubtedly the basis of many of these has been the tendency to cling too closely to the methods and patterns of excavation laid down by Wheeler. There are remarkably few instances of innovation of techniques to meet changing objectives, or for that matter of experimentation with some of the new methods which have been developed and successfully employed elsewhere in the world. Another neglected area is in the adoption of new approaches including those which may be characterized as theoretical archaeology. One consequence of this is the all too frequent absence of a problem-oriented approach. Another is the rarity of the use of statistical methods comparable to those employed by the social sciences. A contributory factor may be the relatively limited interaction with archaeologists from outside South Asia possible under the system prevailing during much of this period. In some cases for example, in India, international exchanges and particularly co-operation in fieldwork were for a time actively discouraged. Happily this situation has now changed.

Such general criticisms of course call for some qualification. First of all, it must be remarked that the situation has differed from country to country within South Asia, some showing greater interest in early historic archaeology and others less. Secondly, it is evident that, for whatever reasons, palaeolithic, prehistoric, protohistoric and even medieval research have almost everywhere received more attention, and consequently have remained more lively than early historic archaeology. Thirdly, there are numerous examples of South Asian archaeologists and institutions whose work transcends our criticisms, even if it often lies outside the narrowly early-historic field. For example, in India, Deccan College, Pune, lovingly developed by the late H. D. Sankalia, stands out as a centre which has consistently sought to arouse public interest and support for all periods of archaeology, and to promote international co-operation and exchange. It has also created a leading South Asian base for scientific specializations in archaeology; and in some of its recent excavations, notably that of the village of Inamgaon, its archaeologists have employed a theoretical approach, and new concepts of excavation and interpretation. Similarly the radiocarbon laboratory established first at the Tata Institute of Fundamental Research, Bombay, and later transferred to the National Physical Laboratory, Ahmedabad, has developed a South Asian centre of repute for physical methods of dating and their applications. In Pakistan, Rafique Mughal's Cholistan survey stands as an outstandingly important and innovative research project, still awaiting final publication, which although largely concerned with the protohistoric period demonstrates how much a problem-oriented approach can accomplish. In Sri Lanka, Siran Deraniyagala's extensive series of cave excavations and the systematic employment of radiocarbon dating in this context offer another outstanding model; so too does the same scholar's major project at Anuradhapura which has been applying modern sampling techniques and a carefully devised strategy of excavation to the rediscovery and study of this early historic city. More such innovative approaches are needed in the early historic field.

The need to enhance early historic archaeology

In the course of writing, we have quite frequently experienced feelings of despair, brought on by the realization of how many opportunities have been lost and how slow has been the advancement of knowledge in so many areas. What makes the situation particularly acute is that, with the continuing population explosion taking place throughout South Asia, whole areas, including ancient cities, which were still reasonably accessible and undamaged in 1947, have since been destroyed or at least put beyond the range of excavation by the process of development. In some cases the extent of change or destruction is extraordinary. For example, Pataliputra was probably the greatest city of South Asia in Mauryan times, and much of it was still available for investigation forty years ago, but since then a great part of the ancient city has been submerged by modern housing and other development as part of the expansion of the city of Patna. In Nepal, the Licchavi capital near the village of Hadigaon, with its royal palace complex, regarding which so much can be learned from inscriptions, has suffered a similar fate. In Pakistan, the second city of Puskalavati (Charsada), at Shaikhan Dheri, was still an open mound of some 36 hectares when we saw it in 1963, at which time the site was declared protected: returning thirty years later we found that nearly the whole mound had since been built on. What makes this case so deplorable is that the buyers of building plots first plunder any ancient remains they can discover and in the course of this excavation most objects and cultural evidence have been destroyed.

Such horrors of course can be found in many parts of the world, and we do not wish to imply that South Asia is in any way unique in this respect. But in some respects the local situation is peculiarly unfavourable to conservation, because of the great density of population in many areas and its continuing growth, and because of the necessarily limited funds and resources available. Moreover, as we have indicated, the wider situation is not as bleak as the more narrowly early historic picture may suggest. Since the middle of the twentieth century there has been a slow, but steadily increasing, momentum of change, and particularly in the past decade the quality and quantity of archaeological publications, both from the Government departments and more particularly from universities, hold out the promise of progress to come. If our present book appears from time to time to be over critical, it is because of our deep concern at the destruction of the cultural heritage which we have witnessed taking place before our eyes during the past decades.

CHAPTER 2

THE ENVIRONMENTAL CONTEXT

B. ALLCHIN

Viewed from outer space, or seen as part of a physical map of Asia, the Indian subcontinent appears as a discrete unit, a triangular peninsula bounded on two sides by the ocean, and divided from the rest of Asia by three great intersecting mountain ranges. Lying approximately between latitudes 5 and 35 north of the equator, much of the peninsula is in the tropics. Within the region there are great climatic variations, providing a whole range of environments from the humid tropical conditions and residual tropical forests of parts of the south, southwest and east to the desert of the northwest, and including mountains, rocky hills and plateaux, dry forest and savanna, and rich alluvial plains some of which are well watered and others completely arid and unproductive unless extensively irrigated. The major rivers are important features of the subcontinent, and one or more of them have been central to each phase of early city development.

South Asia is a land of massive erosion and deposition, processes natural to the arid tropics which have been accentuated, particularly in the northern parts of the subcontinent, by the rapid uplift of the Himalayas. This has been taking place for several million years, and is still taking place. It is due to the ongoing collision of the Indian peninsula, which was formerly a large island, with mainland Asia. This in turn is part of the process of plate tectonics or continental drift whereby major land masses divide, move around the world and re-combine with other blocks of the earth's crust.

The Himalayas, Karakoram, Hindu Kush etc. are all in geological terms young mountain ranges, still being pushed upward by the force of the collision with peninsular India. As a result the rivers and streams that drain them flow with great force, are constantly down-cutting to maintain their level, and at times carry great quantities of silts, gravels and larger pieces of rock out of the mountains. Most of this material is deposited in the plains, and some of the finer silts are carried out to sea. The result is the wide alluvial plains and great deltas of the Indus and Ganges systems; the coastal plain of Gujarat, formed by the Narmada and Tapi (Tapti) rivers; the extensive deltas of the east coast, and the numerous enclaves of fertile alluvial soils in mountain valleys and among the hills of northern and central India and northern Pakistan.

The combination of forces described above, together with a monsoon climate which means long dry periods alternating with heavy seasonal rains, produces a volatile situation. In the normal course of events sudden heavy floods occur following prolonged dry periods, and failure of the monsoon leading to severe droughts is not uncommon. Major rivers regularly deposit vast quantities of silt on their flood plains, so that the soil is constantly revitalized, which helps to account for its apparently inexhaustible fertility. But the same rivers are also prone to change their courses from time to time with catastrophic effects. There is ample geological and geomorphical evidence to show that events of this kind have been taking place at intervals over many thousands of years due to natural causes. Increasingly the effects of erosion, droughts, etc. have been accentuated by human activities such as deforestation. These are all factors which must be borne in mind when considering the environmental conditions of past times and attempting to reconstruct the surroundings in which the cities of the second urbanization came into being.

South India and Sri Lanka are rather different in some respects. The major eastward-flowing rivers of peninsular India have formed considerable deltas along the east coast, but inland the valleys appear to be scoured of major accumulations of alluvial material. There are a number of reasons for this, perhaps the most fundamental being that southern India and Sri Lanka appear to have been relatively stable during the Quaternary.

Enough has already been said to indicate that the South Asian landscape is extremely varied, and that within the subcontinent there is a wide range of environments that have the potential to lend themselves to almost every imaginable human life style. Since the appearance of the first cities, and probably long before, some of the alluvial plains have been intensively cultivated and densely populated by settled village communities. Herdsmen traditionally inhabit certain of the more arid regions, many of them leading partially or completely nomadic lives which are often combined with trading and seasonal work of various kinds. Even today there are communities in the remoter hills and forests who depend upon hunting and gathering for much of their livelihood, and a century ago there were many more. Communities such as these existed alongside cities of the Harappan period (the first urbanization) of the third millennium BC, and alongside those of the second urbanization which is the subject of this book. Many of the cities of the latter group have been steadily expanding since the period dealt with in the following chapters, and some of them are now among the largest and most cosmopolitan cities in the world. Nomadic communities still move around in the countryside, and enter the cities for purposes of trade, and sometimes to work on building sites and other projects.

Before discussing the environment in which the cities of the second urbanization emerged, it may be helpful to look briefly at the rather different setting of the earlier Harappan cities. The major Harappan cities, Mohenjo-daro, Harappa, Kalibangan, Judeirjo-daro, etc. are all situated on rich alluvial soils within the so-called Greater Indus system (i.e. the catchment area of the Indus and its major tributaries, insofar as these are within the plains, and outside the Karakoram and other major mountain ranges). Some of the outlying settlements spill over into adjacent areas such as the plains of Gujarat, and even in one case as far away as the Oxus valley in Central Asia. The ancestral roots of Indus urbanism appear to be in the western borderlands of the Indus region, in Baluchistan, where an unbroken line of development can be traced from the earliest settlements, dating to the sixth or even seventh millennium BC at Mehrgarh, at the head of the Kachi plain where the Bolan river emerges from the Baluchi mountains. So far no such early roots have been traced on the southeastern margin of the Indus plains, nor to the northeast in association with its major tributaries.

The earliest cities of the Indus region have much in common with those of ancient Egypt and Mesopotamia: in each case they were associated with a major perennial river flowing through a desert, and were rooted in the local cultures of their own region. Where the Indus situation differs is in what follows. The cities of the Indus plains, after five thousand years of continuous development, and several periods of more rapid and radical change, seem to peter out from approximately BC 1700 onward: they are neither maintained nor replaced by cities on nearby sites, as sometimes happens elsewhere. When cities reappear up to a thousand years later it is on the Ganges-Yamuna (Jamuna) system several hundred miles to the east, and in a very different environmental region. Why the process of city development in the Indian subcontinent should be arrested, and then restart in another part of the subcontinent, is not at present clear. It seems inescapable that environmental factors must have played some part in the process, directly or indirectly, therefore the causes of the change, insofar as they are known at present are briefly reviewed here (see also chapter 3). They are highly suggestive in general terms, but they do not tell us, any more than does the archaeological evidence, precisely what happened. This is one of the outstanding problems of South Asian prehistory which requires tackling. It calls for a positive problem-oriented approach on several fronts, involving all aspects of archaeological and environmental studies.

At the present time all that can be said is that social, economic, political and military factors may all have contributed to the collapse of Indus urbanism, but it is probable that they coincided with or followed other more basic environmental factors. These could have included general or regional changes of climate, or other types of environmental change, such as a shift in the course of the Indus and/or one or more of its major tributaries. There is also the possibility of a man-induced deterioration of the environment, such as we see today, due to deforestation, overgrazing, etc., resulting in a major environmental crisis.

There is some palaeobotanical evidence for a period of slightly greater humidity in the Indus region, coinciding with the mature Harappan urban phase. This was reversed at about the time that the cities were abandoned, and conditions became generally more arid once again. Archaeological evidence from the former course of the Sarasvati river suggests that, also at about this time, changes took place in river catchment and the headwaters of the Sarasvati were captured by the Yamuna. But the picture is far from complete for the region as a whole, and in any case a situation of such marked cultural change must be highly complex and due to a multiplicity of causes. As far as the geographical aspects of the hiatus in city development are concerned, for the present purpose it is probably more profitable to look at the reasons for its resumption in the central Ganges plains and elsewhere than to speculate on its collapse in the Indus region.

Cities of the second urbanization have already been located in a wide range of different regions. All have one important factor in common: they are regions with fertile soil and a high agricultural potential. Briefly they may be listed as follows (Fig. 2.1):

1. The northwestern borderlands, with the three great Iron Age cities of Kandahar, Charsada and Taxila widely dispersed across the region.
2. The central Ganges plain with its numerous cities and their hierarchies of smaller settlements extending from the Ganges-Yamuna Doab in the west to the frontier of Bengal in the east.
3. The Ganges-Brahmaputra delta with Iron Age cities and smaller settlements strategically sited on the stable older alluvium.
4. The western coastal plain with at least two major Iron Age city sites in its northern section.
5. The great deltas of the east coast, the Mahanadi, the Krishna and the Kaveri, each with their own cities and settlement hierarchies.
6. The Iron Age cities of central and peninsular India occupying some of the fertile regions of the interior, in some cases augmenting productivity by dams or bunds (*bandhs*) providing local irrigation.
7. Sri Lanka with sites such as Anuradhapura, Tissa Maharama and Mantai again occupying regions of considerable agricultural potential, enhanced from an early stage by irrigation.

Each of these regions will be briefly discussed below in terms of the factors that are important to the main subject matter of this book. That is to say an attempt is made to show their relationship to the geography of South Asia, to one another and to the outside world. The aim is briefly to outline the context of the second urbanization of the subcontinent, and to indicate the potential for both internal and external relationships. The factors dealt with in each region vary somewhat according to how they have been treated in the following chapters, and to what in each case appears to be significant to the present purpose.

1. The cities of the northwestern borderlands

These are all situated in localities which combined sufficient acreage of good agricultural soil to support a city of the period, with a position upon which trade

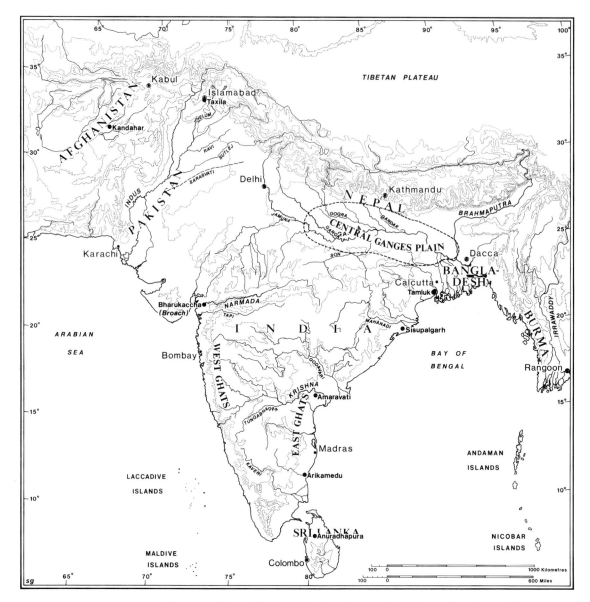

Fig. 2.1.   Map of South Asia showing principal sites referred to in Chapter 2.

routes from various directions could converge. The three major sites, Taxila, Charsada and Kandahar, are associated with routes to the north, northwest and northeast, respectively. The first two are associated with rivers or streams emerging from the mountains into rich piedmont valleys, and Kandahar is an oasis city.

Taxila lies in a basin surrounded by an amphitheatre of rocky hills out of which flow two quite small but constant streams, the Tamra Nala and the Lundi Nala.

The former flows past the Bhir mound (see chapter 8) and the Hellenistic city of Sirkap (see chapter 12) and must have been their main source of water. The latter waters the fertile valley, immediately to the northeast, in which most of the Buddhist monasteries are situated and which today is famous for its citrus orchards. The topography around Taxila is complicated as it has been much affected by the uplift of the Karakoram ranges, and by local folding during Quaternary times both stemming from the ongoing continental collision briefly described above. The soil consists of deep deposits of alluvial silt brought down by the streams from the interior of the hills and colluvial material washed off the surrounding slopes. The site occupies a central position in the enclave formed by the coalescing valleys of the two streams. Due to the proximity of the hills the rainfall is more plentiful and the climate cooler than in the Punjab plains that fall away to the southwest.

The main trade route from north India to Central Asia and China, which follows the open fertile corridor between the Cholistan desert and the Karakoram foothills, divides at Taxila. To the northeast one of the branches of the Silk Route leads, via the central reaches of the Indus valley, through the Karakoram ranges to Kashgar, Tibet and China, approximately along the route now followed by the Karakoram Highway. To the northwest the route continues to further important crossroads in Afghanistan and Central Asia. Crossing the Indus where it spreads out over wide gravel beds between Haro and Attock, it goes directly to Charsada.

Charsada, the ancient city of Puskalavati, is situated where the Kabul river debouches from the mountains of Afghanistan into the broad fertile vale of Peshawar, and is joined by the Swat river (see chapter 8). Today the area is intensively cultivated with the aid of local irrigation of various kinds, and there is every reason to suppose that this was the case in the period with which we are concerned. The urban centre has obviously shifted locally from time to time, but there appears to have been continuous occupation within the locality since the early Iron Age. The importance of the city dwindled somewhat in the early centuries of the Christian era, with the rise of the city of Peshawar twenty miles to the west and the development of the alternative route over the Khyber Pass which joins the Kabul river somewhat higher up, in Afghanistan. These two sites command the large, extremely fertile alluvial plain lying between the northwest bank of the Indus and the mountains of Afghanistan. Densely populated and intensively cultivated today, the wealth of early sites and Buddhist monuments indicates that this was already the case in the early centuries BC. Although not an obvious crossroads of major routes like Taxila, any city in the vale of Peshawar provides a focus for routes from a number of rich valleys in the Karakoram foothills such as Swat and Dir, both of which are very rich in Buddhist sites and monuments, and from inner valleys such as Chitral. Therefore whichever of these two cities commanded the main route from India to the northwest was both an important meeting and trading centre between two very different major geographical regions, the Indian subcontinent and Central Asia, and a centre of trade for the surrounding region.

Taxila and Puskalavati, although far from the Ganges valley heartland of Iron Age Indian urbanism, are nonetheless culturally part of the pre-Mauryan and Mauryan world, as the following chapters demonstrate. Kandahar is situated in what is now southeastern Afghanistan, far to the west of the well-watered vale of Peshawar and the Taxila valley, on the eastern edge of the Dasht-i Margo, the desert basin of the perennial Helmund river which flows out of the Hindu Kush. It has many of the characteristics of an oasis city. Historically it is really the centre of an outlying province of the Iranian world. But it was ceded to the Mauryan empire following Alexander's invasion of the region and his retreat before the forces of Candragupta Maurya, and it remained part of the Mauryan empire for approximately half a century. This gave a certain Indian character to the city which it retains to the present day. It cannot however be regarded as participating in the second urbanization of the Indian subcontinent in the same sense as Taxila and Puskalavati.

2. The central Ganges plain

The most striking feature of this region is its sameness. As an environment for the development of early cities it presents a total contrast to the discrete localities each with a strong individual character in which the cities of the northwestern borderlands were established. Here a successful pattern or hierarchy of a city and ancillary sites can be reproduced endlessly over the vast plain. Individual cities and their satellites will not be discussed in this section as they are more fully dealt with in chapters 6, 7, 10 and 11.

The central Ganges plain, in which the cities and city life of the second urbanization of the Indian subcontinent took shape and established their distinctive character, stretches from Delhi and the Ganges-Yamuna Doab in the west to the borders of Bengal approximately eleven hundred kilometers to the east; and from the foothills of the Himalayas in the north to the escarpment of the Vindhyas in the south, a distance that varies from two hundred and fifty to three hundred kilometers. Once one leaves the margin of the plain it has few features apart from the main river and its tributaries. Being a monsoon climate most of the rainfall is in the summer months, and there are also irregular winter rains. The climate is generally less extreme than in regions to the northwest. Rainfall and humidity increase steadily as one moves eastward. Such natural vegetation as remains in places today includes large forest trees. Originally much of the region must have been heavily forested.

What one sees today is largely a manmade landscape, intensively cultivated and much of it producing several crops in a year; closely studded with villages each with its tank and a few large banyan or mango trees, and with here and there larger groves of mangoes or other large trees. A network of roads and dusty tracks links the villages and converges on the larger towns and cities, some of them still lined with shady trees, recalling Asoka's exhortation to create wells and plant trees to provide shade for the enjoyment of both men and animals. At the western end of the plain a wide variety of crops are grown, and there are open grassy areas where animals graze, but as one travels eastward these disappear and rice takes over more and more until almost the entire landscape consists of paddy fields.

The plain is in fact a deep trough filled with alluvial deposits brought down from the Himalayas on the north and the central Indian plateau on the south. The full depth of the alluvium has not been plumbed, but the major rivers now cut down into it to depths of up to a hundred metres. In places where there is some lateral movement and the rivers are actively cutting back their banks fresh sections through the alluvium show a fairly consistent pattern of alternating heavily rolled gravels and fine alluvial silts. The gravels appear to be associated with old land surfaces, each has a different character and each contains a distinctive assemblage of stone artefacts which together form a developing sequence. When the alluvial sequence has been properly interpreted it should provide a great deal of information regarding the climatic changes and tectonic events that took place during Quaternary, and earlier times, in north India.

The structure of the Gangetic plain indicates a volatile history during Stone Age times. The morphology of its surface on the other hand indicates that throughout the period with which this book is concerned, and perhaps during somewhat earlier times also, it was fairly stable. And it appears to have remained stable, apart from a certain increase in erosion possibly due to human activities, and occasional local changes in the course of certain major tributaries, notably the Son. In contrast to the Indus system, these changes do not appear to have been such as to affect profoundly the distribution of population, nor of major sites. Indications of former courses of rivers and streams in the form of ox-bow lakes are everywhere. Just how numerous these are becomes apparent when flying over the plain on a clear day. They attract game and wild fowl, and appear to have been the favoured camping places of Mesolithic hunters who preceded and no doubt overlapped with the first agriculturalists. Ox-bow lakes also provide water for grazing cattle and sheep, and those that hold water throughout the year are a source of fish.

Throughout the central Ganges plain the principal river and its tributaries have incised their beds, and also their flood plains, into the older alluvium. The normal river bed tends to meander within the flood plain, the margins of which are marked by steep banks or sometimes cliffs of alluvium. Floods may fill the flood plain, and sometimes cut back the banks, but seldom overtop them. Therefore from the beginning of the period we are considering onwards settlements have regularly been situated on the older alluvium, sometimes on the top of a cliff overlooking the flood plain so as to take advantage of its rich and frequently replenished soil for certain types of agriculture.

The various types of alluvium have specific names, and their agricultural potential is well known. The main distinction is that between the old (*bangar*) and new (*khadar*) or floodplain alluvium. There are also important differences between the alluvium derived from the Himalayan mountain system and that from the rocks of central India. This is not the place to go into the details of traditional agricultural practice in the Gangetic plain. It is enough to understand that farmers have a profound and detailed knowledge of the various types of soil, and the ways in which they can be utilized at different times of year and in different climatic conditions. Like the whole of the traditional agriculture of the region this understanding is built on long experience, and undoubtedly has its roots in the period prior to the emergence of the Iron Age cities when the forests were being cleared, the population was building up and new settlements were being established.

In addition to the northwestern land route to Central Asia, Iran, China and Europe, the Ganges cities of the plains had outlets to the east by river to the port of Tamluk on the western margin of the Ganges delta. Land routes starting from various points in the middle Ganges region extended into Central India and the south. An important route was that from Mirzapur, near Allahabad, to Kalyan on the west coast near the present-day city of Bombay. Another appears to have linked the Ganges-Yamuna Doab to Bharukaccha (modern Broach) on the Narmada estuary in central Gujarat.

3. The Ganges-Brahmaputra delta

This region is in many respects a continuation of the central Gangetic plain. The rainfall continues to increase towards the east, and the landscape is flat except where relieved by outliers of the hills to the north, southwest and east. When the eye becomes accustomed to the generally low relief it is possible to pick out the slight undulations that indicate areas of older alluvium, and the lower lying areas that follow the courses of the numerous tributaries and distributaries, some active and some abandoned, of the double delta. The fact that it is the delta of two major river systems each with its catchment in a region with a somewhat different rainfall regime, and that it is an active delta, rapidly growing and building new land in the Bay of Bengal, make for a complex topography. Details of the morphology of Bengal are not so easily understood as in the central Ganges region. In practice, however, the important basic distinction between the older and younger alluvium is much the same for those living in the plains of Bengal as it is further west. The older alluvium is only marginally affected by the annual inundations of the complex interlocking flood plains, during and following the rains. The incursions of the sea which can cause great loss of life and salination of agricultural land scarcely touch it.

The Iron Age cities and major Buddhist sites and monasteries, or at any rate those of them that have survived, are consistently sited on the older alluvium.

(For a discussion of individual cities and religious complexes see chapters 10 and 12.) There seems little doubt that the tendency to establish settlements on the flood plains, and on the new land formed by the growth of the delta, has greatly increased with increasing pressure of population. Again the landscape is largely manmade, and rice is the principal crop. In Bengal boats and river transport are a very important part of life, and fish is an important element of diet. With the north–south-orientated mountain ranges that rise abruptly on the eastern margins of the delta the Indian cultural world ends and the Sino-Tibetan world begins, and the eastern parts of the delta are in some respects the beginning of the transition zone.

Given the unstable nature of the delta, if there were ports on its shores in our period many would have disappeared. One port that has been investigated is Tamluk, situated on the western edge of the delta. It has been excavated and shown to go back to the second century BC. All the evidence points to its being an outlet from the eastern Ganges valley to the world of international sea trade with both the east and the west. Further ports have been recorded on the eastern edge of the delta, but much less is known about them as yet.

4. The west coast

Only limited sections of the west coast of the Indian subcontinent, the central Gujarat plain and the area immediately north of Bombay, appear on the basis of evidence currently available to have supported cities of the second urbanization. Two major sites are known, Bharukaccha (modern Broach) and Sopara near Kalyan, not far from the northern suburbs of Bombay. It is possible that there are further major sites to be discovered in this region, and also further down the coast to the south. In Saurashtra too there is at least one city site of the Mauryan period, Junagarh (see chapter 10), and a number of minor sites.

The Gujarat plain has been formed from the alluvium brought down by two major westward-flowing rivers, the Narmada and Tapi, and a number of minor rivers which enter it from the northeast. The Narmada and Tapi both flow in rift valleys that run east–west across the plateau of central India, and therefore they have catchment areas that extend far across the subcontinent. As a result they have a strong perennial flow, and also carry vast amounts of water during the monsoon which sometimes results in extensive flooding. Both have incised their beds and flood plains into the older alluvium of the plain in a similar manner to the rivers of the Ganges system. The minor northern rivers have their catchment in the much more arid regions of north Gujarat and Rajasthan, and consequently have a different regime and are subject both to sudden flooding and to periods of greatly reduced flow. Going south towards Bombay the coastal plain narrows, and increasingly includes hills and rocky outcrops, peninsulas and offshore islands. There are no major rivers, only minor streams that rise in the Western Ghats for, south of the Tapi, all the major rivers of peninsular India flow in an easterly direction. To the south the annual rainfall increases steadily, there are more large trees, and rice becomes the predominant crop.

The plain of Gujarat is different in many respects to that of the Ganges system, being much smaller in extent, and being a coastal plain open to direct sea contact with the outside world. This has helped to make it a centre of trade as well as agriculture, and today Gujarat is one of the most commercially advanced provinces of India. But in spite of the differences, in agricultural terms the overall environment of the central Gujarat plain is not dissimilar to that of the western Ganges plain. It is not surprising therefore that at least one major Iron Age city was established there. It is more surprising perhaps that there are also Harappan settlements in Gujarat. Thus Gujarat is the only region as far as we know at present in which there is a spatial overlap between the Harappan urban world and that of Iron Age urbanism. Furthermore it seems quite possible that there may have been a certain degree of continuity of settlement. If so Gujarat would be the one region in South Asia where this was the case. This is a question of outstanding interest and it deserves the fullest investigation. These observations could be the beginning of a lengthy and very interesting discussion, but the situation can probably best be summed up for the present purpose by the one word 'trade'.

The modern city of Broach appears to be built on and around an artificially raised mound. This is in fact the accumulated mudbrick and other debris of earlier building periods extending back to the Iron Age, and perhaps earlier, and there seems to have been virtually continuous occupation of the site since that time. The city was probably founded on this spot originally for the same reasons that made it an important centre in recent historical times. It is centrally placed where the plain is at its broadest (c. 80 kilometres from the coast to the escarpment of the central India plateau) and has sufficient rainfall to support fairly intensive agriculture. It is also a port situated on the north bank of the Narmada estuary at the head of navigation for traditional seagoing vessels.

Bharukaccha's connections with the interior are likely to have been along the same routes as those in use today. One route ran northeastwards through north Gujarat and Rajasthan, along the margin of the Thar desert to Jaipur and then due east to Agra on the Yamuna. Agra is and was a great centre of trade where a number of routes converge. These included two very important long-distance routes, one coming from the east up the Ganges and Yamuna, and the other the land route to the northwest described above. Like Puskalavati and Peshawar, Agra must have been a centre of regional trade, in this case from the rich lands of the Doab and the western Ganges plains, the Himalayan valleys immediately to the north such as Kulu and Kangra, and from Rajasthan. The other main land route out of Bharukaccha was that to the Deccan, and ran up the Tapi valley which is relatively open. The Narmada on the other hand flows through a gorge in broken rocky hills for some distance before debouching into the plain, and therefore does not provide a route to the interior.

Sopara, about 50 kilometres north of Bombay, is situated on a small estuary. It too was clearly a port, but little is known about it except that nearby an Asokan inscription was found, and a Buddhist monastic complex and large stupa dating from the second to the ninth century AD. Another site, Kalyan, which is assumed to be the same as the modern Kalyan, is mentioned in the *Periplus*. This is a small port a short distance to the north of Bombay and is now more or less part of the city. If the ancient Kalyan was in the same vicinity it is probably lost beneath subsequent developments, or it may be beneath some part of Bombay island which has an outstanding natural harbour. That there was an important site in the Bombay/Kalyan area is clear from the large number of splendid Buddhist monuments both nearby and on the routes leading up the Western Ghats to the Deccan and then on, via the route followed in later historic times by the Great Deccan road, to Mirzapur near Allahabad in the central Ganges valley. The monuments include the monastic complex and stupa at Sopara mentioned above, and the many large monastic complexes cut out of cliffs and standing rock, in the form of great artificial caves that have been recorded on the islands of the Bombay group and at various points on the ascent up the Ghats. This is not the place for a discussion of monuments themselves, but their presence in this coastal region and on the route to the central Ganges plains, and their splendour, indicative of wealthy patrons over many centuries, cannot be ignored. They are of great significance as indicators of a long period of trade with the west, coinciding with the height of the second urbanization throughout the subcontinent. During this time the financial incentives must have been strong enough to warrant overland transport of goods from the central Ganges region to the west coast, and the profits sufficient to enable merchants and others to construct a whole range of magnificent and enduring religious monuments.

5. The east coast

The east coast in some respects continues the pattern seen in the Ganges-Brahmaputra delta, where cities were established on older alluvium, above the level of serious flooding, and took advantage of both the older and newer alluvium for agricultural purposes; a pattern that, as we have pointed out, in turn appears to have been related to those established in the Ganges plains and the plain of Gujarat. This is a rice-growing region with two monsoons where up to four crops a year are produced on the most productive alluvial soils. Whether so many crops were grown in a year in earlier times we do not know, but there must have been a very high level of productivity then as now. The east coast of peninsular India differs from that of the west in that there is a continuous coastal plain augmented by the deltas of three major rivers.

The first delta is that of the Mahanadi and a number of minor rivers flowing out of eastern central India. Together with its hinterland this is the core of the modern state of Orissa, which forms a link in cultural and linguistic terms between Bengal and Dravidian-speaking Andhra Pradesh. Further south, after an interval, we have the interlinked Krishna-Godavari deltas, and south of Madras that of the Cauvery. In the case of the Krishna, Godavari and Kaveri rivers their catchment extends far west, to the top of the escarpment of the western Ghats. Between them they drain the greater part of the peninsula.

With each of the deltas ports and major inland sites of our period are associated. In the Mahanadi delta there is the large city of Sisupalgarh and its associated sites (see chapters 8 and 10). In the Krishna delta are the two cities of Amaravati and Nagarjunakonda (see chapters 8, 10 and 12), and in the Kaveri delta there are many important sites, particularly Kaveripattanam and Uraiyur. There are probably others in every region which have not yet been discovered. Along the coast between the main deltas, and usually associated with minor rivers and estuaries, are a number of further sites such as for example Kalingapatam south of the Mahanadi delta, or Arikamedu near Pondicherry, which were clearly ports. The whole coast is marked by important ports in later times, some of which are mentioned in early sources such as the *Periplus*, but little archaeological research has been done to establish the dates of their various phases of development or their character in early times. Associated with a number of these early sites are fine Buddhist and Hindu monuments and complexes of religious buildings, such as Amaravati, to mention one of the finest. As in the case of the west coast, this must indicate a high level of prosperity, and both internal and external trade, such as that described in the accounts of early travellers, beginning in our period and continuing for a thousand years or more thereafter. It is probable that in contrast to Bharukaccha and Kalyan, but like the minor ports on the southerly part of the west coast, they primarily served a regional hinterland: that is to say that they do not appear to have served primarily as the termini of land routes to more distant regions such as the Ganges valley or the northwestern borderlands, although there was obviously a network of land routes which ultimately connected the main sites in every part of mainland South Asia.

6. The interior of central and peninsular India

This region forms the collective hinterland to which most of the coastal sites mentioned in the two preceding sections relate. Central and peninsular India together form a great triangular plateau surrounded by alluvial plains on the north, and on the southeast and southwest by coastal plains of varying width and by the ranges known respectively as the Eastern and Western Ghats. The underlying rocks of the plateau vary, and with them the topography and scenery, and the fertility of the soil. The dominant factor climatically is the southwest monsoon which in summer brings a very high rainfall to the west coast and Western Ghats, and a much lower rainfall to the interior. The southeast also receives some rain in winter from the northeast monsoon.

We know from the archaeological record that during Neolithic and Chalcolithic times farming cultures with strong regional individuality flourished in most parts suitable for agriculture. Settlements developed steadily into market towns and centres of local chieftainship. Less hospitable areas were inhabited by hunter-gatherers, as some still are today, or were the grazing grounds of local village herds or of independent pastoral communities. Parts of the region have long been renowned for draught cattle, and it has sources of gold that have been exploited from Chalcolithic times. The peninsula presents a much more varied landscape and range of lifestyles than we see in the great alluvial plains that appear to have been the heartlands of Iron Age urbanism, and which show such a regular pattern of settlement hierarchies and are so universally productive in terms of cereals, cotton and various other crops. In a sense the peninsular plateau together with central India forms a region generally complementary to the major plains in a number of respects, but within it there are many minor regions of high agricultural productivity, some of which were the places where cities arose. Like the Gujarat plain and the great deltas of the east coast they provided environments that could support one or more cities with their satellite sites.

Early Buddhist texts mention three *janapadas* or settled areas in Central India and the Deccan with their accompanying cities: Avanti whose capital was Ujjain, on the route from the central Ganges valley to Kalyan and the west coast; Cedi, around Jabalpur, whose capital may have been at Tripuri, on the more easterly route to the south; and Asmaka in the northern Deccan about which little is known. Other cities of our period, to cite a few examples from various regions, are Vidisa and Eran near Sagar in central India; Pratisthana and Tagara in Maharashtra; Kondapur, Brahmagiri, Maski and Banavasi in Karnataka. There are many more. Those in Central India have earth ramparts like the cities of the northern plains, but we do not know whether those in the Deccan have this feature. From Neolithic times onward there is archaeological evidence for the building of small stone dams or bunds across minor valleys to provide water and local irrigation in the vicinity of settlements. As time went on larger bunds were built, and there is a body of inscriptional evidence for the building of substantial dams by kings from the end of our period. There can be little doubt therefore that irrigation played a role in increasing productivity in the more heavily populated areas of the peninsular plateau.

7. Sri Lanka

Sri Lanka is both an island and part of the Indian subcontinent. The interplay of these two factors has been important in forming its character. Although it shares many of India's environmental and social characteristics, being a relatively small island it has much more coastline in relation to its interior, and therefore has been exposed to much more contact with the outside world. Throughout historical times it has been on the sea route between China and the western world, and all the contacts this involved have left their mark. Within itself also it is divided into two major environmental zones, often referred to as the wet zone and the dry zone. These correspond approximately to regions of higher and lower rainfall and have markedly different characters. The Central and eastern plains, where the rainfall is relatively low, provide an environment similar in many respects to the interior of Peninsular India. This is where the first cities took shape, and it continued to be the region of urban settlement until well into the second millennium AD. From an early stage of urban development, that is from about the third century BC or earlier, large tanks or bands were built with massive, long, low stone dams retaining the water of one or more streams. These supplied water for the cities and also for irrigating quite extensive areas of lower lying ground. Individual sites are discussed in chapter 9.

Conclusions

The core region where the pattern of Iron Age South Asian cities with their hierarchies of smaller settlements took shape is undoubtedly the great alluvial plain of the central Ganges valley, and this is where the story really begins. However, although the region is in certain respects physically isolated from the rest of Asia, and forms the centre of a world of its own, that isolation is never complete and it is through the contemporary cities of the western borderlands of the subcontinent, which are part of the same major complex, that the second urbanization of South Asia maintained land contact with the outside world. These cities were in a sense both its points of reference in terms of world history and its overland commercial links with Central and Western Asia and ultimately with China and Europe. This is a role which they have continued to play until the present day except when communication has been interrupted by political or military pressure.

In a similar way it was through the cities of the west coast that sea trade with the Middle East, the Mediterranean and the Hellenistic world generally must have passed. Little archaeological research has been done on this interesting subject, and at present knowledge of the nature of the trade contacts is limited to a number of historical sources and that provided by a few coins and potsherds. As we have seen, it can be inferred from the magnificence of the Buddhist monuments of the second century BC onward that lie on certain of the routes from the west coast to the interior and the Ganges valley that the volume of sea trade with the western world must have been very considerable over a period of several centuries. Numerous smaller ports have been recorded in the *Periplus* (c. second century BC) and other sources further south down the west coast and in Sri Lanka. The list extends round to the east coast and beyond, making it clear that there was active coastal trade, and probably also a regular flow of trade with more distant places via the east coast.

The first observation that this brief geographical survey evokes is, on the one hand, the presence of so much that continued into recent historic times and, on the other, a number of significant differences. Therein lies the interesting aspect of the subject: in the many questions that it raises. The purpose of this book is to formulate and try to answer some of these questions. One thing is clear, they can only be answered in the context of the subcontinent as a whole, its structure, climate and earlier cultural development, and of its relationship to the outside world.

CHAPTER 3

THE END OF HARAPPAN URBANISM AND ITS LEGACY

F. R. ALLCHIN

The Indus civilization was a period of urbanism, parallel in time to the early urbanism of Mesopotamia, with which it doubtless shared important features. Not the least of these was the fact that in each case there appear to have been fundamental changes, if not an actual break, in the cultural traditions during the period between the city states of the third millennium and the new cities which sprang up during the first millennium BC (Fig. 3.1). We still know comparatively little about the nature of the Harappan state and its structure, or about the society which gave rise to it. We are equally in the dark regarding the factors which led to its end and to the nature of the post-urban society which followed. There has been comparatively little excavation of relevant sites: such excavation has for the most part lacked a problem-oriented approach, and in some important instances remains still largely unpublished. Even where a sufficient body of data exists, its systematic study and interpretation, and hence the research situation, all too often remain inadequate to allow firm conclusions to be drawn. For all these reasons, without further intelligently conceived research, much must remain problematic.

In *The Rise of Civilization in India and Pakistan* (1982) we attempted to present a view of these matters in terms of the available evidence, primarily with a view to setting down the relevant archaeological data without lengthy discussion and with only limited interpretation. There is not as yet much which can be added, although the excavations currently being undertaken at several sites (for example, Naushahro, Harappa, Banavali and Dholavira) will almost certainly provide important new data. In the present context our aim is to offer a tentative outline of the developments which took place in the Indus system between the disappearance of the cities of the Indus civilization and the rise of early historic cities in north India and Pakistan, and thus to point to the archaeological background to the latter events. Our starting point will be the causes that led to the breakdown of the Harappan cities, and following that we shall give a brief survey of the nature of the settlements that remained in the aftermath of this development.

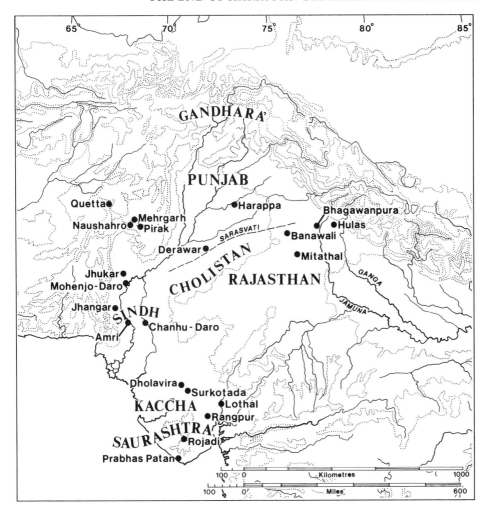

Fig. 3.1.   Map of principal sites of the post-urban period referred to in Chapters 3 and 4.

Possible causes of the breakdown of the Harappan System

There has been much discussion regarding the factors which led to the end of the Indus civilization. We cannot elaborate on this subject here, nor discuss it at any length. Various views have been put forward, and these between them probably offer the beginnings of a proper answer:

– One group sees a variety of natural factors as responsible: a decline in rainfall has been cited as leading to progressive dessication and associated changes; the gradual increase in population, both human and cattle, has been seen as leading to a wearing out of the possible resources, both forest and grassland, and agricultural, thus producing a corresponding weakening of the subsistence base of the economy.

– A second set of postulated causes seeks to find an explanation in more calamitous natural events: a sudden change in the unstable course of the Indus has been invoked to account for the desertion of Mohenjo-daro, the society's epicentre, resulting in a local starving out of the city and a general weakening of the whole society; Dales (1965) and Raikes (1965, 1967a) have postulated powerful tectonic action leading to a damming up of the river Indus with accompanying calamitous inundations at Mohenjo-daro and other settlements. As we shall see below, the gradual drying up of the Sarasvati-Ghaggar river, perhaps linked with the capture of its waters by the Yamuna, may be offered as another calamitous natural event, whose consequences may have occasioned a number of disastrous parallel changes.

– A third set of causes invokes human intervention as leading to the end of the civilization: the movement, for several postulated reasons, of groups of tribesmen into the Indus valley from the hills to the west; or even the arrival of 'Aryans', Indo-Aryan-speaking tribes originating from far to the north and west, has been suggested by some; another suggestion is that the breakdown of trade contacts with Mesopotamia during the opening centuries of the second millennium may have contributed to the weakening of the Indus cities.

– A fourth group of hypothetical causes includes epidemics, supposedly responsible for the presence of bodies lying in the streets, in the final stages of the occupation of Mohenjo-daro; such epidemics may also have led to the society's experiencing a state of inability to change and adapt to the changing conditions of the environment and world outside.

It is evident that any or all of these postulated causes may have operated during the latter stages of the Indus civilization, either singly or in combinations, and contributed to bring it to an end. We shall be arguing below that a series of major tectonic events, leading to the drying up of the Sarasvati, were a powerful factor which operated to bring about changes coinciding with the end of the post-urban period, and may in turn have contributed to a reduction of rainfall in Sindh and neighbouring areas. It seems reasonable to postulate that these or similar factors may have begun to operate several centuries earlier, and have already played their part in the end of Harappan urban society. Even if changes brought about as a result of tectonic events may be postulated as an underlying cause of the end of the civilization, the event itself is likely to have been the product of a multiplicity of causes, operating sometimes together and sometimes separately, perhaps over several centuries, and producing a progressive weakening of the system until its final collapse. We may repeat what we have written elsewhere, that:

> The civilization ... involved a delicate balance of internal relations between cities, towns and villages, and of external relations with neighbouring peasant

societies and with more distant urban societies. The end of the civilization
probaby arose from some major upsetting of this balance. (Allchin 1982b, 329)

There is still great uncertainty regarding the date at which the urban society came
to an end. In the present unsatisfactory research situation, there is as yet an
absence of hard dates derived from contexts which might highlight the events.
We shall content ourselves therefore with a broad observation that the urban
stage appears to have come to a close somewhere between BC 2000 and 1750
and that it is followed in many parts of the Indus region by a post-urban society,
which has been often referred to as Late Harappan.

Post-urban settlements of the Indus System

Possehl (1989, 18) has stated that the term Late Harappan is 'much abused,
misunderstood and confusing', and has proposed as an alternative, 'Post-urban'.
Our own usage has been hitherto somewhat inconsistent and we have sometimes
used Late Harappan, often in ways which are clearly different from the usages of
other scholars. In the light of Possehl's recent contributions (Possehl 1980, 81–5;
Possehl 1989, 17–24) we have come to the conclusion that the second term is to
be preferred, in that it relates to the observable consequences of the breakdown of
the urban structure of society, and as such suggests meaningful and demonstrable
criteria for its use. By comparison the term Late Harappan remains inherently
imprecise and opens the way to semantic confusion.

The post-urban phase covers a number of regional cultural variants: in the
Indus heartland, in Sindh, the group of sites of the Jhukar culture; in the Punjab
and Sarasvati valleys, the sites which may be associated with the Cemetery H
cultures; in the eastern Punjab, the group of sites typified by Banawali and
Mitathal IIb; and in Saurashtra, the group of sites comparable to Rangpur IIb
and III. East of the Punjab, in the Ganges-Yamuna Doab, the sites of the so-
called OCP group also appear to be, at least in part, contemporary with the
post-urban phase, and may be marginally associated with it. As we remarked
above the chronology of the end of the Harappan urban phase and of its
breakdown is not as yet well established. Nor is there any definite evidence that
the end came simultaneously in all parts of the Harappan culture region: the
urban centres in some areas may well have disintegrated before those in others.
In these circumstances we are inclined to think that there is little to be gained in
seeking or attempting to offer any spurious certainty. From the present point of
view it is probably enough to say that the urban phase began to come to an end
around BC 2000 and that it was replaced by the post-urban phase which
continued from that time through to around the last quarter of the second
millennium BC.

What were the main features of the breakdown of the urban society, and what
was the nature of the societies of the post-urban period and how did they differ

from province to province? As we see it there must have been first and foremost a breakdown in the urban structure, involving the abandonment or partial abandonment of the urban centres (Allchin 1982b, 330). This process need not have occurred equally or simultaneously at all centres, and indeed it seems likely that it would have been a progressive decline; but it may be taken as 'an index of change at a basic level of the Harappan socio-cultural system', as Possehl puts it (Possehl and Raval 1989, 24). Next, at least in the archaeological record, the evidence of much of the centralized craft manufactures and extended trade networks would have petered out, and finally come to an end. This would involve both the disappearance of some of the peculiarly urban specialized crafts and their products, and even more clearly the disappearance of evidence of interprovincial and international trade. There is still much systematic work needed to study and plot these things, and to understand their meaning in 'processual' terms. We agree with Possehl's statement that the post-urban picture of the curtailment of such features is not necessarily a sign of economic depression, but rather highlights the fact that the post-urban economies cannot measure up to the dynamism, scale and prosperity of the previous urban phenomenon. Allied with these changes we would expect to find evidence of some changes in the settlement patterns and subsistence economies. In short, there must have been a weakening of those centralized, centripetal forces which throughout the urban phase had encouraged the impression of cultural, and perhaps political and economic unity, and correspondingly an increase of regional diversification (Kenoyer 1991a and b). It has been noticed by several authors, including Allchin (1982b) and Possehl (1977; 1989, 17–27), that this process involved an apparent resurgence of traits of material culture deriving ultimately from the local cultures of the pre-urban phase, and that the boundaries of the post-urban phase reflect a similar phenomenon. This is an interesting feature which has still to be fully explained. What is probably important in terms of understanding the cultural development of the post-urban phase is that throughout every province of the Indus civilization societies survived which, while losing some of the distinctive characteristics of the urban settlements, nonetheless retained a broadly 'Harappan' tradition in other respects. In this way the Indus system differentiates itself from some of the neighbouring areas, such as the northwest frontier region, where during the second millennium societies flourished (i.e. that represented by the Gandhara grave complex) which can scarcely if at all be said to have shared in this distinctive legacy.

When we turn our attention to the post-urban settlements themselves we are struck by the not inconsiderable volume of available evidence, and by the fact that to an extent it proves to be somewhat unhelpful. First, as we have already remarked, much remains to be published, or is only partly published; and second, the limited aims of many of the excavations led to their neglecting some of those categories of evidence which might be most helpful in determining the nature of the settlements and the life of their inhabitants. Nevertheless it is desirable to consider these materials, as archaeologically speaking they certainly provide us with much information and serve as a background to subsequent development. We shall consider each of the regions in turn.

Post-urban sites in Sindh

In the Indus valley itself the post-urban evidence is clearly of outstanding interest and importance, and it is disappointing to discover that of the few excavated sites only Chanhu-daro has been at all fully published (Mackay 1943). Casal's Amri excavations revealed an important post-urban-period occupation, but this part of the excavation was on a small scale and the report is tantalizingly incomplete; the excavations of Dr Mughal at Jhukar, the site which has given its name to the culture period in Sindh, are regrettably still not published, although they are likely to yield extremely important data. The picture that emerges is still incomplete, but it suggests that some fairly tempestuous events have intervened between the mature urban phase and that which succeeded it. At Chanhu-daro there appears to have been a squatter population living amid the ruins of the last urban structures. Their pottery is one category of evidence which provides somewhat confusing indications. Although it represents a style which is clearly distinct from the Harappan pottery, there are enough Harappan, and even pre-Harappan, features to suggest that it was made within the same broad tradition, perhaps by what Piggott calls a 'native, non-Harappa substratum in the local population' (Piggott 1950, 223). Another perplexing feature of the pottery is that in some respects it shows affinities of craft and decoration to those of contemporary western India. What these resemblances signify is not immediately clear, but they certainly convey a sense of a more 'peninsular' (or perhaps we should say 'sub-urban') style, than does the urban Harappan pottery. The most striking aspect of the post-urban material from Chanhu-daro however is the complete absence of any typically Harappan seals or other characteristically Harappan urban craft products. Instead there is a range of stamp seals of terracotta, faience, stone and metal, which, as Piggott recognized, are foreign to India and imply the presence of newcomers, presumably deriving from the west. The parallels of the seals may be found in eastern Iran, Afghanistan and Central Asia. Equally 'foreign' is a range of copper tools and pins whose analogues are also to be found in those regions. While it is possible to argue, as some have done, that the metal artefacts of 'foreign' type may be no more than the products of trade, the presence of the stamp seals is to our mind unequivocal. The absence of Harappan seals, the symbols of the Harappan style and, presumably, of Harappan political and economic power, and their displacement by these foreign seal types, which too were doubtless the symbols of a group with a different identity, must indicate that a new power was dominant at Chanhu-daro and by inference in the middle and lower Indus region.

Rather similar evidence comes from the Kacchi plain, where the Mehrgarh

VIII and Sibri cemeteries contain an assemblage which is also markedly divergent from the Harappan tradition, and whose roots are to be traced in the cemeteries of Uzbeqistan and Bactria (Santoni 1984). Equally foreign to the Indian tradition are many of the objects in the remarkable hoard discovered recently in Quetta (Jarrige and Usman Hassan 1989). The nearby settlement of Pirak, which flourished from around the second quarter of the second millennium, is equally 'outside' the Harappan tradition, and can scarcely be said to belong to the mainstream of the post-urban culture complex as such. Rather it may be seen, along with some of the sites of the eastern borders of the Indus system, as one of the later post-urban adaptations to changing environmental demands.

Post-urban sites in Kacch and Saurashtra

In Kacch and Saurashtra there are traces of local settlements with a distinctive regional character even before the arrival of Harappan influences (which most probably arrived in the form of traders or administrators, with their accompanying lifestyle). These local traits continue at Lothal alongside the predominantly Harappan style. At a certain point in time the Harappan urban elements are withdrawn, leaving a typical post-urban situation, in which 'Late Harappan' features blend with the re-emerging local cultural style. The region has witnessed several major excavations covering this period, and several have been published, including Lothal (Rao 1979; 1985); Rangpur (Rao 1963); Rojdi (Possehl 1989); and Surkotada (Joshi 1972, 98–144; 1990). Further, Possehl has carried out extensive explorations which enable a coherent settlement analysis to be made (Possehl 1980).

From these excavations it is possible to construct a picture of the nature of the pre-urban settlements (as the Prabhas Patan (Nanavati *et al.* 1971)); the arrival of Harappan urban influences around BC 2500; and their withdrawal some five or six centuries thereafter. The upshot of Possehl's research is that there is seen to be a marked increase in the number of settlements in the earlier part of the post-urban phase, with only 18 identified settlements of the period of urban Harappan contact (Rangpur IIA), as against 120 for the succeeding post-urban period (Rangpur IIB–C). A recognizably local, regional character survived throughout all these stages, and remained in the end as the foundation of the cultural style of the region. This style therefore remains as the characteristic form of the post-urban culture of this region. In view of the evidence of contacts with Sindh it is interesting to note that the 'foreign' elements noticed at Chanhu-daro, for instance in the stamp seals, have not so far been found in Saurashtra. One can only speculate on the significance of this: perhaps it indicates that these traits were lost during an initial period of acculturation in Sindh and before an immigrant population spread further east.

Post-urban sites in West Punjab and the Sarasvati Valley

The post-urban phase in the western Punjab is associated with the distinctive style of the pottery first discovered in Cemetery H at Harappa, and hence is often referred to as the Cemetery H culture. Other sites associable with this culture are known from Mughal's explorations in Bahawalpur, but none of these has as yet been excavated (Mughal 1982, 85–95). Evidently related sites also occur in the east Punjab, and these will be mentioned below. But there is to date a paucity of evidence, since apart from Cemetery H only one example of an associated settlement has so far been excavated – the topmost occupation of the Citadel mound (AB) at Harappa. Here Vats reported a mixed ceramic assemblage with some Harappan and some Cemetery H-type pottery found in the 'decadent' structures of reused brick. In Cemetery H, however, the burials contained only the latter type of pottery. Although this is clearly distinguishable from the Harappan, in both range of forms and painted decoration, it represents, from a craft point of view, a closer approximation to it than does the Jhukar ware. Nevertheless, it provides a rather similar indication, that the potters' community was still working within the bounds of the Harappan tradition, but had for whatever reason adopted new forms and decorations, perhaps because they were working for new patrons. The suggestion is, as Vats inferred, that Cemetery H may be regarded as the final stage of the Harappan culture, but that it also represents a time when conquerors or immigrants from outside had captured or dominated the city. We are inclined to agree with Vats's view that these new arrivals may have been Indo-Aryan speakers. It must be remembered that to date the Cemetery H culture does not show some of the exotic features, such as the button seals, which characterize Chanhu-daro during the Jhukar phase, and that there are other marked differences between the two cultures. It is to be hoped that with the current American excavations at Harappa we shall at last learn more about this extremely important period at that site.[1]

Mughal's Cholistan survey has revealed extraordinarily interesting information (Mughal 1990b; 1992). During the antecedent stages of Harappan urbanism a cluster of settlements developed around Derawar, in an area which appears to have been at that time an inland delta of the Hakra-Sarasvati river (99 sites are recorded of the Hakra phase; and 40 of the Early Harappan). Both in terms of site density, and size and gradation of size, these settlements reach a climax during the urban period (174 sites are recorded). In the post-urban phase sites related to Cemetery H occur, but these tend to be both much smaller in size and fewer in number, and to be located mainly along the riverbanks rather than clustered throughout the inland delta. Only 50 sites of this period are recorded. The implications of this appear to be that, for whatever reasons (tectonic, climatic

---

[1]   This was written before the first reports of these excavations had appeared: these seem to emphasize the continuity of this period with the preceding one, and thus to argue against the presence of foreign conquest (Kenoyer 1991b, 56)

or human), the inland delta was in process of drying up and the flow of the Sarasvati was in decline. A further stage of this process can be seen in the distribution of sites of the succeeding 'Painted Gray ware' period, when a few small settlements are found strung out along the Sarasvati, far to the east of the former delta-oasis.

On present showing there are certainly some intriguing lacunae in the evidence from this group of sites. In particular one is inclined to speculate on the reasons for the striking differences between them and the sites of Sind. One may wonder whether the Cemetery H culture is strictly speaking post-urban, or whether it may represent a slightly earlier stage than does the Jhukar culture, and thus be nearer to the final stage of Harappan urban decline. If it be the latter, one has still to account for the almost complete absence of characteristically Harappan urban traits in the graves of the cemetery. Not least, one may wonder why such a potentially important and seminal phase in the cultural history of South Asia should have been for so many years neglected by the archaeologists of both India and Pakistan.

Post-urban sites in the eastern Punjab, northern Rajasthan and Haryana

To the east of Harappa and across the modern Indian border, in the upper reaches of the Hakra-Sarasvati and Drishadvati rivers, another, related situation is found. Here again agricultural settlements occur from pre-urban times. When the full urban stage arose in Sindh and the western Punjab, the sites of this region appear to show two different types: one group continued with a typical pre-urban style, showing at most a small number of urban features, while the other, consisting of the larger sites, shows a more markedly urban style. It has been suggested that this may indicate a process of urban expansion into the region, and that the larger sites may represent a class of Harappan administrative centres imposed from outside.

With the end of the urban phase the situation compares with that of the western Punjab. The size-range of settlements is on the whole smaller, suggesting the disappearance of the large urban, or incipient urban, settlements of the preceding period. Most writers have remarked on the way in which, in this region too, the post-urban pottery reflects the older pre-urban style, while the specifically urban style is eclipsed. On present showing it seems that the sites of this group are particularly to be found in the eastern part of the region, and that there are markedly fewer sites towards the west. Probably the clearest published account to date of an excavated site here is for Banawali (Bisht 1982, 120–2). Here, the first two periods represent the pre-urban and urban phases respectively, and Period III corresponds to the post-urban. Unlike the brick houses of the earlier periods, the post-urban houses are made of pressed earth. The pottery belongs to a typical Mitathal IIB–Cemetery H complex. But, as the excavator remarks, 'the Indus script, seals, clay bangles, steatite disc beads, chert weights, and for that matter stone blades ... are conspicuous by their absence'. Bisht concludes:

> On the whole, this period witnesses an overall disintegration of cities and towns and the emergence of smaller, more nebulous settlements concentrated in fertile areas ... Further, it amply demonstrates that there should be some serious inherent weakness in the socio-economic mechanism of the preceding period. That is why it broke down under its sheer weight and society once again relapsed into its pastoral and agricultural lifestyle.

There has been considerable discussion among Indian scholars regarding the classification and grouping of the many sites which may be assigned to this region. We refer the reader to some representative contributions for further details (Suraj Bhan 1975; Sharma 1982, 142–65; Dikshit 1984, 253–69). An important study of the sites and their relationships has been made by Shaffer (1986, 195–235), and we largely agree with his views. Shaffer points to the absence of any dramatic cultural break between those sites where Mature Harappan interaction networks are in evidence, and those where they are absent. He also suggests that the eastern shift of rivers (to which we shall further allude below) fostered the rise of a new set of cultural interaction networks organized to meet the ecological and cultural conditions related to settlement in the Ganges plains (1986, 228–9).

Sites of the northern Ganges-Yamuna Doab

The easternmost spread of Harappan urbanism appears to have been into the northern parts of the Ganges-Yamuna Doab. There are however very few – if any – sites which actually testify to a Mature Harappan presence in this area. By contrast there are many more sites of the post-urban period, comparing closely with those of the eastern Punjab, and showing marked resemblances of pottery style and decoration to the Cemetery H ware. In this region too the same clear recollections of the pre-urban phase are in evidence. A good representative of a site of this group is Hulas, excavated by K. N. Dikshit, who has also contributed a useful paper on the site and its relations to the post-urban complex (Dikshit 1982, 339–51). It seems clear that the urban Harappan culture scarcely penetrated the Doab, and that the observable influences are more likely to be related to the post-Harappan spread. Similarly, these in their turn scarcely extend east from the Doab, so that in the middle Ganges valley a different cultural style flourished throughout the period preceding the emergence of cities there in the first millennium BC.

The closing stages of the post-urban period

In each of the regions we have been reviewing there appears to have been a somewhat similar pattern with individual variations of detail. There is not as yet sufficiently extensive radiocarbon dating to permit us to determine how far the end of the Harappan urban phase coincided from one region to another; but there appears, in each case, to follow a period which we have been calling post-urban. During this period regional cultures flourished, showing local characters of their own, often recalling the far older pre-urban cultures of the region in question, while retaining some traits of the urban phase, but lacking such specifically urban elements as the use of script and seals. As Possehl remarks, these are, nonetheless, sufficiently distinctive as to be regarded as cultures in their own right.

When we turn to consider the closing stages of the post-urban period, we are struck by a certain feeling of *déjà vu* as if the events which had earlier led to the end of the Harappan urban phase may have been repeating themselves. Although the chronology of the later stages of the post-urban period is still far from firmly established, and many more dates are needed to improve this state of affairs, a number of salient features provide at least an indication of these events. In Sindh there appears to have been a major abandonment of settlements, followed by a temporary occupation by people using crude handmade pottery, named after the type site of Jhangar. Occupation of this sort is found at both Chanhu-daro and Amri. It seems probable that the Jhangar culture represents the campsites of a population which was nomadic and mainly pastoralist. Although this culture has not been properly dated so far, the comparisons of its pottery suggest a date around the end of the second millennium or the opening of the first (Allchin and Allchin 1968, 146–7). The suggestion from Sindh therefore is that there was a deterioration of climate towards the end of the second millennium BC and that this led to a large-scale abandonment of settlements. Such a pattern would be characteristic of areas of marginal rainfall, such as Sindh. The proximity of the Thar desert and the greater variability of annual precipitation means that even a small shift of climate over a period of several years can have far-reaching results. We may recall the rather similar evidence from Maharashtra, where the Late Jorwe culture seems to have witnessed a comparable abandonment of agricultural settlements (Dhavalikar 1988, 71–2), taking place around the end of the second millennium BC and during the opening centuries of the first.

Mughal's dramatic inference of dessication in the Derawar area of Cholistan offers evidence of a related, although quite separate trend, in that here the sites of the post-urban phase seem to have been abandoned mainly because of the gradual drying up of the Sarasvati-Ghaggar river. The absence of sites of the subsequent period (that associated with the Painted Grey ware) in the Derawar 'oasis' or to the west, and their presence at fairly regular intervals along the line of the Ghaggar river, well to the east, may partly relate to this riverine change and partly to climatic (Mughal 1982, 1992). Indeed, this discovery leads us to wonder whether the progressive drying up of the waters of the Sarasvati, perhaps taking place over a period of several successive centuries, or more probably advancing as a series of separate episodes, may not have contributed to the reduction of rainfall in the whole area, and may not already have been a potent factor in the breakdown of the Harappan urban system itself (Raikes 1967a; Allchin, Goudie and Hedge 1978, 17–21; Shaffer 1986, 226–8).

In Saurashtra there does not appear to have been so dramatic a change in rainfall or settlement, but even so the number of settlements associated with the earlier post-urban phases (Rangpur IIb–c) is 120, far greater than the 32 sites of the succeeding phase (Rangpur III). Moreover, there is a reduction in the average size of settlements between the two periods, and the distribution of sites is also over a much reduced area in the later period (Possehl 1980, 56–67). Thus here too there is a suggestion of a comparable climatic shift at this time. However, in this region there is a much stronger indication of continuity of the potter's craft traditions, suggesting a more substantial continuity of population and culture as a whole. There is also some evidence that during the latter stage of the post-urban period, perhaps coinciding with the decline in rainfall, the cultivation of millets, particularly sorghum (*jawar*) and pennisetum typhoideum (*bajra*) gained in importance (Possehl 1986, 237–56).

Farther north, in the west and east Punjab, Haryana and the Ganges Doab, the evidence for the end of the post-urban period is rather different. Here the proximity of the Himalayas produces today a higher and less variable precipitation than farther south, and in the past this situation is likely to have prevailed even when there were periods of aridity around the southern and eastern margins of the desert. Moreover, the tectonic movements which are inferred to have been responsible for the drying up of the Sarasvati were also probably responsible for its capture by the Yamuna, resulting in a new area of fertile, well-watered land which may well have constituted an attraction to those who discovered it. Hence there is not such clear evidence of abandonment of settlements in this region, and there is correspondingly more indication of the continuity of the local population and their culture. The most significant evidence to date comes from sites in the eastern part of the region. At Bhagawanpura in Haryana, J. P. Joshi (1993, 16–17) discovered a sequence beginning with a typical post-urban occupation with many-roomed houses of mud brick; this was succeeded by a second sub-period in which the only recorded structures were single-roomed circular huts of timber and thatch; and this in turn was followed by a further building phase, in which houses were once again built with many rooms, in mud brick or pressed earth. During these two latter phases the ceramic assemblage is augmented by progressively increasing quantities of Painted Grey ware. In the northern parts of the Doab similar evidence is found at other excavated sites, notably at Hulas (Dikshit 1982, 339–51).

Conclusion

We have now reached a point where we may attempt to round off this chapter and arrive at some sort of conclusions. There are some indications that both the end of the Harappan urban period and the end of the subsequent post-urban phase may be linked in one way or another to major changes of environment. The breakdown of the Harappan urban society must have been accompanied by a reversion to a settlement pattern which was in some ways closer to that of the pre-urban stage. The post-urban period witnessed the continuation of many elements of the existing culture, but was accompanied by an almost complete disappearance of some of the specifically urban crafts, and offers no evidence of the continued use of writing. It is probable too that the weakening of the urban culture presented an invitation to some of their predatory neighbours, and thus coincided with incursions of peoples from the hills to the west, who almost certainly established for themselves dominant roles in relation to the existing population of the Indus system. The deterioration of climate may well have been part of a much wider phenomenon, and this may have been a factor which encouraged the population of regions of Central Asia to move southward in search of better living conditions.

During the post-urban period there may have been further episodes in the deterioration of climate, leading to the need for the populations of arid regions to develop new strategies for survival, including a recourse to pastoral nomadism and particularly an increase in the cultivation of millets. It will be interesting, as research continues, to discover how and when this new subsistence basis spread. Around this time it occurs not only in Saurashtra (Possehl 1986; Possehl and Raval 1989, 25); but also in neighbouring southern Rajasthan; on the western edges of the Indus at Pirak (Jarrige 1985, 45–6); and in Maharashtra. At Pirak Jarrige has seen this development as an important adaptation to the arid conditions which prevailed, providing a multi-cropping system which enhanced the food-producing potentials of marginal areas unsuited to wheat or barley.

It appears that the population of Sindh was largely devastated, and this may well account for the rapid disappearance of urban craft specialisms, since the effects of famine would have been felt first in the cities. By comparison the Punjab seems to have offered a more stable climatic regime, and there is every indication that many settlements survived throughout the post-urban period. This is particularly the case in the eastern Punjab, Haryana and the northern part of the Ganges-Yamuna Doab. These areas point towards a general drift of population towards the east, probably in response both to deterioration of climate in the Indus region and to the capture of the waters of the Sarasvati by the Yamuna river. This leads to the exploitation of rice as a cereal crop as another agricultural innovation in this context. These northern regions therefore formed an important centre for the survival of elements of the Indus culture and ideology, and for the new Indo-Aryan cultural synthesis which must have been taking place there. In the south, Saurashtra and southern Rajasthan probably also witnessed a less extreme situation than did Sindh, where the agricultural regime was augmented by cultivation of millets. Here the post-urban cultures seem to have survived right to the end of the second millennium, and once again offer a likely region for the survival and passing on of elements of Indus and post-Indus cultural traditions.

Towards the close of the second millennium the settlements of the post-urban period begin to show a new dynamism, particularly in the eastern Punjab and Ganga-Yamuna Doab. This development is coincidental with the manufacture and spread of the pottery known as Painted Grey ware, and more importantly with the spread and gradual increase in the manufacture of tools and weapons of iron. One of the earliest dated occurrences of this metal is at Pirak, where the first iron occurs early in Period III, perhaps slightly before BC 1000, and iron becomes more common later in the same period, probably from c. BC 900. It is only after this date that ironworking becomes at all common and that its full influence upon the social and economic life begins to exert itself.

Although there is no very good evidence for dating the various cultural phenomena which we have noticed in the different parts of the Indus system, nor even evidence which would allow their sequential ordering, we conclude, on the basis of the above discussion, that the post-urban period may be provisionally divided into three phases, which for want of any other terms we may call early, middle and late post-urban.

– The early phase includes those sites which appear to represent the final urban, or transitional stages and which may well prove difficult to recognize as either specifically urban or post-urban. This phase we may postulate to have extended from c. BC 2000–1600. We believe that the Cemetery H culture at Harappa and elsewhere belongs to it.
– The middle phase by contrast appears to represent already fully sub-urban cultures and we may regard the Jhukar culture of Sindh as typical. This phase also seems to witness a major expansion of population and settlements in several parts of the region, and we postulate that it falls broadly between BC 1600 and 1200.
– The late phase is less uniform than the middle and appears to have coincided with major changes of climate. We may suggest that it dates from c. BC 1200–800. In Singh it is represented by the small, poor settlements of the Jhangar culture; and elsewhere by a broadly new settlement pattern and by the first evidence of the use of iron.

The late phase is important because it appears to mark a series of new cultural adaptations to the deterioration of climate. In some areas, and particularly in the East Punjab, Haryana and Ganga-Yamuna Doab it appears to be the foundation upon which the early urbanism of the first millennium BC was to be built. The period associated with the Painted Grey ware has been widely regarded as one of incipient urbanism in the Ganges valley, and the date of its commencement is still the subject of some discussion. These topics are properly the subject of chapter 6 of this book and will be discussed below. But before we do so we must first consider the controversial subject of the arrival of Indo-Aryan language-speaking people in South Asia and the way in which they achieved a position of cultural dominance and status.

CHAPTER 4

LANGUAGE, CULTURE AND THE CONCEPT OF ETHNICITY

F. R. ALLCHIN

The earliest literary remains from South Asia, excluding the still unread inscriptions of the Indus civilization, are the Vedas, and the first datable and readable inscriptions are those of Asoka in the third century BC. The Vedas, along with the great volume of exegetic literature which follows them, and the Asokan inscriptions, are all in Indo-Aryan languages, and the whole series offers a clear history of language change and development over a period of not less than one thousand years, prior to Asoka. To try to discover whether, how and when these languages arrived in South Asia, took root there and spread over so much of the subcontinent is therefore a matter of interest in its own right, and relevant, even if somewhat indirectly, to the main thrust of this volume – the emergence of cities and states in the first millennium BC. It is also a topic on which there are remarkably divergent views: at one extreme there is the conservative Indian view which regards the Aryans and their languages as indigenous to South Asia; at the other, broadly stated, is the view of western philologists that the Indo-Aryan languages were carried to South Asia around the middle of the second millennium BC, as part of the much wider dispersal of Indo-European languages. Between lie a number of variant views which would have the first Indo-Aryan speakers arrive in South Asia at an earlier date, perhaps even during the lifetime of the Indus civilization. If we conclude that the Indo-Aryan languages cannot have been indigenous to South Asia, the further question of how they came to occupy the dominant position, which for so long they have held there, calls for explanation.

The present chapter is intended to be read in parallel with chapter 3, which is a more or less straight conspectus of archaeological data relating to the post-urban period (i.e. the second millennium BC), in the Indus valley and adjacent regions. In the present chapter we shall consider the evidence of comparative philology, and seek to discover whether there is any relationship between the model it offers and that of archaeology. In this attempt we shall be writing largely at the level of hypothesis. At the outset we wish to dispose of certain 'Aunt Sallies': we cannot agree with the school of thought which maintains that 'the introduction of the Indo-Aryan language family to South Asia was not dependent upon population movement' (Shaffer 1986, 230); we hold the view that the initial introduction of any ancient language to a new area can only have been as a result of the movement of speakers of that language into that area. This in no way disregards the probability that thereafter, increasingly as time went by, the further spread of the languages took place, along with processes of bilingualism and language replacement, meaning that the proportion of original speakers would decline while that of acquired speakers would continue to rise. The discipline of comparative philology, at least as it affects the history of the Indo-European, Indo-Iranian and Indo-Aryan languages, offers a well-established, if conservative, method, but like everything else it has its limitations. It has constructed on philological grounds a sequence of stages in language structure and development which maps out the 'separation' of different branches and sub-branches of these languages. But it has to rely largely on other methods, particularly archaeology, to supply any real chronology for these sequential stages: hence the need to read chapters 3 and 4 in relation to one another.

Discussion of the growth and spread of the Indo-European languages and attempts to relate them to archaeological evidence are quite numerous: the past decade has seen a number of substantial contributions and advances. In the main we shall confine ourselves to reference to a few recent sources:

- Burrow's important short paper on the Proto-Indoaryans (Burrow 1973);
- our own short paper on 'Archaeological and language historical evidence for the movement of Indo-Aryan speaking peoples into India and Pakistan' (Allchin 1980, 1981) and *Rise of Civilization in India and Pakistan* (Allchin and Allchin 1982), both focussing primarily on South Asia;
- Colin Renfrew's *Archaeology and Language, the puzzle of Indo-European Origins* (Renfrew 1987) offers a new and controversial interpretation of the archaeological data which, at least as far as South Asia is concerned, is hard to reconcile with the long-accepted evidence of philology;
- Asko Parpola's important monograph on *The Coming of the Aryans to Iran and India and the Cultural and Ethnic Identity of the Dasas* (Parpola 1988) further develops a consistent line of investigation which its author has followed for nearly two decades (Parpola 1974);
- J. P. Mallory's *In Search of the Indo-Europeans* (Mallory 1989) provides a balanced and reasonable, if somewhat unadventurous, discussion of the whole Indo-European language field, together with a broad survey of the current state of archaeological knowledge, and gives new insights into some aspects of the subject;
- Recently, Harmatta (1981, 1992) has presented a short and masterly synthesis of the relevant philological evidence, integrated with many recent studies. His contribution is particularly helpful for its inclusion of the evidence for borrowings by the Finno-Ugrian languages from Indo-European and even Indo-Iranian.

As the title of this chapter suggests, we shall introduce into this discussion several concepts, apart from languages and their speakers, which require consideration as they are not infrequently used in conjunction with the words 'Indo-Aryan' and 'Aryan'; they include, particularly, the related concepts of culture and ethnicity. Their employment raises delicate questions, whose explosive qualities are apparent both in the heated debates they arouse among scholars, and in the inter-ethnic violence so widely and tragically occurring in the modern world.

We should perhaps begin by indicating how we propose to use these terms. When we are writing of the languages and of the people who were at the time speaking them, *Indo-Aryan* will be used in its well-defined, narrowly linguistic sense. This usage does not carry any physical connotation; but this does not preclude us from recognizing that an Indo-Aryan speaker might be so, either by virtue of birth and family, or of having acquired the speech through interaction with others who already had it. When we refer specifically to the languages of the period prior to their arrival in South Asia, we shall follow Burrow's term Proto-Indoaryan (Burrow 1973).

In using the word culture we shall attempt to elucidate some of our earlier writings (Allchin 1980, 1981, 1982b), in that we envisage a situation in which groups of Indo-Aryan speakers arrived in an area where another language or languages were prevalent, and living there for a period in interaction with the existing population, became involved in a process of acculturation. We are here thinking specifically of the greater Indus system, where archaeology indicates that there was already an extensive population, both settled and nomadic, presumably but by no means certainly speaking a non-Indo-Aryan language or languages, and either still in the Harappan urban stage or in what we are calling the post-urban stage. We previously wrote that this process must have involved:

> a progressive Aryanisation of the existing communities; and a progressive
> Indianisation of the immigrants. The results in either case would be the
> production of a series of related but no doubt individual syntheses, which we
> may expect to be, culturally speaking, Indo-Aryan. (1980, 73)

In our present context we shall seek to avoid such terms as *culturally Aryan* or *culturally Indo-Aryan* for those who we postulate to have belonged to these groups, because we believe that they are likely to be misunderstood or misinterpreted. We choose rather a term which more clearly recognizes the cultural diversity of the resulting society, and shall therefore refer to *acculturated Aryan*.

The terms ethnic and ethnicity have been introduced by Erdosy (1989) in discussing 'Aryan' and 'Arya' and are taken as denoting consciousness of an ethnic identity among the members of the society of the time of the Rigveda and thereafter. This approach is further developed in chapters 6 and 7 below. Erdosy seeks to arrive at a sound conceptual framework for the archaeological consideration of ethnicity, and argues convincingly for adopting the approach of Barth (1969), who had stressed the importance of interaction in the formation of ethnic identities, and writes that 'ethnic groups are categories of ascription and identification by the actors themselves, and thus have the characteristic of organising interaction between people'. We find some difficulties in following this usage. These arise on two main grounds: first, that Erdosy's adaptation of Barth's definition raises the question of how far such categories of ascription and identification can ever be recognized in archaeological contexts or data, in the absence of the actors themselves; and second, that the common usage and understanding of 'ethnicity' in its modern sense is today so widely thought of in relation to the modern situation that its use in an archaeological context is likely to be distorted and profoundly misunderstood. In these circumstances we are inclined to discuss Aryan culture in terms of cultural-pluralism rather than of ethnic identity.

We shall argue in what follows that these several usages probably reflect different aspects and stages of a continuing cultural process, rather than a number of disparate episodes.

Our starting point is the clear assumption that the Indo-Aryan languages were originally brought to India-Pakistan by immigrants or nomads arriving from outside and encountering an already heterogeneous population who spoke other languages, probably, but by no means certainly or exclusively, non-Indo-European. Such movement, certainly is unlikely to have constituted an invasion or invasions, and it may not have involved conquest. This hypothesis also postulates that there must have been a subsequent process of interaction in which the indigenous languages were gradually replaced by the newly introduced language(s).

Mallory (1989, 258–9) provides a lucid discussion of the mechanics of this process. He writes:

> When two languages come into contact, people speaking one of them do not immediately abandon their own and adopt the language of the other. A prerequisite to language shift is societal bilingualism. This may remain quite stable over a long period but in the case of the Indo-European expansions it was obviously a prelude to the adoption of Indo-European. We assume for the expansion of the Indo-European languages that native populations became bilingual for a time, speaking both their own language and adopting that of the intruder. Normally social context determines which language is spoken ... If the intrusive language is employed for more and more different contexts, it will eventually lead to the total replacement, or language death as it is sometimes called, of the native language.

The same author is equally clear in discussing the factors which lead to this kind of language replacement (Mallory 1989, 259):

> It is clear, then, that the crux of the issue is bilingualism and how it is induced. Without state coercion, we do not imagine that second languages are forced upon people. Rather, bilingualism is induced when the context of speech

requires the use of the new language if one wishes to obtain better access to goods, status, ritual or security. The success of Indo-European expansions should have been due to their ability to offer such advantages to the populations with whom they came in contact.

This offers a very plausible hypothesis of what may have happened in northwest India-Pakistan when Indo-Aryan speakers moved into the Indus valley. Renfrew also discusses the phenomenon of language replacement in the context of the Indo-European language spread. Two of the models he proposes in this connection, those of system collapse and elite dominance (Renfrew 1987, 131–7), appear to be those most appropriate to our context. In particular, we regard the collapse of the Harappan urban system, which, as we suggested in the previous chapter, was probably precipitated by major climatic and tectonic events, as providing a favourable backdrop for language replacement of this kind.

The origins of the Indo-Aryan speakers and their arrival in northwest India-Pakistan

There is a fashionable tendency these days to dismiss 'Aryan invasions' as mere myths, the aberrations of 'Diffusionist' thinking (e.g. Shaffer 1984, 77–90). As we have seen above, our view is that if the Indo-Aryan languages were *not* autochthonous to the Indian subcontinent, they must have been brought from outside by people who already spoke them, and who may moreover have already referred to themselves as 'Aryans' (Allchin 1980, 70; Mallory 1989, 257–8). There has been a considerable degree of unanimity regarding this among almost all scholars who have attempted to explain the phenomenon of the Indo-European languages and their spread. Although there has not been comparable agreement regarding the hypothetical Indo-European 'homeland' from which the initial dispersal of the languages is supposed to have taken place, the weight of opinion still looks towards a region extending across from the north of the Black Sea in the west to the north of the Caspian and beyond in the east. There has also been a fairly general agreement that the Proto-Indoaryan speakers at one time lived on the steppes of Central Asia and that at a certain time they moved southwards through Bactria and Afghanistan, and perhaps the Caucasus, into Iran and India–Pakistan (Burrow 1973; Harmatta 1992).

A novel and somewhat revolutionary view has recently been put forward by Renfrew (1987, 189–97) (his 'hypothesis A'), suggesting that the original centre – the Indo-European 'homeland' from which the dispersal began – was in Anatolia and that the eastward spread towards India may have come not from a northerly direction via Central Asia, but rather from a westerly direction across Iran. Renfrew further suggests that this movement may have coincided with and accompanied the spread of early agriculture and must therefore have taken place much earlier than any other writer has so far envisaged. Renfrew (1987, 197–205) allows for the possibility of a second hypothesis (B) which is closer to the more commonly accepted version; or even for a blending of the two hypotheses.

From our point of view there are a number of serious objections to Renfrew's hypothesis A, and we believe that it cannot be sustained so far as the movement of the Indo-Aryan languages into South Asia is concerned. However, because the suggestion has wide ramifications, we shall digress briefly to consider some of the grounds for questioning it. For one thing there is really no evidence that the rise of agriculture in the Indo-Iranian borderlands, approximately ten thousand years ago, was anything other than an indigenous development, and while there is at Mehrgarh very early evidence of long-distance trade and interaction with other regions, there is not as yet anything to suggest that the initial impetus of settled agriculture arose as the result of an outside movement of this kind. Indeed, as Vavilov (1951) long since observed, the Indo-Iranian borderlands are still the home of wild progenitors of wheat and barley, and it is likely that some at least of the cereal grains discovered at Mehrgarh were locally domesticated. A second major consideration is that nearly all the scholarly attempts to pinpoint the language of the Indus seal inscriptions agree (with one to two exceptions) that the evidence points to its being structurally ancestral to Dravidian. While it is to be expected that the seal inscriptions, if and when their reading is achieved, may be found to include loan words from Indo-Aryan and perhaps other languages, the probability remains that the underlying language structure was Dravidian. Regrettably there is not as yet an agreed reading for the inscriptions; nevertheless the arguments of Parpola, Knorosov, Mahadevan, Fairservis and others show considerable areas of agreement regarding the implications of the structure of the language of the inscriptions. A third argument relates to the broad perspective of the history of the Indo-European languages, and of their separation and development through time, as they are reconstructed with the aid of philology. The generally accepted philological view is that the Indo-Iranian branch became separated from the other branches around (?)BC 4000–3000, and that the Indo-Aryan and Iranian speakers themselves separated from each other, to form the Indo-Aryan and Iranian sub-branches, probably during the second half of the third millennium (Burrow 1973; Harmatta 1981, 80–2; and 1992, 370–8). If Renfrew's hypothesis A were viable one would expect to find traces also of a far earlier Indo-European language stratum surviving in Iran and northwest India-Pakistan in fossil form, in toponyms, etc. Likewise one might expect to discover in the Vedas traces of loans or influences from a language belonging to a far earlier stage than that represented by the Early Indo-Aryan of the Vedas. A fourth argument is that the archaeological evidence, as we read it in the previous chapter, points in much the same direction as the generally accepted philological hypothesis for Indo-Aryan origins. For all these reasons therefore we shall assume a hypothesis which follows in broad terms the generally held view.

Once we accept the basic premise that the Indo-Aryan languages were introduced into South Asia by immigrants from outside who already spoke them, we must next consider when and how those immigrants came. It is unlikely that there was any single migration, let alone 'invasion', and our model must be flexible enough to allow for several different types of movement, probably taking place on more than one occasion, and representing a number of stages in time and place. We can see no way in which the philological evidence can supply us with hard dates for the first arrival of Proto-Indoaryan speakers on the northwestern borders of the Indus valley, and the archaeological evidence is as yet only moderately better.

We shall now review some of the evidence we assembled in the previous chapter, in terms of our hypothesis of a number of chronological stages which we may tentatively identify as follows:

1. First encounters (c.? BC 2200–2000)
2. Interaction and conquest (c. BC 2000–1700)
3. Acculturation (c. BC 1700–1200)
4. Emergence of Aryan cultural-pluralism (c. BC 1200–800)

Indo-Aryan advance and acculturation

1. First encounters

Indo-Iranian-speaking tribes of pastoral nomads probably began moving south-wards into southern Central Asia by around the middle of the third millennium, there coming in contact with an existing population who may have spoken either another Indo-European language or, more probably, some other language or languages. As a result of this movement they took to a more settled subsistence in which agriculture played a greater role. Their traces may be seen in Uzbeqistan and Tajikstan in the sites and cemeteries of the Sapalli Tepe group, in Turkmenistan at Namazga V, and in northeastern Iran in Hissar III. We do not mean by this that these sites were exclusively occupied by members of one language group, or that the stable population of these areas was somehow displaced by them; rather we are thinking in terms of typical culture-contact situations, where the nomads established relations with the settled agriculturalists. Somewhere around the middle of the third millennium the Iranian- and the Indian-speaking tribal groups became separated from one another; the former remaining north of the line of the Kopet Dag–Hindu Kush mountains, and the latter moving southwards into the Iranian plateau and spreading out eastwards and westwards, across Afghanistan towards the Indus valley to the east, and towards the Caucasus and Anatolia to the west.

The earliest archaeological traces of this southwards movement into South Asia may be represented by the cemeteries south of Mehrgarh and at nearby Sibri (Santoni 1984, 52–60); in the recently discovered Quetta grave cache (Jarrige and Usman Hassan 1989, 150–66), and in various other assemblages from Baluchistan. None of these is yet firmly dated, but in the light of a single radiocarbon date from Mehrgarh VII, we may expect them to be around 2000–1900 BC (Jarrige and Usman Hassan, 1989). In all these instances, as far as the evidence is available, a major element of the material culture seems to be an imported style, reflecting a probable source of the movement in the Bactrian region. We have as yet no idea of the size of these groups or their numbers. Nor is there any reason to suppose that they were the first such groups to spread southwards from Central Asia. There may well have been earlier groups, both Proto-Indoaryan speaking and others, who followed the same trail. We may enquire what brought these hypothetically Proto-Indoaryan-speaking tribes to the mouth of the Bolan pass at this time, and probable answers are not hard to find. For one thing it seems likely that the Proto-Indoaryans were involved in one way of another in trade, much as some pastoral nomads in South Asia have continued into the present century to take advantage of their mobility to trade profitably with the settled populations. Doubtless this contact would have awakened the visitors to the rich plunder which might be had in the larger settlements, and particularly in the Indus cities, as centres of craft specialism. This role certainly fits the picture which we have from the material record of the Indo-Aryans as mobile and warlike aristocracy. It is tempting to think that such intruders played a part in the sack of many settlements, recorded about this time in Baluchistan, and possibly, as Wheeler opined, in the downfall of the Indus cities themselves. But it seems more plausible, as we suggested in the previous chapter, that their arrival on the western borders of the Indus system more or less coincided with the collapse of the urban Harappan culture (which we believe to have been primarily due to other causes). This collapse would have created a power vacuum in the Indus valley, and offered a powerful centripetal attraction to such groups. Parpola (1988) has suggested that these first Indo-Aryans may have been the *Dasas, Dasyus* and *Panis* who later appear in the Rigveda as the opponents of the Rigvedic Aryans. For this reason he identifies them as 'pre-Vedic' Aryans, and this name may well be correct, although, as we shall argue below, its significance still calls for elucidation.

2. Indo-Aryan conquest and interaction

A rather different picture is presented by the evidence found in the Indus urban settlements. We have discussed this from the archaeological point of view in the previous chapter. At Kalibangan the curious ritual hearths (if indeed they are so) reported in domestic, public and civic situations are suggestive of a practice ancestral to the Indo-Aryan fire sacrifices, and it is tempting to see this as an indication of the presence of Indo-Aryan speakers already during the Harappan urban phase.

At Harappa, Cemetery H appears to represent a transitional urban/post-urban phase. The evidence is admittedly slender, but there appears to be a good case for seeing in the Cemetery H culture the presence of an element of foreign intruders who have dominated the existing population and exploited their craft products, though modified to suit their own tastes. This is suggested to us particularly by such things as the distinctive pottery forms and decoration of the Cemetery, and by the new burial rites of which it provides evidence. The current American excavations at Harappa are clearly of great interest and their outcome is eagerly awaited as hitherto no settlement area of this period has been excavated, apart from the original work of Vats on the upper levels of the Citadel mound, and there are as yet no radiocarbon dates for the Cemetery H phase. The situation at Mohenjo-daro also possibly indicates some sort of violent end to the city, though of what kind is not clear.

At Chanhu-daro and at Amri the Harappan occupation is followed by that known as the Jhukar phase. This appears to represent a slightly later date than does the evidence from the other sites, and probably extends from the second into the third stage.

We may expect, pending more solid dating, that the second stage lasted from c. BC 2000–1700, and coincides with what, in the previous chapter, we have called the Early Post-urban period. Taken together these sites may be interpreted as representing a major stage in the spread of the early Indo-Aryan-speaking tribes, leading to their achieving hegemony over some sections of the existing Indus population and to the beginning of the process of acculturation we have postulated above. During this time many of the distinctive traits of material culture which pointed to the foreign origin of the makers of the Mehrgarh cemeteries disappear. It may be expected that the process of bilingualism which preceded language replacement began to operate in a limited way. By the end of stage 2 the Indo-Aryan speakers would have been substantially different from their ancestors who some centuries earlier had arrived on the frontiers of the Indus valley.

3. Indo-Aryan acculturation and progressive language replacement

The further South Asian dispersal of the Indo-Aryan tribes and their languages may be associated with a third stage of acculturation, represented by the Middle Post-urban settlements of Sindh, Punjab and Haryana, and may probably be dated between c. BC 1700 and c. 1200. We have discussed these cultures in some detail in chapter 3. It is worth recalling that the main excavated site of this period in the Indus valley is Chanhu-daro and that it produced relatively more pronounced Iranian or Central Asian traits than any other Indus site so far excavated. This may indicate either that in this area the exposure to foreign influences was greatest; or that the Jhukar culture phase at Chanhu-daro is slightly earlier than those to the east and represents an earlier stage in the process of acculturation. What we observe in these post-urban settlements suggests that the process of cultural interaction had by this time advanced so far that the different ethnic groups were already becoming integrated into a complex, culturally pluralistic social system. We may also postulate that the process of language replacement was already well advanced in these areas.

It is to be expected that during these centuries rather similar developments would be taking place more widely afield in the Ganga-Yamuna Doab, Saurashtra, Central India and Maharashtra (in the latter probably represented by the settlements of the Jorwe culture). In spite of their individual characters, these regional developments seem to represent an accelerating process of dispersal, and it is to be expected that related language replacement and cultural integration of indigenous population and Aryan immigrants, into characteristically South Asian pluralistic societies, would take place wherever Indo-Aryan bands found themselves. Thus increasingly with time the proportions of hereditary Indo-Aryan speakers would have declined as the numbers of 'new' or acquired Indo-Aryan speakers increased.

The Gandhara grave culture

A rather special case is represented by the Gandhara grave culture of the northwest valleys of Pakistan. This presents us with a clearly defined exotic pattern. Much of the material culture and burial customs revealed in the graves strikingly recalls contemporary developments in northern Iran and the Caucasus. The Gandhara graves are probably the traces of a rather separate group of immigrants who moved into the mountains, probably from the north or northwest, and remained there for centuries, largely shut off from major external influences from the Indus plains and therefore developing in a distinct way. Here again there can be little doubt that the archaeological culture involves two elements, one already locally long present, and the other newly arrived and almost certainly belonging to an Indo-Aryan-speaking group. The dates of the Gandhara grave culture are still not clearly defined, but its distinctive character probably emerges around c. BC 1700–1600. Thereafter the second and third phases of the grave culture offer closely related developing features and continue down into the early first millennium.

The Rigveda

There seems at present no way to determine at what point in this process the Indo-Aryans referred to by Parpola as 'Vedic', as opposed to 'Pre-Vedic', arrived in South Asia. Indeed, the thesis of several distinct waves of Indo-Aryan migration implies that different groups arrived at different times; rather than that different bodies of data reflect a series of developmental stages relating to one major group and their subsequent dispersal and movements. We incline towards the latter hypothesis: that there was probably a long period of movement to and from Central Asia and the frontiers of the Indus; followed by further movements into the Indus heartland; and by a series of later dispersals farther towards the east and south. In each case such movements would not have taken place in a vacuum, but would have involved fresh encounters of various kinds, some peaceful, some warlike, with existing populations and therefore producing varieties of cultural interaction. If we follow Parpola's analysis, we would expect his 'Pre-Vedic' Aryans (representing our Stage 1) to have arrived on the frontiers of the Indus region during or towards the end of the Indus civilization (i.e. c. BC 2000); to be followed after an interval of several centuries by his 'Vedic' Aryans. Formulated in terms of our hypothesis, it may be that the 'Pre-Vedic' and 'Vedic' Aryans represent members of the same group at different stages of their history. From our present point of view this in any case is not a matter of critical concern. For the moment the focus is on those Indo-Aryan speakers, whoever they may have been, who were the authors of the Rigveda.

The evidence of the Rigveda Samhita itself suggests that there were several stages in its formation. The main lines of discussion on their dating and development have changed comparatively little since Keith summarized them in 1925 (Keith 1925). We would expect the initial composition of the early hymns to date from c. BC 1800–1500, although some may be much earlier. The compilation of the hymns into the Samhita, at least in its early form (i.e. excluding Mandalas I, VIII, IX and X), was probably made around BC 1500; and the final additions (i.e. the four remaining Mandalas) were probably complete by BC 1000. Thus we may think of the period c. BC 1750–1500 as Early Vedic, the period from c. BC 1500–1300 as Vedic, and the succeeding centuries as the Late Vedic period.

4. Aryan 'ethnicity' and 'ideology'

The fourth stage in the process is represented archaeologically by the emergence of the new cultural configurations, referred to in the previous chapter, around the last quarter of the second millennium, and in the Ganges-Yamuna Doab by the appearance of the Painted Grey ware pottery. These developments we have associated with the Late Post-urban period, and particularly with its eastern manifestations in the East Punjab and Ganges-Yamuna Doab. In terms of discussion of the stages by which the Indo-Aryans became acculturated, and ultimately absorbed, into the already complex, culturally pluralistic society of north India-Pakistan, the focus now increasingly shifts towards the evidence of literature and tradition, and it is to these that we turn our attention.

As we saw above, Erdosy (1989) has referred to this fourth stage as the emergence of an 'Aryan' ethnic consciousness, and he sees its end result as an expansion of an 'Aryan' culture and the gradual incorporation of diverse ethnic groups into a poly-ethnic society. This process had undoubtedly already started in our second and third stages, but it only reaches maturity in the Late Vedic period, when the Purusa Sukta, probably one of the latest hymns in the Rigveda, appears to recognize a culturally plural, poly-ethnic Aryan society, incorporating

Brahmanas, Ksatriyas, Vis and Sudras. At this point we are on the threshold of the developing social complexity which gave rise to the cities and states of the Ganges basin.

Conclusion

Between the four stages of Indo-Aryan acculturation which we have discussed above, a considerable period had elapsed since the first arrival of Proto-Indoaryan speakers on the frontiers of the Indus system (Table 4.1). During this time they had first co-existed with the local population of the frontier regions, later they had moved on into the Indus heartlands and beyond, probably frequently establishing hegemony over the local population. Acculturation had begun, as a result of interaction with such existing communities. The process of bilingualism leading to language exchange must have continued for decades, if not centuries, and the longer it continued the greater would have been the proportions of the total population who had acquired their Indo-Aryan speech by such means. Thus while some of the older hymns of the Rigveda may date back to a time when the process of cultural interaction had scarcely – if at all – begun, others and indeed a majority, may be expected to show evidence of accruing strata of acculturation.

Table 4.1. *Suggested relationship of archaeological and cultural developments discussed in chapters 3 and 4*

Date BC	Archaeological stages (chapter 3)	Stages of Indo-Aryan acculturation (chapter 4)
2300	Mature Indus urbanism	1. First encounters
2200		Presence of Proto-Indoaryan speakers
2100		on western borders of Indus valley
	Transition to	
2000		
	Early Post-urban	2. Interaction and conquest
1900	period	Start of language replacement and
1800		acculturation
1700		
1600		3. Further advance and acculturation
1500	Middle Post-urban	Progress of language replacement and
1400	period	cultural assimilation
1300		
1200		
1100	Late Post-urban period	4. Emergent culturally-plural 'Aryan' ethnicity
1000		
900		
800		

In these circumstances when we find (as suggested in discussing a seal from Chanhu-daro (Allchin 1985) that a Harappan seal appears to illustrate a recurrent mythological theme of the Rigveda, one interpretation may be that Harappan myths had by the time of its composition become identified with the ideology of the Vedic authors; another possible interpretation is that a Vedic myth had already been absorbed into the Harappan iconography during the life of the Indus civilization; a third interpretation may be in terms of an already prevailing cultural pluralism. Whatever the interpretation may be, this situation points to a fundamentally important conclusion: that this complex culture involved a deeply rooted Indian, even Indus, element as its dominant feature; while its 'Aryan' name derived from the recollection of a remembered, or imagined, ancestry by a tiny proportion of the population, from the language they had transmitted to an ever-growing number of the native population, and from the name by which the minority group referred to themselves, and were no doubt referred to by others eager to associate themselves with the dominant group.

This analysis of the hypothetical stages of Indo-Aryan spread, and of the related chronological and archaeological evidence, should also be considered in relation to the tectonic and climatic events which we have postulated to have been a major factor in the eastwards spread of the Indo-Aryans. The hypothesis also goes some way to explain the context of the absorption of the Indo-Aryan-speaking immigrants into a poly-ethnic society, which in time acquired an ethnic consciousness of its own: a consciousness in which the Indo-Aryan speakers accorded themselves an elite role. It appears to offer an answer to two questions which have puzzled us for many years: how were the Aryans able to bestow their language (albeit in a modified form, with incorporation of some native words and phonemes, almost certainly derived from interaction with Dravidian languages) upon what must have been numerically a much larger indigenous population, including settled agriculturalists and nomadic pastoralists, along with remnants or descendants of the Indus urban population; and second, how did the Vedas achieve and maintain a position where they were regarded by at least a section of the population as the accepted fountainhead of this pluralistic society's tradition and ideology from this time forward?

CHAPTER 5

DARK AGE OR CONTINUUM? AN ARCHAEOLOGICAL ANALYSIS OF THE SECOND EMERGENCE OF URBANISM IN SOUTH ASIA

R. A. E. CONINGHAM

1. Introduction

Before proceeding farther we should give some thought to the question of how cities emerged. Their reappearance in the archaeological sequence seems dramatic, especially in respect to the still unexplained disappearance of the Indus cities. As indicated in chapter 3 it appears that a number of specifically urban traits were lost in the subcontinent after c. BC 1700. However, as Shaffer has pointed out, most of these are again present in the ensuing Early Historic period after c. BC 700 (Shaffer 1993, 59). This re-emergence or 're-urbanization' is more confusing because it occurred after a period during which it has been argued in chapter 4 that there is evidence of complex ethnic, linguistic and cultural change. So as to examine the question of how reurbanization occurred we shall concentrate our analysis on the archaeological material from this intervening period and from the earliest re-emerged urban forms.

Over the past thirty years many attempts have been made to study and identify the local and general causes of urbanization. Many of the early examples were mono-causal in approach. They identified and advocated a single prime mover or catalyst for the emergence of complexity. Wittfogel thus chose to identify irrigation, Carneiro environmental circumscription and Diakonov class conflict (Wittfogel 1957; Carneiro 1970; Diakonov 1969). Further suggested catalysts have included population growth and long-distance trade (Renfrew and Bahn 1991, 419). The reliance upon identifying a single key element in the development of an urban form or city is of course very difficult, notwithstanding the problems of archaeological visibility and artefact survival, and has been widely criticized (Flannery 1968, 85; Wenke 1984, 218–23; Renfrew and Bahn 1991, 421). In light of these weaknesses many archaeologists have adopted the study of multivariate explanations. This form of explanation is based upon systems theory which views a society or culture as a system being made up of a number of smaller sub-systems. These may include, for example, subsistence, technology, social, symbolic, external trade and population (Renfrew and Bahn 1991, 421). In such models a single small change in one sub-system can

54

transform its interactions with other sub-systems in such a way as radically alter the entire system in time. This process is known generally as the multiplier effect (ibid.). However, this form of explanation is difficult to identify archaeologically as the initial changes may be slight and thus explanation remains at a fairly general level. Further criticisms have also been made of this form of assessment (Hodder 1986, 18–33). In view of these criticisms this present chapter will attempt to analyze the archaeological evidence for the emergence of Early Historic urbanism in South Asia from a different perspective.

The methodology we shall follow is threefold. The first section will study current and past attempts to offer definitions for the term urban. These selected examples will be taken from South Asian and more general literature. It is intended, from these examples, to identify and formulate a list of various aspects of material culture which are thought to make up the constituent parts of the South Asian Early Historic city. The second section will select and isolate each of the constituent parts and will attempt to identify their earliest appearance in the archaeological record. It is hoped that this process will allow us to evaluate their individual contribution to the emergence of Early Historic cities in South Asia. The third section will attempt, in the light of the above, to identify which particular aspects of the material culture of the Early Historic period appear to have been most crucial in its formative stages.

2. Definitions

We cannot here attempt a full historical review of urban definitions but we will restrict ourselves to those most relevant to our theme. Following this we shall select those most generally used. One of the fundamental contributions towards the definition of urbanism was made by Childe in 1950. Through a methodology of recording similar features of the earliest civilizations, he formulated a list of criteria which allowed cities to be distinguished from earlier or contemporary settlements (Childe 1950, 15). It appears that he held both terms to be tightly connected and interdependent and that his criteria for the city can be equally applied to urbanism or civilization. His ten points were:

1. Size
2. Inclusion of additional classes (e.g. craftsmen, transporters)
3. Centralization of surplus
4. Monumental public buildings
5. Formulation of ruling class
6. Systems of recording and administration (script)
7. Exact and predictive sciences regulating the cycle of agricultural operation
8. Conceptualized and sophisticated styles of art
9. Long-distance trade importing raw materials
10. Social organization based upon residence rather than kinship.

(Childe 1950, 15–16).

This list has since been criticized by both Western and South Asian archaeologists and anthropologists as being too particular (Chakrabarti 1973a; Ghosh 1973a, 1973b; Joshi 1973; Keesing 1981; Connah 1987). This has led to the development of less prescriptive definitions. One such example is Kluckhohn's criteria of a city as being a settlement with upwards of 5,000 inhabitants, a written language and monumental ceremonial centres (Kluckhohn 1960, 400). This trend culminated in the production of even more widely generalized definitions. Examples would be Erdosy's definition of cities as 'the containers of those institutions that are required for the maintenance of increasingly complex and inegalitarian societies' (Erdosy 1988, 5) or Keesing's of a state as 'A political entity that exercises sovereign rights over a territory and exercises power through centralization, hierarchical political institutions of control, revenue extraction, and enforcement of law and civic duty' (Keesing 1981, 519). The generation of such broad definitions evidently makes them less useful when attempting to apply them to material culture as they might also function as a definition for any form of settlement or for culture itself.

However some South Asian scholars have avoided such generalizations by noting that Childe's criteria do at least present aspects of material culture which can be tested and as such represent an ordered and viable categorization (Chakrabarti 1973a; Ghosh 1973a). Indeed far from abandoning criteria directly applicable to material culture they have attempted to modernize them and apply them to Early Historic archaeology. Allchin thus equates the formation of cities with the following traits:

> an expansion of the site hierarchy to include a new tier of larger settlements
> (cities) at its apex; an increase in social stratification, craft specialization, etc.;
> an increase of craft production of all kinds; evidence of greatly increased trading
> activity, often over long distances; and the emergence of a new political and
> economic system (the state), with an appropriate, accompanying ideology.
> (Allchin 1990, 164)

Joshi has argued for the importance of coinage or rather monetary exchange as an additional criterion (Joshi 1973, 36b), whilst Chakrabarti has advocated the addition of a fortified settlement as a focus for political consolidation (Chakrabarti 1973a, 88). Sharma suggested a further six indicators of an urban site: mounds covering over one square mile; large baked-brick structures; roads; ring wells and tanks; coins; and large furnaces (Sharma 1974, 101). Most recently Shaffer has produced a list of ten criteria shared by both the Harappan and the Early Historic urbanization (Shaffer 1993, 59). The list's debt to Childe is obvious:

1. An economy incorporating agriculturalists and pastoralists
2. Large urban settlements
3. Use of stone, mud and fired bricks
4. Public architecture (e.g. walls and tanks)

5. Development of public and private hydraulic features
6. A highly developed craft industry
7. A homogenous material culture distributed over a large geographical region
8. Long-distance trade
9. A unified system of weights and measures
10. A written script

(Shaffer 1993).

We shall not attempt to formulate our own definition of city or urban place. For the purposes of our discussion we shall use a combination of various past attempts to identify specific criteria, notwithstanding the obvious weaknesses involved. This is done because available generalized definitions are largely incompatible with the archaeological data. From the above review it is possible to identify ten key elements of material culture which are generally held to make up or form a city or urban form. These consist of (1) a large settlement with (2) a degree of internal planning and (3) public architecture (4) at the top of a settlement hierarchy and (5) encircled by defences. Its inhabitants should have access to (6) a script, (7) craft specialization, (8) long-distance trade and (9) a subsistence strategy capable of raising the carrying capacity of the surrounding area in order to support (10) the increasing population.

3. Precursors

Having identified the various elements which define the Early Historic city, we shall now attempt to identify the 'urbanism' of these elements by testing for their presence or absence in the period between the two great South Asian urban civilizations. To this end we shall refer to a number of sites, and nine sites in particular. These are Inamgaon, Navdatoli, Atranjikhera, Anuradhapura, Charsada, Hastinapura, Kausambi, Ahar and Pirak. Their selection is based upon the detail and accessibility of their respective publications rather than as a representative sample of post-urban or non-Harappan Chalcolithic and early Iron Age culture.

3.1 Size

One of the most obvious features of the Early Historic city is its immense size. Of South Asia's Early Historic cities Pataliputra, capital of the Mauryan empire, was the largest, covering some 1,350 hectares (Erdosy 1988, 134). In chapter 10 Allchin offers two further estimates for Pataliputra, of either 2,200 hectares for the larger enclosed area, or 340 hectares for the area enclosed by the city moat. A further ten cities formed a second tier, covering over 100 hectares (ibid.). A number of the cities of the Indus civilization appear to approach these dimensions. Harappa and Mohenjo-daro covered some 85 hectares each whilst Lurewala covered 82 hectares (Chakrabarti 1979, 210–11).

In comparison with these enormous sites, post-urban and non-Harappan Chalcolithic and early Iron age settlements appear to have been small. Chalcolithic Ahar, dated by Sankalia to between c. BC 1200–1500 (Sankalia *et al.* 1969, 6) covered an area of 13.75 hectares (ibid., 7); the Ochre Coloured Pottery (OCP) and Painted Grey Ware (PGW) settlements at Hastinapura, dated respectively by Lal to pre-BC 1200 and between c. BC 1100 and 800 (Lal 1955, 23), appear to have covered c. 6.5 hectares; Kausambi has been estimated by Erdosy to have covered an area of 10 hectares between BC 1000–600 (Erdosy 1988, 51); Pirak, dated by Jarrige and Santoni to between the c. sixteenth century BC and the eighth century BC (Jarrige and Santoni 1979, 352), covered some 9 hectares (ibid.); the Period K settlement at Anuradhapura, dated to between c. BC 600 and 450, covered some 18 hectares (Deraniyagala, pers. comm.); the Red Burnished Ware occupation at the Bala Hisar at Charsada, dated by Allchin to c. pre-BC 400, covered some 13 hectares (Allchin 1989, 7); the Red Burnished Ware settlement at Taxila was approximately the same size as the one at Bala Hisar (Allchin 1982a); Inamgaon, dated by Dhavalikar to between c. BC 1600 and 700 (Dhavalikar *et al.* 1988, 134), appears to have covered some 5 hectares (ibid., 1001) whilst Daimabad appears to have occupied some 30 hectares (ibid.). Although all these settlements fall well below the area covered by the larger cities it should also be noted that a number of Harappan and Early Historic cities were distinctly smaller. Of the former period Chanhu-daro covered 6.5 hectares, Rehman Dheri 20, Lothal 4.7, Kalibangan 15, Surkotada 2.6 and Kot Diji 2.2 (Chakrabarti 1979, 210–12). Of the latter period Bhita covered only 14 hectares (Erdosy 1988, 134), Pushkalavati 25 hectares (Allchin 1989, 7), Eran 10 hectares (Erdosy 1988, 134) and even Ayodhya only 20 hectares (ibid.).

For the purpose of further comparison it is possible to convert these individual areas into terms of average population size, although obvious discrepancies are expected as to the respective densities of each site. For an average population figure per hectare we have selected Dhavalikar's estimate of 200 persons (Dhavalikar *et al.* 1988, 1001). Although this figure was calculated by the authors to apply to small Chalcolithic settlements, it is also held to be applicable to larger urban sites and takes into account open spaces, roads and public architecture (Dhavalikar and Possehl 1974, 40). We should thus expect a population of 1,000 at Inamgaon, 2,750 at Ahar, 1,300 at Hastinapura, 1,800 at Pirak, 2,600 at Bala Hisar, 3,600 at Anuradhapura and perhaps as many as 6,000 at Daimabad. As both Renfrew and Bahn and Kluckhohn refer to cities as being large population centres, often of more than 5,000 inhabitants (Renfrew and Bahn 1991, 156–7; Kluckhohn 1960, 400), this suggests that Daimabad with an estimated 6,000 inhabitants represented an urban form at the very least. It also suggests that to refer to settlements like Bhita, Pushkalavati, Ayodhya, Kot Diji, Chanhu-daro, Kalibangan and Lothal as cities, with estimated populations of 2,800, 5,000, 4,000, 440, 1,300, 3,000 and 940, respectively, one must refer to a characteristic other than size.

3.2 Internal planning

Another striking feature of both Harappan and Early Historic cities is their adoption of rigid cardinal grid plans (Wheeler 1968, 27; Auboyer 1969, 118). Many scholars have illustrated the close regularity of internal planning of the Harappan sites of Harappa, Mohenjo-daro, Kalibangan, Lothal and Surkotada (Allchin & Allchin 1986, 171–6). Similar regularity has been identified at Sisupalgarh (Lal 1949) and Bhita (Marshall 1912). Although our knowledge of the internal layout of post-urban and non-Harappan Chalcolithic and early Iron Age settlements is restricted, it appears that certain aspects of cardinal planning may be identified suggesting that such phenomena were not solely restricted to the Harappan or Early Historic period.

Apparently some such layout was evident at Inamgaon. Its excavators wrote that 'There seems to be some modicum of planning in the settlement for the houses were laid out almost in rows with an open space (about 1–5 m wide) in between which may have served as a road or lane' (Dhavalikar et al. 1988, 1002). It is also interesting to note that the buildings and thus the roads or lanes dividing them were cardinally oriented. The settlement also appears to have been divided internally into areas occupied by specific social groups. The chief's residence stood at the centre of the settlement next to the central granary-temple. The residences of 'well to do farmers' were clustered around these central features (ibid.). Artisans were located to the west of this area and Dhavalikar suggests that the more peripheral areas were occupied by poorer farmers and labourers whilst bonded labourers were located at the extreme west of the settlement (ibid.). Navdatoli appears to have had a similar plan. A building with a ritualistic fire pit was located near the centre of the settlement (Sankalia et al. 1971, 10). As at Inamgaon, rectangular structures, streets and lanes were cardinally planned, suggesting that settlement was constructed to a formal grid plan. Pirak in Baluchistan also appears to illustrate a degree of planning. Individual house units were cardinally planned and, as noted by the excavators, 'houses are part of a closely built area in which streets and lanes that intersect more or less at right angles provide a means of circulation' (Jarrige and Santoni 1979, 390). At Ahar the rectangular buildings were all cardinally orientated with the largest ones in the centre (Sankalia et al. 1969, 11). As rebuildings occurred on the levelled debris of the older houses and often to the same dimensions and plans (ibid., 216) one may suggest that there was some form of planning control. Similarly such control may be suggested from the unblocked and unencroached lanes and roads which served the various post-urban and non-Harappan Chalcolithic settlements.

3.3 Public architecutre

Childe, Shaffer, and Renfrew and Bahn have all commented on the importance of public architecture or constructions to qualify a site as urban (Childe 1950, 15;

Shaffer 1993, 59; Renfrew and Bahn 1991, 157). This certainly appears to be the case for Harappan cities (Wheeler 1968, 26–55) and is widely held to be the same for Early Historic cities (Marshall 1951, 140–1; Auboyer 1969, 124). Mohenjo-daro's citadel must be one of the best examples of the former period. This walled enclosure at the highest point of the city contained a granary, bath, pillared hall and 'college', all of monumental proportions (Wheeler 1968, 41–4). Although the evidence for monumental constructions in the latter period is very restricted, the best-known example is perhaps the pillared hall at Patna, described in chapter 10. It measured 34 m by 43 m and covered an area of 1,462 m² (Altekar and Mishra 1959, fig. 3). Although comparative data from post-urban and non-Harappan Chalcolithic and early Iron Age sites is sparse there is some evidence of public constructions.

The excavators of Pirak identified three types of houses having (1) one or two rooms with niches, (2) a block belonging to craftsmen, and (3) a much larger residence comprising of several rooms without niches (Jarrige and Santoni 1979, 391). The latter complex appears to have functioned as some form of central store and administrative centre. It covered some 400 m² and consisted of a granary (ibid., 367), courtyards, rooms and a store-room with large storage jars (ibid., 368). Finds from the rooms included a copper dagger and axe, an ivory comb, six seals and numerous impressions on clay (ibid.). These prestigious items in combination with the storage facilities suggest that the massive structure may have housed the settlement's centralizing authority. A further example of Chalcolithic public buildings has been identified in the centre of Inamgaon (Dhavalikar *et al.* 1988, 1004). House 51 and 51A, dating to the Early Jorwe period, was identified as a large structure functioning as a granary (ibid., 189). It consisted of two units 51 and 51A. The former covered an area of 54.6 m² and contained two pit silos, a platform for a storage bin and a large fire pit (ibid.). The latter measured 2.18 m long, 0.77 m wide and 0.42 m deep. The second unit 51A covered a further 45.75 m² and contained three storage bin platforms and five pit silos (ibid., 189–93). As the average house covered only 15 m² (ibid., 174) this structure stands out as preeminent within the settlement in terms of size, covering over 100 m². The excavators identified it as a public granary and fire worship temple (ibid., 193). A similar structure may also be identified at Navdatoli. A structure covering some 45 m² was exposed in square A1-T (Sankalia *et al.* 1971, 49). As the average size of structures at the settlement was some 28 m² (ibid., 54) this particular building was large. In the centre was a large fire pit measuring some 2.4 m long, 1.98 m wide and 1.5 m deep which has also been identified by its excavators as having a communal ritual use (ibid., 49).

Further examples of public architecture surely must include, as argued by Dhavalikar (ibid., 1004), the encircling walls and ditches considered below in section 3.5. We must also comment on the provision of drainage at Pirak, as Shaffer includes this as part of his criteria (Shaffer 1993, 59). Whilst excavating structures of period IA, a channel was exposed running along the western side of the settlement (Jarrige and Santoni 1979, 358). It was over 30 m long and was 2 m deep and between 1.1 and 1.7 m wide (ibid.). The excavators suggested that it was probably connected with protecting the low-lying areas of the site from water run-off and flooding (ibid.). This channel may represent far more than an individual effort and may be another communal construction at Pirak.

3.4 Settlement hierarchies

As noted above some scholars believe that cities are obvious as standing at the apex of settlement hierarchies (Allchin 1990, 164). Shaffer has stated further that reurbanization led to the emergence of a four-tier settlement pattern during the Early Historic period (Shaffer 1993, 59). Although, as we shall see in chapter 6, there are data concerning Harappan site hierarchies, the evidence from the Early Historic is clearer. Erdosy's survey of Allahabad district in the Ganges Valley identified a two-tier hierarchy between BC 1000 and 6000 (Erdosy 1988, 46). Fifteen sites occupied less than 6 hectares, with an average of 1.72 hectares, whilst a single site covered 10 hectares (ibid.). During the following period, the Early Historic, between BC 600 and BC 350, Erdosy identified a four-tier settlement hierarchy (ibid., 55). Seventeen sites occupied less than 6 hectares, with an average of 1.51 hectares, whilst two sites occupied 6.75 and 6.12 hectares, one site 12 hectares and one site some 50 hectares (ibid., 569). The evidence thus appears to support Shaffer's claims (Shaffer 1993, 59).

However Lal's survey of Early Historic sites in the Kanpur District of the Ganges Valley appears to have yielded very different data. He failed to identify the presence of any large settlements in the 69,000 km² area sampled. If we apply his data to Erdosy's size categories, a single tier can be postulated for Lal's Black and Red Ware (BRW) and PGW periods, whilst a two-tier hierarchy only emerges during the NBPW period with a single settlement occupying 8.75 hectares (Lal 1984b, 79). In contrast with the latter's results we may review the settlement hierarchies of the non-Harappan Chalcolithic sites. Dhavalikar has identified a three-tier settlement hierarchy in Maharashtra between c. BC 1400 and 1000 (Dhavalikar et al. 1988, 1001). The first tier was formed by a large number of very small settlements, all of which fall within Erdosy's primary category of under 6 hectares. The second tier was provided by Prakash, which covered 10 hectares, although probably Inamgaon also should be included in this tier. The third tier was provided by Daimabad which is identified by Dhavalikar as a 'primary regional centre' (ibid.). Renfrew and Bahn state, regarding early state settlement hierarchies, that there are often three tiers with 'the capital city as the major centre, and with subsidiary or regional centres as well as local villages' (Renfrew and Bahn 1991, 157). Though obviously not as impressive as Allahabad District's four tiers, the three-tier hierarchy of non-Harappan Chalcolithic Maharashtra was a great achievement and suggests some degree of regional power emanating from Daimabad.

3.5 Enclosing walls

Enclosing walls appear to be another of the common morphological features of both Harappan and Early Historic cities. Rehman Dheri has an enclosing wall from the earliest period of occupation (c. BC 3400–3000) (Allchin, pers. comm.) whilst Harappa, Mohenjo-daro, Lothal, Kalibangan and Surkotada were all enclosed by walls (Allchin and Allchin 1986, 172–6) as were Early Historic cities (Allchin 1989, 1990). There is evidence, however, that a number of non-Harappan Chalcolithic and early Iron Age sites were similarly enclosed. The settlement at Inamgaon was located in a meander of the river Ghod and was protected on three sides by it. The settlement appears to have been enclosed on the fourth side by a wall and ditch during Period II, the Early Jorwe period (c. BC 1400–1000) (Dhavalikar *et al.* 1988, 237). The ditch was 195 m long and 20 m wide (ibid.). The excavator of Atranjikhera claimed that he had found evidence of a mud embankment, with an extant height of 1.45 m, dating to the early phase of the Period III, the PGW period (c. BC 1200–600) (Gaur 1983, 126). Other sites appear to have been walled. The PGW settlement at Jakhera is reported as having a width of 4.8 m and height of 1.2 m (Gaur 1983, 4) whilst Sankalia stated that, although there was no trace of a wall at Navdatoli, 'It is possible that the traces of a mud rampart have completely vanished at Navdatoli and similar exposed Chalcolithic sites, but have been preserved at Nagda and Eran because of historical debris over the earlier remains' (Sankalia *et al.* 1971, 411).

3.6 Script

Since early theoretical days archaeologists have identified writing as a mark of civilization or urbanism (Childe 1950, 16). Although this view was criticized later (Wheeler 1956) it appears to have regained its currency in South Asia (Shaffer 1993, 59). That the Harappans possessed a script, notwithstanding the fact that it has never been deciphered, is well known (Wheeler 1968, 107–8; Agrawal 1982, 160–6; Allchin and Allchin 1985, 212–13). Despite attempts by Lal to study the continuation of certain Harappan symbols through the Chalcolithic to the Iron Age (Lal 1960) it appears that a written script was absent between the collapse of the Harappan and the beginning of the Early Historic period.

There is, however, considerable recent evidence from Sri Lanka to suggest that writing had been introduced as early as the fifth century BC (see chapter 9). Anuradhapura's period J, dated to between c. BC 450 and 350, has yielded four Brahmi inscriptions on potsherds and two styli. The early Iron Age settlement at that time covered only 26 hectares (Deraniyagala, pers. comm.) and was not fortified until the next structural period. Other early evidence comes from Hastinapura where possible styli were identified in PGW levels, dated to c. BC 1100–800 (Lal 1955, 144). Similar styli were recovered from PGW levels at Atranjikera (Gaur 1983, 217). Allchin and Allchin have taken these objects to be one of several varieties of bone arrowheads (Allchin and Allchin 1968, 214–8). A large residence in Period II at Pirak yielded six terracotta seals and numerous clay blocks with seal impressions (Jarrige and Santoni 1979, 368). Although the seals bear only geometric patterns it may be supposed that the different seals denote a form of symbol system.

The interpretation of non-scriptual graffiti on Chalcolithic potsherds is more difficult. Although they bear a variety of symbols (Lal 1960) they are not held to represent a script. That they were part of the incipient growth of a demand for a script cannot be doubted. At Anuradhapura the earliest Iron Age settlement (c. BC 600–450) yielded a number of examples of sherds with non-scriptual graffiti whilst during the succeeding period they occurred side by side with sherds with Brahmi inscriptions. It is clear from the ASW2 sequence that as more examples of Brahmi occurred the count of non-scriptual graffiti dropped, evidently as the latter had been superseded. This pattern suggests that the non-scriptual graffiti of the early Iron Age represented the precursor or incipient demand for a script which was met during the following period. A similar phenomenon appears to have occurred in a number of sites, for example Rehman Dheri, in the Indus valley, prior to the emergence of Indus script.

3.7 Craft specialization

Childe believed that as cities emerged there was the creation of additional full-time classes of specialists (Childe 1950, 15). Evidence of this phenomenon has been identified during both the Harappan and Early Historic periods. At Harappa Wheeler and Piggott identified evidence for craft specialization from the complex of barrack-like dwellings, granaries and food-processing equipment to the north of the citadel (Wheeler 1968, 33–4, 54). Evidence for craft specialization has also been predicted for the Early Historic city (Thapar 1961, 73; Auboyer 1969, 121; Ghosh 1973b, 48). There is evidence to suggest that in some cases this phenomenon was present during the post-urban and non-Harappan Chalcolithic and early Iron Age.

The best evidence comes from the Late Jorwe period of Inamgaon (BC 1000–700). Of the 69 houses (Dhavalikar et al. 1988, 204) excavated, nine houses or thirteen per cent belonged to craft specialists. Three belonged to lime-makers (ibid., 222), one to a bone tool-maker (ibid., 237), two to stone blade-makers (ibid., 102, 216) and three to copper- or goldsmiths (ibid., 204, 212, 225). Similar evidence for full-time craft specialists was also found at Pirak during Periods IIIA and B (c. 11th century–8th century BC) at Pirak. The excavators identified a specific craft compound with evidence for bone-, metal- and stone-working and potting (Jarrige and Santoni 1979, 374–5). Note should also be made of the research recently carried out in Rajasthan by Craddock into ancient mining practices (Craddock et al. 1989). It appears that there is evidence for complex mining activities in Rajasthan during the second millennium BC suggesting a strong degree of specialization (ibid., 55). Although these sites show signs of craft specialization, a trait that many archaeologists have identified as complex, there is at least one Early Historic city which shows a different pattern. As noted in chapter 8, Deraniyagala has excavated thirteen sondages in the Citadel of Anuradhapura down to bedrock. Almost every area of the city has thus been subjected to a systematic sample. One of the most surprising results was that metal-working slag was discovered in every sondage from the basal protohistoric levels upwards (Deraniyagala 1990b, 261). This result suggests that at least metal-working was practised throughout the site and not concentrated in a particular quarter. Although one would normally be tempted to interpret such a pattern as having been produced by a settlement of simple self-sufficient economies based upon individual households, the pattern is the same even when the settlement became capital of the entire island and at times of parts of Southern India too.

3.8 Long-distance trade

Long-distance trade is another common criterion for urbanism, statehood and cities (Childe 1950, 16; Shaffer 1993, 59; Allchin 1990, 164). The Harappan cities had trading contacts which appear to have reached as far west as Mesopotamia, as far north as Shortughai in Afghanistan and as far south as Gujarat (Allchin and Allchin 1986, 186–7). Early Historic cities also appear to have participated in long-distance trade. Sri Lanka's first fortified city, Anuradhapura, had imports of carnelian from Gujarat and lapis lazuli from Afghanistan during Period I (c. BC 350–BC 275). It is also notable that if one studies the distribution of Rouletted ware, as an indicator of the trading networks of the Early Historic period, it covers most of India, Sri Lanka and even extends to Bali (Ardika and Bellwood 1991, 221). There is evidence to suggest that the post-urban and non-Harappan Chalcolithic and early Iron Age communities also had extensive communications and trade contacts, however it is unclear how one can distinguish which exotic items have reached a site via the simple process of down-the-line exchange and which via direct trade links. In this case the most we can do is to identify items not available locally.

At the non-Harappan Chalcolithic site of Inamgaon a number of artefact categories present were not available locally. Marine shells were brought there 200 km inland (Dhavalikar et al. 1988, 665), gold and ivory were brought from Karnataka, amazonite from Rajpipla in Gujarat, and copper from Ahar in Rajasthan or Amreli in Gujarat (ibid., 1006). Ahar's exotic imports included a lapis lazuli bead from Afghanistan (Sankalia et al. 1969, 163). At Navdatoli, occupied between BC 1600 and 1300, coral and lapis lazuli were recovered from Period I onwards (Sankalia et al. 1971, 351); other imports included marine shells (ibid., 407), jasper, agate and carnelian from nearby, copper, quartz and steatite from Rajasthan, sandstone from the Vindhyas, and coral and amazonite from

Gujarat (ibid., 367). The BRW deposits (c. BC 1450–1200) at Atranjikera yielded quartz, agate, chalcedony and carnelian from up to 560 km away (Gaur 1983, 473) and imports of stone and copper (ibid., 120). The inland post-urban Chalcolithic site of Pirak yielded marine shell in Period II (Jarrige and Santoni 1979, 401), ivory from the Ganges Valley and carnelian from Gujarat in Period IA (ibid., 363).

3.9 Subsistence strategies

It is very clear that in order to support a large agglomeration of population in one place, for example in a city, an appropriate subsistence strategy must be followed. Harappan subsistence strategy was based largely upon domesticated and wild animals, wheat and barley (Allchin and Allchin 1986, 190–2). It is necessary to understand the importance of subsistence strategy to the survival of cities; this is best illustrated by the many environmental catastrophe theories which have attempted to explain the collapse of the Indus Civilization. As described in chapter 3, they range between the over-cultivation of the land, a drop in rainfall, a tectonic barrier affecting hydrology and river capture. They all reflect, however, the dangers of neglecting the balance between the carrying capacity of the land and the subsistence strategy followed. Some scholars have argued that the new civilization which arose in the first millennium BC was based upon two new elements which helped to raise the carrying capacity of the land and allow cities to be viable again (Kosambi 1956). These two elements were iron and rice. However there is now evidence to show that non-Harappan Chalcolithic subsistence strategies were capable of cultivating not only the alluvial strips of river valleys, but also the heavier and more extensive black cotton soils without the use of iron tools. There is also evidence that rice had been cultivated long before the emergence of the Early Historic city.

The dating of South Asia's first iron tools has long been contested (Chakrabarti 1992), however its importance to this section will necessitate another brief review. Kosambi was perhaps the first scholar to have explained the re-emergence of cities and civilization in South Asia in terms of the introduction of iron tools. In his view iron plough agriculture led to the creation of a regular and large food supply. This in turn led to greater permanent agglomerations of population in single settlements which in turn led to new social needs and organizations (Kosambi 1965, 108). He further believed that iron tools and ploughshares enabled the clearance and colonization of the Doab (Kosambi 1965, 84). Agrawal took a similar stance advocating that copper technology could not cultivate the black cotton soils and that only iron tools could (Agrawal 1971, 228). A number of critical reviews of such ideas have been made (Ghosh 1973a; Chakrabarti 1973b) and their conclusions are fairly convincing.

Chakrabarti noted that the black cotton soils, although more amenable to heavy iron-tipped ploughs, were undoubtedly farmed during the Chalcolithic period (ibid., 336). Dhavalikar and Possehl have found evidence to support this claim by projecting the subsistence pattern of Inamgaon (Dhavalikar and Possehl 1974). They calculated the average daily calorific intake for an individual and multiplied this by the approximate population of Inamgaon. By estimating the extent of land necessary for the production of these calories they calculated that the settlement required up to 2,000 acres of farm land (ibid., 42). As the easily farmed alluvial strip is quite narrow, they calculated that the farmers of Inamgaon would have had to cultivate a strip some 9 km long in order to meet the gross calorific needs of the community (ibid., 43). In such a case they suggested that it would have been more likely that portions of the settlement's population would have split off and founded a new community rather than travelling a possible 18 km per day to the fields and back (ibid.). This data led them to suggest that the black cotton soils were cultivated, perhaps with wooden ploughs or simple hoes.

It is also clear from Lal's survey that the initial colonization or exploitation of the Doab had begun by the PGW phase. During this period the total area occupied by settlement rose by 32 per cent from the preceding BRW period in comparison with the 38 per cent rise from the PGW to the NBPW phase (Lal 1984b, 79). This suggests that the exploitation of new areas had already begun by the early Iron Age. As has been noted by many scholars, iron farming implements do not appear in the sequence until a few centuries later, suggesting that the initial colonization used the implements and methods already available to Chalcolithic farmers. Finally it has been remarked that the addition of iron tools in a number of site sequences does not appear to have had an immediate effect. At Pirak the first iron objects appear in Period III, c. BC 1100, and the other aspects of material culture appear to continue unchanged, Indeed the excavators comment that 'familiarity with iron smelting did not mark an immediate transformation in the way of life of the inhabitants of the site' (Jarrige and Santoni 1979, 398). This leads us to wonder quite what the term Chalcolithic as opposed to Iron Age actually implies. The Chalcolithic settlement of Pirak did not suddenly become Iron Age because of the presence of a few iron objects, the basic infrastructure remained unchanged.

Similarly some have identified the widespread use of rice as a mechanism to raise carrying capacities and to allow the agglomeration of large concentrations of population in a single place: 'the cultivation of rice was a feature of the rise of the Ganges civilization' (Allchin and Allchin 1968, 265). Certainly this must have been the case of the city of Anuradhapura in Sri Lanka's Dry Zone, which, as noted in chapter 8, has a carrying capacity of c. 0.4 individuals per km^2 using natural resources (Deriyanagala 1992, 412). Following a similar methodology to Dhavalikar and Possehl (Dhavalikar and Possehl 1974) it is possible to calculate the different carrying capacities of the Dry Zone using different forms of subsistence strategies.

It has been calculated that the total annual nutritional needs of an individual in the subcontinent in 1964 was 706,640 calories (Holst 1970, 136). As foodgrains make up some 72 per cent of this amount, 508,810 calories annually are needed from them (ibid.). This can be converted to the equivalent of 144.6 kg of foodgrain per year per person (ibid.). If we compare the relative yields of kilograms per acre for rice, wheat, millet and pulses, we can illustrate their effect on the carrying capacity of the land. Dry-system rice will yield between 180 and 230 kg of grain per acre, semi-dry-system rice will yield between 453 and 545 kg, and wet-system rice will yield some 2,267.5 kg (Kumar 1963, 3–7). Dry-system wheat will yield some 725 kg of grain per acre, wet-system wheat will yield some 1,133 kg, millets will yield between 272 kg and 544 kg, and pulses will yield between 136 kg and 272 kg (ibid., 15–47). In terms of population one can therefore calculate that a single crop of wet-system rice from one acre of irrigated land in North Central Province will support some 15 individuals or a carrying capacity of 24,00 people per km² in comparison with the natural carrying capacity of 0.4 per km² (Deraniyagala 1992, 412). This example illustrates the impact that rice cultivation could have upon the viability of cities as centres of population.

However recent evidence suggests that rice was available in the preceding period. It was certainly part of the subsistence strategies of the Harappans. Evidence for rice has been found at Lothal and Rangpur in Gujarat and at Kalibangan in the eastern Punjab in the form of husk and spikelets in potsherds or terracotta cakes (Vishnu-Mittre 1974). Similarly evidence has been found for rice at Neolithic and non-Harappan Chalcolithic sites. The Neolithic sites include Loebanr in Swat, Koldihwa and Mahagara near the confluence of the Ganges, and Yamuna and Chirand in the middle Ganges basin. Chalcolithic sites with rice include Navdatoli and Inamgaon in the Western Deccan, Pirak in Baluchistan, Sonpur in the middle Ganges Valley, Pandu Rajar Dhibi in West Bengal and Ahar in south Rajasthan. As is evident from this brief survey, rice subsistence was available and practised throughout the subcontinent, with the exception of Peninsular India south of the Godavari basin, from at least the second millennium BC. This evidence suggests that rice cannot be identified as a prime mover or catalyst for the re-emergence of cities in South Asia although the development of new varieties of rice and methods of transplanting them undoubtedly contributed to the population explosion of the 5th–6th centuries BC (see chapter 13).

3.10 Population growth

Population growth has been identified as having been intimately linked with the emergence of urbanism, indeed it has been identified as a prime mover by a number of theoretical archaeologists, as summarized in Renfrew and Bahn (Renfrew and Bahn 1991, 417). Certainly it appears as if the loss of the Harappan cities coincided with a general decrease of population in the Indus valley (Shaffer

1993, 54). It also appears that the Early Historic period and the re-emergence of cities was accompanied by considerable population growth between BC 600 and 100 (Erdosy 1988, 129). However Lal's survey data (Lal 1984 a and b) suggests that this growth had begun long before and had its beginnings in the preceding non-Harappan Chalcolithic and early Iron Age periods, itself due to increasingly rising levels of technology and subsistence.

Lal's data show that regardless of the absence of a central place or incipient kingdom in the region surveyed, the number of new settlements increased and began to colonize or rather exploit areas previously ignored, in particular areas away from large river courses. During the BRW phase a total of 17.25 hectares were occupied by settlements. During the PGW phase this had increased to 53.58 hectares, to 140.05 in the NBPW and to 291.12 hectares in the Early Historic (ibid., 79). We may convert this data into possible population densities using Dhavalikar's figure of 200 people per hectare (Dhavalikar *et al.* 1988, 1001). During the BRW period settlements were occupied by some 3,450 people, the PGW period settlements by 10,716, the NBPW period by 28,010 and the Early Historic period by 58,430 people. It is possible to compare these results with those from Erdosy's survey (Erdosy 1988). Lal's BRW period and some of his PGW period correlate with Erdosy's period I; Lal's NBPW period correlates with Erdosy's period II; and Lal's Early Historic period correlated with Erdosy's period III. During Erdosy's Period I (BC 1000–600) (ibid., 46) a total of 35.80 hectares were occupied, 100.5 hectares during II (BC 600–350) (ibid., 56) and 312.51 hectares during III (BC 350–100) (ibid., 66). In terms of population this generates a population of 7,160 in period I, 20,100 in II and 62,502 in III. Although the relative sizes of the survey areas were different we may still compare them in terms of growth. Lal's PGW population increased by 38.26 per cent to reach the NBPW level and again by 47.94 per cent to reach the Early Historic figure of 58,430. During the equivalent periods Erdosy's period I's population rose by 35.62 per cent to reach period II's level and again by 32.16 per cent to reach period III's ceiling.

Two points are clearly illustrated by this discussion. Firstly, Lal's data showed an increase in population of just over 32 per cent between the BRW and PGW periods. This is a considerable increase and suggests that the demographic phenomenon noted by scholars as accompanying the Early Historic period had already begun by the start of the PGW period *circa* the beginning of the first millennium BC. It should also be noted that this expansion must have been based upon the existing post-urban and non-Harappan Chalcolithic subsistence strategies detailed in section 3.9. The second point suggested by Lal's data is that this population growth occurred in Kanpur District without the presence of a nearby city as he failed to find a distinct central place. Indeed it is remarkable how Lal's percentage increases match Erdosy's, suggesting that although cities appeared during this time of remarkable growth they were not necessarily created by it.

4. Summary

The foregoing discussion has expressly attempted to illustrate that the stretch of c. 1000 years between the two great civilizations of the subcontinent was not the 'dark age' as suggested by Wheeler (Wheeler 1959, 114). Indeed, as already noted by Allchin in chapter 3, many areas show distinct continuities from the pre-Harappan to the post-urban period. We must abandon Wheeler's vision of this period as consisting of 'semi-nomadic food-gathering communities, capable of clearing patches of jungle ... but living mainly by hunting and fishing' (ibid., 126) for one of large agglomerations of population in large permanent settlements, some of which surely must be classified as urban, although part of the population undoubtedly still practised hunting and gathering. Indeed this period which straddles the Chalcolithic and early Iron Age appears to have been remarkable consistent, what Allchin has called 'a single broad cultural tradition'. If one leaves the question of iron aside it is possible to conclude that the various sites, with the possible exception of southern India, are unified by a common pool of technology and subsistence although not in regard to specific ceramic types. It can be no coincidence that it was a period during which, as many have pointed out, the foundations for the Early Historic period were laid. Nearly all the traits that we have identified as 'urban' were present in its settlements. At the very least we must be tempted to award the title of 'incipient urbanism' to such sites. However we must not make the mistake of considering that these societies and settlements were in no ways different to the cities of the Early Historic or Harappan civilizations. They were organized on a very different scale. Although some post-urban and non-Harappan Chalcolithic and early Iron Age sites were bigger than a number of Early Historic cities it should be pointed out that they are themselves dwarfed by the larger ones. Some form of dramatic transition separates the Early Historic cities from the settlements of this period.

The nature of this transition may best be examined through the medium of social mobilization. As noted in section 3.1, a number of post-urban and non-Harappan Chalcolithic and early Iron Age settlements had quite sizable populations, ranging from 1,000 at Inamgaon to 6,000 at Daimabad. However these numbers are dwarfed by the enormous populations of the seven largest Early Historic cities. Pataliputra had a possible population of 270,000, Mathura 60,000, Besnagar and Vaisali 48,000, Kausambi and Old Rajgir 40,000, and Ujjain 38,000. This difference is further strengthened if we compare the number of man-days expended in the construction of the defences of the respective settlements. We can calculate the number of man-days taken to build such features using a rate of 0.58 cubic metres per man-day (Erdosy 1988, 113). The ditch at Inamgaon was some 195 m long and 20 m wide (Dhavalikar *et al.* 1988, 237). Unfortunately there is no indication of its depth, however if one assumes it was similar in depth to the irrigation channel one may suggest a depth of some 2.15 m (ibid., 241). As such it represents the removal of 4,192.50 cubic metres or the investment of some 7,228 man-days. If we accept that they were built well within the dry season when excess labour was available, it can be calculated that it represented a possible force of 48 individuals working for 150 days. The rampart at the PGW settlement of Jakhera was 5 m wide and 0.8 m high (Erdosy 1988, 106). As the site covered some 8 hectares (ibid.) and the rampart ran for some 1,200 m it thus appears that it represented some 4,800 cubic metres or the investment of some 8,276 man-days. This would reflect a workforce of 55 individuals working for 150 days.

In comparison the Early Historic city defences are quite vast. Using Sharma's section across the defences (Sharma 1960, fig. 3) it is possible to identify an internal core of packed clay at the centre of Kausambi's Rampart 1 (SP.I.3). It is hypothesized that this feature represents the initial clay bund constructed to defend the settlement. It was some 9 m high and was probably less than 20 m wide (ibid.). As the rampart ran for some 6,200 m it contained some 892,800 cubic metres. It also represents 1,539,310.3 man-days or a possible workforce of 10,262 working for 150 days. Sisupalgarh's first defences were 7.62 m high and 33 m wide (Lal 1949, 74) and ran for some 4,828 m (ibid., 64). It thus contained some 1,214,048 cubic metres of earth and represented a possible 2,093,188 man-days or a labour force of 13,955 working for 150 days. Ujjain's Early Historic ramparts have been calculated as containing some 3,000,000 cubic metres (Erdosy 1988, 113). This is represented by 5,200,000 man-days (ibid.) or a possible workforce of 34,666 individuals working for 150 days.

Further details of political complexity are illustrated when the percentage of the settlement's population reflected in the calculated workforce from the respective settlements is compared. It is hypothesized that the higher the percentage the greater the forces of complexity and centralized organization. Inamgaon's defences could have been constructed in 150 days by a workforce of 48 and Jakhera's by one of 55. As Inamgaon's population can be estimated as being near 1,000 and Jakhera's near 1,600 this suggests that the workforce engaged in the construction of the settlement's defences represented a mobilization of 4.8 per cent and 3.4 per cent of the population. In comparison Kausambi's first Early Historic rampart was constructed by a possible workforce of 10,262 working for 150 days. As only 50 hectares were occupied at the time of the construction of the ramparts (Erdosy 1988, 113) this suggests that even if the entire population of 10,000 were working a further 3 per cent from elsewhere would have to be found. The ramparts at Sisupalgarh represented a possible 2,093,188 man-days or a labour force of 13,955 working for 150 days. They enclosed some 144 hectares (Erdosy 1988, 134) containing a possible population of 28,800. These figures suggest that the ramparts could have been built using 48.45 per cent of the population. Ujjain's Early Historic rampart reflected a possible workforce of 34,666 individuals working for 150 days. The site covered an area of 190 hectares, suggesting a population of 38,000. In terms of the percentage of the entire population it represents 91.22 per cent. These data suggest that, although the Early Historic cities were of a far greater size and contained more inhabitants than earlier settlements, their main difference or transformation was that they could achieve the mobilization of a far greater percentage of the population than before. However the beginning of this transformation is not so clear.

Erdosy appears to share Wheeler's view of the relatively uncomplex nature of the non-Harappan Chalcolithic (Wheeler 1959, 126) by suggesting that chief-doms and social stratification occurred only after c. BC 900 during the PGW or early Iron Age (Erdosy 1988, 21): 'The restoration of stable political structures following the collapse of Harappan urbanism ... required almost a millennium' (Erdosy, this volume, chapter 7). In support of this claim he identifies the following chiefly elements in the PGW: 'an agricultural economy making limited use of iron, by low population density and by a two-tier settlement hierarchy whose central place coordinated the procurement, processing and distribution of vital raw materials' (this volume, chapter 7). He also attributes the emergence of increasing complexity to the role of warfare (1988, 142–8) and comments that until the sixth century BC iron in the Ganga valley was mainly used for the manufacture of weapons (1988, 142). Weapons and warfare were integral elements in his reconstruction of early Iron Age chiefly society in the Ganges Valley (1988).

However, as we have demonstrated, all these elements were present prior to the beginning of the first millennium BC in the post-urban and non-Harappan Chalcolithic. This is, of course, with the exception of iron which as shown in section 3.9 is not considered crucial. Notwithstanding the theoretical problems associated with the application of such definitions as chiefdom to archaeological data (Tainter 1978; Keesing 1981; Earle 1991), why should these earlier societies not also be termed chiefdoms? Dhavalikar has argued that the term chiefdom can be attributed to the Chalcolithic sites of Maharashtra (Dhavalikar *et al.* 1988, 1004). These sites, belonging to the Jorwe period c. BC 1400–1000 (ibid., 1001), were extant at least four centuries before Erdosy's early Iron Age chiefdoms. Dhavalikar based his claims on a number of elements present including settlement hierarchy, public architecture, a ranked society and craft specialization (ibid., 1004–6). Certainly his thesis appears to have been supported by the evidence we presented above in sections 3.1–3.10, which seems to refute Erdosy's claim. Also to restrict the use of metal weapons to the early Iron Age is surely incorrect, as they have also been identified in the copper hoards.

The copper hoards have often been discussed as a separate archaeological phenomenon (Agrawal 1982; Allchin and Allchin 1986). However following the discovery of similar copper objects *in situ* in habitation sites (IAR 1963, 11; Sankalia *et al.* 1971, 90) it now seems fairly certain that they may be associated with the non-Harappan Chalcolithic. In general the objects have comprised the following forms: celts, rings, harpoons, swords, anthropomorphic figures and axes (Lal 1951, 32–7). The most obvious factor therefore is that they are mainly weapons, for precisely the same use as the earliest iron objects. This suggests that the preceding Chalcolithic could have hosted as much conflict as has been attributed to its successor, further strengthened by the presence at some post-urban and non-Harappan Chalcolithic sites of enclosing walls. The hoards also have elements which in combination with weapons may all be described as objects for personal display. These objects have seldom been found in habitation sites but mainly in hoards. This led Wheeler to suggest they represented semi-nomadic food-gathering communities in a period of insecurity and economic instability (Wheeler 1959, 126). However hoards can be deposited either in times of conflict, or as a dedication or an extravagant display of wealth. The deposition of a hoard thus may represent a display of wealth enabling an individual or group to compete directly with other individuals or groups for power and hegemony (Ransborg 1982). It is argued therefore that settlements and societies fitting Erdosy's definition of chiefdoms had developed well before the PGW period.

In conclusion it appears that the foundations for the emergence of the Early Historic city were already being laid during the second millennium BC. All the material aspects which actually constituted an Early Historic city were present during this period of incipient urbanism. During this time only a key for social mobilization was missing causing settlements and societies to remain at a ceiling size. Rather than attributing the actual emergence of this element to the early Iron Age the archaeological evidence suggests that attempts were being made during the post-urban and non-Harappan Chalcolithic to mobilize groups of people in numbers in excess of kinship ties. Perhaps it is no coincidence that one of the largest copper hoards, weighing over 60 kg and consisting of an elephant, a rhinoceros, a buffalo and a man in a buffalo-drawn chariot, came from Daimabad one of the largest known non-Harappan Chalcolithic settlements covering some 30 hectares (Dhavalikar et al. 1988, 134) and standing at the centre of a three-tier settlement hierarchy. It thus appears that the period between the Harappan and Early Historic civilizations was less of a Dark Age but more of a period of gradual stable growth and innovation which culminated in the emergence of the Early Historic world. However until we have the full horizontal excavation sequence of an Early Historic city from its Chalcolithic beginnings we will often just be examining settlements that failed. Only by examining the transition from Chalcolithic village to Early Historic city can we attempt to identify the possible factors involved in the development of a successful city, and until more excavations of the calibre of the one at Inamgaon are carried out it would be presumptuous to suggest any more from the fragmentary data.

PART II

THE RISE OF CITIES AND STATES

CHAPTER 6

THE PRELUDE TO URBANIZATION: ETHNICITY AND THE RISE OF LATE VEDIC CHIEFDOMS

GEORGE ERDOSY

The settlement history of Northern India in the 2nd millennium BC

On the principle that 'there is something in all of us of the decisions made in the flaking of the very first hand-axe' (Hodder 1986, 10) it will be useful to take a long-term perspective on the background to the 'second urbanization of India'. The factors contributing to the decline of the Harappan civilization have already been weighed in chapter 3; the aim here is to amplify its conclusions from the perspective of settlement archaeology, before examining the revival of complex societies from the 10th century BC onwards. While the evidence at our disposal remains a patchwork of surveys over a widely dispersed area, the patterns emerging are sufficiently consistent to be significant. Of particular interest are the surveys of Mughal (1984, 1990b) in the lower Sarasvati (Hakra) valley in Pakistan, those of Bhan and Shaffer (1978) in the upper Sarasvati valley in Haryana, and of Lal (1984a and b) and Erdosy (1988) in the Ganga-Yamuna Doab. Together with the work of Possehl (1980) in Saurashtra, which falls outside the scope of this discussion, these constitute our primary sources at present, along with occasional site lists in *Pakistan Archaeology, Indian Archaeology – A Review*, and individual publications (Lal 1955; Bhan 1975; Shrimali 1983; Joshi *et al.* 1984; Kumar 1987).

Of the two geographical regions of interest the Ganga Valley, prior to BC 1000, presents few difficulties of interpretation. In spite of the impression conveyed by some accounts (especially SB 1.4.1.14 ff) that the area was only brought under plough by advancing 'Aryan' tribes,[1] archaeological research has shown that it was well settled by the 2nd millennium BC.[2] Our knowledge of the

---

[1]   In this chapter the use of the term 'Aryan' in quotes is intended to convey the traditional characterization of the authors of the Rigveda in racial terms. If the alternative categorization, based on cultural criteria (Erdosy 1989) is meant, the term *ārya* (Skt. 'noble') will be employed, since this is what the seers of the Vedic hymns actually call themselves.

[2]   Although the site of Koldihwa produced dates of 8280±210 bp (PRL-224) 6580±215 bc, 7180±230 bp (PRL-100) 6076, 6059, 6043, 6018, 6001 cal. BC and 6300±180 bp (PRL-101) 5240

first phases of colonization comes from excavations at the Mesolithic sites of Chopani Mando, Mahadaha, Sarai Nahar Rai and Damdama (Sharma 1973a and b; Sharma 1980), at the Neolithic sites of Chirand (Verma 1970), Mahagara (Sharma 1980) and Koldihwa (Misra 1977), and at the Chalcolithic sites of Atranjikhera, Period I (Gaur 1983), Narhan, Period I (Singh and Lal 1985), Sohagaura, Period I (Singh and Lal 1985), Sringaverpur, Period I (Dikshit 1981) and Lal Qila (Fig. 6.1). Although lack of a settlement hierarchy points to simple social structures, centred on individual sites, other patterns of culture are already well established. Thus we may infer from the presence of both spring and autumn harvests (wheat and barley on the one hand, rice on the other) that classic cropping practices have already taken root. The range of domesticated animals includes cattle, sheep, goat, pig and dog, to which the horse is the only significant addition in the Iron Age. Likewise, but for the introduction of iron tools, the level of technology changes little in the succeeding millennium. Furthermore, incipient craft specialization and status distinctions may be inferred from the relative sizes and artefact contents of individual dwellings at Mahagara (Sharma 1980, 192 ff). By the so-called Chalcolithic period, datable to the mid-2nd millennium BC and identifiable by the presence of Black and Red ware in the lower Ganga valley and by Ochre Coloured pottery further west, there is a proliferation of settlements, even if central places continue to be absent. Clearly, cultural evolution in the area did not await the 'Aryan' colonists of the Vedic texts. Nevertheless, the picture gleaned is one of very gradual evolution, even taking into account the infancy of research.

By contrast, the Indo-Gangetic divide flourished under the Harappans, and its contribution to the growth of complex societies in early historic times needs to be carefully assessed, in light of the hiatus apparent between the first and second periods of urbanization. It is here that the benefits of settlement pattern studies, which afford a good picture of broad evolutionary trends, become evident. To begin with a summary of the Mature Harappan period (which may be placed in the second half of the 3rd millennium BC) (Possehl 1990), an elaborate settlement hierarchy is a conspicuous feature, whether at regional or supra-regional levels. As regards the latter, Mughal (1990a) has recently pointed out the

cal. BC, from the Neolithic and Chalcolithic levels, the same also yielded measurements of 2380±105 bp (PRL-102), 405 cal. BC, 2050±110 bp (PRL-227), 92 cal. BC, 1990±150 bp (PRL-98) 8 cal. AD and 820±100 bp (PRL-56) 1225 cal. AD. No other site offers support for the earlier set of dates, with the Neolithic levels of Mahagara having four dates of 3330–3190 bp (BS-128; PRL-407 to 409) 1628–1451 cal. BC and the Neolithic of Kunjhun three dates of 4600–3120 bp (BETA-4879, 6414, 6415) 3360–1414 cal. BC, which restricts the span of time occupied by the Vindhyan Neolithic firmly to the late-4th to mid-2nd millennium BC. The Neolithic levels of Chirand produced eight dates between 3600–2715 bp, 1961–845 cal. BC (along with dates of 2485±150 and 2290±110 bp, 761, 681, 659, 596, 577 cal. BC). Finally, the Mesolithic site of Chopani Mando produced a date of 4540±110 bp, 3338, 3213, 3203 cal. BC from its uppermost levels, further strengthening the case for placing the emergence of the Vindhyan Neolithic in the late 4th millennium BC at the earliest. However, even such a conservative estimate well predates the ārya colonists of the Vedic texts.

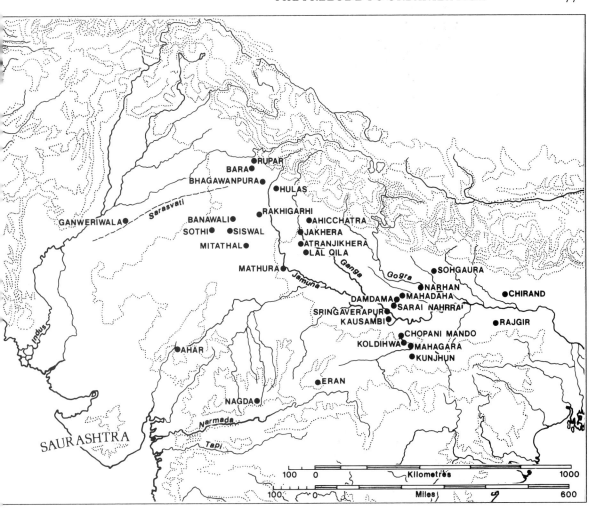

Fig. 6.1.   Map of principal sites referred to in Chapter 6.

fallacy of viewing Mohenjo-daro and Harappa as twin capitals of an empire, given the discovery of similar large and regularly spaced settlements throughout the greater Indus valley. Although the sizes of the former have lately been revised upward (Kenoyer pers. comm.), it may be better to view the Harappan civilization as made up of closely integrated regional polities, with the main cities acting not so much as centres of dominance but as mediators of intensive interregional interaction.

As for regional settlement hierarchies we may note the presence of at least three size categories in the Hakra valley (Mughal 1990b, Shaffer 1993) and four in the upper Sarasvati basin (Shaffer 1986), the two areas which have been well surveyed. In the former, the site of Ganweriwala at 81.5 hectares acts as the central place, followed by one group of settlements measuring 12 to 20 hectares, and another containing sites under 10 hectares in extent. Indeed, given that in some areas, such as Allahabad district (Erdosy 1988), three types of sites were identified within the last size category (with the aid of locational attributes), the presence of additional levels in the settlement hierarchy cannot be ruled out. In the upper Sarasvati basin, Rakhigarhi at 80 hectares is the largest site, followed by Banawali at 25 hectares; both show the characteristic division into citadel and town. Next come sites of 4–8 hectares (Bara, Rupar, Kotla Nihang, Siswal, Mitathlal, Bala and Nauli); the fact that apart from the two largest settlements they were the only ones producing Mature Harappan ceramics supports their claim to a higher status than enjoyed by those sites which not only did not exceed 2 hectares in area, but have yielded exclusively Siswal A-B type ceramics (Shaffer 1986, 224).

The case for cultural complexity is strengthened by the functional diversity of sites that were incorporated into regional networks. In the Hakra valley, out of 174 Mature Harappan sites, 79 were industrial, 33 multi-purpose and only 62 exclusively rural (Mughal 1982). Elsewhere the pattern is less clear, although specialized factory sites have been found in the Punjab as well, exemplified by the large-scale manufacture of faience and stone beads at Dher Majra. That the regional networks were integrated into a wider system is shown by the regular spacing of major centres (Shaffer 1986, 224; Mughal 1990a) as well as by the extensive distribution of such typically Harappan traits as civic planning, seals, weights, triangular terracotta cakes and a variety of painted designs on ceramics.

All this comes to an end by the early 2nd millennium BC. Large centres, such as Mohenjo-daro and Harappa, suffer a 90 per cent reduction in size; others such as Ganweriwala and Rakhigarhi disappear altogether. Indeed, in the upper Sarasvati Basin the top three levels of the settlement hierarchy are obliterated, as shown by the sizes of Late Harappan settlements (Bhan and Shaffer 1978; Kumar 1987), none of which exceeds 6 hectares. In the lower Sarasvati (Hakra) valley the change appears to be more gradual, with the retention of a three-tiered hierarchy crowned by a site of 38 hectares (Kudwala) and showing a cluster of sites between 12 and 20 hectares, just as in the preceding period. However, a significant shift in the locations of central places suggests a discontinuity masked by the consideration of size categories in isolation, an impression reinforced by the disappearance of the intricate network of diverse specialist sites. Furthermore, the disappearance of once widespread traits such as town planning, writing and weights, signals the collapse of supraregional networks. Finally, there occurs a significant population shift towards the northeast, most likely in response to the gradual drying up of the Sarasvati river system in the wake of tectonic action (Yash Pal et al. 1984). This is graphically illustrated within the lower Sarasvati (Hakra) valley (Mughal 1984), as well as by the disappearance of sites in northern Rajasthan and the correspondingly dramatic increase in the number of sites in the eastern Punjab and Haryana (from 34 to 128, and from 44 to 297) (Joshi *et al.* 1984).[3]

On several counts, therefore, we may ascribe a complexity to the Mature Harappan phase which is comparable to state societies elsewhere, and sustain the case for a catastrophic systems collapse in its wake (Renfrew 1979). This is not to deny the individuality of the Harappan civilization, which defies simplistic parallels with the centralized states of the Near East, a point instinctively grasped already by Marshall and recently elaborated by Shaffer (1982, 1986) and others. However, claims of a Harappan antiquity for many of the social and economic institutions of modern India must be viewed with scepticism, in light of the events of the 2nd millennium BC; thus, it would be a mistake to replace Mesopotamian analogies with those drawn from the South Asian present to illuminate less accessible aspects of Harappan society and culture. The continuity, which undeniably exists, is of a different sort. As intimated in recent reviews of the 'Aryan problem' (Shaffer 1984; Erdosy 1989, 1995), neither literature nor the archaeological record requires major population movements (beyond the shift noted within the Sarasvati basin) as an explanatory mechanism for the resurgence of civilization in South Asia. Even if Harappan institutions have been fundamentally altered by the collapse of urban centres and networks of interaction, their successors, in the guise of a self-proclaimed 'Aryan' ideology, gained widespread adoption in the emerging complex societies of the Ganga valley. However, before turning to the processual issues just anticipated, it will first be necessary to outline the literary and material evidence for the rise of Late Vedic chiefdoms.

Settlement patterns and material culture of the Early Iron Age (10th–6th centuries BC)

The very title of this section calls for a few definitions. The appellation 'Early Historic' reflects the nature of our source materials, although the texts supplementing material culture are of a primarily religious orientation, devoid of serious historical content. The beginning of the period coincides with the first appearance of literary works – this means c. BC 1500 for the Punjab (home of the Rigveda) and BC 1000 for the Ganga Valley (home of the later Samhitas and their auxiliary Brahmanas, Aranyakas and Upanisads). However, while the earliest coins (from the 5th–4th centuries BC – see chapters 7, 9 & 10) and the earliest inscriptions (from the 3rd century BC) signal a qualitative improvement in available sources, the most convenient terminus remains the 4th century AD. It is then that an extensive reorganization of politico-economic structures was undertaken by the Guptas, who found the Mauryan pattern of centralized political and economic control to be unworkable.

---

[3] Since the survey of northern Haryana by Suraj Bhan and Shaffer (1978) followed a more rigorous sampling policy, its results are probably more reliable than the global figures quoted by Joshi: in this more restricted area 14 Mature Harappan as opposed to 61 Late Harappan sites were found.

The term 'Early Iron Age' will be used within this span of time to describe the 10th–6th centuries BC whenever material culture is the basis of discussion; with reference to literature the same may be called 'Late Vedic'. The choice of centuries to delineate this period reflects the level of resolution hitherto gained through absolute dating, of the time that elapsed between the respective appearances of Painted Grey ware (PGW) and Northern Black Polished ware (NBP).[4] Although no dates are available from early PGW levels, those from mid-PGW levels fall in the 9th–7th centuries BC;[5] the 10th century BC is, thus, a good estimate for the appearance of the former. As for NBP, radiocarbon measurements (calibrated according to the curve proposed by Stuiver and Becker 1986) suggest the mid-6th century BC as the date of its earliest appearance (see chapter 7). For these reasons the 10th–6th centuries BC form an acceptable, if conservative, temporal span for the Early Iron Age.

It is at this time that the Indo-Gangetic divide and the Ganga valley arrive at similar levels of cultural complexity, from opposing directions. The most striking development is the establishment of closely comparable settlement systems over a wide area. In the Hakra valley, Mughal (1984) noted 13 sites of 4 hectares or less along with one site (Satwali) of 13.7 hectares. In Northern Haryana (Bhan and Shaffer 1978) the site of Bhukari, at 9.6 hectares, stands out among 38 others of 4.3 hectares or less. In Kurukshetra district alone is the pattern three-tiered: the largest settlement (Agaundh) measures 12 hectares, three others fall between 6–8

---

[4]   As the recognition of these two wares played a major part in the establishment of a culture sequence and chronology for the Ganges valley in the period when radiocarbon dating was not yet available, and as they continue to be useful as in providing chronology for sites otherwise not dated, it is worth remarking that they share many common technical features: both are made from very finely sorted or elutriated alluvial clays; both have a limited range of forms, suggesting either wheel throwing or a distinctive technique of turntable building, and closely related to each other; both have been fired in closely controlled reducing conditions, producing a light to medium grey colour. The NBP may be regarded as developing out of the PGW, in that its chief distinguishing feature is its treatment with a fine glossy black dressing which under firing conditions produces a black gloss or glaze. Because of frequent references by some archaeologists to 'PGW' people, we must reaffirm the long-held view of the authors of this book that neither ware should be associated with a 'people'. Nor does one merely succeed the other – there is a considerable overlap between them. Indeed, as Hedge (1975) concluded, NBP represents a minor technological innovation independent of any of the cultural changes (e.g. urbanization) that have been attributed to it. The chronology of NBP will be discussed in chapter 7.

[5]   The only dates from mid-PGW levels come from the site of Noh, in Rajasthan, with TF-993 measuring 2600±145 801 cal. BC and TF-994 2560±100 bp 793 cal. BC. Date TF-191 from Atranjikhera, measuring 2890±105 bp 1057 cal. BC and frequently used to support the dating of early PGW-levels to the 2nd millennium BC, is the only anomalous date in an otherwise consistent series from that site, and cannot be accepted without supporting evidence, which is totally lacking at present. The Early Iron Age of the eastern Ganga Valley has produced radiocarbon dates of 2640±95 bp (TF-336) 809 cal. BC from Chirand, 2620±130 bp (PRL-669) 805 cal. BC from Śringaverpur, 2565±105 (TF-389) 794 cal. BC from Mahisdal and 2510±105 bp 767 cal. BC (TF-376) from Sonpur. Such a dating is supported by thermoluminescence measures from Śringaverpur, five of which came from Period II: 900±300 BC, 789±400 BC, 763±300 BC, 710±280 BC and 680±280 BC, and three from Period I, dating to 1035±280 BC, 920±380 BC and 875±270 BC. For a more exhaustive discussion of chronology see Erdosy (1993), which is based on the list of radiocarbon dates published by Possehl (1989; 1994).

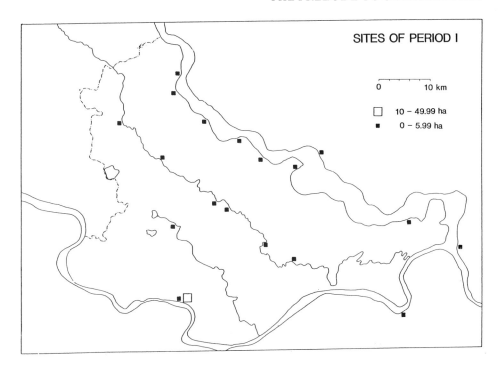

Fig. 6.2. Map of settlement pattern, Allahabad district, Period I, c. BC 1000–600 (after Erdosy 1988)

hectares, while the rest are 5 hectares or less in extent (Kumar 1987). In view of the drastic reorganization of social and political structures following the upheavals of the 2nd millennium BC, it is not surprising that none of the newly emerging central places was occupied in the preceding periods.

The same period also sees the emergence of a hierarchy of settlements in the Ganga valley, out of the previously undifferentiated sites of the Neolithic and Chalcolithic cultures. Once again only two categories, indicative of a simple political structure, may be distinguished, as in Allahabad district (Erdosy 1988), where one site of 10 hectares and 15 others of 2.8 hectares or less were discovered dating to the 10th–6th centuries BC (Fig. 6.2). However, while the number of Early Iron Age sites in some areas of the Indo-Gangetic divide show a decline from Late Harappan levels (Shrimali 1983), the number of sites in the Ganga valley increases dramatically, showing an eastward shift of power that continued up to the time of the Mauryas. That the emerging polities were separated by wide areas of exclusively rural settlements is demonstrated by Lal's survey of Kanpur district (Lal 1984a and b), where not a single site exceeded 4 hectares in an area of 6,000 km², in spite of a fivefold increase in population from the previous period.

Such patterns of settlement have been attributed, in the context of Mesopotamia, to chiefdoms (Johnson 1973, 1987; Earle 1991), which should exhibit a permanent agency of co-ordination, enjoying a monopoly of political, military and judicial power with authority resting rather on religious sanction than on force (Carneiro 1981). These attributes cannot as yet be identified in the archaeological record of the Ganga valley, owing to the absence of extensive excavations at key sites, although they are attested to in the literary sources (see below). What is apparent, is the influence of strategic resources on the location of central places. For example, Kausambi is surrounded by the poorest soils in Allahabad district which only makes sense in light of its consequent proximity to the sources of iron ore and semi-precious stones in the Vindhyas. The anomalous situation of Rajgir (the only major Early Historic city at a great distance from rivers) may likewise be explained by its access to the largest sources of iron ore in India. Mathura is another city lying on the boundary of two ecological zones (Dalal 1989). Thus, the procurement, processing and exchange of raw materials absent in the alluvial plains were clearly among the most important functions of the earliest central places, and set them apart from other settlements. Such a pattern recalls the importance attributed to the interregional exchange of prestige goods during the formative stage of complex societies (Friedman and Rowlands 1978).

We have already suggested above that few advances occur in material culture. Rice, wheat, barley, sesame, gram and cotton had already been known to the inhabitants of Chalcolithic Atranjikhera (Gaur 1983), Sringaverpur (Saraswat 1983), and Chirand, and they continue to be cultivated. The presence of the principal spring (*rabi*) and autumn (*kharif*) crops shows that the agricultural cycle was already well-established, although it is difficult to infer at present whether double-cropping of the land was practised. The horse is the only significant addition to the range of domesticated animals, which from Neolithic times onward had included cattle, sheep, goats and pigs. Ground stone and microlithic tools continue to supplement those fashioned from bone; copper is employed mainly in ornaments, iron in weapons.

Among excavated settlements, only Jakhera (Sahi 1977) shows evidence of a protective rampart of modest proportions.[6] Individual houses continue to be made of wattle and daub, with hearths and beaten earth floors. In the absence of wide exposures it is difficult to argue from negative evidence, but the lack of any facilities of sanitation, contrasted with their prominence from the 6th century BC onwards, is noteworthy. Our knowledge of social divisions is equally scanty. The presence of an ironsmith's workshop at Atranjikhera (Gaur 1983) bespeaks craft specialization on the one hand; its modest size along with the limited repertoire of iron objects suggests the absence of standardization and mass production on the other. A single elaborate structure of mud brick at Bhagwanpura (Bisht and Asthana 1979), consisting of 13 rooms, has been cited as an example of an elite residence,

---

[6]   Although without an accompanying rampart, a ditch found in the earliest PGW-bearing levels at Sonkh (Härtel 1993a, 19) may also represent a defensive structure.

but since it is the only (!) houseplan as yet available for this period, such an interpretation is hazardous. We may certainly note the general absence of luxury goods and a striking poverty of artistic expression. Apart from beads of terracotta and semi-precious stones and trinkets of shell and glass, only the engraved terracotta discs and the wide repertoire of painted designs on PGW may be cited in this context. However, the literary evidence – to be presented below – shows that material culture is not the only carrier of social status and its simplicity does not mean the absence of complex social organization.

One crucial innovation, which merits discussion, is iron smelting. Although the evidence is hardly satisfactory, it permits radical conclusions. The traditional view, that iron was brought into the subcontinent by invading 'Aryans' (Banerjee 1965), is wrong on two counts: there is no evidence of any knowledge of iron in the earliest Vedic texts (Pleiner 1971), where *ayas* stands either for copper or for metals in general, and the idea that the *āryas* of the Rigveda were invaders has become just as questionable. Wheeler's assertion that iron only spread to India with the eastward extension of Achaemenid rule (Wheeler 1962) is even more untenable in the face of radiocarbon dates from early iron-bearing levels. The alternative thesis (Chakrabarti 1977), that iron smelting was developed in the subcontinent, rests on two principal arguments. First, iron ore is found across the length and breadth of India, outside alluvial plains, in quantities that were certainly viable for exploitation by the primitive methods observable even in this century (Ball 1881; Elwin 1942). Ample opportunities thus existed for experimentation, although given the complexity of iron smelting this is not a conclusive point. The second argument, that the earliest evidence for iron comes from the peninsula and not from the northwest, is much more persuasive, even if better examples than quoted by Chakrabarti can be adduced in support of it. Briefly, while the dating of Phase II of Nagda (the earliest iron-bearing level) depends on ceramic analogies, and the stratigraphy of Ahar (another site which is claimed to have produced early evidence for iron) is hopelessly muddled,[7] the testimony of radiocarbon dates is instructive. Iron Age levels have yielded dates of 2970 ± 105 bp (TF-570) 1255, 1240, 1221 cal. BC and 2820 ± 100 bp (TF-573) 993 cal. BC from Hallur, and 2905 ± 105 bp (TF-326) 1096 cal. BC and 3130 ± 105 bp (TF-324) 1420 cal. BC from Eran. They are not only earlier than any date from the Ganga Valley (which dates fall between 2700–2500 bp) but are also earlier than the dates from Pirak in the northwest, with the exception of an

[7] Some of the 'Chalcolithic' levels producing iron objects (e.g. Trench C: Layers 1–3) yielded inscribed seal impressions of the 3rd–2nd centuries BC, while others (e.g. Trench I: Layer 1; Trench H: Layer 1 and Trench F: Layer 2) contained cast copper coins. Acceptance of a Chalcolithic date for these objects would require revisionism of an unprecedented magnitude, comparable only to the assertion of G. R. Sharma (1960) that cast copper coins associated with the lowest levels of Kausambi's rampart could actually be dated by their stratigraphic context to the 8th century BC rather than be used to date the latter itself to the 4th century BC.

anomalous reading of 2970±140 (Ly-1643) 1255, 1240, 1221 cal. BC.[8] Since
the process of diffusion from the west should produce rather the opposite
pattern, a strong case can be made for an indigenous origin of iron smelting,
although it could do with further support given the complexity of this
industrial process which by common consent renders multiple centres of
innovation unlikely.

Indeed, it would be tempting to strengthen Chakrabarti's arguments by pointing
out that until the 6th century BC iron in the Ganga valley was used but sparingly,
principally for the manufacture of weapons (Pleiner 1971). Only the sites of
Central India, in particular Prakash (Thapar 1967), Ujjain (Banerjee 1960) and
Nagda (Banerjee 1986) yielded a wide range of objects such as crowbars, spades,
axes and sickles. On the other hand, the presence of slag at such sites as
Hastinapura and Atranjikhera shows that even societies in the Ganga valley had
access to iron technology and simply chose not to make full use of it until the 6th
century BC. The reasons for this delay will be discussed in the next chapter; here
we must examine Late Vedic institutions as seen through the filter of literature.

Late Vedic polities

We have already discussed the methodological issues involved in the use of
literary sources in archaeological analysis elsewhere (Erdosy 1988). As for the
origin, dating, authorship, transmission and biases of Vedic literature, these are
conveniently summarized in recent syntheses by Gonda (1975) and Witzel (1987,
1989, 1995) and their conclusions need not be repeated here. Suffice it to say that
Vedic texts represent the point of view of the priestly order, whose principal
concern is the justification of the exalted position it has arrogated to itself. They
by and large ignore women, lower castes and people considered non-'Aryan', as
these groups are irrelevant to the principal aim of negotiating the brāhmaṇas'
social position *vis-à-vis* secular authority. The most important texts for our
purposes are the Brahmanas which, in Gonda's words, 'represent the intellectual
activity of a sacerdotal class which had succeeded in arranging and systematizing
the older forms of belief and worship, and in transforming them into a highly
complicated system of sacrificial ceremonies'. Given the monumental proportions of the corpus at hand, I have made extensive use of the *Vedic Index of Names
and Subjects* (Macdonell and Keith 1912), mindful of the limited range of texts
indexed even in that survey.

[8] The date of 2970±140 bp 1255, 1240, 1221 cal. BC (LY-1643) for Pirak III contrasts with the other
dates yielded by this period: 2705±120, 2660±100 and 2650±100 bp 818 and 813 cal. BC (TF-
1109, 861, and 1201). It is, above all, earlier than most of the dates recovered from the Chalcolithic
period which are, in ascending order, 2590±100 799 cal. BC, 2650±150 813 cal. BC, three dates of
2730±100 897 cal. BC, 2940±80 1159, 1142, 1138 cal. BC, and 3150±150 bp 1428 cal. BC. Indeed,
like TF-191 from Atranjikhera, it is the only anomaly in an otherwise consistent series, and cannot be
accepted as a reliable indication of the beginning of the Iron Age in Pirak unless further evidence
emerges in support of it.

It may be recalled briefly that in the Rigveda only the most nebulous ethnic and social categories can be detected (Parpola 1988). A general contrast is made between *aryas* and non-*āryas*, the latter variously described as *dāsas*, *dasyus* and *paṇis*, but this is based on cultural rather than racial or linguistic criteria (Erdosy 1989). Both categories, styled *varnas*, have smaller subdivisions, designated by the term *vis* or by an ethnonym such as Yādvāḥ (Macdonell and Keith 1912.2, 269). Beyond the association of certain tribes and rivers (e.g. the Pūrus with the Sarasvati), and a sentimental regard for the Saptasindhu as the claimed homeland of the *āryas*, ethnic groups are not assigned clearly delineated territories. The references to specific streams clearly mark the Punjab and the present Northwest Frontier Province as the home of the Rigvedic hymns. While the Yamuna appears already in one of the 'family books' (RV VII.18), the Ganga is accorded mention only in a late hymn (RV X.75), dedicated to rivers.

Although it is difficult to reconstruct the Rigvedic antecedents of political institutions, its vestiges survive in an anecdote related in PB XX.12.5 (Macdonell and Keith 1912.1: 262). This concerns Citraratha, who by virtue of a ceremony performed for him becomes the undisputed leader of his clan, in pointed contrast to the sharing of authority by members of other ruling clans, which must reflect an ancestral practice. That oligarchies were giving way to more centralized leadership even in the Rigveda is evident, however, from fragmentary genealogies which in the case of the Pūrus may have extended to five generations.[9] At the same time, leadership was still tempered by popular institutions. The evidence is difficult to interpret and much disputed, but there are unmistakable references to assemblies (*samiti*) of the entire (adult male?) population, whose approval of major decisions was at the least considered desirable, even if they had no legislative authority (cf. RV X.191). Coupled with examples of deposed and exiled rulers (e.g. AV III.3[10]) it shows that leadership had not yet become secure, and depended principally on prowess on the battlefield and generosity with booty.

The picture presented by the Late Vedic texts, datable to the 10th–6th centuries BC and focussing on the Ganga valley (Witzel 1987), shows considerable evolution on all fronts. At first, political boundaries are rarely drawn, unless rivers are conveniently available for the purpose (ŚB I.4.1.17). However, the seeds of change appear in the sudden prominence attached to the horse sacrifice (ŚB XIII.5). As a prelude to this ceremony, a horse is let loose, so that its owner may claim all the territories it wanders over, an assertion that he must be

---

9 According to RV X.33.7 the Pūru king Upamaśravas is the son of Kuruśravaṇa and the grandson of Mitrātithi, while in X.33.4 Kuruśravaṇa is said to be the descendant of Trasadasyu who is, in turn, the son of Purukutsa in RV VIII.19.36. The Bharatas could also boast a genealogy for Sudās, and it is significant that these two tribes were not only the most prominent in the Rigveda but later merged to form the Kuru *janapada*, which played a leading role in Late Vedic texts.

10 The following are the abbreviations used in the following sections: AB=Aitareya Brāhmaṇa; AV=Atharvaveda; ChUp=Chāndogya Upaniṣad; KŚS=Kātyāyana Śrautasūtra; LŚS=Lāṭyāyana Śrautasūtra; PB=Pañcaviṃsa Brāhmaṇa; RV=Rgveda; ŚB=Śatapatha Brāhmaṇa; SŚS=Śānkhāyana Śrautasūtra; TA=Taittirīya Āraṇyaka; TS=Taittirīya Saṃhitā; VS=Vājasaneyī Saṃhitā.

prepared to back up with force. At the conclusion of a victorious campaign the horse is sacrificed in an elaborate ceremony, an event frequently recorded for posterity. Such action symbolizes the newly found desire of polities to carve out mutually recognized territories for themselves. By the time of the Upanisads and the Srautasutras, the earliest of which may date from the 6th century BC, we see the explicit association of polities with territories. As Macdonell and Keith (1912.1: 273) point out, the term *janapada* now acquires its classical meaning of 'realm' (ChUp V.11.4, VIII.1.5). Kuruksetra, home of the most famous of all Late Vedic tribes, may have been the first region to be clearly delineated (TĀ V.1.1). At a slightly later time, the term *māgadha-deśīya* (KŚS XXII.4.22 and LŚS VIII.6.28) also creates a clear association between a *janapada* and the territory it occupies. It is in this vein that polities, small-scale and organized around a single central place according to the archaeological record, begin to fill a previously undifferentiated landscape. The modest nature of central places is confirmed by the late appearance (TĀ I.1.18) of the term *nagara*, the usual Sanskrit designation for town which would, indeed, have been ill applied to any settlement of the PGW phase revealed by archaeological surveys. Also, as regional settlement patterns have shown, wide belts of rural settlement still acted as buffers between evolving polities.

Although settlement patterns show little change during the 10th–6th centuries BC, patterns of political control evolve rapidly. Already in the Atharvaveda (IV.22.1, IV.22.5) the epithet *ekarāj* ('sole ruler') assumes a literal meaning, and becomes part of a ruler's legitimate aspirations. In the Brahmanas references to assemblies all but cease, while hereditary leadership, already detected in Rigvedic genealogies, is now elevated to a principle. Thus, in presenting the ruler to the multitude during his consecration (AB VIII.17) *rājapitṛ* is included among his titles.[11] His functions are also elaborated. In the Rigveda he was principally a leader in battle (e.g. X.173–174) and entitled to tribute (*bali*) from both foes (VII.6.5 and VII.18.19) and subjects (X.173.6). Although vestiges of his military leadership survive in the later Samhitās (Macdonell and Keith 1912.2: 86), a more elaborate theory of kingship emerges in the Brāhmaṇas, culminating in the proclamation of AB VIII.17 in the course of the royal consecration:

> Him do ye proclaim, O men as ... king and father of kings ... the lordly power ... the Kshatriya ... the suzerain of all creation ... the eater of the folk ... the

---

[11] Divine sanction may even be inferred for the principle of primogeniture from the story of Devāpi and Śantanu in the Bṛhaddevatā (VII.155–VIII.9), embellishing a cryptic reference in RV X.98. Devāpi, although the elder son of a departed king, refuses the throne due to his skin disease, which is thus assumed by his younger brother Śantanu. However, Devāpi's dereliction of duty is punished by a series of calamities, as a result of which he is offered the throne again. Although he refuses, he performs a series of expiatory rites to restore happiness to the realm. Apart from confirming the right of primogeniture, this complex story may also carry the seed of the king-*purohita* relationship; it is tempting to equate Devāpi (the elder brother) with the latter, and Śantanu (the younger brother and, thus, Devāpi's inferior) with the former.

slayer of foes ... the guardian of the Brahmans ... the guardian of the law.
(Keith 1920, 334)

In addition, as ŚB V.2.1.25 asserts, the ruler ensures tilling, peaceful dwelling and prosperity within his realm.

However, to the very end of the Late Vedic period, the duties of the ruler are embodied in abstract principles devoid of detail, such as acting for the general welfare of his subjects. Moreover, while they are enjoined to protect the social order and sacred law (*dharma*), the latter are not clearly elucidated until the appearance of the Dharmasūtras from the 6th century BC onwards. The simplicity of the administrative structure is further proof of limited development, in spite of the lofty titles claimed by rulers. Only the list of *ratnins* ('[bearers of] jewels'), whose blessing is sought in the course of the royal consecration, gives any evidence of full-time administrators (TS I.8.9; ŚB V.3.1). These include the royal chaplain, the army commander, the minstrel or court-poet whose high position is not surprising in a pre-literate society, the village headman, the chamberlain, the tax collector,[12] the charioteer, the thrower of dice, the huntsman and the courier. There is no word, unfortunately, on the procedure for appointing officials, or on their patterns of residence, but all of them could have been accommodated even within the modest central places already described.

What the administration lacked in elaboration and power was amply supplied by a cycle of rituals which forms the subject matter of many of the later Saṃhitas and Brāhmaṇas. The most important ceremonies grew up around the royal consecration which, by careful selection of attendance and the assignment of roles to participants, defined the scope of kingship, sanctified the alliance of priestly and secular powers, and reaffirmed the existing social order and the concomitant duties of individuals in the maintenance of society. Although physical evidence is at present lacking,[13] we may recall that a reliance on religious sanction in preference to brute force is one of the distinguishing criteria of chiefdoms, some of whose other attributes (such as a settlement hierarchy of two or three levels) have indeed been identified.

Turning, finally, to the emerging social order, an elaboration of a Rigvedic creation hymn (X.90) encapsulates its principal features:

> Prajāpati desired: 'May I have offspring'. He meted out the Trivṛt [Stoma] from his mouth. After it the God Agni was created ... [and] the Brahman; ...
> therefore are they the chief, for they were produced from the mouth. From the breast and arms he meted out the ... god Indra [and] the Rājanya ... Therefore

---

[12] Such a translation of the term *bhagadugha* is problematic, though the alternative of 'carver' or 'divider of portions' is no more plausible. The character of Pūṣan the divine *bhagadugha*, who places the portions of the gods before them in ceremony, is likewise ambiguous since he may be seen as both the collector and the redistributor of the offerings to deities.

[13] The so-called Śyenaciti at Kausambi has been identified by Lal (1985) as part of the collapsed brick mass of the revetment of the defenses, which is an interpretation suggested even by the drawings of the excavator.

are they strong, for they were created from strength. From the middle he meted out the ... Viśvadevas ... [and] the Vaiśya ... Therefore are they to be eaten, for they were created from the receptacle of food. Therefore are they more numerous than others, for they were created after the most numerous of gods. From his feet ... [came] the Śūdra ... Therefore [is] the Śūdra ... dependent on others. Therefore is the Śūdra not fit for the sacrifice for he was not created after any gods. (TS VII.1.1.3–5 – Keith 1914, 558)

A similar, if more concise version is found in AB VII.29, detailing the calamities awaiting a *kṣatriya* who partakes of improper food at sacrifices:

If the Soma [they bring up to the Kṣatriya] ... in thy offspring one like a Brahman will be born, an acceptor of gifts, a drinker of Soma, a seeker of livelihood, one to be moved at will. If curds ... in thy offspring one like a Vaiśya will be born, tributary to another, to be eaten by another, to be oppressed at will. If water ... in thy offspring one like a Śūdra will be born, the servant of another, to be removed at will, to be slain at will. These are the three foods, O King ... which a Kṣatriya is a sacrificer should not desire. [By contrast, if he eats the right food, the Kṣatriya] establishes himself the lordly power ... In the kingdom he finds support, dread becomes his sway and unassailable. (Keith 1920, 316)

As the quoted passages show, the general principles of ordering social groups and of assigning their inherent rights and responsibilities were certainly in place by the 6th century BC. The four *varnas* have been recognized as distinct and their position in the hierarchy have been fixed. The close co-operation of the lordly and priestly powers, embodied in the king and the *purohita*, has also been prescribed as the key to their dominant position. The general inferiority of the *śūdras*, stemming from their 'godless', 'non-Aryan' origins has been established. At the same time, only a few specific norms of behaviour have been laid down, and these primarily in the conduct of rituals. For example, *śūdras* were not allowed to come into contact with those consecrated for sacrifice; indeed, with the exception of public rituals such as the Rājasūya (in which they were required to act out degrading roles)[14] they were excluded from all sacrifices. This ruling certainly anticipates the elaborate rules of commensality, which are the pillars of the caste system. Modes of address (ŚB I.1.4.12) and the prescribed size of funeral mounds (ŚB XIII.8.3.11) were the only other external symbols of social status, once again strikingly few in comparison with later times, but confirmed by the lack of status symbols in material culture. It is important to note, however, the recognition already in Late Vedic texts (e.g. TS I.8.3.1) that social groups operate under their own internal laws, even if subject to the overriding force of *dharma*.

14   See, for example ŚB II.1.10. Among the roles *śūdras* play in the Rājasūya may be mentioned a fight between a *śūdra* and an *ārya* over a hide (PB V.5.14), which is won by the latter. While the king is required to visit the *śūdras* during his round of the *ratnins*, he must perform expiatory rites afterwards (ŚB V.3.2); this passage, indeed sums up the *śūdra*'s position: on the one hand he is part and parcel of the social system, on the other he is distinctly inferior.

There is complementary evidence that social mobility was still not fully impeded, just as in an earlier period *dāsas* were not categorically prevented from joining *ārya* ranks (Erdosy 1989). Intermarriages are implicitly recognized (TS VII.4.19), although frowned upon and (in the Dharmasūtras) used to explain the proliferation of lowly social groups. Status still, in theory at least, depended on performance: as SB XIII.4.2.17 says, a *brāhmaṇa* is not a *brāhmaṇa* unless he is actually conversant with ritual, while SB XI.6.2.5–10 accords the status of *brāhmaṇa* to the sagacious king Janaka. The stories of Satyakāma Jābāla (Ch Up IV.4) and Kavaśa Ailūṣa (AB II.19), both of whom overcame caste prejudice in being recognized as *brāhmaṇas*, illustrate the same principle. Indeed, both the elaboration of caste rules and their firm application have to await the appearance of legal texts from the 6th century BC onwards, and so we must consider Late Vedic society as being in a formative stage.

Much less, alas, is evident about the economic correlates of social groups. The *Vedic Index* cites the term *pauñjiṣṭha* (son of a *puñjiṣṭha* (fisherman)), found in the Atharvaveda, as evidence of the hereditary nature of at least some occupations; others are only evident in the Buddhist canonical texts (Wagle 1966). Likewise, the economic interdependence of castes, such a crucial feature of later times, occupies little space in Vedic literature. Finally, while private ownership of land is reflected in prescribed rituals for those involved in boundary disputes (TS II.2.1.2 and II.2.3.1) and for those 'desirous of securing a village' (TS II.1.3.2; II.1.6.1; II.5.6.1), the nature of ownership rights – communal or individual; extending to the land or only to usufruct – is nowhere elucidated. About all we can say, based on such passages as KŚS XXII.10–11 and ŚŚS XVI.14.18, is that both land and tenants could be alienated, at least in the form of sacrificial fees, by the end of our period.

Ethnicity

Material culture and the texts show a consistent picture of Early Iron Age (or Late Vedic) society, with one significant exception: while *āryas* figure prominently in literature, they have proved to be exceptionally elusive in the archaeological record. Attempts to saddle them with copper hoards, horses, iron or PGW have all been greeted with justifiable scepticism (Allchin 1980), and by the warning that an obsession with the 'Aryan hypothesis' has channelled archaeologists' energies into an unprofitable dead-end at the expense of other issues (Chakrabarti 1968). Yet the aura of mystery surrounding the *āryas* stems primarily from the defective methodology employed in their pursuit. To wit, archaeologists have neither subjected the literary evidence to critical scrutiny – preferring to accept the conclusions of others – nor developed an adequate procedure for identifying group affiliations in material culture. Taking these points in reverse order, the identification of *āryas* as racial or linguistic groups originating outside South Asia is questionable on the following grounds. First, while the Rigveda contains accounts of migrations and is replete with battles, it preserves no memory of a foreign ancestry; *ārya* tribes appear in the northwest of the subcontinent and from the beginning fight each other as well as non-*āryas*. Second, *āryas* see themselves as subscribers to a set of religious beliefs and social conventions (as opposed to, for example, 'foolish and crooked *paṇis* of insulting speech, not honouring [the Gods, and] not sacrificing . . .' RV VII.6.3), and not as physiologically or linguistically distinct (Parpola 1988; Erdosy 1989).

Coupled with the undeniable fact that *āryas* speak a language with striking structural similarities to languages outside South Asia, the following conclusions seem inescapable: (1) While Indo-European languages may well have spread to South Asia through migration, the *āryas* were not their carriers. (2) *Āryas* do not constitute a racial group; rather, belonging to diverse ethnic groups, they are distinguished by a set of ideas and it is these – instead of the people holding them – which spread rapidly over the subcontinent.[15] The first point has already been discussed in detail elsewhere (Erdosy 1989); elaboration of the second will provide a suitable conclusion to a chapter dealing with the Late Vedic period.

To begin with, apart from the undeniable movement of certain priestly schools, and of the Vedic texts in their care (deducible from both linguistic criteria and explicit references – Witzel 1989), there is little evidence of migrations. It is true that the Kurus are placed in the upper Gaṅgā-Yamunā Doab, while their Rigvedic ancestors (the Pūrus and the Bharatas) had lived between the Sarasvati and the Ravi (RV III.23, III.33, VI.61, VII.18 and VII.96). However, such a localized shift would be expected in light of the drying up of the Sarasvati and is clearly reflected in settlement patterns. By contrast, the most explicit reference to long-distance movement (ŚB I.4.1.14–17) is plainly fictitious since, as the excavations at Chirand have shown, the region of Videha supported permanent settlements even in Neolithic times. Furthermore, while there is an increase in the number of recorded ethnic groups, they are stationary and reflect the expansion in the geographical horizon of the authors of Late Vedic texts.

The postulated conquest of northern India – whether by a single 'Aryan' tribe, or in a succession of waves – also ill fits the pattern of dispersed, small-scale polities, which is demonstrable in both literature and material culture for the 10th–6th centuries BC. It would have called for a much more complex political landscape, along with a rigid social structure which is likewise in conflict with the signs of flexibility evident in the texts. Even a modified theory of 'elite dominance' (Renfrew 1987) is impossible to support. It assumes that the original tripartite society of the 'Aryans' was superimposed as a conquering elite on the native population, resulting in the addition of the 'non-Aryan' *śūdra varṇa* to the

[15] Such conclusions have already been anticipated by Shaffer (1984) who viewed the 'Aryan invasions' as an attempt on the part of the emerging ruling elites of Early Historic societies to enhance their prestige by creating a fictitious foreign ancestry for themselves. While his view is near the mark, it needs to be modified on two counts: it still assumes that Vedic literature actually describes migrations and that 'Aryans' have not left any recognizable traces in material culture.

already existing categories of *brāhmaṇa*, *kṣatriya/rājanya* and *vaiśya*.[16] In such an event one would have expected the lowest *varṇa* to be the most numerous yet, as we have seen (in TS VII.1.1.3–5, quoted above), the texts explicitly refer to the *vaiśyas* as the most numerous and as the chief source of revenue.[17] *Śūdras* are not only fewer in number; their late appearance and lowly status may best be explained as the result of the taking of captives in battles, which would make them the product not of an 'Aryan conquest' but of conflicts normally accompanying the rise of complex societies.

In addition to negative arguments, positive signs of acculturation may also be cited. Among non-*ārya* groups, *vrātyas* were particularly prominent and had a social organization that recalled that of the *āryas* with *arhants*, *yaudhas* and *gṛhapatis* corresponding to the three higher orders (Macdonell and Keith 1912.2: 343). Although called unconsecrated (PB XVII.1.9) they are said to have spoken the language of the consecrated and could become *āryas* through the performance of certain rituals. The fact that 'easterners' (*prācyas*) in general, and Magadhans in particular, were regarded with disapproval by Late Vedic seers shows that the spread of new values had not transcended the Ganga-Yamuna Doab in the 6th century BC, while their eventual conversion to orthodoxy without any reference to an 'Aryan conquest' reinforces the validity of the acculturation model. The movement of priestly schools and of individual *purohitas*, already mentioned, also supports the image of a cultural transformation independent of large-scale migrations or conquests.

Needless to say, none of these theoretical arguments will be convincing in the absence of material evidence. Until now the characterization of *āryas* as invaders has prevented the identification of their physical traces. However, adopting the view that they were indigenous to South Asia, a failure to draw convincing West or Central Asian parallels for supposedly 'Aryan' traits is neither surprising, nor an argument against their existence. It would also eliminate the difficulty posed by the seemingly haphazard appearance of 'Aryan' traits, such as fire-altars, horse burials, and certain painted motifs on pottery, whose chronology does not show the expected northwest–southeast gradient. Since, in addition to being indigenous, *āryas* form a cultural, rather than a racial, category, our task becomes the identification of the material traces of a rapidly spreading ideology which diverse ethnic groups came to adopt. Before proceeding, however, a brief digression regarding the identification of fundamental analytical units in material culture is required.

[16] Or, as Kosambi (1950) suggested, the *brāhmaṇas* may have been indigenous ritual specialists co-opted by the conquering elite composed of *kṣatrīyas*, *vaiśyas* and the now defunct sacrificial priests who died out along with their complex rituals. This is an explanation I have also adopted in an earlier synthesis (Erdosy 1988).

[17] *Vaiśyas* are commonly described as 'food for the king', which refers to their leading role in agriculture. They were allowed to aspire to wealth, but confiscation of their riches was recommended royal policy. *Śūdras* are never so characterized, which underlines their economic insignificance; at best they could aspire to be expert craftsmen and their lot was one of relentless drudgery.

Although it continues to enjoy considerable currency, in practice if not in theory, the concept of archaeological 'culture' defined by Childe (1929) as a recurring assemblage of artefacts,[18] has come under mounting criticism for a variety of reasons. To begin with, if the primary units of analysis are defined in terms of shared material culture traits, which are in turn held to reflect mental templates of their makers, the scope of analysis will be restricted to tracing the flow of ideas and people across space and time. However, while the inadequacy of diffusionist explanations has been recognized in South Asian archaeology (e.g. Shaffer 1978; Chakrabarti 1988), archaeological 'cultures' continue to enjoy respectability, in spite of a recognition elsewhere of their artificial nature, whose imposition on the archaeological record has thoroughly confounded our understanding of the past (Shennan 1989). Apart from their often impressionistic determination, and loose association with social units, their reality has been challenged primarily for two reasons: ethnographic research suggests that assemblages of material culture are rarely coterminous with social boundaries (Hodder 1978), while statistical analysis reveals that they are the aggregates of widely divergent individual distributions (Shennan 1978). Thus, a focus on assemblages has not only distorted the picture but has also submerged a vast quantity of information contained in the spatial distribution of individual traits.

Needless to say, it has been easier to demolish the concept than to replace it. Adherents of the New Archaeology have at times advocated a focus on geographical regions (Binford 1964), which reflects Leslie White's dictum that culture is man's extrasomatic means of adaptation. Elsewhere they separated the information content of artefacts into functional categories – witness Binford's technomic, sociotechnic and ideotechnic artefacts, an idea unhappily resurrected in a recent discussion of ethnicity in archaeology (Schortman 1989). This approach has been rightly criticized by Hodder (1986) for its arbitrary subdivision of human activities into neatly bounded categories and general relegation of stylistic attributes to the level of epiphenomena. A more fruitful remedy, pioneered by Renfrew, starts with the assumption that crucial group affiliations are those which are recognized by both members and non-members (Renfrew 1978, 97). While several cross-cutting circles of affiliation may exist, most likely to be identified (both by actors in the past and observers in the present) are political units, through their reflection in settlement patterns, particularly the distribution of central places. This thread of thinking runs from theoretical assumptions of spatial structure (Renfrew 1978), through the construction of models to derive boundaries from the location of central places (Renfrew and Level 1979) to a demonstration of the role of intensive interaction between polities in producing enduring patterns of culture (Renfrew 1986).

---

[18] Although Childe based his methodology on the work of Gustaf Kossinna, he is the most readily associated with the culture concept as he – unlike Kossinna – wrote in English and, while controversial in his day, was not tainted by his political views.

There is no denying the considerable attraction of this approach for students of South Asia, where one may even test the reliability of using settlement patterns to derive political boundaries against the literary evidence. Moreover, the considerable cultural homogeneity achieved at a time of bitter rivalries recalls the Peer Polity Interaction model. Criticism is thus offered not on grounds of inaccuracy but on those of insufficiency. Renfrew's theoretical models have little to offer scholars interested in societies without hierarchical organization or central places. As for complex formations, political boundaries may enclose a multitude of social groups, of which the power-wielding elite, alone the focus of Renfrew's thrust, is not a sufficient representative. Given the ability of rulers to enforce adherence to a wide range of norms, a knowledge of the political landscape is indeed essential. However, as culture process depends on more than just the matrix of inter-elite relations within and across political boundaries, efforts must be made to identify a wider spectrum of group affiliations even if they do not leave conspicuous traces in material culture. The questions, 'Is not the most important feature of a chiefdom the ... central person?' 'Is not the distinguishing feature of the state generally accepted as the existence of a permanent hierarchical structure of administration ...?' (Renfrew 1978, 101) may, perhaps, be answered in the affirmative if our aim were solely to develop a procedure for identifying highly evolved polities in the archaeological record. They will not, by themselves, lead far in the search for the latter's origins. Given the advocacy of settlement archaeology on the following pages this point is worth stressing. There is no doubt that the former has fostered a good deal of progress in South Asian studies; however, if its limitations are not borne in mind, it will be in danger of becoming a fad, an end in itself, much after the manner of Wheeler's stratigraphic principles. Hence the analyses of settlement patterns presented below may be lauded as significant, but not without stressing that they have, at best, provided a sketchy picture of cultural evolution much in need of refinement.

A promising avenue for proceeding beyond the identification of political structures has been opened by Barth's seminal treatment of ethnicity (Barth 1969). Given the breadth of his theoretical insight, discussion must here be limited to aspects of vital concern to archaeology, though without losing sight of the overall framework. The starting point is Barth's insistence that 'ethnic groups are categories of ascription and identification by the authors themselves' (Barth 1969, 10; cf. Renfrew 1978, 97, paraphrased above). Apart from requiring conscious acceptance of membership, ethnic groups emerge in the context of intense social interaction, and have shifting boundaries consisting of cultural criteria whose maintenance is one of their primary concerns. In Hodder's words, 'ethnicity [is] the mechanism by which interest groups use culture to symbolise their within-group [sic] affiliation in opposition to and in competition with other interest groups' (Hodder 1979, 452). The crucial point for archaeology is twofold: culture (and, by extension, material culture) will be actively engaged in the process of boundary maintenance, but only a few selected traits out of the available spectrum will be called upon to do so (Barth 1969, 14). It follows from this that assemblages of traits will never be adequate expressions of ethnicity. Rather, it will be the distribution of individual items, within the matrix of the distribution of all material culture traits, which will reveal group affiliations.

Since Barth's initial formulation, considerable refinement has been achieved in relating ethnicity to other categorizations, such as economic interdependence (Despres 1975). Archaeologists, for their part, have emphasized that relations within ascriptive units, as much as between them, will determine the material correlates of ethnicity in specific situations, and have also recognized that a wide variety of group affiliations as well as individual strategies may have stylistic consequences. Witness Larick's (1987) study of the influence of age-groups on spear styles in Kenya, or the distinction between 'emblemic' and 'assertive' styles made by Wiessner (1983) in her study of the Kalahari San. There have also emerged attempts to define criteria for suitability as ethnic markers (Buchignani 1987), as well as a parallel corpus of cautionary tales (Sterner 1989). Nevertheless, use of the concept requires further clarification, since there is as yet no agreement either on the relationship of ethnicity to culture, or on what leads to the emergence of ethnicity in the first place. The most successful case studies (e.g. Barth 1969 or Despres 1975) treat the interaction of social groups already characterized by cultural differences which will be called upon to a greater or lesser extent depending on the distribution of power, economic relations between groups, or the perceived distance between their cultural practices. Although it is repeatedly stressed that cultural differences are an insufficient condition for the emergence of ethnic groups, they plainly appear to be necessary. The very view of ethnicity as the social codification of cultural identities (implied in the subtitle to Barth 1969) contradicts the assertion that culture itself is the result of ethnic group organization. It is more likely to support the opposite view, vigorously denied by Barth, that cultural differences emerged initially in situations of relative isolation, even if they were subsequently amplified by boundary maintenance.[19] On a related matter, the view that ethnic groups are the result of cooperation in times of stress to obtain competitive advantage (Hodder 1979) appears simplistic as it downplays the powerful appeal of cultural factors. Were it true, one would not expect so consistently to see the anomaly of disadvantaged members of an ethnic group clinging to their status even if it were to their advantage to align themselves with similarly oppressed members of other ethnic groups.

[19] A good example of changing cultural behaviour in the context of social interaction is furnished by the process of Sanskritization (Srinivas 1966) wherein higher castes have to revise their codes of behaviour continually due to their emulation by economically powerful castes seeking to improve their low ritual status.

My intention here is not to resolve these difficulties; rather, it is to stress that only the study of long-term changes, the unique domain of archaeology, will provide answers to them. An appreciation of these problems should also highlight the fact that, much like central places, ethnic groups only represent one aspect of society, and the assumptions we make about them will set limits on the range of problems their identification will help us solve. Furthermore, the following chapters will make clear that with the emergence of states ethnic groups are superseded by broader circles of allegiance, which incorporate a multitude of ethnic groups in the course of their inevitable expansion. At the very least, this should prevent ethnicity from usurping the role hitherto enjoyed by the archaeological 'culture'. Unlike the latter, it is a concept rooted in careful ethnographic observation and, used in conjunction with other concepts, should contribute to a much refined understanding of past processes.

In the absence of a large published corpus of material, which prevents the study of seemingly mundane objects which often act as signifiers of ethnicity (Wiessner 1983), the task of identifying palaeoethnic groups in South Asia is not an easy one. However, I have already remarked that even considering the paucity of published material, the poverty of material culture in the Early Iron Age is striking. It is not surprising, therefore, that the one outstanding trait, PGW, has received so much attention from archaeologists. While it may be a mistake to equate the distribution of this ware with an effective social group, the coincidence of the territory of *madhyadeśa*, representing the heartland of *ārya* orthodoxy, with it is striking (Witzel 1989, 243).

In describing PGW, however, the diversity of designs from site to site has received little attention. Yet a comparison of corpora from Hastinapura (Lal 1955) and Atranjikhera (Gaur 1983), the only two sites to have been extensively published, yields interesting results. On the one hand one may note the common use of simple geometric designs: parallel lines – straight or wavy, solid or broken, chequerboard patterns and conventionalized swastikas are found at both sites in considerable numbers.[20] On the other hand, many of the more elaborate decorative motifs have limited distributions. For example, tridents, three-armed swastikas and trefoil designs are common at Atranjikhera[21] and absent at Hastinapura, while concentric rings recalling solar or floral designs have the opposite distribution.[22] The treatment of the interiors of bowls and dishes also differs: at Atranjikhera it is common to see three sets of parallel lines converging and occasionally intersecting at the centre of the base, while at Hastinapura concentric rings at the centre act as the foci of decorative motifs, which – including solar/floral motifs, wavy lines or loops – appear to radiate out of

[20]   Compare Lal 1955; Figures 6:14 and 10:64 with Gaur 1983; Figures 42:B-7a, 59:PD-29 and 108:PD-24a. Also Lal 1955, Figure 8:30 with Gaur 1983, Figures 76:VR-1 and 107:PD-19.
[21]   Cf. Gaur 1983, Figures 42:VR-5 and B-6a, 44:B-53. Also Figure 59:PD-2, 2a and 31.
[22]   Cf. Lal 1955, Figure 6:3, 8 and 15.

them.[23] Although circular motifs at the centre of bowls have been found at Atranjikhera, even in the their fragmentary condition they seem to contain either stellar or chariot-wheel designs, which are in turn absent from Hastinapura.[24]

On the whole, not only individual motifs, but entire families, along with principles of design, appear to be restricted to individual sites. At the same time, a common pool of geometric designs is maintained and this is supported by the limited repertoire of motifs published from such sites as Mathura (IAR 1975–76, 54, Figure 5), Sonkh (Härtel 1993a and b) and Ahicchatra (Ghosh and Panigrahi 1946). Although the evidence is too fragmentary to be conclusive, it may be hypothesized that PGW served complementary but opposing ends. The uniformity of its manufacturing process and the use of simple geometric designs over the entire Ganga-Yamuna Doab may perhaps be seen as reflecting the widespread adoption of a new ideology, while the restriction of more complex designs to individual sites may be taken as indications of the diverse ethnic affiliations of the people who subscribed to it.

Such a hypothesis can only be confirmed when more information becomes available. It would be particularly interesting to compare the distribution of designs with those of political boundaries reconstructed from the location of central places. This would afford a better test of the hypothesis than the comparison of distant sites such as Hastinapura and Atranjikhera. The contextual information from individual sites is also missing: was PGW present in all households, or was it – as suggested by its refinement – limited to the tableware of the elite? More extensive publication of the designs on terracotta discs (some of which anticipate the motifs on punchmarked coins – Sinha 1966) may even reveal an alternative set of traits symbolizing group affiliations.

Conclusions

The Late Vedic/Early Iron Age may be best characterized as a period of consolidation following the break up of the Harappan civilization. It witnessed the laying of the ground for renewed urbanization, focussed on the Ganga valley, and the beginning of a cultural tradition which has, in spite of vicissitudes, survived to this day. Since the culmination of this development in early historic South Asia occurred with the rise of the Maurya empire, the factors underlying the emergence of complex societies will be examined at the end of the following chapter. Here, attention will be paid, instead, to a question posed above: how can one explain the rapid spread of a new ideology during the emergence of complex societies, and what were its consequences?

The key to this process must be seen in the system of justifying one's status with reference to cultural criteria, which already guided the authors of the

---

[23]   Compare Gaur 1983, Figures 42:B-5b; 44:B-69; 59:PD-7, PD-21, PD-22 and PD-23 and 107:PD-2 and PD-16 with Lal 1955, Figures 9:59, 61, 62 and 10:65, 66, 67 and 68.

[24]   Cf Gaur 1983, Figure 59:PD-14 and PD-15.

Rigveda, and has remained the fundamental principle of South Asian social organization to this day. Given that the rise of complex societies is accompanied by territorial expansion, leading to the amalgamation of diverse ethnic groups with their diverse practices, a principle of ranking which enshrines already existing cultural differences would provide emerging elites with a means of legitimizing the social order. By presenting status distinctions as the natural outcome of time-honoured cultural diversity, rather than of ephemeral power relations, stability could be imparted to the new system even as it continued to bring new ethnic groups into its orbit. At the same time, adoption of the *ārya* social system entailed the adoption of the language in which it was expressed, namely Old Indo-Aryan, which came to displace all other tongues.[25]

All this could be reinforced by claims of descent from a fictitious foreign ancestor. This is rarely attempted in Vedic literature, although the colonization of Videha is ascribed, in ŚB I.4.1.14–17, to 'Aryan' migrants. Generally speaking, *āryas* persisted as a cultural category, and membership in a common ideology was reinforced rather through the widespread circulation of members of the priestly caste, for which ample evidence exists in the literature. It is in the Pāṇinian tradition of naming *janapadas* after their ruling *kṣatriya* clans (as if these had an external origin) that we witness the first attempts at rewriting history, a trend culminating in the arrangement of purportedly historical traditions in the Purāṇas at the end of the Early Historic period, which provided contemporary rulers with the long genealogies now thought to be commensurate with their status.

Given the constant expansion characterizing the early stages of complex societies, which is amply reflected in the literary tradition, the fluidity of ethnic groups, which were repeatedly reconstituted into larger units, need not surprise us. Since the maintenance of boundaries would remain one of their principal concerns (Barth 1969), one would expect to see periodical changes in material culture to reflect this. It could be postulated that the disappearance of PGW in the 5th century BC is indicative of such a development. Since it overlaps with NBP, the latter is an unlikely candidate for assuming the role of expressing group affiliations. Punchmarked coins, on the other hand, appearing by the end of the 5th century BC, would provide an ideal substitute. They would not only symbolize the emergence of a higher level of political authority, and be instrumental in facilitating the expanding volume of trade on which it depended, but would also suppress the narrower (ethnic) circles of allegiance expressed by PGW designs which had become incorporated into much expanded polities. Such a hypothesis, however, anticipates the changes occurring from the 6th century BC onwards, to which we must now turn.

---

[25] While structural borrowings from Dravidian (which must have previously been spoken in areas presently dominated by Indo-Aryan languages) support this reconstruction, it remains to be explained why the process of language replacement stopped at the Narbada river even if the spread of social institutions did not.

Acknowledgements

The author wishes to express his gratitude to the Social Sciences and Humanities Research Council of Canada and to the University of Toronto for their joint award of a Canada Research Fellowship (1990–93), which enabled him to write chapters 6 and 7 of this volume, not to mention several other papers.

CHAPTER 7

CITY STATES OF NORTH INDIA AND PAKISTAN AT THE TIME OF THE BUDDHA

GEORGE ERDOSY

Introduction

The re-appearance of stable political structures following the collapse of Harappan urbanism, along with an eastward shift in the focus of economic and political power and the spread of a new family of (Indo-Aryan) dialects, required almost a millennium. The emergence of what may be termed simple chiefdoms, datable to c. BC 1000, was the culmination of this process. They were characterized in material culture by an agricultural economy making limited use of iron, by low population density and by a two-tier settlement hierarchy whose central place coordinated the procurement, processing and distribution of vital raw materials. In addition, literary sources speak of social stratification, redistribution, a single level of bureaucracy directly supervised by a (hereditary) ruler and a complex ritual cycle. In spite of the keen rivalries alluded to in the Late Vedic literature, a patchwork of such small-scale political units persisted until c. BC 550, although expanding into the middle and lower Ganga Valley through acculturation, as we have already seen. Lack of environmental or social circumscription (Thapar 1984, after Carneiro 1981) has been held responsible for the slow development: although data on settlement patterns are limited, one may observe low population density, as well as the absence of any central places in vast areas (such as that surveyed by M. Lal (1984a) in his pioneering study). Thus, movement into uninhabited tracts may have offered a viable alternative to political subjection for the junior lineages of Vedic tribes.

By contrast, the next three centuries witnessed dramatic growth in population size and agglomeration, the colonization of fertile but forested tracts away from the principal watercourses (facilitated by the introduction of iron into agricultural production) and the re-emergence of long-distance trade, of a monetary economy and – sometime before BC 250 – of writing (see chapters 9 and 10). Narrow, ethnic allegiances were replaced with submission to the authority of territorially based states. Tradition – principally the Buddhist Pali Canon – speaks of intense political rivalries; unlike previously, these now resulted in steady territorial expansion until one principality attained supremacy over the entire

Ganga Valley and projected its power into both southern India and the northwest. The achievements and legacy of the Mauryan empire are the concerns of chapters 9–10, however; here the aim is to outline both the archaeological record and the literary evidence bearing on the initial stages of state formation,[1] and to account for the emergence of complex societies in light of recent theoretical work on the subject.

Chronology

Given the rapid social and political changes just outlined, it would be desirable to date key developments accurately. However, the chronology of early historic state formation is bedevilled by the retarded appearance of written records, which stands in stark contrast to the antiquity of oral traditions. The earliest monumental inscriptions date to the reign of the Mauryan emperor Aśoka (c. BC 272–232), who ruled with the aid of a bureaucracy that already bore the hallmarks of advanced political organization. Although coins may have been present somewhat earlier, they were initially of the punchmarked or uninscribed cast variety and provide no aid in dating archaeological layers – rather, their own date can only be estimated from their stratigraphic position. As for traditional accounts pertaining to the formative period of states, one need only refer to renewed controversy surrounding the date of Buddha's *nirvāna* (Bechert 1982, 1991) to appreciate their limitations as historical documents. Far from helping us establish a chronological framework, they themselves, in the manner of early coinage, can only be dated with the help of the archaeological record. Finally, even radiocarbon dates are of limited utility due to severe irregularities in the calibration curve around the middle of the first millennium BC (Fig. 7.1)

In spite of these reservations, there are certain patterns in the data which deserve attention. Since all excavators have relied on changes in the ceramic assemblage in their phasing of sites, the dating of Northern Black Polished ware (or NBP) becomes pivotal to a secure chronological framework. First described by Cunningham it was found in a stratigraphic context already by Marshall (1912) at Bhita. However, only after Krishna Deva and Wheeler (Ghosh and Panigrahi 1946, Appendix A) observed its widespread distribution in the Ganga Valley did the ware attract the attention of archaeologists. Apart from its striking appearance, the result of the fusion of its alkaline slip upon firing at high temperatures (Hegde 1975), this easily identifiable artefact occurs in abundance over a wide area. Although representing a minor technological advance, and in no way identifiable with a 'people',[2] most reports, especially the brief accounts

---

[1] Excluding peninsular India and Sri Lanka, which are the respective concerns of chapters 8 and 9.

[2] As advocated by Sita Ram Roy (1969) who tried to equate the 'NBP people' with 'Aryans', an idea that found no favour with his colleagues to judge from comments on his paper (in Sinha 1969).

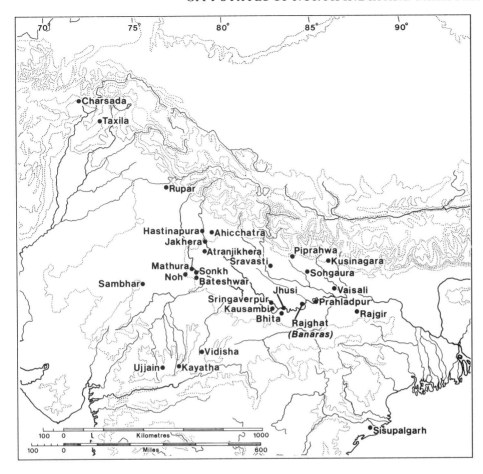

Fig. 7.1.   Map of principal sites referred to in Chapter 7.

submitted to *Indian Archaeology – A Review*, relate important changes in material culture to the date of its introduction. The same practice has spread to identifying the stratigraphic context of radiocarbon samples. Consequently, one must first isolate phases within the NBP-bearing levels at individual sites and then examine the available radiocarbon dates for each.

K. K. Sinha (1969; cf. Sahi 1974) proposed a chronology, placing Sravasti, Rajghat, Vaisali and Kausambi at the core of the NBP culture, and Charsada, Rupar, Ujjain and Hastinapura at the periphery, and dating the appearance of NBP to BC 500 and BC 350, respectively, at the two groups of sites. Although recent radiocarbon dates (including samples from Ujjain and Rupar) throw doubt on his scheme, several of his observations remain valid. To wit, at all sites that have been reported on in detail, the first phase of the occurrence of NBP coincides with the survival of the ceramic industries of earlier periods (PGW and Black Slipped ware (BSW) in the Doāb, BSW and Black and Red ware (BRW) further east, and certain red ware forms in both areas). Although some settlements are already fortified and show increased use of iron, several other traits, such as coins and extensive construction activity in baked bricks, occur only in the succeeding period. It is then, also, that the ceramic industries presaging NBP completely disappear, while certain red ware forms such as carinated cooking pots (*handis*) and piriform water vessels[3] occur for the first time. In the final stage of NBP we enter the realm of history with inscribed seals and sealings providing a secure chronology from the mid-3rd century BC onward.

As regards individual sites, the 'early NBP' phase is represented by Ahicchatra IIIA (Ghosh 1991), Atranjikhera IVA (Gaur 1983), Kausambi PS I–V (Sharma 1969), Mathura IB (Ghosh 1991), Prahladpur IB (Narain and Roy 1967), Rajghat IB (Narain and Roy 1976–78), Sonkh levels 36–35 (Härtel 1993b), Sravasti I (Singha 1967), Sringaverpur IIIA (Lal and Dikshit 1981) and Sugh IA (Ghosh 1991). The 'mid-NBP' phase is found at Ahicchatra IIIB, Atranjikhera IVB, Hastinapura III$_{1-3}$ (Lal 1955), Kausambi SP I$_{A-B}$, Mathura II, Prahladpur IC, Rajghat IC, Sonkh levels 34–33, Sravasti IIA, Sringaverpur IIIB and Sugh IB. 'Late-NBW' levels, dating to Maurya and – in some cases – Sunga times are found at Atranjikhera IVD, Hastinapura III$_{4-6}$, Kausambi SP II–III, Rajghat II, Sonkh levels 32–31, Sravasti IIB and Sringaverpur IIIC.

Determining the absolute ages of the various subdivisions is a more complicated task, in light of comments already made regarding the irregularities of the calibration curve around 2500–2300 bp. The appearance of NBP was first dated to BC 500, based on the evidence from Taxila (Marshall 1951). The date was pushed back to BC 600 by Lal (1955), who assigned 50 years to each structural period at Hastinapura preceding the introduction of inscribed objects in the 3rd century BC. Recently, even a beginning around BC 700 has come to be advocated (Lal and Dikshit 1981) on the basis of the thickness of deposits at Sringaverpur below the first occurrence of punchmarked coins. It is, however, always a dangerous procedure to date sites based on the thickness of deposits, especially when exposure is limited to a few square metres. Neither is there agreement on the date of the first appearance of coinage in South Asia (cp. Gupta 1969; Mitchiner 1973; Dhavalikar 1975; Cribb 1985). As for radiocarbon dates (Erdosy 1993), only the erratic series of measurements from Bateshwar and Mathura place the appearance of NBP prior to the mid-6th century BC. Disregarding these a different pattern emerges and although the evidence is not conclusive, it provides strong support for a relatively short chronology:

---

[3] The so-called type Xa jars from Ahicchatra, where they were first identified (Ghosh and Panigrahi 1946).

To begin with, there are seven[4] dates for the end of the phase immediately preceding the introduction of NBP (marked by PGW in the Indo-Gangetic divide and the Doab and by BSW further east), falling between 2450 and 2350 bp:

Atranjikhera:	TF-291	2415 ± 100 bp	512 cal. BC
	TF-194	2410 ± 85 bp	410 cal. BC
Hastinapura:[5]	TF-91	2450 ± 120 bp	752,709,530 cal. BC
	TF-85	2385 ± 125 bp	406 cal. BC
Khalaua:	TF-1228	2420 ± 95 bp	484,437,424 cal. BC
Noh:	TF-1144	2370 ± 85 bp	403 cal. BC
Rajghat:	TF-292	2350 ± 95 bp	400 cal. BC

A further fifteen dates[6] coming from the early NBP phase of various sites (including dates – identified by an asterisk – from the period of overlap between PGW and NBP) cover an almost identical time-span:

Ahicchatra:	BM-194	2420 ± 150 bp	484,437,424 cal. BC
	WSV-	2400 ± 150 bp*	408 cal. BC*
	TF-311	2360 ± 105 bp*	402 cal. BC*
Besnagar:	TF-387	2350 ± 100 bp	400 cal. BC
Kausambi:	TF-221	2385 ± 100 bp	406 cal. BC
	TF-219	2325 ± 100 bp	396 cal. BC
Kayatha:	TF-394	2380 ± 95 bp	405 cal. BC
	TF-674	2350 ± 95 bp	400 cal. BC
Khalaua:	PRL-67	2450 ± 155 bp*	752,709,530 cal. BC*
	PRL-68	2370 ± 170 bp*	403 cal. BC*
Manjhi:	PRL-983	2350 ± 135 bp	400 cal. BC
Rajghat:	TF-293	2370 ± 105 bp	403 cal. BC
Rupar:	TF-209	2365 ± 100 bp	403 cal. BC
Sohagaura:	PRL-183	2465 ± 105 bp	756,692,541 cal. BC
Ujjain:	TF-409	2335 ± 95 bp	398 cal. BC

4 Omitting dates of 2155 ± 100 bp (194 cal. BC) and 2270 ± 85 bp (383 cal. BC) from Ahicchatra (TF-317), and Allahpur (PRL-81), respectively, which are clearly too late, as well as dates assigned to the period of PGW/NBP overlap which properly belong to the 'early-NBP' period in light of the discussion above. All dates reported from South Asia have been conveniently listed in Possehl 1989, 1994.

5 It has long been assumed that TF-83, 88, 90 and 112 came from the end of the PGW phase, but an examination of the description of their contexts makes it clear that they are from the lowest layers of the NBP deposit of this site. Sample TF-88 is described as coming from Layer 25, the lowest NBP-bearing layer of the site, and this has always been accepted. The other three all come from a context described as 'Layer 26, pit sealed by Layer 25'. Now, even if Layer 26 may be taken to belong to the PGW phase, the pit cutting it comes from the subsequent phase and by simple rules of stratigraphy all finds, including the radiocarbon samples, from it should be assigned to Layer 25, marking the advent of NBP at the site. Apart from making stratigraphic sense, this also removes the potential embarrassment of three very late dates for the PGW period – which has always made archaeologists reluctant to use them – and provides three useful dates for the beginning of the second phase of NBP-bearing deposits in the Ganga valley.

6 Omitting, once again, a date of 2160 ± 105 bp (196 cal. BC) for the PGW/NBP overlap at Allahpur (PRL-83).

Finally, there are eight dates which can be assigned to the next phase of NBP (identified either as 'mid-NBP' or as 'pre-Mauryan' levels in the date lists), and these fall between 2290–2220 bp:

Hastinapura:	TF-88	2225 ± 110 bp	364,279,261 cal. BC
	TF-90	2270 ± 110 bp	383 cal. BC
	TF-112	2260 ± 95 bp	379 cal. BC
	TF-83	2220 ± 110 bp	362,282,258 cal. BC
Kausambi:	TF-103	2295 ± 105 bp	391 cal. BC
	TF-105	2220 ± 100 bp	362,282 cal. BC
	TF-225	2285 ± 105 bp	390 cal. BC
Piprahwa:	PRL-323	2290 ± 100 bp	391 cal. BC

Unfortunately, as already mentioned, the calibration curve for dates falling between 2500–2300 bp is highly irregular, and thus the neat clustering of dates is illusory. Even if one considers the central dates alone, a wide range of possibilities is offered which can only be narrowed by averaging the dates from each period, on the assumption that they are really allowable statistical variations of a hypothetical mean. According to Ward and Wilson (1978), averaging should only be undertaken for dates coming from the same archaeological deposits (indeed, preferably from the same object); even this assumes that a single deposit equals a single moment in time, and ignores the mixing of materials of various ages within the same soil matrix. Averaging dates from different sites makes the additional assumption that both the early and mid-NBP phases began at single instants of time, at numerous settlements distributed over a wide area. The procedure clearly takes for granted something that we must, instead, strive to find out, but until multiple dates from single layers on individual sites are available (as they are for such Chalcolithic settlements as Kalibangan and Inamgaon) this is the best we will be able to do.

The seven dates from the end of the pre-NBP phase average out to 2397 ± 44 bp, which means that at the 95.4 per cent confidence level there is a 30 per cent chance of the true date's falling between BC 761–634 and a 70 per cent chance of its falling between BC 593–395 (Stuiver and Becker 1986). For the 15 dates marking the beginning of the NBP phase the average date is 2379 ± 33 bp, almost identical to the previous estimate, which is not surprising given our assumption that they both really represent the same event. At the 95.4 per cent confidence level a date between BC 758–686 has a 23 per cent chance, between BC 590–527 a 5 per cent chance and between BC 525–390 a 72 per cent chance. Although the results are not conclusive the probability distribution argues against a date in the highest interval. At the same time the lowest estimate, or BC 390, does not leave enough room for both the 'early' and 'mid-NBP phases, which must fit in prior to the mid-3rd century BC, on the basis of firm numismatic and palaeographic evidence. Balancing these criteria, a date in the 2nd half of the 6th century BC – representing the higher end of the lower chronological interval – may provide a realistic estimate for the timing of the appearance of NBP.

Such a hypothesis is supported by the average date of 2246 ± 43 bp for the beginning of the 'mid-NBP' phase, which at the 95.4 per cent confidence level provides a time-span of BC 399–203. Since the phase must have concluded by BC 250, the highest allowable date – or c. BC 400 – is clearly the preferred estimate. Even then, however, if we took the 7th century BC to be the date of appearance of NBP, an unacceptably long duration of 300 years would have to be assumed for the 'early NBP' phase. Therefore this paper will date the 'early-NBP' phase to BC 550–400, the middle phase to BC 400–250, and the late phase to BC 250–100, by which time coins and inscribed seals and sealings provide greater chronological precision than radiocarbon dates.

It only remains to comment briefly on two related issues which have been the subject of much debate. Our chronological scheme suggests that the introduction of coinage into the subcontinent could be dated to BC 400 at the earliest – close to Cribb's rather conservative estimate of the mid-4th century BC on numismatic grounds. This hypothesis remains to be reconciled with the Achaemenid inspiration of the earliest bent-bar coins from Taxila, whose introduction should fall in the 5th century BC, and underscores the uncertainties surrounding the absolute chronology of state formation in the Iron Age of South Asia (see also chapter 10, p. 218). On the other hand, radiocarbon dates clearly agree with the recently proposed short chronology for Buddha's *nirvāna* of c. BC 358–378 (Bechert 1982), which thereby provides a much better fit with every aspect of the archaeological record than the traditionally favoured date of BC 486 (Erdosy 1993).

Settlement patterns in 550–250 BC

For reasons outlined above, regional settlement patterns provide the most reliable index to the evolution of complex societies in prehistoric contexts. Their study is rapidly gaining ground in South Asia, as elsewhere, and even if the evidence is at present limited, it is sufficient to set the stage for our discussion. The evolution of settlement hierarchies remains most clearly documented in Allahabad district (Erdosy 1988) – where sites yielding NBP were assigned to 'early' and 'late' phases, instead of being grouped in a single, long chronological unit. The 'early' phase (period II) corresponds to the 'early NBP' levels of excavations, dated above to BC 550–400; the 'late' phase (period III) encompasses both the 'mid' and 'late NBP' levels of excavations, and spans the period between 400–100 BC.[7] While the survey could not, thus, fully employ the refined chronology of

---

[7] The 'early' NBP phase in the survey was called Period II; its original dating to BC 600–350 should be revised to BC 550–400 in light of the discussion above. Dating of the 'late' NBP phase – or Period III – of the survey should also be revised, from BC 350–100 to BC 400–100. Since the late phase in the survey includes both the 'mid' and 'late' phases of NBP, discussion of settlement patterns here anticipates some aspects of the Maurya period. It is due to the revision of dates that the rates of population growth computed here differ from those given in the original report (Erdosy 1988).

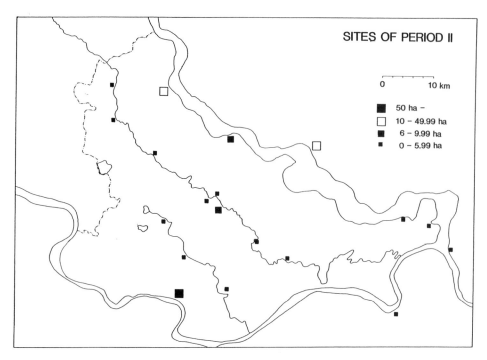

Fig 7.2. Map of settlement pattern, Allahabad district, period II, c. BC 550–400 (after Erdosy 1988).

excavations, it nevertheless revealed processes that were obscured elsewhere, and its results will be discussed first.

It is significant to note at the outset that modern Allahabad district corresponds with the heartland of the Early Historic Vatsa *janapada*, and its largest site – Kausambi – is known from literary sources to have been the latter's capital. This settlement, which already stood apart from others in period I on account of its size, now grows to 50 hectares and is surrounded, by BC 400 at the latest, by a monumental earthen rampart.[8] Secondary centres, each measuring 12 hectares, emerged at Kara and Sringaverpur on the Ganga, localities with their own historical and legendary associations.[9] One settlement of 6.12 hectares was equidistant from these, while another of 6.75 hectares was similarly placed

[8]   The date of the fortifications at Kausambi has been a subject of controversy ever since its excavator placed it in the second millennium BC (Sharma 1960), a date that has been conclusively dismissed (Allchin and Allchin 1968; Sinha 1973; Lal 1982). As suggested elsewhere (Erdosy 1987), a date in the late 5th century BC at the earliest is suggested by the appearance of punchmarked coins (as well as of certain Red ware shapes associated with the second phase of NBP) just after the construction of the rampart.

[9]   As the site of Jhusi is completely covered by a modern village it is difficult to estimate if it had reached its maximum extent of c. 30 hectares already by BC 550–400, or whether it only expanded to this size in the following period. Bhita, which also became an important centre in the next period, however, shows an occupied area of only 3.5 hectares in this period, which places it in the lowest settlement category.

between Sringaverpur and Kausambi; this combination of size and location establishes a third distinct category. The rest of the sites (16 in number) measured .42–2.0 hectares in size and were randomly distributed along watercourses (Fig. 7.2).

Period II shows an exceptionally high increase of size, and therefore rate of population growth, at .68 per cent per annum, much of which is absorbed through agglomeration – the total occupied area changes from 35.8 to 100 hectares, but the number of sites grows only by five, to 21. Clearly we are witnessing rapid political and economic centralization: the concentration of population in sites clearly graded in size, the regular spacing of central places along all major arteries of communication, and the overwhelming dominance of the largest settlement all point to this. Literary sources suggest that such a concentration of power was necessitated by incessant competition between the leading polities of Buddha's time, and this is supported by the proliferation of massive ramparts, as well as by the concentration of larger settlements in restricted areas.

Although the functions of various settlement categories remain to be confirmed by excavation, they can be approximated through a consideration of surface finds, settlement location and literary evidence. On the lowest rung of the ladder were villages, predominantly nucleated and inhabited by those practising agriculture and herding. Above them were minor centres which revealed traces of the manufacture of ceramics and lithic blades, as well as of iron-smelting, and to which marketing, policing and tax-collecting functions may also be attributed on the basis of the literary evidence.[10] Next in the scale were towns providing a full complement of manufacturing activities, including the production of luxury items: unfinished beads of semi-precious stones and shell, as well as copper slag, were among the surface finds at such sites as Kara. Although several of these towns were fortified, they were dwarfed in size by the capital city of Kausambi which, in addition to possessing all the functions of smaller settlements, acted as the centre of political power.

In general the distribution of functions confirms the basic premise of Central Place Theory, that sites of a higher order will contain larger populations and perform all the functions of smaller settlements in addition to some unique to themselves. Although the settlement hierarchy is thus well established by BC 400, the next period (III) sees important changes (Fig. 7.3). To begin with, a fifth category of settlement emerges: newly founded in the midst of rural habitations and measuring 3–5 hectares, thus probably dispersing primary administrative and service functions over wider areas. The number of secondary centres increases to four with the addition of the settlements of Bhita, now fortified and measuring some 19 ha (Marshall 1912), and Jhusi, extending over 30 ha. They,

[10] In particular, the Kautilya Arthasastra (Kangle 1963), whose final compilation may date from the 2nd century AD, but whose description of political and economic organization in the context of polities fighting for supremacy best suits the city-states of the pre-Maurya period (see chapter 10).

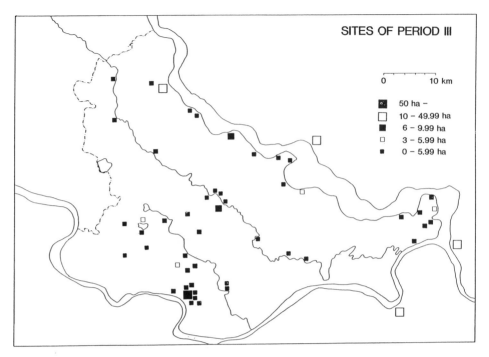

Fig. 7.3   Map of settlement pattern, Allahabad district, period III, c. BC 400–
100 (after Erdosy 1988).

along with Kausambi, are distributed with striking regularity along the Ganga
and the Yamuna, at approximately 35 km from one another.[11] Judging by the
results of Marshall's excavations at Bhita, which yielded the coins of diverse
principalities (Marshall 1912), secondary centres now participate in long-distance
trade, which further sets them apart from smaller settlements. Finally, there is a
proliferation of villages, which may have been behind the establishment of a new
level in the settlement hierarchy, dispensing low-level service function over a
wide area.

It is also in period III that areas away from rivers and lakes are colonized. Such
a development entailed large-scale forest clearance and the ploughing of stiff,
clayey soils, which was facilitated by the large-scale use of iron implements,
confirmed from BC 550 onwards at all major excavated sites. Not surprisingly, it
is in the hinterland of Kausambi that the earliest traces of forest clearance are
found, necessitated by the demands of a fast-growing urban population. By
period IV (BC 100–AD 300) one-third of all villages were to be found away from
watercourses, reflecting a desire to colonize fertile but hitherto inaccessible areas.
That the process took centuries to complete is shown, nevertheless, by Yüan-

[11]   Lacchagiri, measuring at least 30 hectares in area and found 30 km downstream from Jhusi, may well
be part of the same settlement system. Unfortunately, it could not be visited in the course of our
fieldwork.

tsang's account – in the 7th century AD – of extensive forests between the cities of Prayaga (Allahabad) and Kauśāmbī (Beal 1884). Indeed, the last vestiges of the ancient vegetation cover were not obliterated until the large-scale construction of railways in the 19th century.

Although the rate of population growth falls to .37 per cent per annum, even such a rate would have been exceptional in the long run; had it been sustained since BC 550, the population of Allahabad district today would have been around 50 million![12] Not surprisingly, therefore, after the consolidation of urban life around BC 100 the population growth rate falls dramatically, to .0.5 per cent per annum. More to the point, while period II was characterized by agglomeration, period III sees a proliferation of villages, even if higher order settlements themselves grow in size. That the centralization of political institutions should be followed by a great extension in cultivation is hardly surprising, since an expanding bureaucracy had to be sustained by greatly increased primary production. Also, as the Arthasastra states, agriculture is the foundation of a country's wealth and, by extension, the true measure of its economic and political power, which needed to be maximized at a time of keen rivalries.

That the pattern of settlement found in Allahabad district is not unique can only be confirmed with reference to another important *janapada*, that of Pancala (Singh 1981). Significantly, the largest settlement of the region, Ahicchatra, once again coincides with the capital city named in literature. Unfortunately, its excavations have yet to be published in detail, although by the 3rd century BC at the latest, it is a fortified city of some 180 hectares in extent. The secondary centre of the area, Atranjikhera, measures c. 64 hectares (Gaur 1983); it is likewise defended, and contains evidence for a wide range of craft and trading activities. At least one fortified site of 8.0 hectares – Jakhera (Singh 1981; Sahi 1978) – represents a further level in the settlement hierarchy; the rest of the settlements hitherto discovered measure less than 4 hectares each and fall in the category of villages. Unfortunately, Singh's survey did not attempt to divide the NBP-bearing sites into early and late period, and at the moment we can only hypothesize that the timing of population agglomeration and subsequent dispersal corresponds to observations in Allahabad district.

Although further direct evidence of settlement hierarchies is lacking, fortified sites of considerable size are found throughout Northern India, and one may assume that they sat atop integrated networks of settlements graded by size and the range of their functions, in a manner similar to that observed in the Vatsa *janapada*. In addition to Atranjikhera, at least four are stated to have been fortified by c. BC 550: Rajgir, Campa (Sinha 1979), Ujjain (Banerjee 1960) and

---

[12] This estimate is based on a total occupied area of 35.8 hectares at BC 550 (clearly only a fraction of the total as the survey did not achieve 100 per cent coverage), and a density of 120 persons per hectare (Adams 1981), giving a base population of 4,300. As for growth rates, Feinmann (1991) provides figures for the period of state formation in Mesoamerica, which show the same wild fluctuations as found in Allahabad district.

Rajghat (ancient Kās'ī – Narain and Roy 1976–78). It can hardly be a coincidence that they are capital cities of some of the key principalities known from literature: Rajgir (until superseded by Pataliputra) was the seat of the rulers of Magadha, Campā of Aṅga, Ujjain of Avanti and Rajghat of Kasi. Taxila in the northwest may be added to this list, although its 'Achaemenid' strata are only exposed in a limited area (Marshall 1951). Sravasti (Sinha 1967) was the last of the six great cities of Buddha's time to emerge, but it was certainly fortified by the end of the 'early NBP' period (or c. BC 400). To this list may be added, by BC 300 or so, Besnagar (Ghosh 1991), Mathura (Joshi 1991), Tripuri (Ghosh 1991) and Vaisali (Sinha 1969), not to mention the imperial capital of Pataliputra which, according to the soundings of Spooner (1914), Altekar and Misra (1959) and Sinha and Narain (1970), and the accounts of the Greek envoy Megasthenes (McCrindle 1926 (1877)), was one of the largest cities of its time.

Not all areas shared in the rapid evolution of urban centres, however, as is clear from a survey of Kanpur district by Lal (1984a). Here, in an area of 6,000 km², the largest site measured 8.75 hectares in area and 98 others showed a continuum of sizes between .5 and 5.0 hectares. At the most, two levels of a settlement hierarchy can be detected, with the possible addition of a third in the post-NBP period. Population grew at an even rate, computed at .26 per cent per annum in BC 1000–550, and at .21 per cent per annum in BC 550–100. Such rates were well below the levels reached in Allahabad district, although they declined only marginally after BC 100, to .18 per cent per annum. The contrast afforded by this image of stability, in wide belts of rural settlement still surrounding areas of significant population agglomeration, could not be more striking. Unlike previously, however, underdeveloped areas no longer acted as buffer zones between emerging states, preventing neither the outbreak of hostilities nor the absorption of weaker polities in more powerful ones. If anything, the existence of central places, however small, in such rural areas points to efforts to bring even outlying areas under centralized control.

Economic life and social organization

The evidence of settlement patterns pointing towards economic and political centralization remains to be confirmed by archaeological excavations. In part, this results from the durability of Early Historic cities, several of which survive as viable settlements to this day, obscuring earlier habitation. However, one may also regret the reverential attitude of excavators to exposed structural remains – while some of these merit conservation, most act only to impede access to the lower strata of archaeological sites. To this day not a single house-plan is available for pre-Mauryan levels, not to mention evidence for the internal zoning of settlements. Inferences must still be drawn solely from summarily published lists of artefacts, bereft of context. Under such circumstances the analysis of intra-assemblage variability, so crucial to settling questions of economic, ethnic and social stratification, remains an important desideratum.

Bearing in mind these limitations, a few regularities can be pointed out, beginning with the monumental nature of early historic fortifications. The largest of these – at Ujjain – measures 75 m at the base, soars to a height of 14 m, and stretches for over 5 km; several others – at, for example Kausambi, Rajgir, Ahicchatra, Mathura, Atranjikhera – extend for up to 40 m across the base, 15 m in height, and 6 km in length. Even a cursory estimate of the manpower needed to erect such features is sufficient to postulate a high degree of socio-political organization. Some of these fortifications – for example, at Kausambi (Lal 1982) – utilized existing undulations in the landscape, which could be found even in the Ganga Valley. Their ramparts were occasionally revetted with baked bricks (as at Kausambi), or supported internally with wooden planks (as at Ujjain and Pataliputra), and in later stages of their lives were surmounted by parapet walls of baked brick or – in the case of Rajgir – stone.

Their enormous size suggests that, in addition to defending settlements (from both attackers and floods), ramparts may have served a symbolic function, delineating cities as islands of order in an otherwise chaotic landscape. Unlike Chinese cities (Wheatley 1971), however, only one site – that of Sisupalgarh in Orissa (Lal 1949) – shows evidence of careful planning. Its walls enclose a perfect square, which on each side (1.1 km in length) is pierced by two evenly spaced gateways; consequently, streets connecting each opposing pair divide the town into nine equal squares, which recalls the ideal type advocated in the Arthasastra (Kangle 1963). There is reason to believe that the city was erected just after the conquest of Kalinga by Asoka, which could account for its plan. Not even at Sisupalgarh, however, was there evidence of a ceremonial centre, which was a central feature – indeed the *raison d'être* – of early Chinese cities; only medieval Hindu dynasties attempted to create viable urban centres around monumental religious structures.

As for the layout of cities, we have only the testimony of Marshall's excavations at Bhita (Marshall 1912). Although his finds date primarily from the Maurya and post-Maurya periods, the durability of the city plan over centuries, coupled with fragmentary evidence from the 'mid-NBP' levels at Kausambi (Structural periods IA and IB: Sharma 1969) suggests a greater antiquity for the layout of individual houses and of the settlement itself, and as it is the only source of information at present, it may be briefly summarized (Figs. 11.9 and 11.10). At Bhita, streets leading to the major gateways were flanked by shops – to what extent Marshall (1912) was guided by his observations of modern settlements is not clear, although the layout of rooms along his 'main street' lends support to his interpretations. The houses behind the shops lined up in orderly fashion with lanes separating them, were well served by wells, drains and paved courtyards, and succeeded one another with little change in plan. By contrast, the one trench placed near the centre of the settlement showed a palimpsest of poorly constructed walls; this area was occupied by poorer habitations and showed a lack of planning and of civic facilities such as well-maintained streets, wells and drains. Such differences in living conditions would clearly be expected from a stratified society, although they remain to be corroborated by evidence from other sites, or even by a detailed inventory of artefacts from individual living quarters.

The evidence from Bhita is further discussed in chapter 11 (p. 231–3). What preceded such house types is not clear. At Sonkh there is evidence of single-roomed circular and oval structures of wattle and daub in the pre-Maurya levels, each served by a hearth. At Bhagwanpura, however, at least one rectangular structure centred on an open courtyard was found already in the PGW period (Bisht and Asthana 1979). More excavated data are needed.

Information is likewise scanty about craft activities. From several sites – especially Ujjain (Banerjee 1960), Sambhar and Rairh (Ghosh 1991) – massive quantities of iron slag were reported. The scale of the operations suggests full-time craft specialization and production for a wide market, an impression reinforced by the discovery of hundreds of silver punchmarked coins in hoards at Rairh. By contrast, the blacksmith's furnaces recovered from Period IV in Atranjikhera continue the tradition of small-scale operations begun in the preceding period, workshops apparently being located in the midst of a residential area. Coppersmith's furnaces along with moulds were found at Mathura, factories for bone arrowheads at Rajghat, evidence for the manufacture of beads at Ujjain (whose fame reached even the Mediterranean by the 1st century AD), and a unique set of jeweller's moulds from Campa.

With the exception of Atranjikhera, excavation reports have yet to yield contextual information on the location of workshops within settlements. However, there is a general association of craft activities with larger settlements; the survey in Allahabad district, for example, failed to locate small sites specializing in large-scale manufacture of a restricted range of artefacts, which had been so common in the Harappan civilization (Mughal 1982). With the exception of ceramic slag and lithic debitage, only sites in the top three levels of the settlement hierarchy yielded surface traces of manufacturing activities. Given the strict bureaucratic controls advocated by the Arthasastra on the production and distribution of manufactured goods, the concentration of workshops in a few, easily supervised locations would be expected. However, apart from possible granaries discovered at Atranjikhera and Mathura, there is as yet no evidence for the extensive storage facilities which were also prescribed by Kautilya.

The lists of objects recovered from individual sites show a great expansion from the 'early NBP' period onwards. Above all, as already indicated, there is widespread use of iron tools: while chisels, axes, knives and ploughshares occur only from BC 550 onwards. Bone points and blade tools, while surviving into medieval times, decline in popularity and copper is used – as in previous periods – in ornaments and toiletries. Beads are manufactured out of a wide range of semi-previous stones (agate, amethyst, carnelian, chalcedony, garnet, jasper, lapis, onyx, quartz and rock crystal – Hasan 1982), in addition to coral, copper, glass, ivory, bone, shell, terracotta and – occasionally – gold. Although these are widely available in the hilly regions flanking the alluvial plains, their procurement would have had to be organized – as already stressed in chapter 6, the location of several key cities on ecological boundaries suggests that the procurement, processing and distribution of key raw materials was one of the first functions arrogated by the emerging central places of the Early Historic period.

Finally, as regards trade, the appearance of coinage could not but enhance its efficiency and facilitate its control, although literary evidence suggests that much tax was still received, and many artisans in state employ paid, in kind. The date of the introduction of the first coins remains a bone of contention. As we have already seen, the radiocarbon chronology, coupled with evidence for the stratigraphic position of the first coins in the mid-NBP levels, indicates BC 400 as the likeliest date of appearance. This agrees rather well with Cribb's assertion – on numismatic grounds – that the earliest undisputed coin hoard (at Taxila) dates to the mid-4th century BC, but not so well with the clear Achaemenid derivation of the bent-bar coins of Taxila: since Gandhara reportedly became a Persian province in the region of Darius (BC 522–486), a somewhat earlier date for the introduction of coins may be posited. Unfortunately, since we no longer know the code employed by the makers of punchmarked coins, and lack stratigraphic context for the majority of all coins recovered, it is impossible to decide with certainty.

Cities and states in early historic literature

Dramatic changes in settlement patterns and material culture are mirrored in the literature of the 6th–4th centuries BC. Although the texts remain deficient in historical information, they throw a welcome light on social and political institutions, which had featured only incidentally in the Vedic tradition. Being transmitted orally until the post-Maurya period, controversies surrounding their provenance and dating are yet to be fully resolved. Nevertheless, the information offered by the Dharmasūtras of Āpastamba, Baudhāyana and Gautama (representing the final stratum of Vedic literature), along with the Aṣṭādhyāyī of Pāṇini, may be considered relevant to the 'early NBP' phase. As for the succeeding period, the Buddhist (Pali) Canon and certain chapters (especially those dealing with diplomacy and internal administration – Erdosy 1988) of Kautilya's Arthasastra likewise contain much useful detail. Since Thapar (1984) offers an exhaustive discussion of the available sources, the reader is referred to her account for further information. Here, attention will centre on the literary evidence for settlement patterns and political organization, with questions of social and economic stratification reserved for the concluding comments, dealing with processual issues.

A brief note on geography is required to introduce the discussion. It may be recalled that, with the exception of its latest book (X), the world of the Rigveda extended from the Indo-Iranian borderlands to the Yamuna. Then, around BC 1000 (Witzel 1980), a considerable expansion of horizons was marked by a hymn of the Atharvaveda (V.22), which listed regions at the periphery of the Vedic world beyond which fever was to be banished: in the northwest, these included Balhika (or Bactriana) and in the east, Anga and Magadha (both in Bihar). Towards the end of the Vedic age, the appearance of the Andhras of the southern Deccan and of the Pundras of northeast India (in AB VII.18) marked another step forward. Now, at the outset of the post-Vedic period, Panini's Astadhyayi shows an awareness of even Ferghana (or Prakanva – VI.1.153), Begram (or Kapisi – IV.2.99) and the Pamirs (or Kamboja – IV.1.175) in the northwest, Kacch and Sindh in the southwest, and Asmaka along the Godavari river in peninsular India (Agrawala 1953, 37). Remaining patches of *terra incognita* entered the orbit of the Dharmasutras and the Arthasastra soon thereafter. The wide geographical horizons of the times are personified by the physician Jivaka, an early patron of Buddhism, who is said to have been trained in Taxila but plied his trade in the principal cities of eastern India.

In keeping with the evidence for urban centres in the archaeological record, several settlement types are mentioned in literature. Villages (*gāma/grāma*) clearly remained the most numerous and, according to Wagle's analysis of early Buddhist literature (Wagle 1966), were inhabited by extended kin-groups. Their revenues, if not the titles to their lands, were frequently granted to Brahmins; this was only one process hastening the emergence of private property out of communal (lineage) ownership. Under the rubric of villages, forest dwellings and cattle camps were also included; only Panini distinguishes additional rural settlement types such as hamlets (*kheta*) and herdsmen's camps (*ghoṣa*). Significantly, *mahāgrāmas* were no longer recognized as a distinct category, undoubtedly reflecting the emergence of qualitative distinctions in addition to size differences. Instead, the literature speaks of *nigamas*, *puras* and *nagaras*. The first of these terms appears to have had several meanings: it could denote a residential ward within a city, a larger village inhabited by a socially heterogenous population and – particularly in later periods – a market-town. The other two represented urban centres. Although *pura* previously specified a fortified settlement, it now merged with *nagara*, a designation which had appeared for the first time at the end of the Vedic age (in the Taittirīya Āraṇyaka).

Unfortunately, few details are provided in early literature on the appearance or functions of cities. They are said to be populous, well defended and teeming with craftsmen and merchants; if the memory of the Jatakas be accurate, they were inhabited principally by the heads of leading families along with their retinues of followers. It is in the Kautilya Arthasastra that a hierarchy of administrative centres is discussed for the first time, along with the layout of an ideal capital city. Buddhist tradition does, however recognise six cities of outstanding importance which would have been fit to receive the mortal remains of Buddha: Campa, Kasi, Sravasti, Kausambi, Rajagriha and Saketa. That the first five of these correspond to the earliest urban centres reconstructed from archaeological evidence, omitting only Ujjain, attests eloquently to the value of literary sources. By contrast, lesser settlements such as Kusinagara, although themselves capitals of *janapadas*, received the diminutive appellation of *nagaraka*.

The appearance of urban centres could not have taken place without significant changes in political organization (Fig. 7.4). By Panini's time much of South Asia was parcelled out among *janapadas*, representing clearly demarcated territorial units (Agrawala 1953, 424), rather than, as previously, mere aggregations of people.[13] A proliferation of small-scale polities, particularly in the familiar regions of the northwest, surfaces in the Astadhyayi; they were likely organized on a lineage basis (Thapar 1984), although in the Ganga Valley one may already discern nascent monarchies. That *janapadas* were rapidly coalescing, through conquest, into larger units is shown by the emergence of 16 *mahājanapadas* in Buddhist and Jain sources, post-dating Panini by perhaps two centuries. By now, painted grey ware had disappeared and coinage had been introduced, signalling among other things that narrow circles of affiliation, based on ethnicity, were being supplanted by allegiance to territorially organized polities.

Some of the *mahājanapadas* (Kamboja and Gandhara) were found in the northwest, others in the Indo-Gangetic divide (Kuru, Matsya and Surasena), in central India (Avanti, Cedi), in the south (Asmaka) and – above all – in the Ganga valley (Pancala, Vatsa, Kasi, Kosala, Magadha, Vrijji, Malla and Anga) (Fig. 7.1). Soon only four major players – Avanti, Vatsa, Kosala and Magadha – remained on the field, and by BC 321 an uncontested victor (Magadha) emerged, taking the principle of *mātsya nyāya* to its logical extreme. Although the political struggles are seldom detailed, they are frequently alluded to in Buddhist literature. The spirit of the age also infuses the treatment of foreign policy in the Arthasastra, with its stress on the cultivation of allies and the timely conduct of military – and diplomatic – campaigns. As Renfrew and Cherry (1986) have shown, ferocious competition for power by polities sharing in the same cultural tradition is a common consequence of the emergence of complex societies, but this is anticipating matters. Of more immediate interest, here, is evidence for alternative means of political control, designated *rājya* and *gaṇa*, among the *janapadas*. Their changing fortunes may provide valuable insights into the evolution of state societies in general.

---

[13] This is reinforced by the attribute *bhupati* ('lord of the earth'), accorded to rulers by Panini (VI.2.19 – Agrawala 1953, 398). A little later, the Pali Canon lists *janapada* as the largest in a series of administrative units which also includes *gāma*, *nigama* and *nagara*. Finally, in the Kautilya Arthasastra, *janapada* is listed among the seven constituents ('limbs') of a state, representing the territory it occupies; apart from this rather specialized usage the term disappears from the political vocabulary by the end of the Early Historic period.

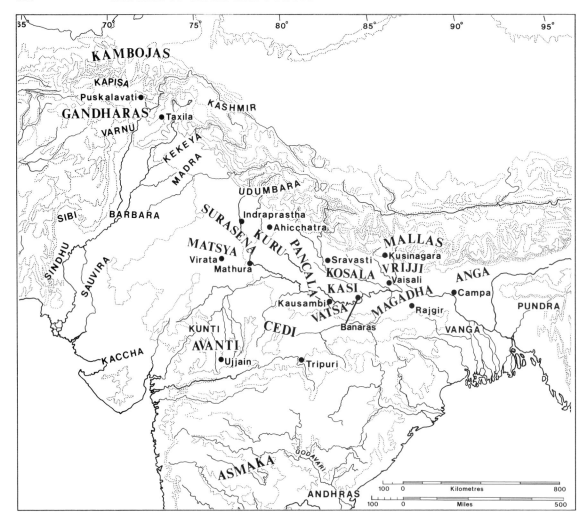

Fig. 7.4. Map of the Sixteen Mahajanapadas (great states): Anga, Magadha, Kasi, Kosala, Vrijji (Vajji), Malla, Cedi, Vatsa, Kuru, Pancala, Matsya, Surasena, Asvaka (Asmaka), Avanti, Gandhara and Kamboja; their capital cities; and other janapadas and tribal names.

The first phenomenon – monarchy or *rājya* – is undoubtedly the more familiar, not the least because it dominates the attention of all, except Buddhist, accounts. Already present in embryonic form in the Late Vedic period, it is characterized by hereditary rulers, whose tasks have evolved from leadership in war and largesse with booty to the protection of life and property and the enforcement of sacred law (*dharma*). A well-developed legal code, incorporating the customs of the various social and ethnic groups making up each *janapada*, was complemented by the granting of coercive powers to the ruler for efficient fulfilment of his duties, and this marks the transition from chiefdoms to states. The administration has grown from a few general office-holders under the ruler's direct command to a hierarchically structured bureaucracy, whose principal constituents are listed by Panini (Agrawala 1953), although described in detail only by Kautilya. The ruler, the chief minister, the *purohita* (chaplain) and the crown prince may be placed in the upper echelons of administration, followed by a council of ministers, heads of departments, officers performing general as well as specific administrative tasks, and the palace staff. The military as well as the judiciary were organized along similarly rigorous lines, and the ruler appears to have had the power to make all key appointments.

This administrative machinery, characterized by extreme centralization and a strict hierarchy, was supported by regularly collected taxes: including a poll tax, manufacturing and sales taxes, a tax on agricultural produce, toll charges and customs duties. Society was stratified, and private property emerged alongside state institutions financed through the redistribution of wealth. Rituals remained important, but no longer played a vital guiding role – clearly, hereditary leadership had less need for legitimation. In all respects we are dealing with a state level of political organization, in spite of the absence of writing and the restriction of monumental architecture to the ramparts surrounding major settlements. This is confirmed by the archaeological evidence for a complex hierarchy of central places, often concentrated in a relatively small area, emerging after BC 550.

The alternative form of political organization, designated *gana*, in the literature, is documented principally in Buddhist sources, since its pattern of decision making duplicated the procedures of the monastic orders. Instead of a hereditary ruler, leaders were elected to a limited term by the heads of families of the ruling lineage. While full-time administrative, judicial and military officials were employed, an assembly of notables – presumably guided by the ruler – took all major decisions of state according to strict guidelines. In other respects, however, oligarchies differed little from monarchies. They had a full complement of social classes, issued their own (punchmarked) coins and supported significant urban centres such as Vaisali. Although viewed as early manifestations of democratic institutions in India, sober analysis suggests that their assemblies sustained a sharp cleavage between rulers and the ruled. Thapar (1984), for example, would limit decision-making powers to the heads of families of the principal *kṣatriya* lineage. Yet, considering that 500 such 'rajas' existed among the Mallas, 5,000 among the Yaudheyas and 7,707 among the Licchavis, oligarchies of early historic South Asia may bear some comparison with ancient Athens.

Of greater interest here, however, is the historical role of oligarchies: did they preserve ancient popular institutions, and were they antecedents of, or alternatives to, monarchies? We have already seen that even if major decisions were taken by a limited circle in Rigvedic times, their approval by a wider body, be it *sabhā* or *samiti*, was at the very least considered desirable. Such assemblies may have also had the power to remove leaders who failed to perform their duties adequately. That their membership was restricted even then is further suggested by the epithet *sabhya* ('fit for the assembly'), although the conditions of enfranchisement cannot be reconstructed. Analogies, therefore, are not lacking between *ganas* and Rigvedic polities. However, most controls on centralized leadership vanished in the intervening Late Vedic period, and by the time assemblies reappeared on the scene, they had to oversee societies which had considerably increased in complexity. The degree of representation among the population had also become restricted, reflecting an increasingly stratified society.

Therefore, to posit, (with Sharma 1968) a direct line of descent, we must assume that the absence of popular institutions in Late Vedic literature is due to the texts' limited focus. Certainly, both the northeastern and western regions of South Asia, where the *ganas* were concentrated, were regarded with disapproval by the seers of *madhyadeśa*, who may have deliberately omitted surviving tribal institutions from their traditions. However, one must also entertain the possibility of political institutions developing altogether outside the sphere of Vedic society; as suggested elsewhere (Erdosy 1988), it would be a mistake to assume that the evolution of the latter constitutes the sum total of South Asian history simply because it monopolizes literary accounts. In any case, oligarchies may be viewed as either antecedents or alternatives to monarchies, even if they survived alongside the latter for nearly a millennium. To begin with, differences between them were limited to the political sphere. Although both relied on a professional bureaucracy, in monarchies the ruler was able to free himself from interference by his kinsmen in decision making, in oligarchies he was not. That the former state of affairs grew out of the latter explains why some oligarchies (for example of the Yaudheyas or the Malavas – Altekar 1949, 137) eventually developed into monarchies, while two of the most famous kingdoms of Late Vedic times (Kuru and Pancala) came to be listed as oligarchies in the Arthasastra.

Most oligarchies, however, had no chance to evolve into monarchies as they were conquered before completing the transition. Clearly, their decentralized decision-making process – a hostage to dissent as recognized by the eleventh chapter of the Arthasastra – placed severe limits on their territorial extent and – by extension – on their economic and political power. Even a confederation of oligarchies under the Licchavis could not resist the advances of Magadha, where a centralized political system strove to maximize economic resources in the service of the state. The competitive advantages thus conferred explain efforts at the concentration of power, which could already be deduced from the study of settlement patterns, and is confirmed by the prevailing political wisdom of the early historic period, as summarized in the Arthasastra. Although not operating with the inevitability of a natural law, the absorption of less advanced polities by those more advanced is a common phenomenon and explains why there are so few examples of pristine state formation throughout history. It must be added, however, that while the hierarchical nature of South Asian states facilitated conquest, excessive concentration of power led to the creation of an unwieldy bureaucracy which could not be sustained long. And, since absorption into a wider polity meant the mere superimposition of additional layers of bureaucracy on local institutions, many of the *janapadas* – including some of the oligarchies – of the early historic period reappeared after the demise of the Mauryas. Such instability was not, however, an obstacle to sustained prosperity in the Sunga-Kusana period; although patterns of political control fluctuated, the foundations of economic prosperity were solidly laid by the third century BC.

Conclusions

Although Early Historic state formation is well documented, especially in literature if not yet archaeologically, it remains to be convincingly explained. Materialist historians, inspired by the ideas of V. Gordon Childe, were the first to provide a coherent synthesis, centred on the invention of iron smelting as a prime mover. Such a technological revolution, in their view, enabled the clearance of forests and the cultivation of the fertile soils of the Ganga basin. The resultant surplus was duly appropriated by a ruling elite, leading to the development of the state to protect, and of a national ideology to sanctify, inequality (e.g. Kosambi 1956; 1963). In response, several archaeologists (e.g. Chakrabarti 1972; Ghosh 1973b) pointed to the long delay in introducing iron tools into agriculture, and argued that even major inventions had little impact until changes in the socio-political sphere prompted their full utilization. In a similar vein they preferred to view surplus as a social, rather than an economic, product. Unfortunately, having, with the aid of the archaeological record, effectively dismissed technological change as a prime mover, they failed to provide an adequate substitute, never specifying what crucial changes in the socio-political sphere actually led to the emergence of complex societies. As a result, competing explanations were repeatedly reiterated without advancing our understanding (Joshi 1974, Chakrabarti 1974; Ray 1976; Sharma 1983; etc).

This impasse between rival theories was first transcended by Thapar's synthesis, which provided a detailed analysis of changing social and political structures in light of the findings of evolutionary anthropologists (Thapar 1984). Her analysis of the evolution of lineage societies into state societies is certainly convincing; however, serious difficulties remain in validating population pressure, expressed in the form of social circumscription (Carneiro 1981), as the source of increasing social complexity. Operational difficulties alone, in estimating past populations and carrying capacity, make it doubtful that population pressure will ever be proven. Indirect evidence, such as the exploitation of marginal areas, is equally inconclusive, at least in South Asia. On the one hand, it cannot be demonstrated prior to BC 400 (when forested areas were first colonized). On the other, we may postulate that as state formation was well under way by then, it – rather than the exploitation of marginal areas – was the preferred initial response to population pressure. What is clear, however, is that rapid population growth alternating with periods of stagnation accompanied the emergence of central places in the Ganga valley, in striking contrast with the slow and steady growth rate seen in exclusively rural areas. It is unfortunate that we lack data for the period just preceding the emergence of settlement hierarchies; only with its aid may the issue of population pressure be finally resolved.

A different situation obtains with warfare. Although the frequently invoked model of an 'Aryan' conquest can no longer be accepted, warfare between social groups (both 'Aryan' and 'non-Aryan') had been common since Rigvedic times, and changing in nature with the evolution of political systems. At first, fights were over pasture-land and such mobile prizes as cattle, horses, chariots and slaves (Thapar 1984). Then, in the Late Vedic period, polities began to carve out mutually recognized boundaries, until the permanent conquest of rivals came into vogue in the 6th century BC. The effects of such competition also varied from one period to another. In the Rigveda, warfare played a crucial role in the selection of leaders who were expected, above all, to be victorious in battle and generous with booty. By the Late Vedic period, captives contributed to the emergence of a *śūdra* underclass, although polities still lacked the necessary administrative structure actually to absorb one another. Only in the post-Vedic world did the conquest of rivals emerge as a viable policy: not only was it, according to the Arthasastra, an effective diversion from internal discontent, but it also justified the policy of centralization, as the most effective means of maximizing a state's resources.

While a causal link is yet to be demonstrated, warfare clearly preceded the evolution of complex societies. However, its changing character alone demonstrates the simplicity of viewing it as a prime mover; it was embedded in a web of relations between gradually evolving institutions, and identifying it as a prime mover would beg the question of what caused it in turn. Indeed, even an external stimulus, that most convenient category of prime movers, would be a mere link in a chain of causation which can only terminate (for social scientists, at least) in an uncontestable natural law.[14] For these reasons, the search for solitary causes, let alone those which operated universally, appears misguided. At the same time, the evolution of social systems shows regularities across a broad geographical and cultural range (Claessen and Skalnik 1978), since the stresses provoked by the emergence of complex, inegalitarian societies can only be resolved in a limited number of ways. Thus, the present study may fittingly conclude with an examination of how well early historic state formation corresponds to the models of evolutionary anthropology, at least within the relatively well-documented region of the Ganga basin.

[14]   Perhaps it is this which makes population pressure so popular, since population growth could be viewed as the unavoidable consequence of sedentism.

In Chapter 6, the polities of the Late Vedic period were characterized as chiefdoms, the penultimate stage in Service's (1975) ascending sequence. To them were ascribed hereditary leadership, a rudimentary bureaucracy directly supervised by the ruler and a common ideology which legitimized the social order. Authority rested rather on religious sanction than on brute force and, judging by the proliferation of small-scale polities, was insufficient to prevent fission, a key distinguishing mark of chiefdoms in some eyes (Cohen 1978). The additional criterion of a basic cleavage between ruler and ruled, supported by an irregularly extracted surplus (Claessen and Skalnik 1981, 490–1), can also be satisfied. By Late Vedic times the lineage society characterizing the Rigveda (Thapar 1984) was breaking down into senior and junior lineages, determined by distance from a mythical founding ancestor. The former evolved into the *kṣatriya* and the latter into the *vaiśya varṇa*, with ritual specialists added to the top of the social hierarchy and *śūdras*, as yet few in number and perhaps representing captives of war, to the bottom. The practice of naming *janapadas* after the dominant (*kṣatriya*) lineage, which continued to the time of Pāṇini (Agrawala 1953) and the monopoly of *kṣatriyas* on the office of the chief testify to a dichotomy of rulers and ruled, reinforced by explicit statements in the course of the royal consecration on the rights and duties of various constituents of society.

In the post-Vedic period, beginning around BC 550, an explicit legal code is first laid down in the Dharmasūtras. At the same time, powers of coercion are granted to the ruler to aid him in upholding the sacred law. The transition from chiefdoms to states thus conforms to expectations; furthermore, fission is replaced by amalgamation, testifying to the growing effectiveness of political control. Land ownership becomes vested in extended families who are effective cultivators (Thapar 1984); crown lands (which may have been acquired through conquest now that rulers were no longer required to part with a large share of the spoils), and lands (or revenues therefrom) granted to priests also emerge. Taxation becomes regular, although the principle of (unequal) reciprocity is maintained, in that the ruler affords protection in return for the wealth flowing to him. Stratification of society is thus accentuated along economic lines, with the heads of wealthier families (*grihapatis*) remaining part of the *vaiśya varṇa*, and the rest joining the *śūdra* ranks of tenant farmers, landless labourers and craftsmen (Thapar 1984). Nevertheless, the ruling elite continues to consist of the king, his close kin, the heads of major lineages and the holders of high office. Markets and a professional trader class are yet to emerge and central places perform primarily administrative functions, all conforming to the 'inchoate' stage of early states (Claessen 1978). It is only around BC 400 that the emergence of large, fortified urban centres, the introduction of coinage, the literary evidence for a professional, salaried bureaucracy and the growth of the Magadhan kingdom confirm the accelerating progress of state formation. These trends culminated in the victorious campaigns of Candragupta Maurya, leading to the foundation of the first South Asian empire by BC 321.

By and large, therefore, the emergence of Early Historic states proceeded by stages familiar from the classificatory schemes of evolutionary anthropologists, especially those inspired by the ideas of Elman Service (1975). One would, therefore, also expect Service's 'integrationist' explanation for the emergence of complex societies to hold true, according to which chiefdoms and their successor states emerged because of the organizational advantages they offered, rather than to protect a stratified, and hence inegalitarian social order. Certainly, as the survey of Claessen and Skalnik (1978) has shown, while a dichotomy between rulers and the ruled preceded the emergence of even early states, economic stratification (through private property and the regular extraction of surplus through taxation) developed subsequently, a pattern which holds true for South Asia. However, we are once again left with the task of answering such questions as: what led to the initial cleavage in society between rulers and the ruled which, presumably, brought forward the need for greater administrative efficiency? We may answer that by pointing to the qualities of leadership favoured in the Rigveda, namely bravery in battle and generosity with the spoils; individuals possessed of those qualities may have been able to assume leadership in times of crisis (as seen in the Rigveda), and in the course of time may have been able to perpetuate their positions. Once safely established, they could – in Flannery's words (Flannery 1972) – convert their positions from 'system-serving' to 'self-serving', and buttress their authority with economic measures; thus setting in motion a chain of events leading to complex societies and equally complex administrative structures controlling them.

Whether such a hypothesis convinces or not, one must remember that archaeologists are often blinded by hindsight, their ability to perceive long-term trends that could have remained hidden to the subjects of their studies. The gradual and simultaneous evolution of a complex of institutions, punctuated perhaps by sudden leaps in levels of socio-cultural integration, certainly shows unconscious actors at work. The fact that South Asian tradition, Buddhist as well as Hindu, did not attempt to justify the emergence of complex, inegalitarian societies until the process had long been completed also points to a delayed realization of the cumulative significance of seemingly trifling changes. Only by remembering this point will we progress towards an explanation of the origin of Early Historic states. Our aim, in the preceding discussion has, however, been more modest: to show that we can now isolate several stages in the development of Early Historic states, and that these stages confirm to expectations derived from the comparative study of a significant sample of the world's complex societies.

CHAPTER 8

EARLY CITIES AND STATES BEYOND THE GANGES VALLEY

F. R. ALLCHIN

Introductory

In the foregoing chapters we have been taking an increasingly – but by no means exclusively – Ganges-centred approach to the development of early historic Indian civilization. This does not mean that we have neglected the other regions, but rather that the mass of evidence which we possess from all sources, historical as well as archaeological, points to the major role which the Ganges valley played in the process of early South Asian city development and state formation. In the present chapter we shall adopt a somewhat different viewpoint, and try to discover when and how cities arose in India beyond the Ganges plains. To this end we must think on rather different lines, concerning ourselves as much with hypotheses and relationships as with straight descriptions.

In this chapter we shall also be using certain terms in a particular way, and it will probably be helpful that we define the usage at the outset. We shall employ 'colonization' in two ways, first to describe the settlement of ethnic or cultural groups in an area to which they chose to move for whatever reason. There is, in some sections of Indian archaeological literature, discussion of such a colonization of the Deccan by 'Harappans'; we are doubtful how far this notion has validity, in the face of the absence of unequivocal archaeological data supporting any demonstrable Harappan presence in the region, or for that matter supporting any real evidence of such a presence. A more convincing example of this kind of colonization would seem to be the appearance of Harappan settlements, represented by a characteristic assemblage of many major traits of Harappan material culture, around Shortughai near the lapis lazuli mines of Badakshan in north Afghanistan. We may postulate an 'Indo-Aryan' colonization of the Deccan, using this term with reference to a hypothetical movement of Indo-Aryan-speaking groups along the lines envisaged in chapter 4. This movement would probably bring no more than small numbers of Indo-Aryan speakers into contact with the relatively more numerous existing population in that area. In the same way one may refer to a 'Gangetic' colonization of, for example, parts of Central India, the coastal strips or the Deccan, when we postulate that groups of

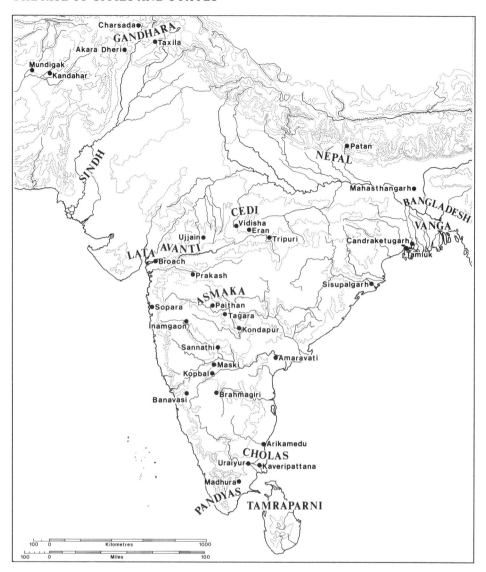

Fig. 8.1.   Map of regions and sites referred to in Chapter 8.

people moved from the Ganges plains into any of these areas and established agricultural settlements there.

Thinking of the way in which cities arose we suggested three alternatives as possible causes (Allchin 1990, 162–5). First is indigenous development, where a city emerges more or less spontaneously as the centre of a group of smaller settlements, without major external stimuli. The second is in terms of city colonization, where a city arises, or at least its development is enhanced, as a result of a colonial movement, even if it may hitherto have been supported by other factors, for example as part of the indigenous development of society in that area. Probably this would have involved a group of settlers moving out from a parent city and establishing a new 'colony' city in an area either where there were no cities, or where an indigenous city was available for conquest. A third way is perhaps a special extension of the second, it is in terms of what we called imperial expansion. By this we mean, for example, that the reappearance of cities in the northwest of Pakistan in post-Indus times may have been bolstered by the Achaemenid imperial expansion into that region. Another, widely relevant example of this process must have been as a result of Mauryan imperial conquest and expansion throughout large parts of the subcontinent. This we shall discuss in chapters 9 and 10. These various causes need not be seen as mutually exclusive. There can be no reason to doubt that many factors were at work at any given time and place, and any attempt to see the process of city formation as the outcome of one exclusive prime mover will almost certainly distort the actuality. Nor must we lose sight of the broad geographical framework presented in Chapter 2, and particularly of the land and sea routes and trade routes which connected the different parts of South Asia with one another. Nor should one fail to remember the practical difficulties which travel over long distances must have involved. Figure 8.1 shows the areas covered by this chapter.

Development of cities outside the Ganges system

Early cities of the Northwest

We noticed above in chapter 3 a marked difference in the cultural development of Sindh, on the one hand, and the Northwest Frontier and Punjab, on the other, during the late phase of the post-urban period. This seems to have arisen as a direct result of the decline of rainfall and consequent dessication of the southern areas, while the northern parts of the Indus system appear to have been less affected by the climatic change and dessication. This is probably the reason why the latter witnessed during this period a growth of settlements which may be interpreted as laying the foundation of city development there; while in the south in Sindh there is still little evidence of any comparable process.

The development we refer to is that associated with a mainly hand-made or turntable-built, coarse red burnished pottery which appears to be characteristic of the later stages of the Gandhara grave 'culture' and which probably belongs to c. BC 1000–500. As yet, there are few relevant radiocarbon dates for this period and the chronology remains vague. The classic sites at which these settlements have been discovered are Taxila and Charsada (Bala Hisar), but several other sites in Swat and neighbouring valleys appear also to go back to this time (Allchin 1982a, 8–14; 1993, 69–80). The radiocarbon dating from Taxila provides the fullest evidence so far available on this region. The earliest period of occupation is at neighbouring Sarai Khola where period I may be described as Neolithic and dated between 3360 and 3000 cal. BC. This is followed by an Early Harappan

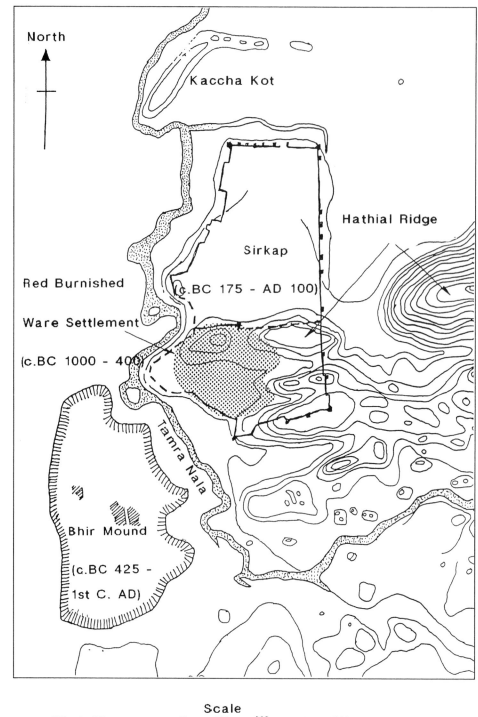

Fig. 8.2. Taxila, map showing the Red Burnished ware in the Hathial settlement area in relation to Bhir mound and Sirkap (Allchin).

period dating between 2909 and 2630 cal. BC. Neither of these periods is found within the Taxila settlement area. The third period at Sarai Khola is described as Late Kot Dijian and this is also represented at Taxila in a small occupation deposit on the Hathial spur (Fig. 8.2). This period is defined by dates between 2460 and 2090 cal. BC at Sarai Khola, and between 2550 and 2288 cal. BC at Hathial.

The ensuing sequence charts the subsequent stages at Hathial. The Red Burnished ware occupation produced two radiocarbon dates:

BM 2198R 1003 cal. BC
BM 2199R   516 cal. BC

These reasonably conform to our expectations, as indicating the span of the period. The radiocarbon dating of the next major period of occupation, that of the Bhir mound, will be discussed below. There appears to be a hiatus between the Late Kot Dijian and the Red Burnished ware periods. The Red Burnished ware settlement is represented by a surface scatter of sherds over an area of c. 13 hectares, but very little more can be said regarding it, in the absence of proper excavations. The area is naturally protected by the rising hills of the Hathial ridge, and this may have been a reason why it was chosen for settlement. This may also explain why it was, later, more or less exactly taken into the southwestern defences of the city of Sirkap. Whether there was already any sort of defensive wall around it in the early stage remains unknown. It is interesting to note that there is not as yet any evidence of a continuous sequence covering the Red Burnished ware settlement. Rather, it seems that this part of the site was for a time left virtually unoccupied, and was only again occupied as part of the building of Sirkap. In the interval between these events the main settlement shifted to the other side of the Tamra stream and is to be found in the then newly constructed city known as the Bhir mound.

Even less can be said regarding the dates of the comparable settlement at Puskalavati (Charsada) (Wheeler 1962). This was discovered in 1958 by Wheeler in the lower levels of his deep cutting through the high Bala Hisar mound, and the distinctive pottery was named by him 'Soapy Red ware' (i.e. what we refer to as Red Burnished ware). There is no way, without more fieldwork, of establishing the extent of the settlement of that period. What is however certain is that the ceramics of the Red Burnished ware settlements at these two sites are very close to each other, and thus it seems reasonable to accept them as of approximately the same period and duration. Whether either constituted a 'city', or whether both are incipient cities, is something we can only speculate on at this time.

If we seek a settlement already deserving the title of city in this early period (i.e. before BC 600), in the sense discussed in chapter 5, we must look far to the southwest, to Kandahar in southern Afghanistan. Here the British excavations of the seventies (still only partly published) suggest that there was a major fortified settlement in pre-Achaemenid times (Figs 8.3 and 8.4). In the earliest

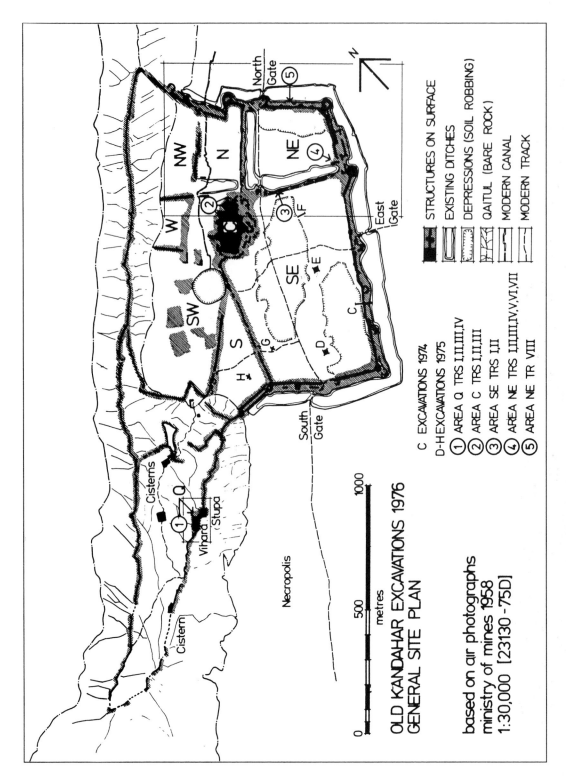

Fig. 8.3.   Kandahar, plan of early fortifications (after Helms 1979).

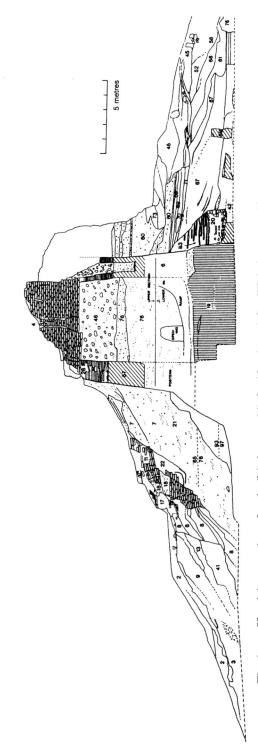

Fig. 8.4. Kandahar, section of early (?Achaemenid) fortifications (after Whitehouse 1978).

phase evidence was found of an already substantial fortification, associated with ceramics which may be compared with that of the last two periods of Mundigak, not as yet dated by radiocarbon, but probably assignable to the first quarter of the first millennium BC (Helms 1979). Most significantly Helms remarked that architecturally and in terms of planning this stage was 'entirely comparable' in conception to the subsequent building period. The latter we may assign, in the absence of any contradictory indications, to the Achaemenid period. We may thus conclude that Kandahar has claim to have been a city at a time when there were perhaps no other cities throughout South Asia; and it is certainly reasonable to see in the establishment of Achaemenid, and even pre-Achaemenid, centres of this kind a strong stimulus towards the growth of cities in the northwest of Pakistan. But, as we have seen, there is other evidence which seems to indicate a more or less contemporary development taking place spontaneously in north India, and it seems improbable that this arose as a result of foreign influence. The material culture of Mundigak and Kandahar at this time is very different from that of contemporary sites farther east, and we should perhaps regard the Indo-Iranian borderlands as more closely linked to eastern Iran. We may also remark that the contemporary material culture of the northwest frontier areas of Pakistan has its own distinctive local character, and this emphasizes the distance between itself and the contemporary cultures of Kandahar on the one hand and Gangetic India on the other.

The northwest parts of South Asia enter the pages of history only with the Achaemenids, who, following the conquests of Cyrus and Cambyses in the west, extended to the east into Central Asia and India, under Darius. Their rule was extended throughout the Indo-Iranian borderlands, and led to the establishment of a group of Satrapies which are still ill-defined, and thence into India proper, where we can recognize the Satrapies of Gandhara and Hindush, the latter being identified with the Indus valley. It is evident that from c. BC 520 until the fall of the Empire at the hands of Alexander the Great, these Satrapies formed a part of it, and it may be expected that the capitals of the various Satrapies would be likely centres for the development of cities. It is regrettably not possible to say much regarding the majority of these eastern capitals, but one may safely assume that Kandahar, the capital of Arachosia, was one of them: it seems probable that other little-excavated and therefore poorly known sites, such as Akara (Akra) Dheri in Bannu District of Pakistan, may also be found to have been other Achaemenid regional centres.

The situation in Gandhara and Sindh is only a little clearer. In Gandhara there was an unbroken occupation at Puskalavati through from the early Red Burnished ware period, which we have identified as originating prior to the Achaemenid rule, into a successor which must span the years until the time of Alexander. But in the very limited excavation done so far at Puskalavati there is little or no evidence of anything which can be identified as specifically Achaemenid, in particular there are no coins. At Taxila the evidence is somewhat more substantial. Here at a certain date a new city, now known as the Bhir Mound, was built on a level plain above the Tamra Nala. The date of this event has long been open to argument, but in recent years a small group of radiocarbon samples from the lowest occupation levels of the site has given dates around the last two decades of the fifth century BC. It might be expected that here one would encounter evidence of the final century of Achaemenid rule, but in fact there are very few indications of an Achaemenid presence, and the cultural character of the finds points in a quite different direction. The relevant radiocarbon dates from the Bhir mound are as follows:

BM2195R 405–402 cal. BC
BM1965R 395 cal. BC
BM1964R 394 cal. BC
BM1963R 399 cal. BC

These four samples all come from the earliest levels of the occupation and may therefore be taken as indicating the date of the foundation of this city.

Although without excavation there is no clear evidence of the former existence of a defensive wall around the Bhir mound, there are numerous things which suggest the survival of the remains of such a wall until comparatively recent times. The sequence of occupation has, following Marshall, usually been treated in terms of four strata, I–IV, the latter being the oldest. From the very beginning there is a major new element in the pottery, alongside the local burnished ware: this is a fine grey or black ware, doubtless locally made in imitation of Northern Black Polished ware (NBP), and sharing with it its limited range of shallow *thali* bowls and deeper *vati* bowls (Fig. 8.5). Some of this pottery is noticeably Gangetic in character. This impression is greatly strengthened in the next stratum (III) when typical single moulded terracotta figurines occur of a purely Gangetic character, along with such typically Gangetic features as terracotta ring-wells. This period may be expected to date from c. BC 320–250. Also present from the very beginning (if we accept Marshall's report) are silver bar punchmarked coins and other associated types. These we believe were locally developed first during the late Achaemenid period, and may be seen as almost the only substantial evidence of an Achaemenid presence in the early Bhir Mound. The excavation at Puskalavati was too limited to obtain comparable evidence of any category except ceramic. The clear published sequence of this material shows a close parallelism to that of Taxila, and leads us to expect a similar sequence there too, when once excavation is undertaken.

We are thus left in a somewhat unclear situation. It would appear as though from the beginning of the first millennium there was a local development of settlements of a markedly local 'Gandharan' character. Somewhere around, or slightly before, BC 400 a new city of Bhir Mound was laid out at Taxila and almost from the start it had a strongly Gangetic flavour. This suggests that well before the time of Candragupta Maurya there had already been some sort of

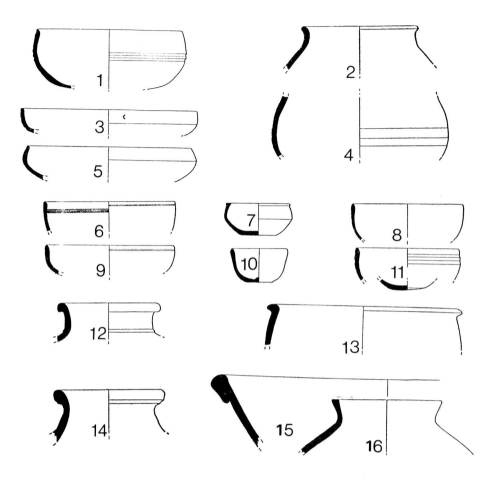

Fig. 8.5. Taxila, Bhir mound, pottery from Period IV, c. BC 400–320 (after Sharif 1969): 1–12, grey ware and black ware; 13–16, red ware (1:3).

Gangetic thrust into this area, of the kind which is suggested by the India epic legends of Janamejaya's conquest of Taxila, and of Bharata's foundation of both Taxila and Puskalavati. It is evident that some such movement must be invoked to account for the steady process of Indianization which accompanied this period. As yet the material traces of the Achaemenids in this area are very slight, but this is no reason to doubt the evidence of history, or to question the Achaemenids' claim to sovereignty over Gandhara from the time of Darius. If evidence for the latter is required it is to be sought in the Asokan inscriptions, and their recognition of Aramaic as a valid local script in Kandahar, Nagarahara and Taxila. Although this evidence comes from the third century BC, the inscriptions stand as records to the erstwhile presence of Achaemenid administrators in these areas.

The further history of this process of Indianization lies in the absorption of the northwest into a wider Indian cultural region, and from Mauryan times deserves to be seen in a wider north Indian context.

Urban expansion to the north and east of the Ganga basin

In view of the proximity of the great Himalayan wall along the northern edges of the Ganges valley, and of its evident inspiration to the early inhabitants of the Ganges plains, one would expect to find evidence of a general northern expansion during the course of the first millennium BC. We have already seen that there are clear hints of such a development in some of the wider and more productive valleys of the northwest. One would expect to find similar evidence in the vale of Kashmir, although archaeology is not yet able to provide it. That there was a northward thrust to extend Indian influence in other valleys, and no doubt to gain control of whatever foreign trade passed through them from the north, may also be inferred from Mauryan times in the placing of Asokan edicts at such strategic places as Mansehra, on the old road towards the upper Indus valley and Gilgit; but we know virtually nothing of the growth of population or settlements in early times in these areas. The early Buddhist tradition suggests that Kashmir was one of the outlying regions to which missionaries were sent by Asoka. Farther east the presence of the Asokan edicts at Kalsi, near the route which led up the Yamuna valley, presumably carries the same implications of Mauryan expansion towards the north.

Still farther east one reaches the valley of Nepal. Here again tradition affirms that there was interest and activity during Mauryan times, and the presence of the four stupas beside the approaches to the city of Patan seems to indicate that this city may well have developed before the time of Asoka. But once again there has been little excavation, and at the time of writing no solid archaeological data exist to support the legends.

The eastern expansion of these urban influences is currently more or less confined to the Ganges-Brahmaputra plains. The easternmost early city of the group is at Mahasthangarh, in the Bagura district of Bangladesh. This large city, with its impressive moat and rampart, has as yet barely been sampled by excavation, but there is solid evidence of pottery related to, if not actually, NBP and other objects which can be reasonably confidently assigned to the Mauryan period, including the stone inscription in early Brahmi with its reference to the maintenance of a storehouse against times of famine (Fig. 10.11). The inscription is important also for another reason: it refers to a city, Pudanagala (Pundrana-gara), which must supply us with its ancient name (Chakrabarti 1992a, 48). We understand that a French team has recently started an excavation project there. Beyond Mahasthangarh there is not as yet much evidence of any comparable urban sites in this area.

The development of cities to the south of the Ganges system

Cities of Central India

Along the southern borders of the Ganges plains there is a less dramatic but no less clearly recognizable abutment with the ranges of hills and forests which divide them from peninsular India. Much of this 'Central belt of hills and forests', as it was named by F. J. Richards (1933), has remained relatively a backwater and, at least since the cultivation of rice began on the plains, less densely populated and with fewer early cities than its northern neighbour. The belt of hills is however in no way so formidable a barrier as are the Himalayas, and from early times has been traversed by major routes linking the Ganges valley with sources of raw materials and centres of population farther south. Another aspect of the settlement history of the peninsula as a whole is that there is very widely dispersed evidence of early settlements there, linked to a combined agricultural and pastoral subsistence base. This too offers a marked contrast to much of the Himalayan zone, and it suggests that the rise of cities in the south is likely to be a more complex affair than in the northern borderlands, with indigenous populations contributing their own important element, alongside the possible stimulus produced by movements of peoples originating in the north or northwest.

In the lists of Mahajanapadas, or centres of population of the time of the Buddha, three at least appear to belong to Central India; they are Ceti or Cedi, Avanti and Asmaka (Fig. 7.4). The first was situated somewhere in Madhya Pradesh but its extent is not clearly known. It seems likely that the ancient cities of Tripuri, near modern Jabalpur, and Airikina, modern Eran, near Sagar, were both included in its territories. The former is in the valley of the Narmada river. Excavation suggests that it goes back to the second millennium BC, but it is still not clear at what date it assumed its role as a city. Eran has been more extensively excavated, but little has as yet been published. Recent excavations (IAR 1987–88, 76–8) confirm that the early occupation goes back to the first half of the second millennium BC, and the settlement seems to have had an unbroken development thereafter. From what is available it appears that at least by Mauryan times a small city was established here, probably producing its own coins, and in touch with the Ganges valley to the extent of importing Gangetic Northern Black Polished ware. The siting of Eran on a fertile open plain surrounded by scattered small hills and anciently also by extensive forests, leads us to regard it as an island of agricultural occupation set in a wider sea of hills and forests.

The second of the Janapadas mentioned above was Avanti, and two substantial early cities may be assigned to it. The first of these, Ujjayini (Ujjain), was probably its capital, or at least became its capital in Mauryan times; although the second, Vidisa, appears to have been the larger city. Ujjain was surrounded by a substantial moat and rampart (Fig. 8.6), probably constructed

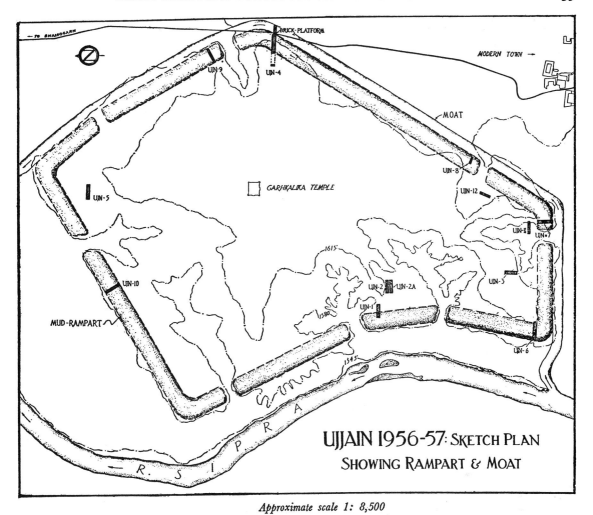

Approximate scale 1: 8,500

Fig. 8.6.   Ujjain, plan of ramparts (courtesy Archaeological Survey of India).

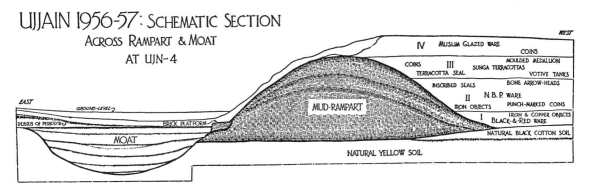

Fig. 8.7.   Ujjain, section of rampart (courtesy Archaeological Survey of India).

in the sixth–fourth centuries BC and enclosing an area of around 95 ha (IAR 1955–56; 56–57; 57–58). This site has been excavated to the extent of a section cut through the rampart, and from the published account it can be seen that this early period was characterized by stone and burnt-brick structures, iron tools and weapons, and Black and Red burnished ware (Fig. 8.7). In the subsequent period the pottery was augmented by imported NBP, copper coins, bone and ivory points or styli and terracotta ring-wells. Another important find of this period was of two small ivory seals with their owners' names inscribed in early Brahmi script. All told it seems probable that the second period represents the time of Mauryan rule, when Ujjain became the administrative centre of this region. This important centre has not yet been dated by radiocarbon.

The second city of this region was Vidisa (formerly referred to as Besnagar), where the area enclosed by the ramparts is c. 240 ha, making it the largest city enclosure in South Asia outside the Ganges valley. Excavations have been done at several places, particularly in the neighbourhood of the Bhagavata shrine where the inscription of Heliodorus the Greek ambassador of Antialkidas from Taxila was discovered (described below in chapter 10), which lies a short distance outside the fortified area. At one place a section was cut through the city rampart (IAR 1964, 65–66, 75–76). It is reported that the rampart was built in the second century BC on top of regular occupation of the previous period, which was associated with NBP, etc. We are inclined to believe that the sequence here may be found to parallel that of Ujjain. The results of this work are only published in summary form and are not altogether clear, but there appears to have been a settlement already during the second millennium BC; with a second developmental stage which is described as pre-Mauryan to Mauryan, in which imported NBP is found along with Black and Red ware, iron objects and punchmarked coins. This in turn is followed by a 'Sunga' period and later occupation. From this it appears that Vidisa was a settlement already during the second millennium BC, and that during the first millennium BC it achieved its full extent.

The cities of central India which we have described appear to share certain distinctive features: they are situated on major roads which linked the Ganges valley with the southern peninsula and the coasts; they are found in fertile areas of agricultural land surrounded by hilly country and/or forests; they appear to have developed first as independent settlements which were at a later stage taken over or 'colonized' from the Ganges valley. Where descriptions of the fortifications are available they appear in several instances to have been surrounded by massive moat and rampart complexes.

Cities of the Deccan

The Deccan plateau lies south of the Narmada river, and constitutes a wide region having many common features. It corresponds approximately with the modern states of Maharashtra, Karnataka and Andhra Pradesh. As we noticed above, it shares with Central India the presence of scattered groups of settled communities with varieties of mixed agricultural-pastoral subsistence going back into the third millennium. As a result of the research programmes of the Deccan College, Pune, and others, we know relatively more about the distribution and numbers of these sites and their culture sequence than about those of the central belt of hills and forests. The areas settled appear to have been considerably greater and the settlements more numerous than those of the Central Indian belt.

The excavations at Inamgaon are particularly helpful in understanding the changes which occurred during the course of the second millennium BC and the early part of the first (Dhavalikar 1988; Dhavalikar et al. 1988). A settlement flourished here during the second millennium, reaching considerable size and structure (see above, Chapter 5, pp. 57 ff.). Towards the end of the second millennium there is something of a decline, and there was a period of relatively lower rainfall around the opening of the first millennium BC, when many of the older settlements in the area were abandoned. But other sites, perhaps where water supplies were more plentiful and reliable, certainly continued to be occupied through into the later centuries of the first millennium. Another clear example of this part of the sequence, which is particularly useful in that it covers the whole of the first millennium, is found in the deep section excavated at Prakash in the Tapti valley (Thapar et al. 1967). This site has so far only been excavated in a very limited area and comparatively little information is available regarding most aspects of the life style of the first millennium BC, but it appears that there was a deposit of some 4 m in depth associated with typical burnished Black and Red ware (Fig. 8.8) and objects of iron. Above this the material culture was augmented by what must be regarded as imported Northern Black Polished ware (probably representing trade contacts with the Ganges valley).

Around this time (the end of the second and the opening century of the first millennium BC), a change becomes noticeable throughout much of peninsular India. Where evidence is available it appears that the change accompanied the beginnings of iron smelting and the subsequent gradual increase in the use of iron (Chakrabarti 1992a, 78–9). For reasons that are not as yet at all clear, it also more or less coincided with the adoption of a common group of ceramics, including the burnished Black and Red ware, made predominantly on a turntable and only occasionally wheel thrown and displaying a cluster of pot forms which are common over a very wide area. Another more or less contemporary development was the growing currency of a whole complex of burial practices which are those often called 'Megalithic' although not all of the contemporary burial practices involved the employment of great stones. For want of a better name this period has been called the Indian peninsular Iron Age. Much more work is called for to establish the phases of the development of this cultural complex and the dates at which they occur from region to region. The picture we

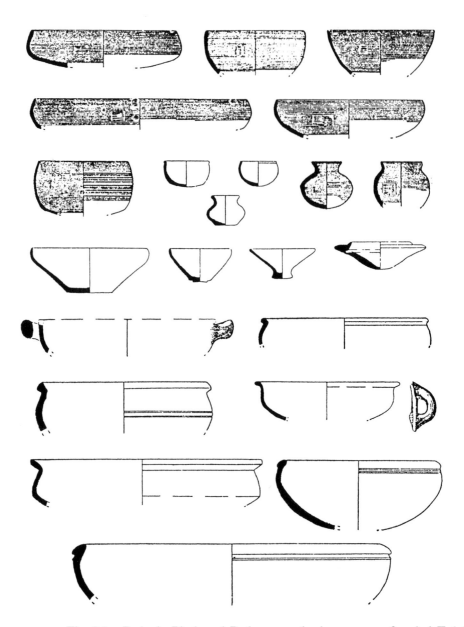

Fig. 8.8. Prakash, Black and Red ware and other pottery of period II (after Allchin and Allchin 1982).

have sketched is essentially very general and lacking in precision, but it is nonetheless, we believe, reasonably correct.

It might be expected that with so much evidence of a long background of settled life, these parts of the Deccan would show early evidence of an indigenous emergence of cities. Whether this was indeed the case is difficult to say, in the light of the curious neglect of this aspect of the archaeological record by local archaeologists. The lists of the 16 Mahajanapadas often include Asmaka (Assaka), and this has been variously interpreted as representing the stony areas of Andhra Pradesh and Karnataka, or Maharashtra. In this context Pratisthana (modern Paithan) is generally agreed to have been a capital city: in spite of reportedly being of considerable extent, the extensive mounds of Paithan have so far not, to our knowledge, been properly described, let alone investigated by archaeologists. We have no archaeological evidence of the date of the first spread of Buddhism into this region. Traditionally it is associated with the story of Bavari, who travelled down to the south from Sravasti; somewhat later his disciples returned to the north in order to have contact with the Buddha, and on their way passed through Pratisthana. If this story actually relates to the time of the Buddha, it would suggest that Pratisthana had already assumed local importance; but it seems probable that the major spread of Buddhism into this area occurred somewhat later during Mauryan times. Subsequently, under the Satavahanas, Paithan certainly became a capital city. It is therefore an important target for research into the rise and spread of urbanism in the Deccan.

By the first century AD, according to the *Periplus of the Erythraean Sea*, there were two important inland markets in the Dakkhinapatha, or Deccan, Pratisthana (Paithan) and Tagara (Ter) (Huntingford 1980). The latter is also known as a major settlement, but here too comparatively little has been published regarding what excavations have been conducted. According to the summary report published in *Indian Archaeology 1974–75 a Review*, there are three main periods of occupation at Tagara, the earliest being associated with the presence of NBP along with Black and Red burnished ware. No Satavahana coins were discovered in this period and the excavators conclude that it dates from the third to second centuries BC. The second and third periods are associated with succeeding phases of Satavahana rule.

Moving farther to the south into Karnataka and Andhra, several more major settlements deserve to be considered as candidates for the emergence of cities. Among them is Sannathi, where a stone rampart encloses an area of about 40 hectares. Although this settlement has not so far been excavated, a copy of an Asokan edict was recently discovered on a floor slab, built into a later shrine. Thus the settlement may well be found to go back to Mauryan times, and was certainly an important centre during the rule of the Satavahanas, as is shown by inscriptions and coin finds. Farther to the east Kondapur is another important settlement of considerable size. Here the sequence is still to be established, in spite of earlier excavations, but there appears to have been a settlement, perhaps established on a Mesolithic camp site, which flourished particularly during the Mauryan to Satavahana periods. Another large settlement within well laid out house plans is at Madhavpur, near Belgaum (Sundara, 1981). Here too a similar sequence appears to exist, with the first period suggesting Mauryan contacts, including reports of punchmarked coins, and the later period coinciding with the Satavahanas, whose coins occur along with evidence of Roman trade. Farther to the south is Banavasi, another important site, notable for its finding mention in the Asokan edicts. Here there is a report of a moat and rampart around at least part of the site (the area enclosed is not recorded), and a similar sequence of Black and Red ware followed by Rouletted ware and materials indicative of the Satavahana period (including coins) is reported (IAR 1970–71, 28–29). Several other sites may be mentioned because of their association with Asokan inscriptions. At Maski, Kopbal and Brahmagiri there were major settlements at least since the second millennium, and there is ample evidence of a pre-Mauryan occupation, associated with black and red ware and Megalithic graves; as yet evidence of Mauryan contact is primarily to be found in the presence of the Asokan inscriptions and until more excavation is done little more can be said. At all these sites there followed a period of settlement datable to Satavahana times.

This cursory survey indicates the large number of major settlements which arose in the Deccan plateau, both in Maharashtra and in Andhra-Karnataka, and the great potential that this area has for further research into the emergence of cities there. On present showing it seems that many settlements enjoyed a long and stable existence in pre-Mauryan times, and in consequence of their size and prestige some of these were chosen as administrative centres by the Mauryans. This early development corresponds with a widely spread and remarkably consistent early Iron Age assemblage, with Black and Red burnished ware and evidence of iron working, and in the absence of adequate radiocarbon dating may be expected to date back to the second quarter of the first millennium (i.e. between BC 750 and 500). In the post-Mauryan period this whole area was included in the Satavahana empire and enjoyed unprecedented affluence during the period of Roman contact (see chapter 12, pp. 305–6).

The western and eastern coastal strips

The peninsular coastal strips, both eastern and western, offer a quite different picture to that of the interior of the Deccan plateau. It appears that maritime trade offered a long-standing stimulus to ports in the coastal zones; and this was augmented by the domestication and cultivation of rice, with resultant increase in population. The sea trade may have involved coastal links originating outside South Asia, mainly at this period in the Red Sea and Persian Gulf, and more distantly with the Mediterranean world; and local trade, originating in the Ganges valley or northwest of South Asia, and passing through major ports on its way to other coastal harbours farther south. Some of these ports would have become cities in their own right, while at other times they may have been colonized by adventurers from the Ganges world, or taken over by local governors or administrators from the Mauryan empire.

On the west coast by far the most important port was Bharukaccha (Broach), near the mouth of the Narmada river. Comparatively little archaeological research has been carried out there, perhaps because the modern town stands on top of the high mound which represents its earlier history. A small excavation was done there in 1959–60 (IAR 1959–60, 19), and another smaller site was excavated at Nagal on the south bank of the river, opposite Broach (IAR 1961–62, 11–12).

Nagal appears to have been a typical ferry point on the river's edge. The excavator identified three phases of occupation, the earliest associated with Black and Red burnished ware, bone arrowheads and points; the second saw a continuation of the Black and Red ware, but now often bearing scratched graffiti; and the third showed a continuation of the Black and Red ware and other features. Iron was present in all but the lowest levels of the site, in which microliths are reported. At Broach itself the earliest levels reported appear to belong to the third of these phases, and unfortunately until more work is done there little can be said regarding its chronology or features. It seems reasonable to assume that the early period at Nagal may go back to a fairly early date (perhaps 8th–6th century BC), and thus there is a real prospect of these sites showing a continuous development through from that time until contacts during the Mauryan period.

The next significant port, going southwards, appears to be Sopara where the discovery of Asokan edicts indicates its importance in Mauryan times. But little if any relevant archaeological research has been done there. In 1993 a British and Indian team started exploratory excavations, and without such work little can be added to the limited information available in early textual sources. Although the *Periplus* mentions a number of further ports on the west coast south of Sopara, none to date is known to have yielded any data relating to its occupation in the period under review.

The eastern coastal strip of the peninsula offers rather more substantial evidence than does the western. In the north, in the Ganges delta region, the excavation of a port site at Tamluk (IAR 1954–55, 19–20), and of a major early city site at Chandraketugarh (IAR 1956–67), demonstrate that this area must at an early date have formed part of the eastern expansion of the Gangetic city complex. Chandraketugarh has been excavated over more than a decade, but so far no satisfactory reports have been published. This is all the more to be regretted because of the quantities of fine ceramics and Early Historic terracottas discovered there, and the fact that they include both peninsular wares, such as Rouletted ware, and what appears to be Eastern Hellenistic pottery, alongside typical Gangetic wares, suggests that this city was at the meeting place of two major regions. Tamluk, as a port, may be seen as simultaneously a major maritime outlet and entrepot for the Ganges valley, and as the northern terminus of the east coast sea trade. The excavations carried out so far highlight the need for more research in the field. The earliest occupation at Tamluk contained Black and Red ware, small stone celts and a variety of bone tools. This is followed by a second period in which NBP occurs in association with timber-framed structures: this may be broadly dated to the pre-Mauryan and Mauryan period. The third period contained numbers of beautiful terracotta figurines, of a style which is characteristic of the early Ganges cities, some of which may be assigned on grounds of style to the Mauryan period, and others to the Sunga; cast copper coins also occur. This was followed by the fourth period in which quantities of Rouletted and Red Polished ware were found, giving evidence of the Roman-Hellenistic trade contacts of the first two centuries AD. This short account is tantalizing because of the many questions which it leaves unanswered, and at the same time because of the broad similarity of the sequence with that of other sites throughout Peninsular India.

Travelling southwards down the east coast the first major region is Orissa. Here the ancient city of Tosali (modern Sisupalgarh), otherwise known as the city of Kalinga, is not only referred to in the local Asokan inscriptions, but appears to be a pre-Mauryan foundation. A reference in the famous but problematic Kharavela inscription, which may be dated to the middle to late first century BC, mentions Kharavela's improvement of a water channel (*panadi*, i.e. *pranali*) which had been constructed by the 'Nanda king' three hundred years earlier and which he now extended into the city (Sircar 1965, 213–20). This suggests that there was an incursion into this region by a Nanda king from Magadha (where the Nandas ruled for a still undefined period of time prior to the accession of Candragupta Maurya in c. BC 324). The site was excavated and studied by B. B. Lal in 1948 (Lal 1949): it is surrounded by a massive defensive rampart and moat, laid out on a square plan with two gates on each wall (Figs. 8.9 and 8.10). The enclosed area occupies c. 130 ha. The gateways are constructed of massive blocks of laterite (Fig. 8.11). The same material was used for some of the houses excavated in the interior of the city. The chronology of the defenses and of the habitation deposits, which were sampled within the enclosed area, is stratigraphically clear, but still uncertain in terms of absolute dates, since the excavations have never been dated by radiocarbon. The deep section shows a deposit of about 8 m and is divided into four periods. The earliest is not well represented, but dates from prior to the construction of the first ramparts. It is followed by two phases of c. 4 m and 1 m depth, respectively, characterized by the presence of Black and Red burnished ware throughout, augmented in the upper period by Rouletted ware, together with a few sherds identified as NBP. Our suggestion for dating this sequence would expect period IIA to extend from c. BC 500–200; and period IIB to extend from c. BC 200–AD 200. But it is really only possible to guess at the chronology in the absence of radiocarbon dating, more extensive work and more objective criteria for dating.

Fig. 8.9.   Sisupalgarh, aerial photograph of the city (courtesy Archaeological Survey of India.

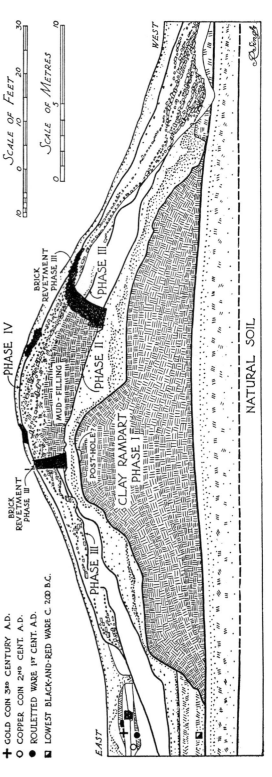

SISUPÁLGARH (ORISSA) 1948: SECTION ACROSS THE DEFENCES AT SP II

+ GOLD COIN 3RD CENTURY A.D.
O COPPER COIN 2ND CENT. A.D.
● ROULETTED WARE 1ST CENT. A.D.
▣ LOWEST BLACK-AND-RED WARE C. 200 B.C.

SCALE OF FEET
10   0   10   20   30

SCALE OF METRES
0   5   10

EAST

BRICK
REVETMENT
PHASE III

BRICK
REVETMENT
PHASE III

PHASE IV

PHASE III

MUD-FILLING

POST-HOLE?

PHASE II

BRICK
REVETMENT
PHASE III

PHASE III

CLAY RAMPART
PHASE I

NATURAL SOIL

WEST

R.Singh

Fig. 8.10.   Sisupalgarh, section of ramparts (courtesy Archaeological Survey of India).

Fig. 8.11. Sisupalgarh, photograph of excavated gateway (courtesy Archaeological Survey of India).

The remains of the fortified city of Tosali are only part of the evidence for the development of the urban complex in its wider context. The city lay on a plain between the Bhargavi river to the east and Gangua Nali which flows close to the western ramparts. There are traces of an ancient moat. Outside the city there is evidence of several religious centres. Two miles to the south lies Dhauli hill with its Minor Rock Edict of Asoka and the carved stone elephant beside it (Mitra 1958). Some five miles to the west lie the twin hills of Udayagiri and Khandagiri with their many Jaina caves and their important inscriptions of king Kharavela and his family (belonging to the first century BC). Within a quarter of a mile to the north of the ramparts, in the vicinity of the medieval Brahmeshwara temple, there is an area where carved stone railings of the first two centuries BC have been discovered, suggesting a Buddhist or Jain stupa close to the northwestern gate. Equally suggestive of the antiquity of the city are the number of large irrigation tanks which lie nearby. These certainly need further attention to establish their antiquity.

Another ancient city has been identified at Jaugada, northwest of Ganjam and about 100 km southwest of Sisupalgarh (IAR 1956–57, 31). This is almost certainly the Samapa of the Dhauli Asokan inscriptions. Here a massive earth rampart, enlarged over several periods, enclosed an area of c. 64 ha. The earliest period contained plain Black and Red ware pottery and iron; post holes suggest simple timber-framed houses, no brick was recovered. The second period produced sherds of typical Hellenistic types of ceramic, with bowls with central omphalos. Houses of brick and stone are reported. The Jaugada Asokan inscription is on a nearby hill.

Travelling southwards little can be said regarding Kalingapatnam near the mouth of the Vamshadhara river. That there was a major settlement can be inferred, but the site has not been investigated so far. The neighbouring Buddhist monastic complex of a hill beside the river suggests only occupation from post-Mauryan times. The next important early city site to the south is Dhanykataka (Amaravati) in Andhra Pradesh. The site is on the right bank of the river Krishna: it includes a square rampart (known as Dharanikota) enclosing an area of c. 33 ha. This is without doubt the ancient Dhanyakataka. Nearby is a second mound which marks the remains of the great Stupa of Amaravati. Among important finds in the neighbourhood is a stone block, part broken and on one side rounded, used until recently as a washerman's block, which bears a short and problematic inscription in early Brahmi. This has been generally accepted as being of the time of Asoka, perhaps even part of an edict, but this remains to be firmly established. Both the ramparts of the town and the stupa area have recently been partly excavated and, although only short summaries are published and these are not always fully clear, a reasonably complete picture of the early sequence can be obtained (for Dharanikota, IAR 1962–63, 1963–64, 1964–65; for Amaravati, IAR 1958–59, 1973–74, 1975–76; Sarma 1985). The earliest occupation (Period Ia) was accompanied by typical Black and Red ware, apparently accompanied by NBP. Several potsherds were found bearing Brahmi inscriptions, remarkably reminiscent of those found at Anuradhapura. The second sub-period (Ib) continued with the same ceramics, but showed the first pieces of monumental stonework from the stupa area, including an inscribed slab. The excavator modestly dates these two phases to early Mauryan and later Mauryan times, and dates the occupation back to the fourth century BC. We are inclined to accept these dates, although when better radiocarbon dating is available it may show that the beginning was somewhat earlier. The next period (II) shows a continuation of the same ceramic wares, although the NBP is less common. Silver punchmarked coins occur, as does more substantial architectural evidence, comparable to that of other early Buddhist sites, particularly Bharhut, and this may well be dated to the second to first centuries BC. Period III introduces the Rouletted ware and typical objects made of kaolin, along with coins attributable to the Satavahana dynasty. The following period (IV) almost certainly represents the period of the Iksvaku dynasty. The chronology of these periods, which are more or less paralleled in the rampart excavation, is partly established by two series of radiocarbon dates: those for the stupa area lie between the first and fourth centuries AD, and scarcely relate to any periods as such; but those from the Dharanikota rampart suggest that the early occupation goes back to the fourth to fifth centuries BC, while the fortification building of the Satavahana period belongs to the late second century BC. These dates appear reasonably convincing. Thus this site introduces two important categories of information in apposition to each other, one relating to the foundation and growth of the settlement, and the other to the monumental history of the great Stupa. What remains to be more clearly established is whether the early settlement at Dhanyakataka is contemporary with, and possibly a result of, Mauryan colonial expansion into the south, or whether – as the radiocarbon dates suggest – Amaravati was already a local settlement of importance at an earlier date.

South of the Krishna river there are many ports mentioned in the *Periplus*, but it is not easy to identify them on the ground. Several sites deserve notice, some of primarily archaeological and others of mainly historical importance. The first is Arikamedu, south of Pondicherry, where the excavations of Wheeler and Casal (Wheeler 1946; Casal 1949, 1956) revealed a sequence beginning with an early period accompanied by black and red ware (Fig. 8.12). This is followed by one in which the local pottery is augmented by imported Arretine ware, amphorae and a group of exotic pottery in a finely levigated clay, including rouletted ware, stamp impressed bowls (referred to as 'type 10') and other pottery of distinctly Hellenistic facies (Figs. 8.13–14). Another striking piece of evidence is provided by the potsherds carrying scratched inscriptions. These are in early Brahmi script adapted for writing in Tamil; several of the longer inscriptions are probably in that language (Fig. 8.15). The chronological position of the sherds is not clearly

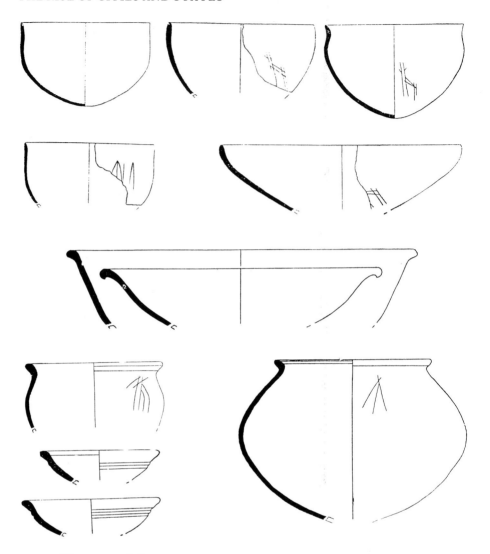

Fig. 8.12.   Arikamedu, Black and Red ware, showing examples of scratched graffiti from early period (after Casal 1949).

stated, but palaeographically the inscriptions comprise a considerable time bracket, the earliest probably belonging to the last two centuries BC and the larger part to the first two centuries AD. There are as yet no radiocarbon dates for Arikamedu, and until fresh excavations are published even the details of the sequence remain somewhat obscure (Begley 1983, 1986). The upshot of work to date is that Arikamedu was a small coastal settlement from early times which at a certain date became involved in the Hellenistic-Roman trade.

The delta of the Kaveri river is in a real sense the homeland of the Cholas who ruled both around the beginning of the Christian era and again around the end of

Fig. 8.13.   Arikamedu, rouletted ware (courtesy Archaeological Survey of India).

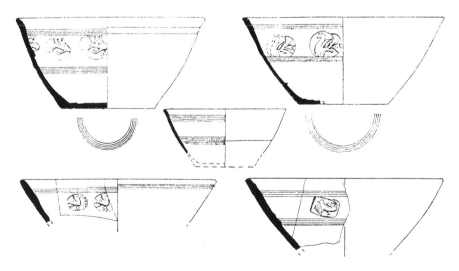

Fig. 8.14.   Arikamedu, stamp decorated grey ware of Wheeler's 'type 10' (courtesy Archaeological Survey of India).

Fig. 8.15. Arikamedu, potsherds with scratched inscriptions in Brahmi script, some in Tamil, c. AD 1st–2nd century, (courtesy Archaeological Survey of India).

the first millennium AD. Several important sites have been excavated in this area, but as yet we are not aware of any major publications. The most important, historically, must be Kaveripattana, which as an early capital of the Chola kingdom must have been a candidate for the rank of city. As yet there is no clear report of the archaeological sequence or its chronology, but there appears to have been an early period of black and red ware, succeeded by a period of Roman contact (IAR 1963–64, 64–65, 65–66). The same is apparently true of some of the other settlements excavated in the Kaveri delta region: at Uraiyur, another ancient capital of the Cholas, excavations have revealed a somewhat similar sequence, but once again there is a lack of clarity in the reports published to date (IAR 1964–65, 65–66, 67–68). Here too potsherds inscribed in early Brahmi with inscriptions in Tamil are reported. Palaeographically these appear to belong to the late centuries BC and early centuries AD. These are potentially important and deserve study in comparison with those of Anuradhapura (see below, chapter 9).

This brief survey of the peninsular coastal plains leaves us with a feeling of perplexity that there is such a wealth of material, that so many of the excavations are incompletely published, and that so many sites cry out for proper archaeological investigation before they are destroyed by modern population growth and industrialization. We cannot but remark, moreover, that there appears to be an absence of clarity in discussing the early sequence at many of these settlements: few if any have been dated by radiocarbon, even the sequences are still unclear, and little progress appears to have been made beyond the point reached by Wheeler and Casal four decades ago! However this may be, the developments we have seen in all parts of peninsular India, and particularly in the coastal plains, provide a useful background against which to turn, in the following chapter, to the rise of cities in Sri Lanka.

One point which emerges from this survey of the early cities in those parts of South Asia which lie outside the Ganges basin is that there are several complementary processes at work. First, it appears that similar technological and cultural changes occurred very widely, for example as a result of the introduction of improved agricultural techniques and tools of iron, and gave rise to similar or at least related changes in the population and the settlement pattern in many parts of South Asia. This is to be expected in view of the fact that these regions were all along open to contacts and influences with one another. Thus broadly parallel changes seem to have occurred in markedly different environments. A second and quite different factor appears to have been the way in which, in the Ganges valley and the northwest of India-Pakistan generally, the end of Achaemenid rule, and the attendant campaigns of Alexander the Great, paved the way for the rise of Mauryan imperialism. We would argue that this development can only have occurred because the ground was already prepared for it in those regions; but it cannot be questioned that the development of Mauryan imperial rule led to a further profound expansion of cities and urban life throughout all parts of South Asia. As an aftermath of this development Mauryan imperial administration became for a time established over much of South Asia. With the parallel conversion of Asoka to Buddhism, Buddhist missionary activity also spread throughout these provinces and beyond. Thus the Mauryan period saw a quite unprecedented expansion of the material and cultural aspirations of the Ganges valley throughout South Asia. Our review of developments in the western and eastern peninsular coastal strips draws our attention to a third influencing factor in the process of cultural change throughout South Asia: this was the greatly increased economic stimulus provided, probably from the time of Alexander on, by trade contacts originating in the Mediterranean. From the start these must have been largely with Greeks or persons calling themselves Greeks (hence the general use of the word Yavana for foreign traders), and there can be no doubt that this trade received a powerful stimulus and expansion during Roman times.

CHAPTER 9

THE RISE OF CITIES IN SRI LANKA

R. A. E. CONINGHAM AND F. R. ALLCHIN

The separateness of Sri Lanka

The sources of our knowledge of Sri Lanka's past are similar to those for the rest of South Asia, primarily archaeological for the earlier period, and augmented by textual and literary references from the early historic period onwards. Of particular significance for the early history are the two chronicles, the Mahavamsa (Geiger 1950 (1912)) and the Dipavamsa (Law 1959), and the somewhat later Rajavaliya (Gunasekara 1900). These chronicles, which were without doubt added to reign by reign or from time to time, and probably also amended or embroidered as time went by, so that no section can be said actually to date from a given period, purport to contain an account of the early colonization of the island by a party of north Indian settlers under the leadership of a certain Vijaya, and of its subsequent history, as it was seen through the eyes of the monks of the Mahavihara or Great Monastery at Anuradhapura. The beginnings of this account include materials that are probably more mythic than historical, but they are none the less of crucial interest. From the time of king Devanampiya Tissa, the contemporary of Asoka and the inaugurator of the Sri Lankan Buddhist state, the history becomes more firmly based, and is augmented by large numbers of inscriptions.

Sri Lanka stands out in South Asia as occupying a position which is in many ways singular. Viewed in terms of its geographical location it is the southernmost extension of the Indian peninsula, and constitutes as much a part of the peninsula as does the mainland; but its position as an island separated from the mainland already suggests that this is not the whole story. Its anthropological and cultural situation both present a similar dynamic tension in that while Sri Lanka is essentially a part of the wider South Asian culture, she possesses a distinct character of her own. The same is no doubt also at least partly true of many of the cultural regions of the peninsula mainland, but the added factor of Sri Lanka's insularity heightens its sense of difference. This is the context in which modern linguistic and religious divisions deserve to be considered. Ethnicity and religion appear to be interlocked in an ancient and peculiarly enduring set of relations, whose history and origins demand careful and systematic research if they are to be unravelled.

The archaeological background

The archaeological background to the rise of cities in Sri Lanka is in some respects different from that of related parts of peninsular India, and deserves to be considered before the main topic is discussed. Since the early part of the twentieth century, and as a result of the researches of the Sarasin brothers (1908), Hartley (1913) and others, a prominent feature of the later prehistory of Sri Lanka has been the role of Mesolithic sites, yielding stone tools predominantly made of quartz, and of a distinctive facies, which most nearly compare with the stone industries of the so-called Teri (sand dune) sites of littoral southeast India. The sites are found widely distributed through Sri Lanka (Fig. 9.1), and include dune sites, comparable to the Indian Teris, caves and open-air factories. A much more detailed knowledge of the nature of the Mesolithic sites, and conclusive proof of their great antiquity has come in recent decades with a series of cave excavations by S. Deraniyagala (1990a–c, 1992). A large number of radiometric samples has shown consistent evidence that the earliest sites were occupied by c. 30,000 years bp; while other dates indicate the continuation of what is evidently an ongoing cultural tradition right down to the first millennium BC. It has generally been believed that the Mesolithic sites may represent the occupation of a people ancestral to the modern Veddas. Interesting new light is thrown on this stage by the discovery of an extensive scatter of microlithic tools stratified below the earliest settled occupation at Anuradhapura, Mantai and other sites. Whatever the nature of the settlement and population of that stage, the indications are that it did not consist solely of small, isolated groups dwelling in caves and rock shelters, but also of sites which served as a meeting point for a not insubstantial population. Indeed, the evidence may further suggest a direct continuity linking the Mesolithic culture with that of the succeeding Iron Age.

While there is thus clear evidence of a long-lived and stable Mesolithic occupation of Sri Lanka, there is not as yet equivalent evidence of early pastoral or mixed agricultural-pastoral settlements, of the kind found throughout much of mainland South Asia and associated with what is generally called the Neolithic–Chalcolithic cultural complex. On present showing the earliest South Asian evidence of these developments is on the western borders of Pakistan, in the seventh millennium BC or even earlier. It would appear that only somewhat later did any related culture complex spread more widely in northern India-Pakistan. This whole development was significant in that it coincided with the rise of the Indus civilization and consequently the special developments of the second millennium which we considered in chapters 3 and 4 above. By comparison developments in the central and southern parts of the peninsula currently appear to have been considerably later, and the earliest Neolithic–Chalcolithic sites so far

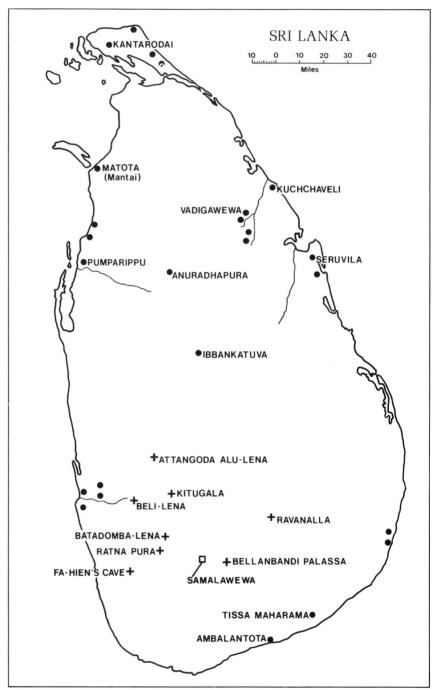

Fig. 9.1. Map of Sri Lanka showing principal sites.

attested are as yet not before BC 3000. It is noticeable that in the southernmost parts of the peninsular mainland there is until now even more uncertain evidence of Neolithic or Chalcolithic settlements, and little if any evidence of early dates. We may hypothesize that comparable processes to those occurring in the south were also present in Sri Lanka. Although there is not conclusive evidence that this spread of agricultural and pastoral cultures throughout South Asia was associated with a comparable spread of new populations moving down into the peninsula, this appears to be the most likely explanation of the development. A note of caution must however be struck, since it is always possible that what appears to be a complete absence of evidence is actually no more than a result of the unsystematic and almost capricious way in which research has hitherto been carried on in these regions.

It has often been remarked that during the historical period movements of immigrant peoples southwards into the peninsula, deriving mainly from the northwest, are attested. This same tendency is also recorded in the traditional histories of many caste groups in the Indian peninsula, where vaguely remembered origins are almost invariably said to have been in the north or northwest. This does not mean that such movements alone were responsible for bringing about cultural changes, or that the existing local populations were either ineffective, insignificant or even wiped out. Rather it suggests that in some situations the arrival of new groups played a part in the process.

As indicated in chapter 8, around the end of the second millennium BC, or during the opening century of the first millennium, a change begins to become noticeable throughout much of peninsular India: this coincided with the gradual spread of iron working and the growing increase in the use of iron. It also more or less coincided with the adoption of a common group of ceramics, including the burnished Black and Red ware, made predominantly on a turntable and only occasionally wheel thrown, and displaying a cluster of pot forms which are common over a very wide area. Another more or less contemporary development was the growing currency of a whole complex of distinctive burial patterns, belonging to the peninsular burial complex and generally referred to as Megalithic. Another striking feature was the remarkable extension of many uniform types of craft products throughout almost all parts of the peninsula.

The existence of a similar complex in Sri Lanka, involving the early use of iron, of black and red burnished ware and the occurrence of megalithic burials has been gradually coming into focus. The discovery of stone cist graves and in some cases of Black and Red ware pottery and objects of iron has been not infrequently reported in the various archaeological publications over the years, but until very recently absolute dating was lacking. Some distortion has been caused by the lack of information regarding contemporary settlements, and undue concentration on burial sites. A similar imbalance of available data is also to be noticed in peninsular India. In recent years useful advances have been made in these respects. Seneviratne has written a recent synthesis of the evidence available to date (1984). Moreover, excavations at a number of early settlements, at sites such as Kantarodai, Ibbankatuva and above all the Citadel mound at Anuradhapura, have supplied new data, some still to be published, and much-needed radiocarbon dates. Thus the situation is now markedly more clear than it was even a decade ago.

What is emerging from this research is that in the early centuries of the first millennium BC there was a widespread dispersal of early iron-using people throughout many parts of Sri Lanka, employing ceramic craft products which along with the other aspects of their culture shared to a large extent in the common aspects of the Indian peninsular Iron Age complex. By contrast with the mainland however, where this development took place in some cases in areas where there had been many centuries of settled or semi-settled agricultural and pastoral life, and where it may be assumed that there was already a stable, settled population, there is not (as we remarked above) as yet any comparable evidence from Sri Lanka. This must raise the question of whether the spread of something so closely resembling the Indian peninsular iron culture was brought to Sri Lanka by actual movements of people, and if so from what direction they may have come. This is a difficult and delicate question to which we shall return later. We shall first consider the traditional evidence for the rise of city life in Sri Lanka, and then go on to examine the archaeological evidence in greater detail.

The tradition of the Sri Lankan chronicles

The early history of Sri Lanka, as given in the Mahavamsa and Dipavamsa, contains a number of episodes which are relevant for our discussion. Three in particular are important:
- the mythological account of the division of the island into three zones, a lowland zone (*Lanka tala* or *dipa*), a mountain zone (*Giri dipa*) and a third, less clearly defined zone (perhaps one might say, *Naga dipa*);
- the story of the conquest of Sri Lanka by Vijaya and a group of north Indian colonists; and
- the account of the establishment of Buddhism as a national religion at Anuradhapura in the third century BC.

Overshadowing the whole context of these three episodes is a peculiarly difficult problem: the historical dates of the Buddha and their relationship to the dates of Vijaya's landing in Sri Lanka and the reign of Asoka. We have touched on these matters several times above and need not repeat them here, except to note that there are broadly two schools of thought, one following a longer chronology which accepts that there was an approximately 218 years' interval between the Mahaparinirvana of the Buddha and the consecration of Asoka (which took place c. BC 268); and a shorter chronology placing the interval between these events at around 100–110 years (Bechert 1982, 1990). Obviously this difference will ultimately have to be resolved if the early history of both India and Sri Lanka is to be given more objective precision; but its resolution is not within our present scope and we can do no more than indicate our own inclination towards the shorter chronology. We are now ready briefly to discuss each of the three episodes.

1. The division of the island

The earliest of the episodes has a timeless almost mythical character and envisages the Buddha seeing with the eye of wisdom the island of Sri Lanka, remarking on its excellence and on its being well cultivated (*sukkheta*) and a dwelling suitable for Ariyas (Aryans). However, it was at that time inhabited by Yakkhas (Yaksas), Bhutas (spirits or ghosts) and Rakkhasas (demons). He therefore resolved to remove these latter groups and to people the island with men (Dipvamsa 1.19–21). The method he chose to achieve this aim was to create another island, *Giri Dipa*, consisting of mountains, and to merge it with the Lanka plains (*Lanka tala*). This done he ordained that the mountainous region should provide a home for the Yakkhas, Bhutas and Rakkhasas, while the plains (*tala*) were peopled with men (*manusa*) (Dipavamsa 1.45–81). This passage also refers to Sri Lanka as being *cira nivasita*, long inhabited (Dipavamsa 1.72).

The following chapter of the Dipavamsa (2) contains the episode of the battles of the Nagas (serpents) and of their being brought under control by the Buddha. An actual Naga settlement is referred to (Dipavamsa 2.42), and it seems probable that those referred to as Nagas, here as in other early South Asian textual contexts, are not actually serpents, but rather distinct ethnic, probably non-Indoaryan-speaking, groups.

These episodes have been often seen as indicating that the Yakkhas and the other named groups were aboriginal forest-dwelling tribes, comparable to the Veddas. But this interpretation is not altogether clear. What the story probably indicates is that at some date a part of the existing population was driven into the mountainous regions, so that the agriculturally more attractive plains might be exploited for settlement by a later population. The story does not clearly indicate whether there were, in addition to aboriginal tribes, already in Sri Lanka earlier agricultural colonizers, perhaps the groups designated as Nagas, who may have crossed the straits from the adjacent parts of South India, as part of an earlier spread of agricultural population. As evidence of such a spread has been found in many parts of mainland peninsula India, such a possibility must also be accepted for Sri Lanka. It is also possible that this development involved the north Indian colonists. Thus, this suggestive and admittedly partisan narrative remains in some respects unclear for want of detail and archaeological support.

2. Vijaya's expedition and the north Indian colonization

The story of Vijaya is well known and has been often told, but in view of its importance for our subject it may be helpful to repeat it, in a succinct form.

Vijaya's grandmother was the daughter of the king of Vanga (Bengal), who according to the story was abducted by a lion (*siha*), while she was travelling across India to Lata (Gujarat). She had two offspring by the lion, one a son named Sihabahu (Lion-armed) because his arms were like those of a lion. This son established a city *Sihapura* (*Sinhapura*, lion city) in the Lata region and founded villages in the forests all around. Later his son Vijaya was banished because of his misdemeanors and with a group of companions travelled by sea down the west coast of India, stopping on the way at Broach and Suppara. They arrived in Sri Lanka on the very day of the Buddha's Mahaparinirvana, and landed at a place called *Tambapanni* (so named because the red dust there stained their hands and feet), possibly represented by the archaeological site of Kantarodai. Here he established a city of Tambapanni and in due course sent out his companions to settle or conquer the remainder of the island. Among the settlements thus established was Anuradhapura. The Dipavamsa refers to Tambapanni as *pathamam nagaram*, the first city in Sri Lanka (Dipavamsa 9.31), but other references in the Mahavamsa suggest that there may already have been a 'city' of the Yakkhas at Sirisavatthu. Vijaya appears initially to have united with a Yakkha woman, by whom he had two children, but later he married the daughter of the Pandava king from the neighbouring mainland city of Madhura, and obtained also many maidens from the same source, along with a thousand families of the eighteen craft guilds. In his old age Vijaya wrote to his brother who still ruled in his father's city of Sihapura in western India and requested him to come and take over the rule of Sri Lanka. In response he sent his youngest son Panduvasudeva and he became king in succession to Vijaya.

The story of Vijaya is significant for a number of reasons. First, it offers three distinct instances of colonization and city founding: of Sinhapura in western India, of Tambapanni in Sri Lanka, and of Anuradhapura and other settlements in other parts of the island. Such colonization recalls the policy of *janapada nivesa* advocated by Kautilya (see below, chapter 10). In addition it tells us that Vijaya first married a local woman, a Yakkhini, and secondly a princess from the neighbouring Pandya kingdom, from whence he also invited a thousand families from different occupations. In this way intermarriage both with indigenous and with presumably Dravidian-speaking women from the mainland is referred to. Although the Chronicle is written from a distinctly partisan point of view, it nevertheless offers important clues to the complex, pluralistic society which was emerging during this time.

3. Mahinda's mission and the establishment of Buddhism

The third episode, that of the establishment of Buddhism in the island, brings us much closer to externally verifiable historical facts. It tells how in the reign of Asoka of Magadha a great council was held at the capital city, Pataliputra, at which it was decided to send out missionaries to convert many neighbouring lands. These included Gandhara in the northwest, Mahisa and Maharattha (Maharashtra) in the Indian peninsula, Aparantaka in western India, Yonaka and Himalaya in the north, Suvannabhumi (Burma) in the east, and Lanka in the far south. Asoka's own son Mahinda was chosen to head the Sri Lankan mission. The Mahavamsa account describes in great detail the missionaries' arrival in the city of Anuradhapura in c. BC 246, and gives much incidental information concerning the city and its surroundings. We are told of the establishment there of the Bodhi tree brought from Bodh Gaya as a scion of the original Bodhi tree, the establishment of the Mahavihara, and various other monasteries and stupas.

These three episodes provide us with a series of examples of the textual tradition and the problems raised by its interpretation for historical or archaeological purposes. They suggest that even in the earliest and most cryptic of the three there is significant information, if only it is possible to interpret it. Obviously nothing should be accepted without critical evaluation; but equally nothing should be rejected without reasonable and proper consideration. The need for an addition of sound archaeological data is obvious.

As we have seen above Anuradhapura appears in the chronicles as one of a number of village settlements founded by Vijaya's companions, shortly after his landing in the island. It is referred to again as a settlement in the time of Vijaya's successor, and again in his great-nephew Pandukabhaya's time, when the text informs us that it was transformed and laid out on properly planned lines. Pandukabhaya made it into a 'capital city', and appointed his uncle as the city guardian (nagaraguttika). In this context we also find reference to his enlargement of an existing irrigation tank, the Jayavapi. The city and its environs are described as having various precincts, including an area set apart for Yonas (i.e. Greeks or foreigners). We obtain further details of the city in his grandson Devanam-piya Tissa's time, when the capital received the mission of Mahinda, the son of Asoka, and when Buddhism was accepted as a state religion. There is thus an expectation that the archaeological record may be able to provide data on the growth of the city for comparison with the traditional history.

Archaeological evidence from Anuradhapura

Looking at Anuradhapura today, it is not difficult to recognize that there are two main sectors: the central mound, known as the Citadel, which can be identified as the ancient city; and a peripheral zone which includes many remains of monastic complexes, including the four great stupas, with their respective monasteries, the Maha Thupa (Ruvanvalisaya), Jetavanaramaya, Mirisavati and Abhayagiriya (Fig. 9.2). In this surrounding zone too there are a number of irrigation works, some of undoubted antiquity and historical significance. We shall refer to these below.

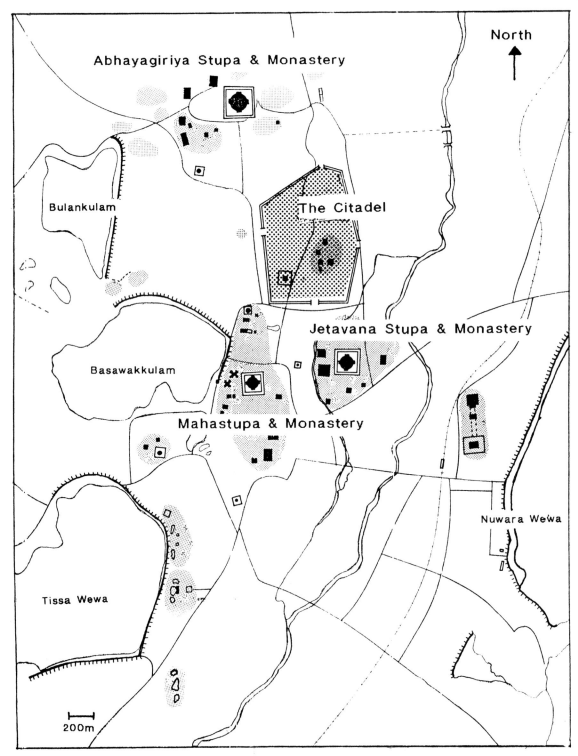

North

Abhayagiriya Stupa & Monastery

Bulankulam

The Citadel

Jetavana Stupa & Monastery

Basawakkulam

Mahastupa & Monastery

Nuwara Wewa

Tissa Wewa

200m

Fig. 9.2. Plan of the city of Anuradhapura and its surroundings, showing principal early monasteries and irrigation works.

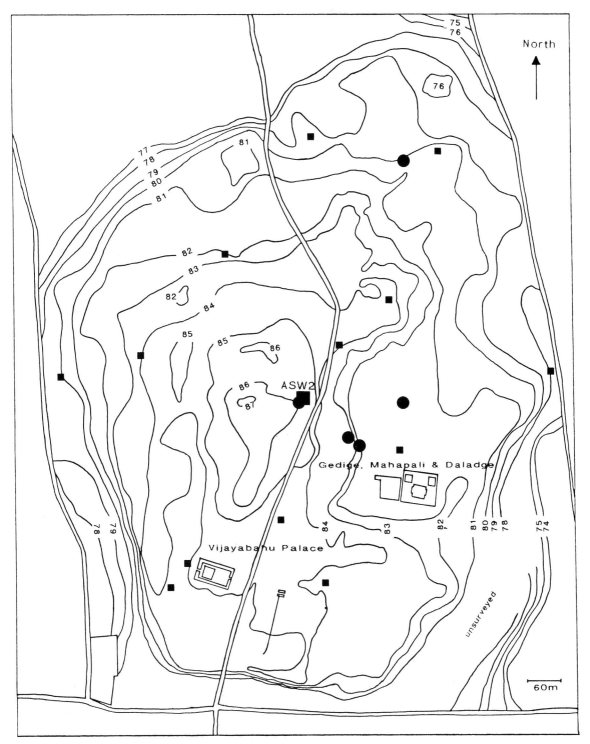

Fig. 9.3. Plan of the citadel at Anuradhapura, showing excavated sites. Small squares represent the location of sondages and circles represent the location of stone pillared halls.

Period

A

B - F

G - H

I

J

K

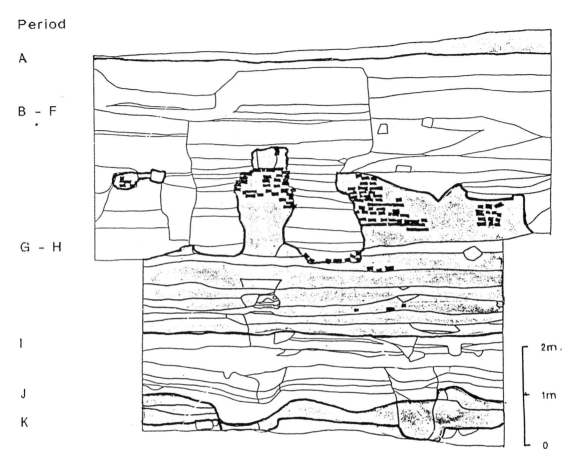

2m

1m

0

Fig. 9.4. Anuradhapura excavation at ASW2, southern section.

To begin to understand the growth of the city we must first consider the development of the main settlement, as it appears in the light of recent and current excavations. The mound occupies some 100 hectares. Deraniyagala has carried out excavations there since 1969 (Deraniyagala 1972), and more recently has made a series of deep sondages in different parts of the mound (Fig. 9.3) (Deraniyagala 1986; 1990c). These sondages were of limited size (3 × 3 m) and the data they yield is thus restricted, although they provide the basis for a clear understanding of the sequence of occupation of different parts of the mound, and therefore of the extent of the settlement at different times. Since 1990 a Sri Lankan–British team has been carrying out a somewhat larger excavation (10 × 10 m), identified as ASW2 at Salgaha Watta, adjacent to one of the earlier sondages, with a view to providing comparative information and a bigger volume of cultural data (Coningham 1990; 1991; in press; Coningham and Allchin 1992). In the light of these excavations the following sequence may be reconstructed (Fig. 9.4). We shall review the evidence in chronological order, starting at the beginning and describing it period by period, generally following or adapting the period names and numbers employed by Deraniyagala (1990a and b):

Period L. Mesolithic (from ? early second millennium BC)

The earliest human occupation at the site is found in the gravels lying beneath all the subsequent occupation in two of the other sondages and in the ASW2 pit. It takes the form of quartz or quartzite tools, scrapers, points, flakes, cores, hammer stones and waste materials, suggesting an already considerable area of occupation, implying something more than a casual camp site. The presence of cores and waste materials indicates local manufacture of stone tools. Although no dating samples were obtained from ASW2, this period is dated by a number of radiometric samples from the other sondages, suggesting that the Mesolithic occupation dates back to the early second millennium BC (Deraniyagala 1992, 700, 709). As we saw above comparable Mesolithic assemblages are found elsewhere in Sri Lanka from very early times through to the beginnings of Iron Age settlement.

Period K. Iron Age (c. BC 600–450)

The second period coincides with ASW2 structural period K and is found in the form of occupation on and dug into a reddish brown old soil on top of the gravels. This occupation is in evidence in several of the sondages and indicates that it covered an already extensive area (more than 18 hectares) (Deraniyagala, pers. comm.). In ASW2 three superimposed phases of insubstantial structures were found, partially sheltered by an outcrop of gneiss boulders on the south. The latest of these structures took the form of a circle of postholes, 2.5 m in diameter, with another line of postholes extending towards it on one side. Finds associated with this period include typical Black and Red burnished ware, some sherds with scratched graffiti, iron slag and iron artefacts, and bones of cattle. There are several radiocarbon dates, both from the earlier sondages and from ASW2. The former samples suggest that, taking the site as a whole, the period may well go back as far as c. BC 800 and continue until c. BC 450. The ASW2 samples agree with this long time span, although the earliest dates obtained so far suggest that the period extends from c. BC 600–450.

Period J. Early Historic 1 (BC 450–350)

The succeeding period witnessed a modest expansion of the site to c. 26 hectares (Deraniyagala, pers. comm.). In ASW2 it coincides with structural period J and contains five further structural phases, still involving circular huts, but now constructed with larger timber posts and having more deeply dug postholes. In the second building phase a circular structure of c. 5 m was encountered, with a circular pit of 1.25 m diameter beside it. This pit was filled with ash and sealed

Fig. 9.5.   Burial pit in ASW2, period J (photograph Coningham).

with red grit (Fig. 9.5). On excavation it was found to contain an iron arrowhead, a small copper alloy object, a polished rubbingstone, three Black and Red ware cups with small holes bored in their bellies, and three other vessels with graffiti scratched on them. Although no bones were found this assemblage is strongly suggestive of South Indian Iron Age burials of the Megalithic series, and particularly reminiscent of examples excavated at Pomparippu and at Maski. From the third structural phase comes the first of a series of pit hearths or furnaces. Slag continues to occur. In the fourth building phase a replacement circular house had a diameter of 5.5 m with a line of four posts in the centre, conjecturally for timber roof supports (Fig. 9.6). The absence of wattle and daub in this and the subsequent period I is noticeable, in contrast to later periods; this suggests that roofs and walls were covered with palm leaves or grass.

The pottery of this period is still dominated by Black and Red burnished ware, but some relatively fine grey ware also occurs. Iron, copper and slag occur, as well as disc beads of paste, horse bones and styli (or arrowheads) of bone and ivory. The presence of waste and finished products of conch shell, iron ore, amethyst and quartz indicates a major expansion of trade and the increasing role

Fig. 9.6. Plan of part of a circular house from ASW2, period J (photograph Coningham).

of Anuradhapura at the centre of manufacturing and distribution. A further important find is of four potsherds scratched with portions of Brahmi inscriptions, cut in ill-formed but nonetheless convincing letters. Despite the appearance of Brahmi inscriptions of potsherds, the remaining features of the material culture remain largely as in the previous period, and still deserve to be equated with the Peninsular Iron Age complex. The radiometric determinations for this period are somewhat unclear, and offer dates between BC 450 and 350 (Deraniyagala dates his equivalent period to BC 600–500).

Period I. Early Historic 2 (BC 350–275)

The fourth period, coinciding with ASW2 structural period I, represents a major expansion of the settlement which now occupies an area of more than 66 hectares, an increase of some 60 per cent (Deraniyagala, pers. comm.). In ASW2 the round timber structures of the earlier period are now replaced by oblong ones cardinally oriented, of which the period witnessed no less than eight phases of construction and reconstruction. In the first phase a single room of 5.7 m^2 was found, defined by

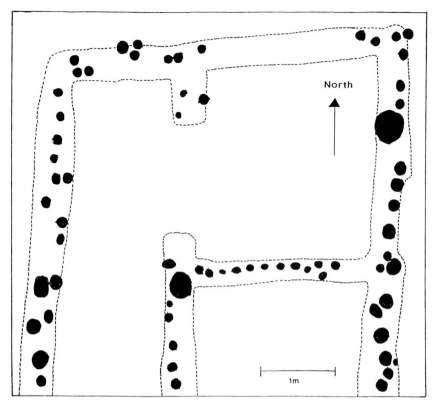

Fig. 9.7.   Plan of part of a rectangular house, ASW2, period I.

post holes and wall slots. During the fourth phase the structure was substantially enlarged to cover 40m². The original first-phase room was retained at the core of the house but another room was built on to its northern wall; a verandah or corridor was added to the western walls of both rooms (Fig. 9.7). Although much of the structure remains unexcavated under the southern side of the pit, it is interesting to note that the configuration of inner rooms and connecting verandah is one of the key units of both historic and contemporary Sinhalese architecture. This example from the fourth century BC may therefore represent a prototype. The walls of the oblong buildings were made of wattle and daub spread over post and stake alignments. The roofs may have been made of grass or palm, but in the fourth phase kiln-fired tiles appear for the first time.

Period I is dated between the mid-fourth century BC and the last quarter of the third century BC (Deraniyagala dates his equivalent period to BC 500–250). It also represents a watershed as far as the position of Anuradhapura in inter-regional trade networks is concerned. The houses are associated with quantities of waste and finished products of garnet, amethyst and quartz from the uplands; iron ore from sites at least fifty miles away; mother of pearl, cowrie and conch shells from the west coast; and ivory and horn from the surrounding forests. More exotic finds of lapis lazuli from Afghanistan or Pakistan and carnelian from Gujarat were also recovered. Rouletted ware occurs alongside the earlier fine grey ware and indeed appears to have developed from it. A greyware bowl portrays a sea-going vessel with a high prow and stern, a single mast and double steering oar at the stern. Five Brahmi inscriptions on potsherds, and five ivory and bone styli were also recovered. ASW2's earliest coins also occur towards the end of the period. They are of a copper alloy and bear a single arched hill or caitya.

This period of urban development at Anuradhapura may now be compared with that of the Early Historic city states of the Ganges plains and other parts of peninsular India. These are in many cases surrounded by great moats (technically referred to as *parikha*) and ramparts (*vapra*), surmounted by walls (*prakara*). A recent series of sondages on the southern side of the Citadel mound of Anuradhapura have exposed part of an 8 m high sequence of earthen ramparts and capping walls (Coningham, 1993). The earliest phase is represented by a 2.5 m thick inside toe of a rampart of reconstituted reddish-brown earth and bedrock. This soil is presumed to have been the spoil of a ditch or moat to the immediate south, which still awaits excavation. The height and width of the rampart was then increased by a further 0.50 m thick layer of mixed reddish-brown earth and bedrock. A third phase of construction increased the height of the toe of the rampart to 3 m and its width to 13 m. The first phase was artefactually sterile, the second contained minor inclusions of fragments of tile and black and red ware, the third phase contained also rouletted ware. From this evidence it appears that the first rampart was constructed not later than our period I. A contour survey has shown that the ramparts enclosed a cardinally oriented rectangular area of c. 100 hectares. The later city phases, from period G onwards, may indicate that the city was subdivided into blocks by a series of cardinal roads: the cardinally oriented buildings encountered in period I may be the first evidence of the introduction of such a layout. Until the discovery of these features, datable to between the mid-fourth century BC and the last quarter of the third century BC, the most southerly identified walled urban complexes were those of Dhanyakataka on the river Krishna in Andhra Pradesh and Banavasi in North Kanara district of Karnataka (see above pp. 146 and 140). With the extension of the distribution to Sri Lanka it is now clear that the so-called 'second' emergence of urbanism and complex societies in South Asia was not just the result of Mauryan imperial conquest, nor exclusively a northern phenomenon.

Periods H and G. Early Historic 3 and 4 (BC 275–225 and BC 225–150)

The two succeeding periods (coinciding with ASW2 structural periods H and G) represent the florescence of the early settlement, with the site increasing in area by a further 4.7 per cent to its maximum extent of c. 71 hectares (Deraniyagala,

Fig. 9.8.   Clay sealing inscription from ASW2, period H, scale 1/1 (photograph Coningham).

pers. comm.). The sondages on the southern rampart show that a fourth, brick-built, stage was constructed during this period; the toe of the rampart was increased to 4.75 m in height and to over 15 m in width.

The domestic structural phases of periods H and G are subdivided into two main parts, the earlier, H, datable to c. BC 275–c. 225, and the later, G, from c. BC 225–AD 150 (Deraniyagala dates the two structural phases as apparently constituting a single period, from BC 250–AD 100). The first building phase of the former represents an anomaly in comparison to other periods and phases. No house remains occurred, and the only structural features encountered were nine shallow troughs cut into the subsoil. All are perfectly oriented east–west. They are not all exactly contemporary, but appeared to have been phased. The troughs were filled with wood and then burned, the heat oxidizing and reducing the surrounding soil. Their sections suggest that they were filled in almost immediately after a single activity of burning. Considering their short exposure they produced a disproportionately high concentration of special finds, including beads, iron, rouletted ware, mica, a conch shell, pottery and a clay sealing with Brahmi inscription (Fig. 9.8) (see below pp. 178–79). They are unlike any domestic hearths or furnaces encountered during the excavation, and initially it seemed tempting to interpret them as cremation sites, since their size and shape were almost exactly anthropomorphic. However, it seems more probable that they had some specialized industrial use, and one may note that similar trough furnaces have been found in early historic excavations in India.

Normal occupation of the site continues in the succeeding period G with a sequence of five rebuildings of houses of the same plan. These structures represent the first use of bricks and limestone blocks. The best preserved structure is the final one consisting of a brick-paved floor, covering 16 m², with three large ceramic vessels sunk in it. The pavement's western edge was defined by a brick wall. Beyond the wall a narrow lane separates the structure from a further series of foundations to its west, probably representing another compound. This lane is the first indication in the excavation of the wider division of the city into blocks separated by streets or lanes. The area to the south and east of the paved room consisted of a north–south range of four cells. The walls were constructed of stakes with a plaster coating and whitewash. The building was roofed with ceramic tiles.

Finds from this period included rouletted ware, black slipped wares with an as yet undefined Hellenistic affinity, pottery of Arikamedu type 10, and glass. Varieties of coinage multiplied during this period, with the following types in evidence (in order of antiquity): triple arched hills, elephant and svastika, Buddhist cakram, mini Laksmi and Laksmi coins. The majority of the prestigious finds were found within the paved area: they included imported pottery, semi-precious stones, conch shells, horn, ivory and whale-bone. Although Brahmi inscriptions were still found at the opening of the period, their absence in succeeding phases combined with finds of bone and whale-bone book-covers suggests that the writing medium had now changed. The glass, Eastern Hellenistic or Indo-Greek black slipped ware, Arikamedu type 10 pottery and a carved ivory mirror base all belong to the Hellenistic culture complex which was generally prevalent in western Asia at this time. The appearance of the Tree and Svastika coins early in this period may provide some archaeological corroboration of the Mahavamsa's record of the bringing of a scion of the original Bodhi tree from Bodh Gaya to Anuradhapura by Sanghamitta, the daughter of the Mauryan ruler Asoka.

Period F. The opening of the Anuradhapura period

The final stage of the Early Historic period is represented in the ASW2 excavations by structural phase F, and marks the beginning of the golden age of the city. Numismatic and ceramic evidence combine to suggest a date for the construction of this phase in the first half of the third century AD and its conclusion in the sixth century AD. The preceding experiments in brick and limestone construction culminated in the extensive use of ashlar slabs and pillars of gneiss. The single structure encountered in ASW2 was a square hall comprised of five rows of five such pillars. Each was 4.6 m long, 0.25 m wide and 0.20 m thick. The portion exposed above the floor level was dressed and plastered whilst the portion below was left undressed. The building was oriented on cardinal axes.

Other Early Historic settlements in Sri Lanka

The known settlements of the Early Historic period appear to be divided into two clear categories, urban and rural. It is also clear that rather than forming a distinct cultural horizon, the Sri Lankan Megalithic sites straddle the Iron Age and Early Historic city sites. The twenty two known megalithic cemeteries vary greatly in appearance; consisting of either extended burials, pit burials, cairn circles or cist burials (Seneviratne 1984). Pomparippu covered 4 acres and contained an estimated 8,000 burial urns, while Vadigawewa contained only 15 burial cists. In date some of the artefacts from Pomparippu belong to the Early Historic period while the radiocarbon dates from Ibbankatuva are somewhat earlier (Deraniyagala 1992, 734). Such cemeteries are probably the most obvious markers of the rural settlements, which due to monsoon climate, use of organic building materials and density of scrub or jungle cover are almost invisible. Indeed the obvious correlations between megalithic cemeteries, irrigation tanks and early Buddhist viharas suggest at least an early interdependence or transition between the two.

Although recorded and investigated for many decades, a large amount of data has been recovered from two major excavations carried out in the past twenty years. Pomparippu was excavated for a single season by members of the University of Pennsylvania and Sri Lankan Archaeological Department in 1970 (Begley *et al.*, 1981). Finds included paste beads, copper bracelets, seven quartz microliths, iron objects, a spear head, five kohl sticks and possibly a single bell. Unfortunately no radiometric dating material was obtained, but the bell and kohl sticks suggest that some urn burials date between the first quarter of the third century BC and the latter half of the second century AD. Ibbankatuva was excavated between 1983 and 1990 for five seasons by members of KAVA and the Universities of Kelaniya and Peradeniya; the report is awaited (Fig. 9.9). There are four radiocarbon dates clustering between the late fourth century BC and the mid to late seventh century BC (Deraniyagala 1992, 734). Finds included iron, copper, gold and carnelian, agate, quartz, ivory, glass and gilt beads (Bandaranayake 1992).

The cemeteries provide the bulk of the available evidence for rural settlement during this period, although other surveys, such as that of the University of Jaffna in the Jaffna peninsula yielded eighteen Early Historic and Megalithic sites (Ragupathy 1987). Further evidence has come from large-scale development projects, such as the Samanalawewa dam project in the central highlands, where a single iron-processing site has been identified, dating from the fourth century BC, along with many later such sites (Juleff 1990). Similarly the expansion of Colombo has led to the discovery of at least four sites yielding Black and Red burnished ware in the Kelaniya valley (Seneviratne, 1984).

Our second category of sites, major or urban settlements, appears to have been

Fig. 9.9.   Ibbankatuva, megalithic graves (photograph Coningham).

more thoroughly investigated than the rural category, with excavations at Kantarodai, Ambalantota, Mantai and Tissamaharama. With the addition of a suspected major settlement in the vicinity of the present Kelaniya temple, these four sites represent the island's major proto- and early historic centres.

Kantarodai consists of a 2 m high mound covering some 25 hectares, situated in the centre of the Jaffna peninsula. It is located in a belt of fertile paddy land and is near a major tank, the Kantarodai *kulam*, of some 40 acres. It was excavated by members of the Sri Lankan Archaeological Department and the University of Pennsylvania (Orton 1993). A ceramic sequence remarkably similar to that of Arikamedu was identified, with a pre-rouletted ware period, subdivided into earlier 'megalithic' and later pre-rouletted ware phases, and followed by a rouletted ware period. The pre-rouletted ware period is dated by the excavators to between c. BC 480 and BC 130, and includes finds of black and red ware, fine grey ware (from the very early levels), bronze and iron. The succeeding period is dated between c. BC 100 and BC 10, and yielded in addition to Black and Red and fine grey wares, rouletted ware, Arikamedu type 10 pottery, postulated Eastern Hellenistic wares, glass and semi-precious stone beads, a carnelian intaglio depicting Nike, coral blocks and Lakshmi plaques. This second period appears to be contemporary with the adjacent Buddhist complex of Kantarodai. Brahmi graffiti are reported on sherds of the rouletted ware period. Whether they occur in the earlier period is not clear. Beads were found in all stages of manufacture, and included imported lapis lazuli and carnelian. Details of coins recovered in the 1970 excavations have not been fully published, but they include silver and copper punchmarked, Buddhist cakram, elephant and svastika, tree and svastika, Indo-Roman, maneless lion coins and Laksmi plaques. The faunal subsistence pattern appears to be similar to that of Anuradhapura, with both domestic and wild species represented.

Mantai, the historical port of Mahatittha, is an 8 m high mound covering some 30 hectares on the northwest coast, just opposite the southern tip of Mannar island. The location of the city at the crucial break-of-bulk point between the Middle East and Far East, and between the east and west coasts of India can be interpreted as fundamental for the role of Sri Lanka in international trade and must have been one of the prime reasons for the evolution of the site. Environmentally this major settlement is located in an arid zone, but it is only some 10 km from one of the largest irrigation tanks in Sri Lanka, the Giant's tank with an extent of 7.75 hectares. Much of the mound is enclosed by a second to fourth century AD cardinally oriented double moat in the shape of a horseshoe, with the medieval temple of Tirukketisvaram standing at the centre of the site. Several earlier excavations were made, but have not been published: it was more recently excavated by members of the Archaeological Department of Sri Lanka and the Mantai Project in 1980–84 (Carswell and Prickett 1984).

The earliest occupation is indicated by remains of a mesolithic hunting camp, in the form of a scatter of microlithic tools, and animal and fish bones, at the bottom of the mound sequence. Following a hiatus the excavators divide the periods thereafter into early historic, intermediate and early medieval: the absence of an iron age or equivalent period is noteworthy. Although the later periods occupy some 7 m of deposits, the early historic is represented only by 1 m depth. It contained quantities of rouletted ware, postulated eastern hellenistic ware, beads, slag, metal objects, ivory, shell bangles, tree and svastika coins and Laksmi plaques. Elephant and svastika, maneless lion and Indo-Roman coins are also known from the site.

Mahagama, the capital of the southern sub-kingdom of Ruhuna, first mentioned in the Mahavamsa as the seat of Mahanaga, the brother of the ruler at Anuradhapura, Devanampiya Tissa (c. BC 250–210), has been identified with the modern town of Tissa. The site is a 6 m high mound covering a considerable area. As in the case of Anuradhapura it is surrounded by an outer zone of monasteries and four large tanks, of which the largest, Tissawewa, covers some 600 acres. The chronicles record that the southern province continued to expand until its ruler Dutthagamani (BC 161–137) defeated Elara, the king of Anuradhapura, and installed himself in the northern capital. The city remained an important administrative centre for successive independent or Anuradhapura-backed regimes until the collapse of the Dry Zone civilization. The site has been investigated for over a century and finds included rouletted ware, Black and Red ware, Brahmi graffiti on pottery, Laksmi plaques, elephant and svastika, tree and svastika coins, Indo-roman and copper punchmarked coins (Parker 1909). As yet there is no clear evidence of any Iron Age occupation. Currently excavations are in progress by members of the Sri Lanka Archaeological Department and KAVA.

Ambalantota, also on the southern coast, was investigated by the Archaeological Department in the 1960s. This site has been identified as the historic Mahanagahula, a twelfth-century royal capital of southwest Ruhuna, but excavations have revealed a considerable depth of Early Historic occupation. Finds included rouletted ware and Black and Red ware. A hoard of over 25,000 Indo-Roman coins was discovered near the site in 1985 (Silva 1988, 9).

Accompanying aspects of early Sri Lankan cities

Early evidence of the use of irrigation works in Sri Lanka

We have had occasion to notice in several earlier chapters of this book that various types of irrigation played a part in the development of early historic cities and agriculture in South Asia. Just how large a part this was, or how significant in terms of the development of the state, has still to be objectively established. It is perhaps not necessary to state that the scale of the works, as far as can be ascertained, was for the most part decidedly smaller than that of comparable works of the medieval period. The situation was probably much the same in Sri Lanka, where the surviving evidence, for one reason or another, is clearer and more comprehensive than in other parts of South Asia (Brohier 1934). This is partly because of the greater volume of historical or inscriptional data, and partly because once the water management system in the dry zone collapsed large agglomerations of people were no longer possible and the entire system was overgrown by the jungle rather than being reused or demolished.

The city of Anuradhapura offers a clear example of the role of irrigation in an urban context, of the evident antiquity of certain tanks and their continuous existence down to modern times. Anuradhapura is located in the North Central Province of Sri Lanka and in the island's dry zone. It has an annual rainfall of 127 cm from the northeastern monsoon, between October and February, and a distinct water deficit throughout the rest of the year. As the water catchments of many of the province's rivers are in the rain shadow of the southwestern monsoon, most become shallowly linked pools during the summer months. The only other perennial or semi-perennial water sources available are natural 'cisterns' in rocky outcrops, small natural shallow pools or villus (*vila*), limited to the western part of the province, and freshwater lenses in unconsolidated sand along the western seaboard (Deraniyagala, 1992, 372). In view of this it has been calculated that the province has a carrying capacity of no more than c. 0.4 individuals per square kilometre, using natural resources (ibid., 412). It should also be noted that widespread and destructive flooding is common during the northeastern monsoon.

It is obvious that in order to support large sedentary communities a degree of water management is necessary to overcome the summer deficit and winter surplus and regulate the flow for watering of people, animals and crops. There is either of two techniques to do so, first to conserve a proportion of the surplus rainfall by damming valleys with an embankment or bund, thus creating a surface drainage tank; and second to divert water to tanks from other tanks by the use of channels. It is to be expected that the former was the simpler and earlier of the two techniques and that the latter was a later development. In the absence of archaeological evidence it is necessary to refer to textual sources for further data regarding this topic.

During the initial colonization of the island it is recorded that a number of settlements were established in the northern part of the dry zone by Vijaya and his ministers. Among these it is recorded that Tambapanni (Dipavamsa 9. 34), Anuradhagama and Upatissa (Mahavamsa 7, 43–44) were all built on the banks of rivers, evidently so as to be near water sources which could be manipulated. The first reference to the management of water resources is found in the description of the refounding of Anuradhapura by prince Anuradha, a generation later. The Mahavamsa states that he settled there and built a tank and a palace to the south of it (9. 11). Pandukabhaya, Anuradha's great-nephew and Devanam-piya Tissa's grandfather, further developed the settlement by enlarging it to become his capital, and at the same time enlarging its water supply systems. He had a natural pond near the city deepened and renamed *Jayavapi*, Victory tank (9, 59–60), and also had the Abhaya tank constructed (9, 88). The latter may be identified with the modern Bassavakulam, which is situated at the southwest corner of the city, from the discovery of a tenth-century inscription on its bund referring to it as the *Abhayavapi* (Fig. 9.10). The identification of prince Anuradha's tank or the *Jayavapi* is more difficult; however, Parker (1909, 361) suggested that it might be identified with the Tissawewa. He based this partly on the discovery of a natural pool in its bed, prior to its repair and refilling, and partly because the fifth-century AD channel feeding water from the Kalawewa to the Tissawewa was named the Jaya Ganga. He also suggested that this tank was enlarged c. BC 250, during the reign of Devanampiya Tissa, and renamed after that king. The Nuwarawewa was an even later construction, being built, according to Parker, in the early part of the first century BC (ibid., 364–65).

Archaeologically there is also evidence that significant changes occurred in the watertable at Anuradhapura in early historic times. During period I at ASW2 the shallow wells and watering holes of the two previous periods, cut only to the underlying gravels, were replaced by a deep well cut through the underlying occupation levels, the gravels and some 2 m into bedrock. This may have been as

Fig. 9.10. Anuradhapura, Bassavakulam tank from the embankment (photograph Coningham).

a result of a drop in the watertable. This development is accompanied by a change in the soil matrix from humus-rich reddish-brown earth to a sterile grey soil. It is hypothesized that this change was due to the construction of large tanks near the city and the subsequent retention of the water which otherwise would have passed directly into the watertable. A similar pattern has been found in localized watertables in the Eastern province since the Mahaweli irrigation project started reclaiming abandoned tanks (Sirisena, pers. comm.).

The picture that we gain from all these data is that there was probably some water management already during the very early part of the settlement of Sri Lanka, and that this received two major boosts: first during the reign of Pandukabhaya, and then during the time of Devanampiya Tissa. This is evident from the increase in the size of individual tanks and from their proliferation. While the natural pools or villus (*vila*) in the province cover an average size of 2 acres, the Abhayavapi covers 225 acres, the Tissawewa 396 acres and the Nuwarawewa 3,180 acres (Parker 1909, 360, 364, 400). That the water was supplied not only for men and animals, but also for crops cannot be doubted. This becomes increasingly apparent in the inscriptions of the last century BC and early centuries AD, when many references to tanks (*vapi*, *vava*), and irrigation channels (*adi*, *ali*) may be found. There is also evidence for rice in the early levels of the citadel at Anuradhapura. At ASW2 the earliest examples of carbonized rice grains and quantities of rice husk as temper in roof tiles come from period I, while Deraniyagala recovered rice husk temper in the 1969 Gedige excavation from stratum 3B onwards, that is from c. BC 500 (Deraniyagala 1990b, 266–9).

However, the textual and archaeological evidence does not clearly indicate, apart from the basic premise that without water management no large settlements could exist in the dry zone, how far the role of irrigation was in any way fundamental to the development of the cities and state in Sri Lanka, nor does it appear to validate the claim that irrigation was the hallmark of a 'hydraulic' society and state. Water management was of course carried out at two levels in the dry zone, the monumental tanks and channels necessary for high densities of population in the city, and the vast system of smaller village tanks often covering an average of two to three acres. Whilst at Anuradhapura there were three large tanks by the beginning of the Christian era, a survey of North Central province identified just under 3,000 village tanks (Brohier 1934, II,2). Although the water management of urban areas appears to have been a kingly duty, that of the rural areas was probably a more local affair which in course of later centuries might in some cases also become a receiver of royal support and patronage. Thus the picture we gain from Sri Lanka is largely parallel to that inferred for India and from Kautilya, on which we comment in Chapters 10 and 11. We may recall Romila Thapar's sensible assessment of the limited role of irrigation in determining the character of society as a whole in these contexts (Thapar 1984, 75).

The early use of writing and inscriptions

As we have seen the recent excavations at Anuradhapura have yielded a substantial body of important data relating to the rise of the city and its absolute chronology. They have also provided remarkable evidence for the appearance and early use of writing. The first report of this work was by Deraniyagala, to whom credit for the discovery must be given (Deraniyagala 1990c). It has been confirmed by the current Sri Lankan British excavations. Inscriptions on pottery begin during the course of period J, which is dated by radiocarbon to between BC 450 and BC 350, if not earlier (as suggested by Deraniyagala 1992, 739–48). The earliest indication comes from the first phase of this period, but it is only a single letter; other examples come from later phases: the first fragments of full inscriptions occur in the uppermost, fourth and fifth, phases (Fig. 9.11). This would indicate that the use of writing began some two centuries earlier than the first datable inscriptions currently known from any other part of South Asia. The inscriptions are found on sherds of local pottery, being throughout scratched with a sharp point after firing, and as such almost all are incomplete. They are

Fig. 9.11. Early Brahmi inscriptions on potsherds, from Anuradhapura ASW2:
1 and 2. period J.5 (c. BC 370); 3. period I.5 (c. BC 300); 4. period G.5 (c. AD
100) (photographs Coningham) (1:1).

also regrettably short, none of those discovered in ASW2 to date is of more than six syllables, and many consist of only one or two syllables. There can however be little doubt that these single or double letters or syllables are parts or inscriptions, and are not to be confused with a second series of signs which are less certainly letters. The script in all cases appears to be an early stage of the Indian Brahmi alphabet, written from left to right. With one or two problematic exceptions the language, wherever enough letters are present to make identification possible, appears to be Prakrit, that is an early Middle Indo-Aryan language rather than a Dravidian or other language. Probably even the originally complete inscriptions were short and apparently often consisted of a single name, sometimes given in the dative case. The indications of an early form of Tamil, such as those discovered at Arikamedu, belonging to the early centuries AD and already employing a number of specially adapted letters, are quite absent from the Anuradhapura inscriptions. Taken as a series they show a clear development from larger and more crudely formed letters at the beginning to smaller and more regularly formed letters at the end of the series. The latest well-stratified inscriptions probably belong to the first two centuries of the Christian era. Of special interest is the clay sealing from one of the trough pits in period H (Fig. 9.8). This reads 'Magaha, the *Purumaka*, son of Tisa', and appears to have belonged to a person who styled himself in the same way and who dedicated a cave at Mihintale to the Buddhist Sangha. As this cave is one of a group assigned by Paranavitane to the final decades of the third century BC, the sealing of Magaha dating to perhaps a decade or two earlier offers a striking example of history and radiocarbon dating nearly coinciding.

After the early centuries AD the inscribed potsherds decline in frequency. This decline coincides with the increasing use of palm-leaf manuscripts, attested in the excavations by the first appearance of ivory manuscript covers designed to protect the leaves of this material.

In Chapter 10 we shall compare the results of this closely stratified excavation with our hypothesis regarding the 'prehistory' of the Brahmi script in South Asia. Briefly, following the lead of Buhler and Winternitz, we propose that the early use of the borrowed, and at first only partly adapted, script was primarily for mercantile purposes. In the course of time the use of writing was extended to include various official and state purposes; it was almost certainly at this time that it was elaborated and refined by the North Indian grammarians. We infer that it was only centuries later employed for the copying and transmission of religious texts. It seems reasonable to see in the early pots, inscribed with owners' marks and names, the earliest stage of this process, augmented around the mid-third century BC by official use in the production of seals and sealings. As and when it becomes possible to divide up chronologically the mass of cave epigraphs in Sri Lanka it may be possible to elaborate the hypothesis into other spheres of activity.

It should be recalled that in the Anuradhapura excavations a parallel series of graffiti of a non-scriptual character is found, also scratched on local pottery. These signs are generally single, and show numerous similarities to the incised graffiti found on the Black and Red pottery of the Megalithic graves and associated settlements throughout peninsular India, as well as in Sri Lanka. The earliest of these graffiti more or less coincide with the first structural remains in period K, and are thus prior to the earliest definitely identifiable inscriptions in period J. The graffiti continue side by side with the inscriptions, up to and even beyond the latest inscribed potsherds.

The graffiti thus appear to represent a form of non-scriptual pottery marking, perhaps of owners' marks, antedating the earliest inscriptions, and analogous to and even sharing many of the same motifs as those found on the Black and Red ware of the peninsular Megalithic graves. It is interesting to note that from the excavation at ASW2 out of some 250 examples of graffiti no fewer than 46 are variants or portions of a single complex mark (which the excavators dubbed the 'dominant sign'). The sign consists of two elements, an angular sign resembling the Brahmi letter *ma* but of a type not found in early Sri Lankan Brahmi inscriptions, placed inside an open pot-shaped sign, in some cases with double or triple branched ends. This sign occurs in the excavated area repeatedly from structural phases J1 through to the end of period G, that is from c. BC 450 to c. AD 200.

The early use of coinage in Sri Lanka

Unlike the early occurrence of inscriptions at Anuradhapura, the appearance of coinage is more in conformity with our general expectations. The study of the coins from our current excavations is still incomplete, and what we now write must be regarded as somewhat tentative. It may well be that the fuller study will allow considerably greater precision in dating and in typological development.

The earliest coins appear in the final stage of period I, structural phase I.8, i.e. c. BC 275. Thereafter coins occur more or less continuously throughout the occupation. The great majority of the coins of the earlier periods are of copper, although rarely silver punchmarked coins are also found. Unfortunately so far these latter are not from well-stratified contexts. The indications are therefore that coinage only became at all current around the time of Mahinda's mission to Sri Lanka, and of the expansion of North Indian, or more precisely Mauryan, influence there (Fig. 9.12).

A total of 48 coins were recovered from periods I, H, G and F (structural periods I, H, G and F). From table 9.1 their periodised distribution is clear. The first coin was recovered in a well-stratified context in I.8, i.e. the youngest phase of period I. It is a small square copper plate with a single indistinct sign in the centre of the obverse face. The sign appears to be a single arched hill. During the succeeding period H, similar sized coins occurred, with a triple arched hill in the centre of the obverse. From period G come a wider variety of square and circular

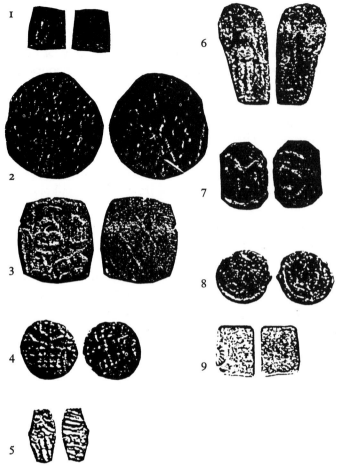

Fig. 9.12.   Early coins from Anuradhapura ASW2 excavations: 1. copper coin, triple arched hill or caitya; 2. copper coin, elephant and svastika; 3. copper, 'Buddhist cakram' coin; 4. copper, tree and svastika coin; 5. copper, miniature Laksmi plaque; 6. copper, Laksmi plaque; 7. copper, maneless lion; 8. copper, Indo-Roman coin; 9. silver punchmarked coin. (photographs Coningham) (1:1).

copper coins with one or more signs on the obverse, including elephants, trees-in-railings, svastikas-in-railings, and other signs. The earliest example, an elephant and svastika coin, was recovered from the oldest phase of this period. From the succeeding phase, G.2, a total of nine coins were recovered. They consisted of the latest occurrence of a triple arched hill, two elephant and svastika, three unidentified signs and svastika, and the earliest three examples of tree and svastika coins. G.4 yielded a further two tree and svastika coins, and one 'Buddhist cakram' coin, the latter perhaps representing a Pandyan issue. The youngest phase of period G, G.5, yielded a mixture of coins with the older issues of elephant and svastika, tree and svastika, and unidentified signs and svastika coins, alongside the earliest examples of punchmarked coins and Laksmi plaques. The latter appear to be divided into two series, one minute and the other full sized. The largest coin collection came from the foundations of the pillared hall of period F. A total of 19 coins were recovered. They consisted of one tree and svastika, seven punchmarked coins, eight full sized Laksmi plaques, one Indo-Roman, and two maneless lion coins.

Generally this sequence appears to correspond with that suggested by Codrington (1924), although our series is constructed from an excavation, and the latter from collections. The one contradiction is that Codrington rightly hypothesized that the earliest Sri Lankan examples would be silver punchmarked coins. At Anuradhapura, ASW2, these do not occur until structural period G.5. They are also very worn with few symbols distinguishable. Although there is a possibility that earlier examples exist in the Citadel (although not so far found by either Deraniyagala or the British team) it is also possible that, as Indian imports, they may have come into Sri Lanka only at a later date.

Codrington's chronology for the coins also corresponds fairly closely with that of ASW2, although the latter is based on a combination of ceramic, numismatic and chronometric sources. He dated the punchmarked coins in India between the fifth century BC and AD 300, but believed that the Sri Lankan examples were later imports; the elephant and svastika coins to the second century BC, the tree and svastika coins and Laksmi plaques to the beginning of the Christian era, the maneless lion coins to c. the third century AD, and the Indo-Roman coins mainly between the last half of the fourth century and the first half of the seventh century AD. In ASW2 the earliest elephant and svastika coins occur c. BC 225, followed in about the middle of the second century BC by the tree and svastika coins and Buddhist cakram coin. The latter was identified by Codrington as representing an early Pandyan issue. Miniature and regular Laksmi plaques first occurred about the beginning of the Christian era. The evidence from period F, the pillared hall, similarly appears to corroborate Codrington's chronology. We have dated the construction of the monumental building to the first half of the third century AD. As is evident from table 9.1 the first Indo-Roman and maneless lion coins occur in this structure.

It is hoped that with the completion of the study of the many coins from the various recent excavations at the Anuradhapura Citadel site a fuller chronological sequence of these coins will be forthcoming.

The development of civic and religious architecture and art

The civilization of Sri Lanka in the later Early Historic and Medieval periods was distinguished by the remarkable quantity and quality of its monumental architecture, both secular and religious, much of which still survives to this day. As we saw above, the ramparts of Anuradhapura bear evidence of a still earlier construction, and of several subsequent periods of enlargement and raising of

Table 9.1. *Coins from Anuradhapura (ASW2)*

Period	I8	H1	H2	H3	G1	G2	G3	G4	G5	F	Total
Type											
Single hill	1										1
Triple hill				2		2					4
Elephant and Svastika					1	1			1		3
Tree and Svastika						3		2	2	1	8
? and Svastika						3			1		4
'Buddhist Cakram'								1			1
Minute Laksmi plaque									4		4
Laksmi plaque									4	8	12
Silver punchmarked									1	7	8
Indo-Roman										1	1
Maneless lion										2	2
Bull and fish										1	1
Other									2	6	8
Total	1	–	–	2	1	9	–	3	15	26	57

their height. They appear to have been first laid out and constructed around the middle of the fourth century BC, and coincide remarkably with the Mahavamsa's reference to the laying out of the city by an expert learned in *Vastu-sastra* (the science of construction) on behalf of king Pandukabhaya. To the same early date may also be attributed the beginning of the regular, cardinally oriented, plan of the city, its streets and houses.

The beginnings of religious architecture may also be ascribed to the same period, since the Mahavamsa (X.96–102) relates that Pandukabhaya, in laying out his newly created city, established separate areas for numerous groups, for *Brahmanas* (presumably orthodox Hindus), *Niganthas* (*Nirgranthas*, *Jainas*), *Ajivakas*, and orders of *Samanas* and *Paribrajakas* (wandering ascetics, presumably Buddhists). This passage expressly mentions the construction of a temple (*devakula*) for a *Nigantha* (this seems something of a contradiction in terms!). Guruge (1989, 791, Note 76) has pointed to the significance of this passage as revealing the heterogeneous nature of society in the pre-Mahinda era, when Buddhism was only one among many sects. As yet however, we cannot point to archaeological data or actual monuments belonging to this early period, and to find them must remain a target for future field research.

For the more substantial development of Buddhist architecture, however, one must await the time of Devamanpiya Tissa, some two generations later, when the mission of Mahinda led to the establishment of Buddhism as the major religion of the ruler and his people. According to tradition the first stupa to be constructed at Anuradhapura was the *Thuparama Dagaba*, whose foundation dates from the time of Mahinda's visit (i.e. c. BC 246). The present form of the stupa represents the outcome of several later reconstructions. The Mahabodhi tree, a scion of the original tree in Bodh Gaya, was brought from India during Mahinda's lifetime, and established with its associated shrine nearby. From this time or shortly after we find the establishment of the *Mahavihara* (Great Monastery) and some time later of its stupa (the *Mahathupa*). With the contemporary establishment of the *Cetiya vihara* at Mihintale, with its associated monuments, and its large number of natural or partly natural caves, we find the beginnings of the tradition of predominantly Buddhist monumental activity in Sri Lanka, whose record continues and flourishes throughout the later chapters of the Mahavamsa, and even till today. Great interest clearly attends the identification of the *Loha Pasada* or 'Metal palace' originally constructed as a chapter house for the *Mahavihara*, but reputedly transformed into a nine-storeyed palace by king Dutthagamini (c. 100 BC). In the early centuries of the Christian era, both the Jetavana monastery, with its enormous stupa and its extensive ranges of accompanying monastic buildings, and the Abhayagiriya monastery with its still larger stupa and further extensive monuments, were established. Thus we see how at Anuradhapura a whole complex of Buddhist monuments was created during these centuries, and how the city became the centre of a whole outer ring of monasteries and other architectural features.

PART III

THE MAURYAN EMPIRE AND ITS AFTERMATH

CHAPTER 10

THE MAURYAN STATE AND EMPIRE

F. R. ALLCHIN

1. Introduction

The period of Mauryan rule, arising in the aftermath of Alexander the Great's campaigns in northwestern India-Pakistan and his subsequent withdrawal, represents the culmination of the developmental processes which we have witnessed in the previous chapters. We have already discussed in chapters 6 and 7 the stages by which the social and political entities which developed across northern India-Pakistan, involving the emergence of *janapadas* – probably this term implies areas settled, or colonized, by groups who had formerly been or regarded themselves as *janas*, tribes – gave rise to a new phenomenon, in the form of states with cities, centres of population, surrounded by agricultural land and networks of villages. Between the *janapadas* there developed a process of internecine warfare, from which there emerged around BC 350 a dominant metropolitan power, Magadha, with its capital at Pataliputra, achieving for a few decades rule and control over a far larger surrounding area which is generally regarded as deserving the title 'empire'. This process coincides with all sorts of other developments: thus apart from the growth of cities, the Mauryan period witnesses the first appearance in northern India-Pakistan of monumental architecture, stone sculpture and other arts, together with the growing importance of coinage in the economic life, and of writing in all aspects of urban life.

Sources

The sources for reconstructing the Mauryan period are far more numerous and varied than those for the earlier periods. They involve several types of written evidence in addition to archaeological. The first category of written evidence includes indigenous sources. These are almost all of a kind which demands that they are used with great caution, but their value, once they can be accepted, is very considerable. A prime example of such a source is the Arthasastra of Kautilya (Kangle 1960–65; Rangarajan 1992). Tradition has it that this treatise was written by the chief minister of Candragupta Maurya, and although there is no way of proving this, there is equally no good reason to doubt it. Kangle the editor and translator of the text, offers a lengthy and detached discussion of its author and date, and sums up by stating that 'we may therefore conclude that there is no convincing reason why this work should not be regarded as the work of Kautilya who helped Candragupta to come to power in Magadha' (Kangle 1965, vol 3, 59–115, 106). One cannot but be struck by the many close correspondences between the Arthasastra and the two other major sources the Asokan inscriptions and Megasthenes text, and by the many correspondences between it and archaeological or numismatic data. Even so, there is also no reason to doubt that the text may have been added to or amended in later times. We shall make considerable use of the Arthasastra, in spite of such doubts, because in our view a great part of its contents relates directly to the Mauryan period. For this reason we shall for chapters 10 and 11 treat it as effectively a Mauryan document. The early texts of the Pali canon are probably at least in part pre-Mauryan in terms of their composition, but it is generally agreed that they were originally passed down in oral form, and only committed to writing in or after the Mauryan period; a second, later, group of Buddhist canonical texts was probably composed during the Mauryan period and, if these could be identified with any certainty, should provide a useful source. The Puranas provide us with the bare bones of the Mauryan king-list, and offer a minimal chronology which, so long as it can be tied in to events in the world outside, provides some basis for dating (Smith 1957). Another useful, if indirect, source for the time of Asoka is provided by the Ceylon chronicles, to which we have referred particularly in chapter 9.

A second category of written evidence includes references to India and the Mauryans in classical literature. The prime sources are to be found in those authors who wrote concerning Alexander's campaigns in India and their aftermath. Of particular note are the accounts of India by Megasthenes, the envoy of king Seleucus, one of the successors of Alexander, whose lost treatise is preserved in a number of extracts quoted by later Greek writers, such as Arrian and Strabo (McCrindle 1877). Much later, but also not without relevance for the history of the Mauryan period are the records of Chinese Buddhist pilgrims, notably Fa Xian (Fa Hsien) and Xuan Zang (Hsuan-tsang), who travelled to India to visit the Buddhist holy sites and incidentally recorded many observations relating to Asoka's pious acts and his dedication of monuments.

Another prime body of written sources is to be found in contemporary inscriptions. Of these the edicts of Asoka are of the greatest importance because almost alone among early India inscriptions they are datable by internal historical means. Other inscriptions may be assigned to the time of the Mauryans epigraphically or inferentially, among them the Mahasthangarh stone plaque inscription (Sircar 1965, 79–80) and the Sohgaura copper or bronze plaque inscription (Sircar 1965, 82–3), both of which combine a technical terminology which accords to that of the Arthasastra with other features recalling the Asokan inscriptions; a further group includes inscriptions which, although of later date, refer to the Mauryans or to datable events, an example of this class is the Rudradaman inscription at Girnar (Sircar 1965, 175–80), which recalls the repair and enlargement of an irrigation tank constructed four hundred years earlier by Candragupta Maurya and later enhanced by Asoka.

The archaeological sources are more plentiful but still must be handled with due care. For instance, when Asoka placed an inscribed column at the gateway of a stupa or by a monument, it seems reasonable to assume that the stupa or shrine was either already in existence, or was founded in Asoka's time.

Historical summary

The chronology of the Mauryan rulers may be summarily stated as follows:

Candragupta Maurya	c.325–321	– c.297 BC
Bindusara	c.297	– c.272 BC
Asoka	c.272–268	– c.235 BC
Dasaratha	c.235	– c.221 BC
? Brihadratha	?	– c.185 BC

We shall not expand on the history here, for want of space, but readers are directed to reliable sources for further detail, particularly Raychaudhari (1972); Thapar (1961; 1987); Kosambi (1956); Mookerji (1953).

2. The Mauryan state as seen by the Arthasastra

Ideology, social and political institutions

Before reviewing the predominantly archaeological evidence relating to life in Mauryan times, we shall first outline the character of the Mauryan state as it emerges from our literary sources. For further discussion of this subject the reader is recommended to consult Romila Thapar's *From Lineage to State* (1984), where the emergence of the early Indian state is discussed in its wider context. In the present section we shall mainly limit ourselves to a consideration of the Arthasastra's treatment of the state, accepting as we are doing that this text has considerable internal coherence and probably represents the individual, and even somewhat idiosyncratic, views of its author Kautilya. In quoting it we shall sometimes follow the recently published translation of L. N. Rangarajan (1992) which, although in some respects overstepping the bounds of scholarly convention, strikingly succeeds in bringing out the meaning in terms understandable to a modern reader. We shall also on other occasions choose to quote and refer to Kangle's monumental edition and translation. It must be recalled that the Arthasastra was reputedly composed as a textbook to instruct a prince in the art of statecraft: expressly it concludes by stating that

> this treatise has been composed by one who, resenting the misrule of the Nanda kings, rescued this neglected science and used it as a weapon to destroy them and save the kingdom. (15.1.73)

More specifically, tradition asserts that Kautilya's aim was to establish his master Candragupta Maurya as a universal ruler or Cakravarti. As such his text is more prescriptive than descriptive. That he deserves a place as the outstanding political economist of early historic South Asia is universally acknowledged.

The definition of a state is not given in the Arthasastra in the way one might expect, and it is not altogether clear which single term may best be translated by 'state'. But the character of the state which emerges is nevertheless clear and comprehensive. The state is defined in terms of seven constituent elements (*prakritis*), which are listed in order (6.1.1). These are: the king (*svami*); the council of ministers (*amatya*); the territory (*janapada*); the fortified settlements (*durga*); the treasury (*kosa*); the forces (*danda*); and the ally (*mitra*). This formulation was no doubt of recent origin in Mauryan times, although it is evident that it emerged from a line of earlier scholars' works, and subsequently became imbedded in the standard pattern of the '*saptanga*' or seven elements of the state. To understand the elements in the context of the Arthasastra some further commentary is required.

(A) Svami

It may seem strange that for the first element the word *svami*, master, is used in preference to king, but the reality of kingship is nonetheless not in question. The Arthasastra's norm for a state is a kingdom, ruled over by a ruler (*raja*); and in this role the state is also referred to as a kingdom (*rastra*). Elsewhere in the text another type of society is mentioned, *sangha*, union, sometimes translated, perhaps misleadingly as 'oligarchy'. These *sanghas* were evidently tribal societies which still retained something of their older character.

(B) Amatya

The various ministers (*amatya*) and functionaries of the state are described in the Arthasastra, together with the many other grades of officials and civil servants, down to village headmen. The text goes into considerable detail in giving their job descriptions and salaries.

(C) Janapada

The *janapada* (already discussed briefly in chapter 7) is perhaps the most basic element of the state and needs some elucidation. The precise significance of the term is not easy to determine, but it appears to mean territory, settled territory, countryside, country. The *janapada's* importance for the practically minded Kautilya can be gauged from such words as 'all economic activities have their source in the *janapada*' (8.1.29). As we shall see below the *janapada* is a territory which is regarded as ripe for *nivesa*, entering into, settlement or colonization; and ripe for economic exploitation.

(D) Durga

The fourth element is given as *durga*, that which is difficult of access, and may more narrowly be translated as fort. But its usage in the Arthasastra is far wider than what is commonly understood by fort, and indeed it is used for any fortified settlement, including a capital city, any city or administrative headquarters, varieties of border forts and forts in natural fastnesses, mountains or islands, etc. Kautilya uses the technical term without clarifying its relation to the concept of the city. We shall see below (in chapter 11) that the Arthasastra describes in detail the construction of the moats and ramparts of such forts, and gives details of the layout to the plan, gates, streets, allocation of different areas for different communities or purposes, etc.

(E) Kosa

The treasury (*kosa*) is described in detail and instructions for its construction, location, security and staffing are given. The treasury was conceived as one of the elements contained within a fortified city.

(F) Danda

The sixth element, *danda*, also needs clarification. Literally *danda* means a rod or staff, and in the Arthasastra it means force, as well as forces and physical coercion. Hence both the operation of the law and of the army can be included within its scope.

(G) Mitra

The final element is given as *mitra*, friend or ally, and here too its significance for the text is far wider than the word, at first sight, implies. It relates to the whole complex of external relations of a king, and hence to foreign policy. Viewed in this context it can be also referred to as the theory of the circle of states, and thus as a vital aspect of Kautilya's instruction to the would-be successful prince.

Colonization of territory and of cities

It is apparent that in the main the Arthasastra presents a view of a certain stage in the expansion of the early Indian states and their civilization. This is the point which approaches the end of the process of the swallowing up of the smaller by the bigger units, and the achievement of a unified empire holding the many smaller units in a controlled balance. This situation is particularly recognizable in the section of the Arthasastra entitled *janapada nivesa*, settling a territory (2.1):

> The king shall populate the countryside by creating villages on virgin land or by reviving abandoned village sites. Settlement can be effected either by shifting some of the population of his own country or by immigration of foreigners. The settlers in the villages shall mainly be Sudra agriculturalists ... The villages shall be sited so as to provide mutual protection. (2.1.1–3)

The text goes on to instruct the king to establish a progression of larger settlements to serve as the centres for each group of ten, two hundred, four hundred and eight hundred villages. These clearly represent different levels of administrative and fiscal activity, and the apex of the hierarchy, the *sthaniya* or regional centre, is clearly envisaged as a fortified city. On the frontiers of the state the king is also advised to build fortresses to guard the entrances to the kingdom.

Bearing in mind Kautilya's dictum that all economic activities have their source in the *janapada* one can readily appreciate the importance of conquest or colonization of territory and of its economic exploitation. In another part of the text the author discusses the relative merits of land watered by rain or by flowing rivers. He concludes that the latter is to be preferred. In the case of rain-watered land he prefers an area in which two crops per annum can be raised, without too great a use of labour (7.11.3–17). The first aim being to establish agriculture, land grants are to be made to Brahmans and to local officers, while others are allotted land for their lifetime on payment of tax. When new land is to be developed encouragement to the colonists shall be given in the form of grants. In spite of his mention of land grants to Brahmans, Kautilya is inclined to favour the more practical course of settling members of the lower castes because of the benefits (in the form of work and hence wealth production) which flow from them. He repeats the importance of a working population because, 'like a barren cow, a kingdom without people yields nothing'.

In view of the importance Kautilya attaches to agriculture it is interesting to note the various aspects of the subject which are addressed in different parts of the Arthasastra. In the section detailing the duties of the Director of Agriculture (2.24), which read, one may feel, very much as those of his modern Indian counterpart's may do (!), it is clear that the author recognizes the supremacy of environmental and climatic factors in the success of agricultural operations. This approach seems appropriate for a work which envisages the Mauryan empire at its height, when the empire included many different climatic and environmental zones, each with its own features. The Director may not actually engage in the business of getting his hands dirty, but at least he must be educated enough to know the characteristics of different crops, so that he may be able to communicate with the experts who are appointed to advise him. The text envisages a full range of crops. These include two varieties of rice, *vrihi* and *sali*, wheat, barley, *kodrava* (paspalum scrobiculatum), *priyangu* (panicum italicum), some six sorts of pulses or beans, four oilseeds, mustard, sesame, linseed and safflower, various vegetables, herbs and spices. Each should be sown on appropriately selected soils, in areas with the right climate and rainfall. Where rainfall is not satisfactory, irrigation should be resorted to.

Kautilya stresses the importance of increasing agricultural production by means of irrigation, and the king is recommended either to construct irrigation works himself, or to offer inducements to others to do so (2.1.20–24). The almost casual way in which the subject of tank construction for irrigation is introduced certainly does not suggest that this subject occupied a role of pivotal importance in the economy, and we agree with Thapar's assessment.

> That irrigation was a significant variable in social change does not necessarily imply a link between irrigation and despotism but rather suggests a relation between water control and the sources of power among ruling elites. (Thapar 1984, 75)

Elsewhere in the text indications are given of the sophisticated inducements to be offered in this connection. For instance, for building or improving irrigation facilities there shall be exemption from payment of water rates for a given number of years; or again, irrigation tanks may be privately owned, and the owner is free to sell them (3.9.33–36). Also there are details of the customary conduct of irrigation and of fines for its neglect.

Apart from agriculture, suitable areas of the newly colonized land should also be apportioned for pastoralism, and forest areas should be allocated for other productive purposes, royal hunts and for the production of elephants. Forest produce is an important source of revenue and appropriate factories should be established where the materials may be processed before sale. The author frequently reminds the prince that mines are an important source of wealth, and that they constitute a main reason for seeking to conquer new territory. Among the metals referred to are gold and silver, copper, lead, tin, iron and zinc: precious stones are also obtained from mines. Recent research by Craddock has revealed extensive archaeological evidence of mining and metallurgy of the Mauryan period, including remarkably preserved copper, lead and zinc mines, dated by radiocarbon to this period (Craddock *et al.* 1989).

Trade and foreign contacts

We mentioned above the foreign policy of the Arthasastra and its system of establishing sets of relations with neighbouring princes: this system is usually referred to as the circle of states. Its exposition in the text is described by Rangarajan (1992, 542) as 'a brilliant, comprehensive, cohesive and logical analysis of all aspects of relations between states'. The reader wishing to learn more is advised to consult the text itself, through the medium of one of the standard translations. Our present concern is more narrowly with aspects of the subject which are reflected in the archaeological record, and thus we shall pass over foreign relations rather briefly. Suffice it to remark that if Kautilya was indeed the minister of Candragupta Maurya, then it was presumably his conduct of foreign policy, and in particular of his relations with his neighbours in South Asia, which contributed to his success in establishing so large and prosperous an empire.

On the subject of trade the Arthasastra has much to offer. Book 2 contains a mass of detailed information regarding almost every class of economic activity carried on by the state. They include practical details of coinage and exchange, detailed descriptions of weights and measures, and of the apparatus used to weigh goods (we shall discuss these further later in this chapter), as well as details of actual industrial processes, and of the sources of different raw materials. This section therefore refers to many places both within and outside the Mauryan state from which goods or raw materials were obtained. Of the external countries Sri Lanka, Barbara (?), Burma or Sumatra, Pasa (?Persia), Nepal, China, Kapisa and Harahura (Afghanistan), Bahlika (Bactria) and Kamboja (also to the northwest of India) are mentioned. Also on the subject of trade Kautilya is interested in the different routes and methods of travel. He discusses whether land routes are to be preferred to water, and concludes that they are. He prefers the southern routes to the northern ones, because of the wealth of their products and the number of their mines. He prefers roads suitable for carts to those allowing the passage of only pack animals.

3. The imperial structure and the settlement hierarchy

The settlement terminology

It is evident from even the oldest stratum of the Pali canon that already in pre-Mauryan times the settlement hierarchy in the central Ganges valley had developed so as to include at least three main tiers, cities, towns and villages (see chapter 7). The terminology which may be derived from these sources is in some respects surprisingly different from that employed by Kautilya: it seems that the author of the Arthasastra, not unlike some modern social scientist, preferred to coin his own set of special terms for describing settlements viewed as administrative or economic categories, rather than as common settlements. At the head of the pyramid in the Pali canon are cities, for which the most common term is *nagara* (Wagle, 1966, 12–43; Sarao, 1990, 36–47). *Nagara* is further divided into several classificatory levels, suggesting that a further hierarchical division may have divided major cities and capital cities from the main series: thus the term *mahanagara*, great city, is reserved for certain major cities in the Ganges valley; *rajadhaniya nagara* or simply *rajadhani*, capital, for cities which were the seat of a king or other ruler; *mula nagara*, original or root city, apparently also carried a special meaning, although it is not clear exactly what is signified. The simple term *nagara* was the common form, while another term, *nagaraka*, is generally taken to mean small city or perhaps suburb. We also find *sakha nagaraka*, branch city, apparently used in a similar way. A general word which occurs frequently in these texts is *pura*, which probably combines the meaning settlement, in a broad and undefined way, with occasional use in contexts signifying city or town.

There are a number of terms which appear to have been associated with specialized settlements of one kind or another. One is *pattana* which means a port or harbour, generally on the sea, but also sometimes on a river. This is apparently used for an independent settlement, but it may also have been used for a harbour associated with or belonging to a larger settlement. A second term is *puta-bhedana*. The indications are that this too meant a riverside wharf or trading area, and that it was associated with specialized mercantile communities. In the Pali canon Pataliputra is significantly referred to as a *puta-bhedana*, emphasizing its riverine location.

A second major tier in the site hierarchy is represented by another main term in the Pali canon, *nigama*. This is generally taken to mean a settlement somewhere between a city and a village in size, but having a more specific meaning as a market and/or administrative centre, or as a trading community specializing in the manufacture or distribution of a specific commodity (Thapar 1984, 90). *Nigama* often occurs as one of a group, as *gama*, *nigama* and *nagara*, thus suggesting that these refer to three major stages of the settlement hierarchy.

The third major division of the hierarchy is *gama*, the village, then, as ever since, the most numerous class of settlements in South Asia. The Pali canon specifies various categories of village, depending on the materials of which the houses are built – brick, stone or wood; or upon the occupation or caste status of its inhabitants – carpenters, Brahmanas, Candalas, and so on; or on its position in relation to a city, such as near the gates, outside the walls, etc. Villages are also sometimes referred to according to their size, as comprising only one hut, two huts, and so on.

The term *janapada* calls for some further consideration in relation to the hierarchy of settlements in the Pali canon (see also chapter 7). There is a good discussion of its usage and meaning in Wagle (1966, 29–43). At root it seems to have meant something akin to populace or community, but to have acquired a broadly geographical and ethnic meaning which Wagle describes as 'a socio-cultural group, presumably with a territory of their own'. It was probably already an old and well-established word by Mauryan times. It appears that originally it was used to refer to the movement into or colonization of land by tribal groups; but that increasingly during the second half of the first millennium BC such groups settled down and transformed themselves or were transformed into emergent states. Both *janapada* and *mahajanapada* (great *janapada*) appear, in the course of time, to have acquired a quasi-political significance in some contexts. In the end, as we have seen, by the Mauryan period the meaning came to include also the imperial takeover of adjacent independent states and their absorption into the empire.

We noted above that the Arthasastra (Kangle 1963) provides its own perspective on the settlement hierarchy, in that it introduces, in addition to occasional use of common terms, special or technical terms of its own, often with an administrative or fiscal slant (Fig. 10.1). As we saw, the *janapada nivesa* section of the second book (2.1) literally describes the colonization or 'settlement of the countryside'. The text prescribes the establishment of a network of villages (*grama*) each of one hundred to five hundred families of agriculturalists. Groups of such villages were to be served by markets or by administrative or fiscal centres, for ten, two hundred and four hundred villages. Such centres were known respectively as *samgrahana*, *karvatika* and *dronamukha*. A central, district town or settlement, the *sthaniya*, was to be established for each group of eight hundred villages. The term *sthaniya* is apparently used to signify not merely a district headquarters, but also a fortified city.

The following section of the Arthasastra (2.2) discusses the creation of fortified places (*durga*), including the fortification of the *sthaniya* established in the heart of a *janapada*'s territories. We shall discuss this evidence in more detail in the next chapter. It is strange that the Arthasastra does not mention certain common settlement terms, for example *nigama*; but such things apart, the data supplied help to elucidate, from what we take to be a contemporary source, the conception of the hierarchy of settlements within a *janapada*. We shall compare below this evidence with that afforded by archaeology.

The settlement archaeology

It will have become apparent in chapters 6 and 7 that the application of what has been called 'settlement archaeology' to the problem of understanding the early urban development of South Asia is still very much in its infancy. There are indeed a few major studies of early historic settlement development in the Ganges plains, including those of Makkhan Lal (1984a) and Erdosy (1988), for Kanpur and Allahabad districts respectively. There is a real need for further studies of this kind in other districts, in varying environmental settings, for example in the manifestly different environment of eastern Uttar Pradesh and Bihar; and in other areas, outside the Ganges valley, for example in the Northwest Frontier province of Pakistan, and in the Punjab. There is also still much research required to refine the means available for determining what settlements may be ascribed to what actual periods, such as the Mauryan.

The work of Makkhan Lal and Erdosy provides a sound material basis against which to test the indications derived from the literary sources, and confirms the expectation that during the Mauryan period the total settlement hierarchy not only showed an expanding number of larger settlements, but also witnessed the

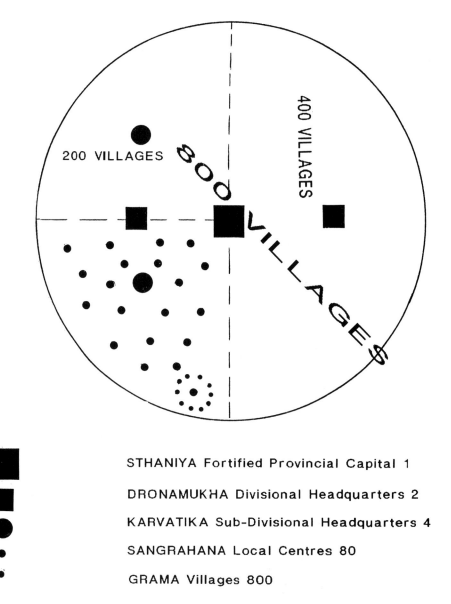

STHANIYA Fortified Provincial Capital 1

DRONAMUKHA Divisional Headquarters 2

KARVATIKA Sub-Divisional Headquarters 4

SANGRAHANA Local Centres 80

GRAMA Villages 800

Fig. 10.1. Diagrammatic representation of administrative and settlement hierarchy of a janapada (after Kautilya).

emergence of distinct networks of settlements, with groupings clustering around the major cities. In Allahabad district comparison of the settlement map of this period (Fig. 7.4) with those of the preceding two (see above Figs 6.2 and 7.3) illustrates the point well: Kausambi remains the only city of its size in the area, but there are now four other cities, all sited on major rivers, and several clusters of villages around larger settlements. In this way a hierarchy of three or four levels can be recognized, and one may speculate on its relationship to the Arthasastra's administrative hierarchy.

The imperial structure from inscriptional sources

There are some topics on which the Arthasastra is sadly lacking. Any straightforward description of the actual, as opposed to theoretically desirable, administrative structure achieved by Candragupta, or of the various cities which occupied different roles, is not even hinted at. As we approach wider aspects of the structure of the state and settlement hierarchy it is interesting therefore to consider the contrast offered by the inscriptions of Asoka, the grandson of Candragupta, who came to rule about a quarter of a century after Candragupta's death (Fig. 10.2).

In his numerous inscriptions, or edicts (*sasana*), Asoka usually uses the title 'King Priyadarsi (piyadassi raja), the beloved of the gods'. He also refers to himself as the Magadhan king (or king of Magadha). The name of the metropolis, Pataliputra, is referred to, evidently in its capital role. There are also references to certain cities as the seats of princes appointed as regional or provincial governors. These are Taksasila (Taxila), Ujjayini (Ujjain), Tosali (near Bhubaneshwara, Orissa), and Suvarnagiri (probably in Karnataka, perhaps Maski). These are thus taken to indicate the headquarters of four provinces. Other cities are mentioned in connection with resident ministers; among them are Kausambi, Samapa (presumably Jaugada in Orissa), and Risila (also in Karnataka, perhaps Brahmagiri). A further inscriptional city is Mahasthangarh whose name is mentioned in the fragmentary small stone inscription as *Pudanagala* (Pundranagara): we agree with Sircar that this inscription should be assigned to the Mauryan period (Sircar 1965, 79).

Further evidence on the structure of the empire can be obtained by plotting the sites of the identified Asokan inscriptions and noticing their proximity to archaeologically recognizable major settlements or cities datable to that period. Among these are Girinagara (Girnar, near modern Junagarh in Saurastra), Sopara (Suppara) on the coastal strip north of Bombay, Kandahar (in Arachosia, Afghanistan, one of the provinces ceded to Candragupta by Seleucus), Kopbal in Karnataka, Virata (Bairat) in Rajasthan, Brahmagiri in Karnataka, Vidisa (near Sanchi in Madhya Pradesh), Varanasi (Banaras), the city near which is situated the famous Buddhist pilgrim spot, Sarnath.

Another interesting line of evidence for the scale of the empire is afforded by references to various neighbouring peoples who are classed as *Aparantas*, 'western borderers'. These include Yonas or Yavanas (Greeks) and Kambojas in the northwest, and such peoples (some perhaps still tribal) as the Andhras, Paradas, Chodas (Cholas), Keralaputras and Satiyaputras in the south. Tamraparni (Sri Lanka) is mentioned also in this context. Of particular significance are Asoka's reference to his armies having earlier conquered

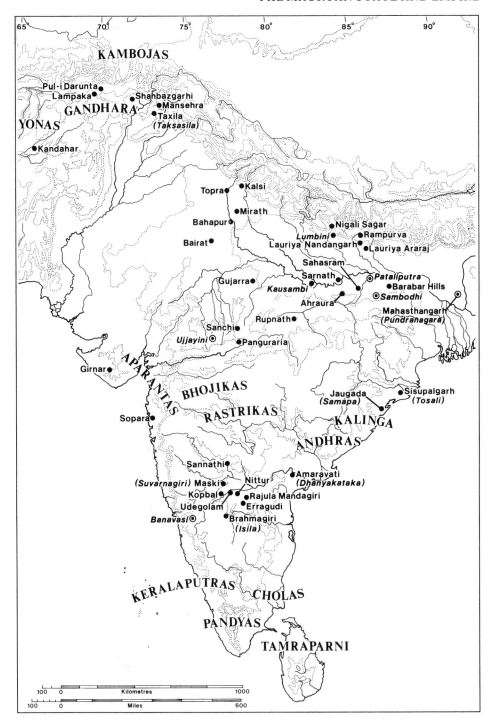

Fig. 10.2. Map of findspots of Asokan edicts; of place-names (in italics) and other tribal or regional names (in large type) occurring in Mauryan inscriptions.

Kalinga, for which he later repented, regretting the loss of life, and the inscriptional reference by Kharavela (c. 1st century BC) to the supposed conquest of Orissa by a Nanda king, whose date can be calculated to be in the fourth century BC. These references demonstrate the active outward thrust of Magadhan imperialism, in both pre-Mauryan and Mauryan times, and the conquest of desirable regions, probably attended by the superimposition of a Kautilyan pattern of settlement. Bearing in mind Kautilya's frequent references to border states one may safely infer that these and similar states or tribal peoples were on the frontiers of the Mauryan empire, though whether within the empire or as its neighbours is not at all clear.

From this review there emerges a view of the extent of the Mauryan empire and of its probable provinces. In the Ganges valley one must conceive the older *mahajanapadas* as now absorbed within the main Magadhan state, or into what we may call its metropolitan province. Beyond that there seem to have been at least four major provincial groupings: (a) in the northwest, the cities of Taxila, Puskalavati and probably the other cities of the Indo-Afghan border regions, comprising the *janapadas* of Gandhara, perhaps Kamboja and others; (b) in Madhya Pradesh (Central India), the cities established in the largely forested zone south of the Ganges valley, such as Ujjain and Vidisa, comprising the *janapadas* of Avanti and probably Cedi; (c) on the east coast, the area of Kalinga including the cities of Tosali and Samapa; and (d) in the southern Deccan a whole series of settlements including Suvarnagiri, Isila and probably Vanavasi.

Pataliputra, the Mauryan Metropolis

Having discussed the settlement hierarchy, as it appears in some of our more reliable sources, we may now turn our attention to some actual examples of the major sites known from archaeological and traditional sources. The first of these must be Pataliputra, the metropolitan centre of the Mauryan empire (Fig. 10.3). The ancient city was first identified with modern Patna by Rennell (1783), but it took more than a century before the explorations of an inspired amateur archaeologist, Waddell, revealed more or less conclusive proof of the correctness of this view (1903). As we remarked in chapter 1, the neglect of this city by archaeologists is difficult to understand. That so important a centre should remain virtually unexcavated, and that there is not a single properly excavated domestic house, let alone religious monument or royal palace to which we can point, would in the context of any other of the great civilizations of antiquity be almost unthinkable. In spite of this neglect, Pataliputra has one great advantage over almost every other city of early historic South Asia – that it was visited by a Greek envoy, Megasthenes, who left a detailed written description of his observations, regarding both the city and the state of which it was the centre (McCrindle, 1877). In our description of the city we shall compare Megasthenes's account with modern observations.

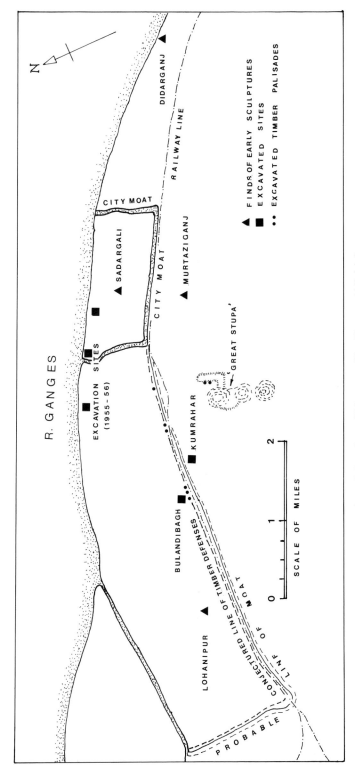

Fig. 10.3. Conjectural reconstruction of the plan of Mauryan Pataliputra (Allchin).

The earliest history of the city is associated with the story of the Buddha's prophesy of its future greatness. Standing as it did on a ferry point across the Ganges, and less than thirty miles from Vaisali, the rival capital city of the Vajjian confederation, the then village of Pataligama was an obvious place to establish a fortified settlement, and this evidently was done, with the construction of the first wooden ramparts, during the time of Ajatasatru (i.e. c. BC 400, according to the chronology we have adopted for the Buddha). This new riverside settlement enjoyed the protection of the Son and Punpun rivers on the south and west, as well as the defensive protection of the Ganges on its north, thereby benefitting the river trade which it commanded. Its promotion to the role of capital city of Magadha evidently occurred in the subsequent reign of Udayin, some half a century later, when it is believed that the capital was shifted from Rajagriha. Buddhist sources suggest that the construction of timber fortifications began as early as the Buddha's time, and were certainly greatly expanded by Ajatasatru.

Megasthenes informs us that by the time of Candragupta the city was, like the modern Patna, long and narrow, being 80 stadia in length (c. 8–9 miles), and 15 stadia in width (around 1.7 miles), with a circumference of around 21 miles. This compares with our own conjecture of the original fortified area, which today measures c. 7 miles on each side, and between 1.5 miles on the west end and one mile on the east. It was surrounded on all sides by a broad moat, some 600 feet wide and 45 feet deep, and protected by a timber palisade, interspersed with 570 towers and 64 gates. Erdosy has attempted to estimate the area enclosed by the city defenses; he believes that Megasthenes's account envisages a total area of some 4,500 hectares, while a more modest computation, based upon the size of the conjectured area enclosed by the wooden ramparts detected in modern times, would still comprise between 1,200 and 1,350 hectares (Erdosy, 1987, 18; 1988, 134). Our own estimate is slightly different, being either 2,200 hectares including the whole area conjectured as enclosed by timber ramparts, or some 340 hectares limited to the area enclosed by the 'city moat'. Even if the more modest figures are anywhere near correct, Pataliputra would have been far larger than any other South Asian city of its day, and on this score alone would certainly qualify for the title of Metropolis.

Archaeology was slow to reveal traces of the timber palisades, but since their first discovery in 1876 quantities of buried timber, presumably preserved by the height of the watertable, have been discovered (Fig. 10.4). The palisades seem to have consisted of a double line of timber, about 4 m in width, presumably originally having an earth infilling (Gupta 1980, 230–5). Slower still has been the search for other structural remains which must have occupied parts of the city. The discovery of the remains of a pillared hall, resting upon a substructure of timber, and consisting of pillars of Chunar sandstone bearing a distinctive polish, was made by Spooner, an officer of the Archaeological Department, in 1913, working thanks to the enthusiastic benefaction of a Parsi industrialist, Ratan Tata (Gupta 1980, 228; Spooner 1913, 56–86); but Spooner's work was not above

Fig. 10.4. Bulandibagh, Patna, remains of timber rampart excavated in 1927–28 (Wheeler Archive, Faculty of Oriental Studies, Cambridge).

criticism, and his interpretation of the discovery left much to be desired. The fuller significance of the find only becomes apparent in the report of its reinvestigation by Altekar and Mishra (1959). The conclusion is beyond doubt that this magnificent monument was the work of the early Mauryan period and that the hall was destroyed by fire around BC 150. We shall describe the structure in greater detail in Chapter 11. There has been much conjecture concerning its nature and function: its resemblance to Achaemenid structures at Persepolis and elsewhere has often been noted, and it seemed logical, in view of Megasthenes's reports on Pataliputra's containing many sumptuous palaces, to regard it as a part of the royal palace. But others have seen it as a religious edifice, perhaps a Buddhist Uposatha hall; S. P. Gupta regards it as more probably a pavilion for royal relaxation. As yet no comparable stone structures associated with the Mauryan period are known from Pataliputra, but in the absence of systematic search this is scarcely unexpected. From the other excavations conducted there from time to time, and from the chance finds of public works in various parts of the city, a number of striking and suggestive fragments of polished stone sculptures and architectural elements have been discovered. Some of these we have indicated on our plan (Fig. 10.3). We shall review them in the next chapter.

Cities, provincial capitals and administrative centres

The archaeological identification of the major cities of the Mauryan empire can be fairly confidently made. As we saw above, many are marked by the proximity of Asokan inscriptions, some even recording their names of other cities. Others are identifiable as already cities in pre-Mauryan times, and as recognizably still occupied during the Mauryan period. Once they have been identified one may consider how they may be grouped, both geographically and typologically. In the second Mauryan map (Fig. 10.5) we have shown many of these sites graded according to the area enclosed by the ramparts, there are without doubt many more sites which still await either discovery or proper mapping and identification, and this work would seem to be an urgent desideratum as expanding population and housing, and economic development, offer a continually growing threat to such sites.

Geographically the division may reflect the administrative divisions of the empire at its height. But we are reluctant to impose too close an affiliation of the urban groupings with the administrative provinces. In view of their uncertainty, we would rather choose a more pragmatic division, based on the broad geographical groupings envisaged in chapter 2, and on the sites themselves. These may be further subdivided as required:

1. Gangetic (or Metropolitan) Province

First, there is a large group of cities located in the Ganges valley, and in many cases older than the Mauryan age. Most if not all of these appear to have been the capitals of previously independent *janapadas*, and these number several of the largest enclosed settlements in all South Asia. A systematic study of these sites has been made by Roy (Roy, T. N. 1983). A few sites which are peripheral to the Ganges alluvial plains are noticeably smaller. They extend in the west into the Doab of the Ganga and Yamuna rivers, and in the east beyond the Ganga into the complex river system of the Ganga-Brahmaputra deltas. Among the cities of this province are Rajagriha (Rajgir), the earlier capital of Magadha, Kausambi, Sravasti, Ahicchatra, Mathura, Sankissa, Kapilavastu, on the northern edges of the Gangetic plains, Balirajgarh and Bangarh in the northeast, and Mahasthangarh in the east. In addition there are many other ancient cities, whose size and/or age have not been definitely ascertained: among these are ancient Varanasi (Banaras), Jhusi, Masaon, Buxar, Champa, Ayodhya, Atranji-khera and Vaisali.

2. *Northwestern (or Gandharan) Province*

A second group of cities is situated in the northwest, in Pakistan and Afghanistan, and includes a small number of cities, mainly of considerably smaller size than those of the first group. The principal cities of this group are Taxila, represented by the Bhir mound, and Puskalavati (Charsada) represented by the Bala Hissar group of mounds, in ancient Gandhara, Nagarahara, near modern Jalalabad and, by temporary adoption during the Mauryan period, Kandahar. Once again there are a number of other possible candidates for inclusion in the list. Among these is Akara Dheri, the great mound in the fertile Bannu basin: there can be little doubt that this was already a city during Mauryan times, but until excavations are done the evidence is somewhat tentative.

3. *Central (perhaps Ujjain) Province*

A third group of cities, also mainly associated with identifiable *janapadas*, lie in the territories to the south and southwest of the Ganges valley; as we know them they are with one exception smaller than the Ganges cities. The main cites of this province are Virata (Bairat) to the northeast of Jaipur, Vidisha and Ujjayini (Ujjain) in the west, Airakana (modern Eran) and Tripuri near modern Jabalpur.

4. *Southern (perhaps Suvarnagiri) Province*

A fourth group includes a large number of major sites which with one or two exceptions cannot be specifically related to known *janapadas*. One of these is Pratisthana in the north of the province, all others are either of as yet undetermined size, or of distinctly small size. Other major city sites are Tagara, Kondapur, Sannathi (c. 40 hectares), Madhavpur (near Belgaum) (c. 40 hectares), Maski, Brahmagiri, Kopbal and Banavasi.

5. *Western coastal (perhaps Aparanta) Province*

A small number of sites can be identified as belonging to a western province, which is closely associated with the coastal region and therefore presumably with sea trade. The modern site of Junagarh, near Girnar, marks the ancient Girinagara, Bharukaccha on the bank of the Narmada river, and probably Suppara, although the actual habitation area of this site is still not clear. No major sites have been discovered south of Suppara, although Kalyan northeast of Bombay is another obvious location where an important ancient city must once have existed.

6. Eastern coastal (perhaps Tosali) Province

Another small number of sites can be identified as belonging to an eastern coastal province. In the Ganges delta a major city was at Candraketugarh, northeast of Calcutta, while Tamluk marks the site of the ancient port of Tamralipti. To the south, and close to the coast, is Sisupalgarh, near modern Bhubaneshwar, beyond that lies the ramparted city of Samapa, near Jaugada. The situation of Dhanyakataka, known from the modern name of Amaravati, is somewhat unclear, it might also be associated with the southern province; but when its position is compared with that of Sisupalgarh in Orissa, it seems rather to belong to a coastal provincial group. It would seem reasonable, in view of the terms of our geographical classification, to recognize Sri Lanka as a further province, but as there is no reason to see the island as ever forming a part of the Mauryan empire we do not include it.

The typology of the cities

It is difficult to decide by what criteria – if any – one should classify the typology of the cities outlined above. As a starting point we believe that it is probable that all, or at least nearly all, were originally surrounded by defensive walls, or moats and ramparts. Cities constructed on alluvial plains were endowed with sometimes enormous ramparts and moats. This is true at nearly all the Gangetic cities, with odd exceptions, such as Ahicchatra, where a rampart has not as yet been demonstrated archaeologically (although Cunningham certainly believed that there was one). Where a city was constructed in a rocky terrain, as was the case at old Rajagriha (Rajgir), the original capital of Magadha, a solid stone wall with regular square bastions, built on rock, formed a double line of defense around the older city. The neighbouring fortification of New Rajgir on the other hand was built on open ground and had a regular moat and rampart. Another doubtful case is at Taxila, where the Mauryan city was undoubtedly located in the Bhir mound which today offers no visible sign of either a wall or rampart. But Cunningham, who visited it in the 19th century, found some traces then still visible, and our own view after repeated walking around its circumference is that it once had a wall, most likely of stone rubble, which probably survived into fairly recent times, but has now been robbed for use as building material. Such defenses are helpful to the archaeologist, as when they are intact they provide a good indication of the area enclosed, and indeed most of the calculations of area we have cited from time to time have been arrived at in this way.

Perhaps a better criterion for classifying cities is in terms of their outline plans. We would expect, from the Arthasastra, a city to be square with three gates along each side, and roads dividing it into regular square blocks. In the standard Arthasastra city there is a central square in the middle of the city, with the royal palace on its north side. But few if any of these features can so far be recognized in actual sites studied by archaeology, as little or no problem-oriented research has been made on this matter. The square plan is most nearly represented at Sisupalgarh, where each side of a near-perfect square is divided by two gates into three sections (Fig. 8.9); the same plan is reasonably closely approached at Mahasthangarh, where four sides make a near-square, and at Kausambi where there are three sides suggestive of a regular rectangular plan, although it is irregular on the side bounded by the Yamuna river. But other cities have quite different plans: Sravasti has a roughly moon-shaped rampart, Ahicchatra approaches an equilateral triangle, and Sankissa has a more or less circular rampart. It would be interesting to discover whether the square plans are the products of a later period, while the other forms may have been relatively earlier.

Another way of classifying cities is in terms of the area enclosed by their ramparts, when these are ascertainable, or recorded. We have indicated these in Fig. 10.5, where cities are graded in six categories according to size. The cities thus listed are as follows:

Grade 1. Above 241 hectares
  Pataliputra (enclosed area estimated to be c. 2,200 ha *in toto*; area enclosed by the 'city moat' is c. 340 ha;

Grade 2. 181–240 ha
  Rajgir, Kausambi and Vidisa;

Grade 3. 121–180 ha
  Ahicchatra, Sravasti, Tosali (Sisupalgarh), and Mahasthangarh;

Grade 4. 61–120 ha
  Ujjain, Jaugada (Samapa), Pratisthana (Paithan), Anuradhapura;

Grade 5. 31–60 ha
  Kandahar, Taxila, Balirajgarh, Sannathi, Madhavpur, Dhanyakataka (Amaravati);

Grade 6. 16–30 ha
  Kapilavastu, Puskalavati.

This pattern is highly suggestive. The Mauryan Metropolis is by far the largest city known in South Asia at that time. The former capital of Magadha, Rajgir, and Kausambi are in the second grade, along with Vidisa, the only city of such a size outside the Ganges valley. Of the third grade two are among the great cities of the Ganges valley, Sravasti and Ahicchatra, together with Mahasthangarh in the eastern extension of the Ganges plains, and Sisupalgarh in Orissa. The fourth grade takes us even farther from the centre, with Ujjain, Paithan and Jaugada, and Anuradhapura; and the fifth grade similarly with Balirajgarh on the northern fringes of the Ganges plains, Taxila and Kandahar in the far northwest, and Amaravati, Sannathi and Madhavpur in the southern Deccan. Finally grade six is represented by two

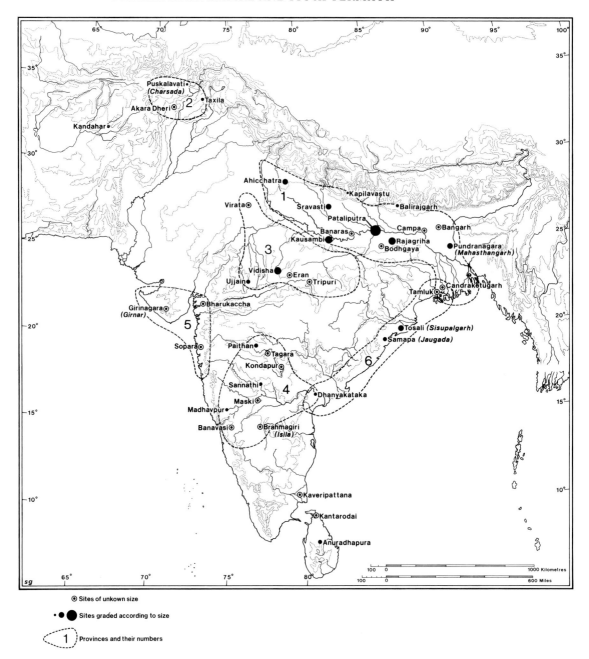

Fig. 10.5. Map of probable provincial groupings of the Mauryan empire, with cities graded according to their size (see p. 207).

sites, Puskalavati also in the far northwest and Kapilavastu on the northern Ganges fringes.

Smaller settlements and forts

There are a number of smaller settlements which may belong to intermediate places in the hierarchy, somewhere between the full-fledged city and the village. An example of such a settlement is Bhita, south of Allahabad. This small settlement was protected by a fortified rampart and its excavation by Marshall in 1912 was a major landmark in the archaeology of the early historical period, regrettably since then left without proper continuation or development. It occupies approximately 14 hectares (Erdosy 1988, 70), and may have been a small *sthaniya* or one of the other intermediate administrative centres, perhaps a *nigama*. Another comparable example of a small settlement of the Mauryan period is Prahladpur, on the banks of the Ganga east of Banaras, where there appears to have been a fortified settlement of c. 4 hectares. There are doubtless many other such sites awaiting systematic study and survey; and as yet the archaeology of village settlements of the Mauryan period has scarcely begun.

4. The infrastructure of urbanism

The complex urban society whose widely diffused remains we have been reviewing, and whose organization as a state and empire we have been examining, could scarcely have functioned without a foundation of science and learning, and without the benefit of the 'Three Rs', reading, writing and arithmetic. We cannot involve ourselves here in an exhaustive discussion of these subjects, but we can at least consider how far textual and archaeological evidence compare in defining the role and extent of the use of writing, the regulation of weights and measures, and the use of properly controlled coinage in Mauryan India. As we noticed above these things are an inseparable part of Kautilya's concept of society and of its underlying function of the creation of *artha*, wealth.

The use of writing

We saw in chapter 9 that archaeological evidence has recently been obtained to show that the Brahmi script began to be used in Sri Lanka *at least* a century and a half before the start of the Mauryan rule in Magadha, and perhaps as early as three centuries before that event. We have long admired the brilliant analysis of Buhler, originally published in 1898 (1962, 38–9), who reached the conclusion that the Indian script had been first introduced into South Asia by merchants around BC 800, in the form of borrowings of a nucleus of letters from a North Semitic alphabet, which some time later was adapted by Brahman scholars and

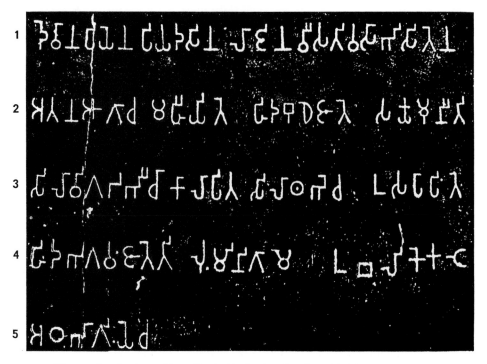

Fig. 10.6.   Asokan pillar edict in Brahmi script, Lumbini, Nepal.

transformed into a script well suited to represent the phonetic structure of both Sanskrit and Prakrit. This transformation may, he hazarded, have been completed by c. BC 500. In spite of this plausible hypothesis, it is surprising how frequently later scholars have accepted the absence of positive evidence of the use of writing as indicating that the Brahmi script was virtually an invention of the time of Asoka, and have shown little or no awareness of the difficulties this view puts in the way of reaching an understanding of the early history of Indian civilization. Winternitz (1927), accepting Buhler's hypothesis without reservations, has an interesting discussion of the problem. He concludes that writing was probably not used for copying or transmitting sacred texts until some centuries later, and points particularly to the absence of references to the copying or writing of texts or books in early textual sources. Following Winternitz's argument, we shall assert that the early use of the adapted script may not long have been restricted to mercantile purposes, but may soon have been expanded to cover a wider range of secular functions. It seems likely that such secular activities as governmental account or record keeping would have been inaugurated well before the transcription of religious texts. We may therefore expect that it was only after a further interval that the unorthodox sects, including the Buddhists, accepted the use of writing for copying texts, and that the most

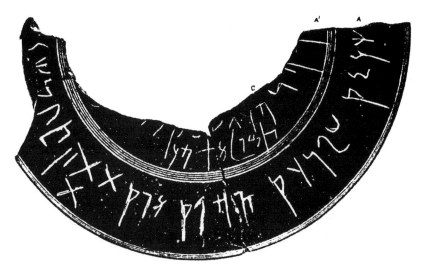

Fig. 10.7. Kharosthi inscription of Menander (c. BC 175), Bajaur, Northwest Frontier Province, Pakistan.

tenacious stronghold of the oral tradition, and therefore the latest to adopt the new fashion, would have been maintained by the schools of Vedic transmission.

It must be admitted that the archaeological evidence available to date is surprisingly limited. For reasons which we have already discussed, archaeologists in India have neglected to obtain absolute dating for many categories of finds from this period, inscriptions among them. For whatever reason, for nearly a century after Buhler wrote, archaeologists produced no concrete evidence of any pre-Asokan inscriptions, and instituted no problem-oriented research designed to investigate the question. This state of affairs continued until, within the past decade, Deraniyagala's excavations at Anuradhapura, subsequently reinforced by those of the British team, have revealed for the first time Brahmi inscriptions on potsherds dated by a large number of radiocarbon samples at least to the 4th–5th centuries BC, if not earlier (see above, pp. 176–79). We suspect that with more critical use of radiocarbon dating a number of excavated sites in India, which have produced inscribed potsherds, seals or sealings from hitherto imprecisely dated contexts, may also be found to yield pre-Mauryan as well as Mauryan materials.

The following categories of written material deserve to be considered in the context of the use of writing in Mauryan times:

(A) The body of Asokan edicts

Carved on rocks and pillars, in caves and on stone slabs, this constitutes the most solid and best-dated material for the use of writing at this time (Fig. 10.6).

Whatever may be said regarding the suggested borrowing of the idea of such public edicts, or their phraseology, from the Achaemenids, the fact remains that the Asokan edicts offer an example of the way in which an exotic culture trait can be introduced and almost instantly transformed into an indigenous concept. Throughout South Asia the Asokan inscriptions are in Prakrit, written in Brahmi script, except for those in the northwest. These latter are either in Prakrit, written in Kharosthi, a script derived from Aramaic script, adapted for writing an Indian language (Fig. 10.7); or translated directly into Aramaic, the language of the Achaemenid administrative class (Fig. 10.8); or into Greek (Fig. 10.9) at Kandahar, no doubt as a result of the establishment of a Greek colony there by Alexander, and where there must still have been a substantial Greek population living (Allchin and Norman 1985). That the Brahmi script was generally employed in South Asia, outside the northwest, suggests that it must already have been established there before the adaptation of Kharosthi from Aramaic took place. One of the salient features of all the Asokan inscriptions is of their being deeply imbued with a Buddhist ethic. In this respect they are unique, and strikingly suggest that Asoka was rather a disciple of the Buddha than of Kautilya.

(B) A miniature stone slab from Mahasthangarh

This provides another type of inscription, almost certainly a special variant of the Asokan series (Sircar 1965, 79–80) (Fig. 10.10).

(C) The Sohgaura copper plate inscription

A further important piece which may be regarded as Mauryan is the Sohgaura copper plate inscription (Sircar 1965, 79–80). Like the previous example this appears to have been a unique type of Asokan inscription anticipating the copper plates of later centuries (Fig. 10.11).

(D) The Piprahwa relic casket inscription

We may also follow Sircar in accepting the Piprahwa relic casket inscription as of Mauryan date (Sircar 1965, 81).

(E) Small seals

There are numbers of small seals of ivory, bone, stone, or terracotta, from excavated sites and contexts, many of which may confidently be accepted as Mauryan: one may cite examples from Rupar, Ujjain, Bhita, Vaisali, etc. These generally contain short inscriptions in the genitive case, giving the name of their owner.

Fig. 10.8.   Aramaic inscription of Asoka, Pul-i Darunta, Afghanistan.

Fig. 10.9.   Bilingual Greek and Aramaic inscription of Asoka, Kandahar, Afghanistan.

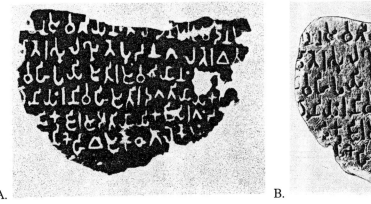

A.   B.

Fig. 10.10. Mahasthangarh, Bangladesh, stone inscription in Brahmi script, 3rd century BC. (A. Rubbing; B. Photographic print)

Fig. 10.11. Sohgaura copper plate inscription in Brahmi script, 3rd century BC.

(F) Inscribed potsherds

From a number of excavated sites come occasional reports of finds of potsherds with short inscriptions in Brahmi, usually not firmly dated. Unfortunately the examples known to us are too few and too scattered for any useful comparison with the more massive and solidly dated evidence from Anuradhapura. However, it seems probable that these short inscriptions may be the traces of a much wider use of writing during the Mauryan and pre-Mauryan periods than has hitherto been supposed.

In sum, this evidence indicates two kinds of usage for writing: official, on the part of the king or his servants; and mercantile or domestic, in the small inscribed seals and potsherds.

The use of writing during the Mauryan period

We now turn to the evidence of literature. We have accepted earlier the Arthasastra as a reliable source for information regarding the Mauryan period. The text is in Sanskrit, and thus differentiated from the majority of available near-contemporary written sources which are in Prakrit. This need not pose a problem since Sanskrit had long been in use among Brahman scholars. It is certainly not easy to imagine that either this treatise, or the others which its author claims to have used, can have existed merely as oral texts. We are tempted to take this as support for our hypothesis that during this period the range and variety of uses of writing may have been steadily expanding, and may even have gone so far as to include the compilation of secular books. In the Arthasastra, for example, one reads (2.7) of the construction of a record office as a place for keeping record books (*pustaka*), into which the requisite evidence of state financial business should be entered. Accepting that there may be some doubt about the antiquity of the word *pustaka* (at least for religious texts) this seems reasonably clear, and acceptable for secular usage, particularly as the account of the structure of the administrative departments is more or less supported by Megasthenes. A second important passage is with regard to the issuing of *sasana*, edicts (2.10). These are so named because they are used by the king to give commands. For a king such orders are of prime importance since peace and war may depend on them. Therefore the scribe (*lekhaka*) should be endowed with the excellencies of a minister and be able to read, understand and write well. The remainder of the passage describes the structure and contents of an edict. The ordering of the material, the expression and the legibility are stressed. From this passage it seems quite clear that writing played a major role in the life and work of the king and his government. One is forcefully reminded of the edicts (*sasana*) of Asoka in this context. A further group of Arthasastra references relates to the use of seals to check the entry and exit of goods, in the course of trade, for foreign travel (on passports), the transport of merchandise, etc. Slight as these passages are, they provide apparent corroboration from the Arthasastra of the archaeological evidence.

We conclude this short section by noticing that there is a clear harmony of the two types of evidence in indicating that throughout the Mauryan period writing played a major part in public and royal life.

The regulation of weights and measures

Vasudeva Saran Agrawala (1953) notes that the Kāśikā Vritti (a commentary on Pāṇini's Aṣṭādhyāyi, dating from c. 7th century AD, but regarded as being both authoritative and incorporating much earlier material) includes a *mūrddha abhiṣikta* (head anointed, i.e. universally cited) example which includes the words 'the Nandas regulated the weights and measures'; this he interprets as indicating that in the decades preceding the time of Alexander the growing power and urban structure of the Nanda rulers of Magadha led them to institute a regulation of weights and measures.

Archaeological evidence to support this state of affairs for the succeeding Mauryan period is still not sufficient to allow much meaningful comment. From sites such as Vaisali and Kumrahar there are large numbers of well-made stone weights, usually of discoidal form, and reportedly made from jasper. These come from various periods but mainly, we are informed, from the period of the NBP. We know of no proper comparative, let alone metrological, study of these weights, but obviously a comparison with the weights of the Arthasastra and other texts is demanded. It is therefore to the Arthasastra that we must again turn for further information regarding the regulation of weights and measures. The Arthasastra offers a wealth of evidence for the wide varieties of standardized weights and measures of the time. Officers were appointed to control their use and standardization. The measurements include those of length (2.20), divided into several series, rising from those below the standard *angula*, defined as 'the middle joint of the middle finger of a man of average size'; to those above, including the span and the cubit, and ending with the rod (*danda*) or bow (*dhanus*) of around 180 cm; and above this measurements of longer distance, the *goruta* or *krosa* and the *yojana*. Various special measurements are mentioned, for instance for digging moats, making roads or city walls. Measurements of capacity were set on several different standards, for revenue, trade, payments or palace purposes: these were applicable for both liquids and solids. Weights, too, were in several series: for precious substances there were three, for gold, silver and diamonds (2.19.2–7); another series was for weights for general purposes (2.19.19–20). Weights should be made of iron or of stone from the Mekhala hills (presumably the modern Maikal hills, south of the source of the Narbada river). Considerable attention is given to the types of weighing machines employed: one is a balance (*tula*) with two pans, for which ten different sizes are recommended for weighing different quantities; and another a sort of steelyard, in two sizes. A steelyard is used as a symbol on the *negama* coins from Taxila, suggesting their clear mercantile connotation (Allan 1936, cxxvi, 214–15). Equal attention is given to the measurement of time, based on a device named the *nalika*, being the time taken for one *adhaka* of water to flow out of a pot through a hole of the same diameter as that of a wire 4 *angulas* long, made from 4 *masas* of gold.

That these systematic measurements were not solely the invention of Kautilya may be gauged from the fact that earlier sources, including Panini's grammar, mention some of them, incidentally. But these early references are scarcely enough to reconstruct the whole system. Further, the textual references of slightly later date involve numerous variants, and a comprehensive study of this subject is still called for. We have in mind particularly such works as the Manava Dharmasastra and the Caraka Samhita, as worthy of comparison.

Coinage in the Mauryan period

In chapter 7 (p. 113) we have seen how evidence suggests that the first introduction of coinage in its proper sense to South Asia almost certainly took place during the period of Achaemenid rule. This does not mean that the early coinage was narrowly copied from the Achaemenids, on the contrary it appears from the beginning to bear a style and ethos of its own; but nevertheless there are clear indications of the direction from which the idea of coinage reached India. The first beginnings of Indian coinage have been set variously between the sixth and fourth centuries BC; Cribb (1985, 550) in particular has argued that the first silver punchmarked coins belong to the early fourth century BC, and this is probably very near the actual date. Our personal view would favour a slightly earlier date around or a little before BC 400. The upshot of this would be that for at least a century before the beginning of Mauryan rule coinage had been in use in the northwest, and that it soon spread to the Ganges valley. Moreover, although very few Achaemenid coins have been discovered in the Indian provinces over which they ruled, it is reasonably certain that their coinage must have been familiar in these regions, as must the pre-Alexander Greek coins which also occur in small numbers in early contexts.

Before we consider the archaeological evidence for Mauryan coinage we should first discuss the evidence provided by the Arthasastra. In the text as we have it the whole concept of the work of society revolves around money and monetary values: every worker, from the highest minister down to the humblest worker, for example the washerman, is assigned his appropriate salary in *panas*; every offence is given its appropriate fine in *panas*. Kautilya has an earthily realistic attitude to wealth and therefore to the state's role in producing and exploiting it. So long as we accept the Arthasastra as a contemporary expression of the state ideology of the Mauryan period, the expectation that its statements on the use of money reflect that age seems altogether acceptable. However, we must not forget that the Arthasastra is a prescriptive text, setting out what its author doubtless wished to present to his readers, the princes of a royal family, an idealized picture of an ideal state.

The Arthasastra regards the manufacture and control of coinage as coming under the authority of the Chief Controller of Mining and Metallurgy. Under him the Chief Master of the Mint is responsible for the minting of coins of copper and silver. The silver coins are to be made up of (an alloy consisting of) $\frac{11}{16}$th part silver, $\frac{1}{4}$th part copper, and $\frac{1}{16}$th part hardening metal (such as iron, tin or antimony); and issued in the following denominations: 1 *pana*, $\frac{1}{2}$ *pana*, $\frac{1}{4}$ *pana* and $\frac{1}{8}$ *pana*. Copper coins, made up of $\frac{3}{4}$ copper and $\frac{1}{4}$ hardening metal are to be issued in the following denominations: 1 *masaka* (equalling $\frac{1}{16}$ silver *pana*),

$\frac{1}{2}$ *masaka*, 1 *kakini* (equal to $\frac{1}{4}$ *masaka*) and $\frac{1}{2}$ *kakini*. Another post, the Examiner of Coins, is responsible for certifying the coins used in trade and in payments to the Treasury, and in charging for his services, for issuing new coins and for certifying them. In this succinct passage the text sets out the basis of the currency. The silver punch marked coin, or *pana*, is in other texts and later times generally referred to as *karsapana* (*kahapana*), while the pre-Mauryan silver bars are referred to as *purana*, ancient coins.

The archaeological and numismatic evidence necessarily presents a different picture. We refer the reader to a number of useful numismatic contributions for further reading, particularly to P. L. Gupta's *Coins* (1969); D. D. Kosambi's *Introduction to the study of Indian History* (1956); J. Cribb (1985); a useful study of the stratigraphic occurrences of coins by S. C. Ray (1959) and Sir John Marshall's *Taxila* (1951).

Kosambi had argued that it was possible to identify groups of silver punchmarked coins with actual dynasties and even rulers. In particular he had used the evidence of hoard finds at Taxila to show that there were three series of coins: the silver bars and associated coins of smaller denominations; silver punchmarked coins of an earlier; and of a later series. Cribb and P. L. Gupta (1969) have shown that the later series has an interregional distribution and have therefore called it a 'national' coinage, while the earlier series had mainly localized distributions, hence called 'local'. Cribb also argued that the coinage had probably first been issued in the early 4th century BC. It is not unreasonable to conclude that the 'national' series of coins belong to the first really inter-regional national rule known to us, i.e. the Mauryan; and that the earlier local coins were issued by separate authorities in the days of the Mahajanapadas. Ray's work showed that at many excavated sites the earliest occurrence of punchmarked coins was in the early stages of the levels containing NBP, and thus should be datable to somewhere between c. BC 550–400 (see Chapter 7); but we must confess to some doubt whether the period was strictly the early subdivision of NBP, viewed globally, or merely early in its occurrence in a particular site and excavation. In this case it may be safer to assign such finds to the early to middle stages of NBP, and allow the first NBP to occur somewhere between BC 550 and 250. Ray also shows that the cast copper coins occur in the same period as the silver punchmarked ones.

We are prevented from arriving at more precise dating by the tradition of using NBP as a type fossil. It would be interesting to have actual dates for strata providing the earliest occurrences of coins, among other more significant classes of artefacts. Since Ray's contribution (1959) much additional information has been obtained. It seems clear that at Taxila, for example, where the foundation of the first city in the Bhir mound (period BM IV) has been dated by radiocarbon to the late fifth century BC (see above, p. 131), BM III coincides with the pre-Mauryan and perhaps early Mauryan occupation, while BM II coincides with the later Mauryan occupation. Silver bar and round and concave silver coins occur

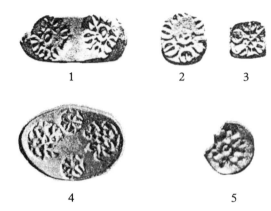

Fig. 10.12.   Coinage ascribable to the pre-Mauryan period (c. BC 4th century). Northwestern regions: 1. silver bar coin (double standard); 2. silver round coin (half standard); 3. silver square coin. Ganges valley (Kasi): 4. cup-shaped silver punchmarked coin; 5. silver punchmarked coin. (1:1)

first in BM IV and are certainly pre-Mauryan (Fig. 10.12); while the earlier silver punchmarked occur in BM III; and the later class of punchmarked silver occurs first in BM II (Allchin 1968, 6–7). Moreover, the coins of the later hoard are made of silver alloyed with copper, and therefore debased. The copper coinage occurs in small quantities in BM III, and more plentifully in BM II. A problem raised by the attempt to associate the coinage of the Mauryan period with that of the Arthasastra is that the four silver denominations mentioned by Kautilya do not occur in actual coins, where there are at most two denominations, the unit and its sixteenth. Our knowledge of the copper coinage is even less than of the silver. Far too little study has been made, even for accurate metrological analysis to be made.

The silver coins are on a uniform standard of 54 grains (Fig. 10.13). Those of the later (Mauryan) series are thicker than the earlier, and consequently smaller in size; they tend towards square or rectangular forms. Gupta divides the whole category of silver punchmarked coins into six chronological series, the older being thin, and the younger progressively thicker. They uniformly have five symbols punched on the obverse with five separate punches. These have often been taken to represent the royal marks of different kings. The reverse side is left plain, but in the course of time many minute marks have been added, presumably by the sort of moneyer's check called for in the Arthasastra. The copper coins are generally made by casting, although punchmarked and even what appear to be die-struck coins also occur. They include some with a central main sign, often a lion or an elephant, and some with groups of signs. None of the coins which are attributable to the Mauryan period are inscribed.

To conclude this brief survey of the coinage of the Mauryan period, we must agree with much of Cribb's criticism. More research is needed, including

Fig. 10.13. Coinage ascribable to the Mauryan and immediately post-Mauryan period. 6, 7, 8. silver punchmarked coins, national series; 9, 10, 11. copper cast coins; 12, 13, 15, 16. die-struck copper coins; 14. inscribed copper coin, Taxila: obv. *negama* (Brahmi script), rev. *kojaka* (Kharosthi script). (1:1)

metallurgical analysis and typological and distributional studies; and more detailed archaeological dating, before it will be possible to establish more definitely the association of coins with the Mauryan period. However, in the broader context of our study, this limitation extends also to much of the data available on other parts of the subject. We believe it is reasonable to conclude that during the Mauryan period silver punchmarked coins of the national series were very widely distributed in South Asia, and were accompanied by coins of the cast copper varieties.

CHAPTER 11

MAURYAN ARCHITECTURE AND ART

F. R. ALLCHIN

Taking a broad view of the role of the Mauryan period in the rise and spread of cities and states in South Asia, it cannot be contested that in both architecture and art it witnessed the first flowering of styles ancestral to those not only of the succeeding centuries, but of the subsequent course of Indian art thereafter. This aspect is most clearly in evidence in the stone sculpture which has about it what Stella Kramrisch referred to as a quality of Indianness by which it may be at once recognized, but it is no less true of the distinctive forms of the architecture of early Buddhism and of the rock-cut architecture (Kramrisch 1933, ix). In this sense Mauryan architecture and art offer a foundation upon which the whole subsequent superstructure of Indian architecture and art rest.

1. Secular architecture

The creation of monumental architecture was cited in Chapter 5 as one of the characteristics of a nascent civilization. We are now in a position to see how far this is true of the architecture of the Mauryan period. We shall first consider secular architecture and then religious. In chapter 10, the social and political role of cities and their defences was considered; we shall now proceed to look more closely at their layout and construction, first in terms of the evidence of texts and then of archaeology.

City defences

The Arthasastra (2.3) describes the excavation of the moat (*parikha*) and consequent banking up of the rampart (*vapra*), so as to make a fortified settlement (*durga*) or city: it recommends three concentric moats, although we know of no surviving fortification which displays this feature, or where it has been revealed by excavation. The initial construction and excavation of a moat depended upon the available depth of alluvial soil (Fig. 11.1). Where the ground was deep and alluvial, the soil excavated from the moat was used to pile up the rampart. At Mahasthangarh the moat, now more or less silted up, is still clearly

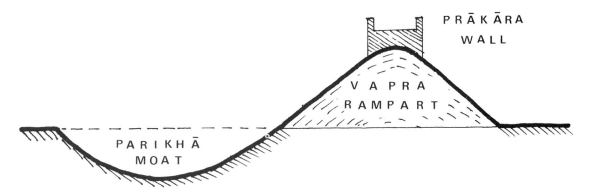

Fig. 11.1. Diagrammatic section of a typical city fortification.

visible (Fig. 11.2). Where the ground was rocky and moat digging was impractical, the earth rampart was dispensed with and a stone wall (*prakara*) was built, as at Rajgir (Fig. 11.3). Earth ramparts might be faced with burnt brick or stone, as in the excavated rampart at Kausambi (Fig. 11.4) (Sharma 1960); while the crowning walls (*prakara*) were to be either of brick, as at New Rajgir, Sisupalgarh, etc., or of stone. On no account, adds Kautilya, should the walls be made of timber (as, according to Megasthenes and the testimony of archaeology, they were at Pataliputra!). The wall should be strengthened by the construction of turrets and towers at intervals, calling to mind the square bastions found at Rajgir. Access to the interior was to be by three gateways on each of the four sides of the square city plan. The text describes the layout of a gateway in some detail, with several variations of design. Various excavated examples of gates are known, at Bhita, Sisupalgarh, Tilaura Kot and New Rajgir, but so far no comparative study has been made of them.

The text also describes (2.4) the internal layout of such a fortified settlement (Fig. 11.5). There are to be three major roads running at right angles to each other, leading to the gateways in each section of the rampart. Provision should be made for deities of the quarters to be established at the gates. The whole plan is centred upon a central square which should contain shrines or temples of a number of deities. The royal palace and its component parts should be located on the north side of the central square. Other sectors of the city are allotted to different castes and activities. They include provision of areas for animals, stores, etc. Quarters are reserved for craft guilds and for the residence of foreign merchants. To date little investigative excavation has been carried out inside any of the cities, and their potentials for providing further information on a whole range of aspects of planning and life touched on by Kautilya remain almost entirely untapped. Even where excavation was done on any scale, as for instance at the Bhir mound, Taxila, it was scarcely conceived in terms likely to produce such results.

Fig. 11.2. The silted-up moat at Mahasthangarh, viewed from the rampart (photograph Allchin).

The Arthasastra tells us that certain urban components should be located outside the city walls (2.4.20–21) (Fig. 11.6). These include varieties of religious settlements, gardens and groves, as well as cremation grounds. Separate settlements for certain low caste groups, including Candalas, evidently already treated as outcasts, and heretical sects are mentioned. Irrigation tanks (*setu-bandha*) are also to be established around the periphery of a fortified city. Archaeology can supply many examples of both irrigation works and religious foundations in such contexts, but as yet few if any systematic attempts have been made to date or study them in the context of their role or function as parts of an urban environment. Many examples of what are probably ancient irrigation works lie neglected and unstudied, many must have been destroyed in recent developments; nor have the collaborative services of archaeologists, geomorphologists or modern irrigation engineers been enlisted to help in their investigation. Purposeful mapping of such evidence, for example that which can be seen or inferred around such places as Sravasti or Sisupalgarh, would almost certainly produce interesting results. Early inscriptions sometimes provide valuable pointers: the Rudradaman inscription (c. AD 150) at Girnar (Girinagara in the

Fig. 11.3. View of stone walls surrounding the valley of Rajagriha (Rajgir) (photograph Allchin).

inscription) refers to the enlargement of an irrigation tank (*tadaka*) which had been founded by Asoka, and this ancient embankment is one of the few to have been actually studied by an archaeologist (Mehta 1968). The Hathigumpha inscription of Kharavela mentions the extension of a waterchannel created some three centuries earlier by a Nanda king, and here too a little exploration and purposeful excavation might produce interesting results (Sircar 1965, 213–21).

Examples of outlying religious settlements occurring in the vicinity of major cities are also numerous. The Deer Park at Sarnath lies some four miles from the ancient city of Banaras; the Dharmarajika stupa complex some two miles from the Mauryan city of Taxila; the Jetavana monastic complex is a short distance outside the ramparts of Sravasti; the Sanchi monastic complex is some five miles from the gates of the city of Vidisa; and several religious complexes occur near Sisupalgarh, including the Asokan edict site at Dhauli (Fig. 11.7). Perhaps the most complete example of a city complex of this kind is that already mentioned at Anuradhapura in Sri Lanka, illustrated in Figure 9.2. One may remark in passing how much more has survived in Sri Lanka, with its living Buddhist tradition, than in either India or Pakistan.

Fig. 11.4.   Early brick rampart of Kausambi (after Sharma 1960).

CITY PLANNING

{2.4.8-16}

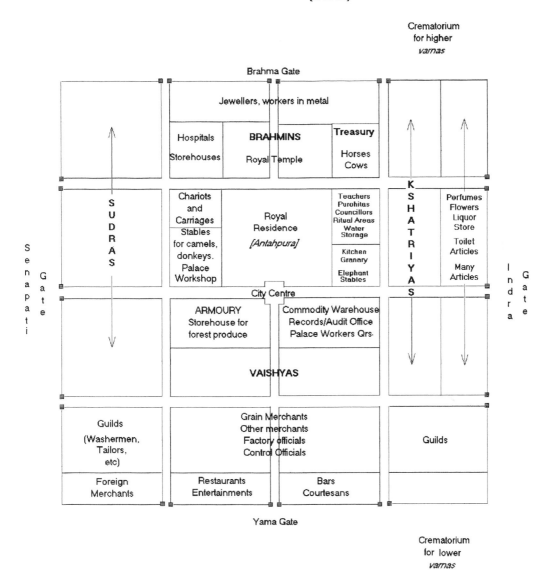

Fig. 11.5. Layout of a fortified settlement, according to the Arthasastra (courtesy L. N. Rangarajan).

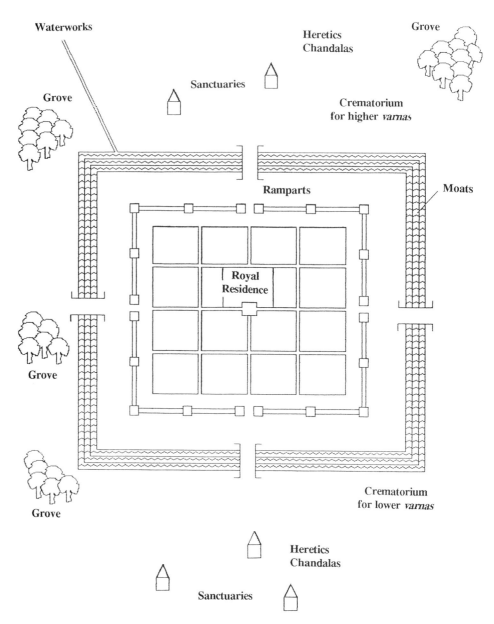

Fig. 11.6.   A city and its surroundings, after the Arthasastra (courtesy L. N. Rangarajan).

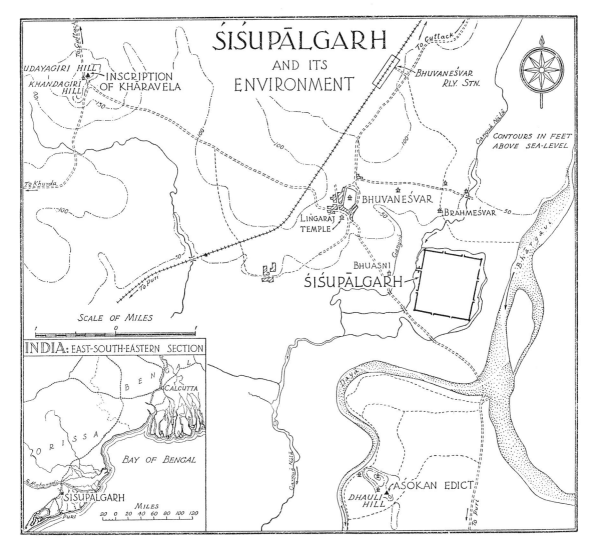

Fig. 11.7. Sisupalgarh, the city and its surroundings (courtesy Archaeological Survey of India).

City planning

From the literary sources it emerges that by Mauryan times the planning and layout of a city were already regarded as specialized activities, for which suitably qualified experts were to be employed. Thus the selection of the site for a city must be chosen with the assistance of an expert in planning and architecture. It seems likely that there were already technical texts, ancestral to the *Silpa sastras* of later centuries, which contained such information and which were presumably available for a researcher such as the author of the Arthasastra, to consult, before

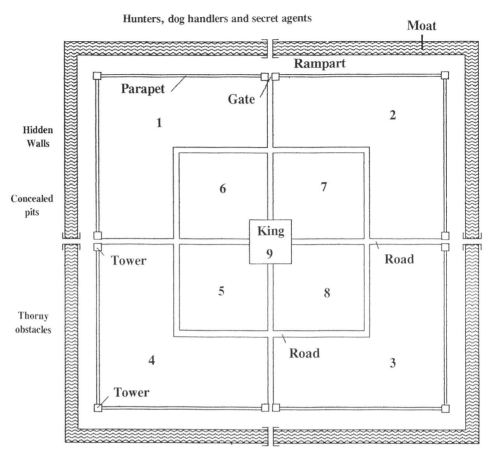

Fig. 11.8. Plan of a fortified camp site, according to the Arthasastra (after L. N. Rangarajan).

he wrote his chapter on the layout of the city. The Arthasastra has several references to this topic. The first is relating to the creation of fortified settlements (including cities and forts) (2.2), another to the construction of royal camps (10.1). This is interesting because it shows that although the camp is constructed as a temporary site, it is modelled on a permanent fort (Fig. 11.8). Surprisingly, similar care is lavished on its planning. The site is chosen with the agreement of 'experts in planning' (*vastuka*), the army commander, carpenters and astrologers, and it should be measured and laid out according to a set plan, as either circular, square, etc. Its construction involves a moat, rampart and walls, and a disposition of gates, roads and quarters for various sections of the army. Once again the royal quarters are placed to the north of the centre point of the demarcated area. Thus the camp is nothing but a less permanent fort, following an accepted design and planning concept. One of the visible results of this specialized expertise can be observed in the way that, at a certain date, attempts were made to provide cities with straight, regularly oriented streets and perhaps, too, ramparts: this certainly appears to have been the case in the Mauryan, and perhaps even pre-Mauryan, reconstruction of the Bhir mound at Taxila, at Bhita and elsewhere. An indication of this process can be seen in the way in which the later *Silpa sastras* continue to use some of the earlier terms with their original meanings, while other terms have strayed away from their original meanings. We interpret such phenomena as consistent indications of the emerging complexity of society and the growing evidence of planning and constructional specialism during these centuries. The cities of the Mauryan period represent an advanced stage of a development that had already started in pre-Mauryan times, and which was to continue in the centuries to come. Thus the architecture and planning of the Mauryan cities appear to be a part of this process, with their own early history, and their elements were still operating in medieval and later times.

Domestic houses

In spite of the large number of excavations of early historic sites carried out in what are now India and Pakistan during the course of this century, few appear ever to have included the laying bare of complete houses, let alone blocks of houses, of either the Mauryan or for that matter any other period. Two major exceptions are Sir John Marshall's excavations at Bhita, (Figs. 11.9 and 11.10) and at Taxila, where in the Bhir mound several large blocks of housing, covering the 4th–2nd centuries BC, were excavated (Fig. 11.11). The Bhita houses have been referred to by Erdosy in chapter 7 (above, pp. 111–12), where it was suggested that such house plans were already established in pre-Mauryan times. The Bhita houses belong to the Mauryan and post-Mauryan period and we may therefore cite them here as town houses of the Ganges plains. They are generally more or less square in plan, measuring around 10 × 10 to 15 × 15 m. A house consisted of up to 15 rooms arranged on three sides of a large, open courtyard paved with bricks and roofed with terracotta tiles. Similar houses are documented (albeit mainly for the post-Mauryan period) at Kausambi (Sharma 1969), Ahicchatra (Shrimali 1983), Sonkh (Hartel 1993a), Rajghat (Narain and Roy 1976–78), and Vaisali (Sinha and Roy 1969). They are well served with drains, wells and storage jars; later rectangular Buddhist monasteries suggest elaborations of such a plan. The Bhir mound houses are less regular in form, but have a generally oblong plan. One is struck by how great are the potentials of this aspect of settlement excavation.

From the Bhita excavations it is evident that the regular orientation of streets and houses goes back to a Mauryan, if not pre-Mauryan, date, and continues into the post-Mauryan period. The Bhita brick houses appear to have retained a more or less regular pattern of rooms around a central courtyard throughout the whole of the occupation, while the Bhir mound houses are built of stone rubble and are considerably less regular. Marshall identified a number of small separate structures facing the street as shops, while the courtyard houses were approached

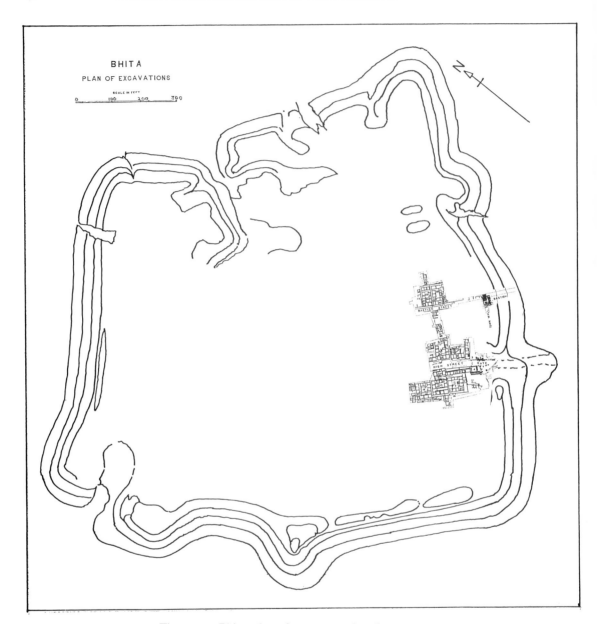

Fig. 11.9. Bhita, plan of rampart and settlement.

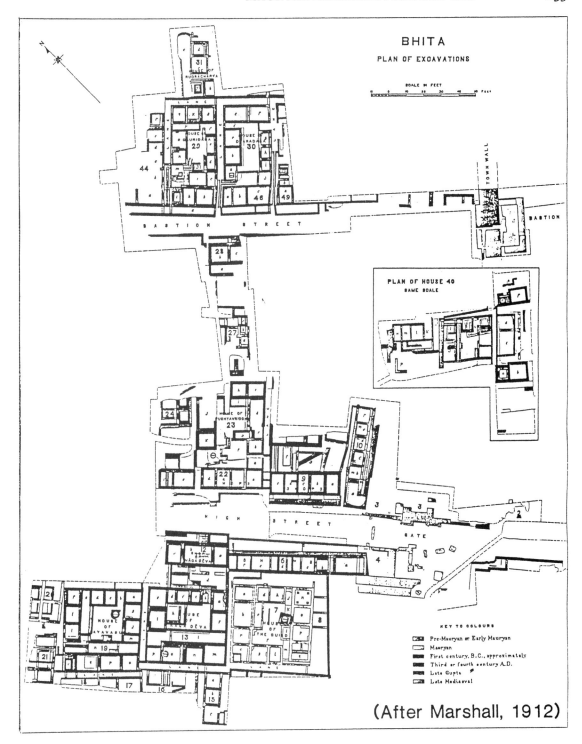

Fig. 11.10.   House plans of the 3rd to 2nd centuries BC, Bhita (after Marshall).

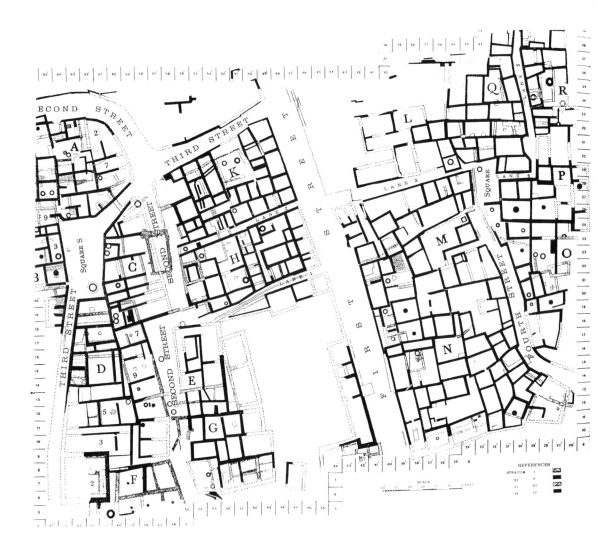

Fig. 11.11.   House plans of the 3rd to 2nd centuries BC, Bhir Mound, Taxila (after Marshall).

by narrow alleys leading off the streets. At Taxila too there is some evidence that a regular grid pattern of main streets was established by Mauryan times, although neither the smaller lanes nor the houses themselves altogether conform to this plan. Strangely, the orientation of the main streets bears little relationship to the surviving outlines of the mound. In Wheeler's unpublished excavations of 1945, a curious curved or even perhaps apsidal structure was found amidst regular housing but no description or explanation has been published (Fig. 11.12). Elsewhere, structures were made of burnt brick, unburnt brick or stone,

Fig 11.12. Taxila, Bhir Mound, excavations of 1944–45, view of excavated structures assignable to the Mauryan period (Wheeler Archive, Faculty of Oriental Studies, Cambridge).

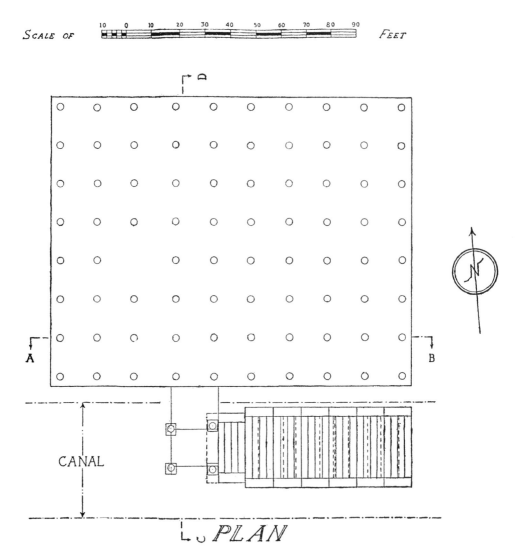

Fig. 11.13.   Pataliputra, Kumrahar, plan of the pillared hall (after Altekar and Mishra).

depending on local availability of materials. In both Bhita and Taxila terracotta ringwells occur from Mauryan times, both within the confines of courtyard houses and outside. There has been much discussion of the function of these ringwells; but there is evidence that the same structures were employed in several different functional contexts: some being used for drawing water; others to provide soakage pits for sullage; and a third group used as latrines (Roy 1983, 139–47). One of the clues to this latter function is the occasional discovery in the Ganges valley of terracotta slabs with a central hole and raised foot emplacements, more or less identical to their modern ceramic counter-

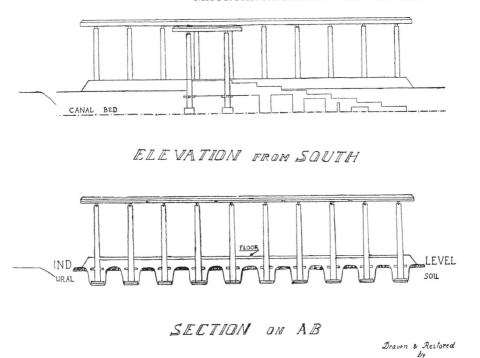

Fig. 11.14. Pataliputra, Kumrahar, side elevation of the pillared hall (after Altekar and Mishra).

parts. We are not aware that illustrations of such specimens have ever been published but we were shown an example of Vaisali.

The pillared hall at Pataliputra

We referred in the previous chapter to the mysterious pillared hall at Kumrahar and as it is probably the earliest building in South Asia, employing monolithic stone pillars, one needs to understand more regarding its nature and construction. In this task the original excavation report of Spooner in 1912–14 is less helpful than the brilliant re-examination of the site by Vijaykanta Mishra and A. S. Altekar in 1959 (Figs. 11.13 & 11.14). These excavations revealed that the pillared hall was constructed by digging a series of 80 foundation pits in the alluvial silt, each between 1.52 and 1.83 m in depth and about five feet square. In each pit a 15 cm layer of rammed blue clay was laid and on this bed a timber platform of c. 1.4 m² was placed, consisting of at least two layers, at right angles to each other. The pillars were erected on these platforms. Over this foundation a plinth, about 1.07 m in height, was raised and a further section of the shafts of the pillars was therefore buried. The excavators estimated that a complete pillar was probably c. 9.6 m in length, but that about 2.7 m of this total was buried beneath the floor of the raised plinth. To the southeast of the hall, a canal of c. 3 m depth and 12.6 m in width had been excavated. The excavators conjecture that the massive timber platform found by Spooner immediately south of the hall formed the foundation for a broad ramp or stairway leading up from the ground level to the floor. The hall had a fairly short life and appears to have been destroyed by fire some time in the second century BC. A thick layer of burnt material and particularly of wood ash led the excavators to conclude that the stone pillars had supported a massive timber superstructure or roof.

In sum, this pillared hall combines certain features which recall the pillared halls of the Achaemenid palaces and others which show a distinctly local improvization. The concept of a more or less square hall, raised on a plinth and approached up a monumental ramp on one side appears to us to be distinctly Achaemenid; but the way in which the structure was achieved suggests that it was the work of local craftsmen who had been given a description of the Persian halls and who created their own solution while reproducing them on the alluvial banks of the Ganga. We are unable to determine the function of the hall: S. P. Gupta (1980) in a characteristically spirited discussion suggests that it may have been a canal-side pavilion rather than one of the formal halls of the palace. Clearly this site calls for exploratory excavation so that further structural remains may be uncovered.

2. Religious architecture

The introduction of stone

Before considering the different categories of early religious monuments and their affiliations, we must first point out that the introduction of cut stone as a building material in religious, no less than secular, architecture and sculpture appears to have first occurred during the Mauryan period. There is no evidence that the rare occurrence of architectural stonework in the Indus civilization, as for example that recently discovered at Dholavira, formed the beginning of a lasting tradition; and thereafter there is no further evidence of such monumental stonework until the Mauryan period. We are therefore inclined to follow the views of Vincent Smith) (1914, 140–3), and to associate the beginnings of stone architecture and sculpture in India with the stimulus provided by the Achaemenid empire and particularly as a result of Alexander's invasion of India. These events at the very least opened the way for travellers to move between India and the countries to the west and thus may be seen as creating a climate for new ideas to be disseminated. This in turn may have coincided with the emergence of a group of craftsmen who translated what had been either seen or heard of elsewhere into actual craft skills, and into something peculiarly Indian. We find it difficult to accept Irwin's view that:

the alleged 'foreign' inspiration of the style had nothing whatever to do with Perso-Hellenistic art of the post-Alexanderian period, but is traceable to an earlier epoch when India was already linked culturally, as well as economically, with the civilizations of the ancient Near East. (Irwin 1974, 712)

That there was in India already a flourishing architectural tradition in wood, as Fergusson long ago argued (Fergusson 1910, 51–3), seems to us quite acceptable. We believe that this tradition arose as a concomitant of the emerging city states of the Ganges valley during the century or so which preceded the Mauryans. Its traces are clearly to be seen in the typically timber structural forms which are translated into stone in the early Buddhist rock-cut apsidal 'caitya' halls and monasteries. They are also in evidence on the early structural stone railings and toranas of Mauryan and later times. The point, however, remains that there is no solid evidence for the use of monumental stonework or sculpture in the Ganges valley prior to the time of Candragupta; and until its existence can be demonstrated, it seems premature to postulate shadowy borrowings from an 'earlier epoch' (see also Gupta 1980, 43–7).

For an overview of Mauryan architecture we recommend the reader to consult some of the principal expositions to date: notably Percy Brown's *Indian Architecture (Hindu and Buddhist)* (n.d.), and S. P. Gupta's *Roots of Indian Art*, 1980, where the subject is discussed with great authority and in considerable detail. For early Buddhist architecture a shorter but authoritative source is Debala Mitra's *Buddhist Monuments* (1971).

Early Buddhist architecture

The appearance of religious architecture during the Mauryan period may be linked in no small degree with Asoka's conversion to Buddhism. It is thanks to this event that the emperor established or enlarged many Buddhist sites, and set about disseminating his beliefs, in the form of rock inscriptions. The presence of such inscriptions on stone columns or rocks, and their apposition to monuments or monument complexes, provides us with a challenge to discover at what point in the history of such monuments the Asokan intervention took place. A few major examples will suffice to show our meaning.

> At Lumbini, the birthplace of the Buddha, a stone column bears a seminal inscription of Asoka, stating that he visited the place in the twentieth year of his reign (c. 249 BC) and worshipped, because 'Here Buddha was born, the Sakya Muni. A stone pillar was set up and a stone wall was made.' The pillar stands beside the small shrine, now entirely masked in later construction, on a raised platform which marks the sacred spot.

At the nearby Nigali Sagar an inscribed pillar was erected in the same year, when Asoka visited the site and worshipped. This states that here a stupa of the former Buddha, Konagamana (Kanakamuni), was enlarged twofold (or, for the second time). The stupa itself has now disappeared.

At Sarnath, in the Deer Park where the Buddha preached his First Sermon, turning the Wheel of the Dharma, an inscribed column was set up on the west side of the main shrine marking no doubt the actual spot associated with this momentous event. Excavation revealed, on the same axis but a short distance farther west, the foundations of an early brick apsidal caitya hall (Fig. 11.15). In this part of the site a number of early stone sculptures, some probably Mauryan and some slightly later, were found. To the south of the main shrine, on the north–south axis, the earliest structural stage of the nearby Dharmarajika stupa was also found to belong to the Mauryan period.

At Sanchi, beside the great stupa on the hilltop monastic site outside the city of Vidisa, an inscribed column was erected beside the south gateway of the stupa, and excavation revealed that both the stupa and an apsidal hall in front of the gateway had been founded in the Mauryan period (Fig. 11.16).

In all of these, and many other instances, it can be safely assumed that the inscribed pillars in their monumental settings and their careful siting in relation to major shrines, stupas and apsidal caitya halls, formed part of the great constructional activity inaugurated by Asoka. Indeed the only instance where one may with any confidence postulate an earlier date for the foundation of a stone monument is the pillared hall at Pataliputra, which may date from the time of Candragupta Maurya.

Main types of monument

It may be accepted that certain types of Buddhist structures go back to the founder's lifetime. Unfortunately archaeology can as yet tell us little or nothing about the forms of these early structures. While it seems reasonable to expect that some at least were made of transitory materials such as bamboo, thatch, etc., this can scarcely excuse archaeologists for their lack of a more enquiring, problem-oriented, approach to research on such matters. It might be expected for example that at the Jetavana monastery at Sravasti, where according to ancient tradition the Buddha spent much time in residence, excavation would reveal evidence of the earliest structural remains, which as they may be expected to date from the time of the Buddha would be of particular importance. In the time of Asoka, when more solid materials, brick and stone, began to be employed, three main types of structures emerge: these are the stupa, the apsidal caitya hall, and the monastery. The Mauryan columns constitute a fourth structural form, but we shall discuss them below in the context of sculpture.

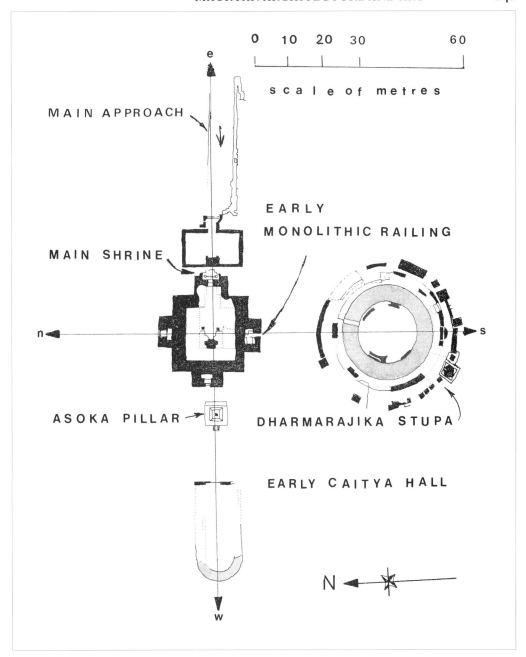

Fig. 11.15. Central elements of the religious complex at Sarnath in the Mauryan period (based on excavation reports).

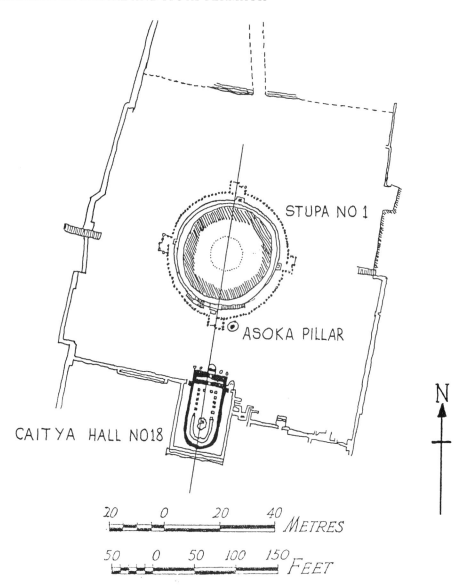

Fig. 11.16. Sanchi, relative position of the great stupa, Asokan column and caitya hall No. 18.

The stupa

The stupa is essentially a heaped-up mound of earth over the ashes of a cremation. Its Buddhist connotation doubtless arose at the time of the Mahaparinirvana, when the ashes of the Buddha were collected, divided and ceremonially buried in seven places, including Rajgir, Vaisali and Kapilavastu. These seven places must have been the earliest Buddhist stupas. Perhaps the

Fig. 11.17. Vaisali, early brick stupa showing projections at the cardinal points and periods of reconstruction (after Sinha and Roy).

oldest surviving stupa, though whether it is one of those referred to above cannot be proven, has been discovered and excavated at Vaisali (Sinha and Roy 1969, 16–23). This was originally a simple heap of clayey earth, some 7.8 m in diameter and at maximum 3.3 m in height; subsequently it was enlarged with burnt bricks on three occasions (Fig. 11.17). The first enlargement may well have been pre-Mauryan, in the light of associated finds of NBP, and the second was probably of the time of Asoka. A fragment of polished Chunar sandstone was found stratified above this level. A peculiar feature of this stupa, found in the original clay structure and repeated in each of the brick enlargements, is the presence of small projecting platforms on the cardinal points, similar to the *ayaka* platforms of Sri Lankan stupas.

We cannot point to a single stupa which preserves unchanged the original form of the Asoka period, as in almost every case subsequent rebuilding and enlargement have taken place. However, we would agree with Debala Mitra's conclusion regarding the Dharmarajika stupa at Sarnath (Mitra 1971, 24):

> The Asokan nucleus of the Dharmarajika is somewhat better documented. It was a hemispherical dome (nearly 46 ft in diameter) of brickwork, with a terraced

drum or *medhi* (less than 60 ft in diameter) as the base; the dome was surmounted by one or more umbrellas (*chatravali*), the latter set within a square railing.

Whether the idea of casing a stupa in stone, as we find in some later instances, began as early as the Mauryan period, cannot at present be said. The further development of the stupa, with its regional variations, must belong to subsequent periods.

The apsidal caitya hall

A second class of monument found in early Buddhist contexts is that known from inscriptions as *caitya griha* or caitya hall. These halls had in the main an oblong body with one apsidal end. From the detail recovered from rock-cut architecture of a slightly later date we know that substantial parts of such structures were of timber, although the walls might well have been made of brick, or brick and timber. Certainly, wherever evidence survives it appears that the apsidal end was intended to house a stupa, and therefore the hall as a whole must have been intended for purposes of worship. We have no definite evidence that any of the earliest surviving examples actually date from Mauryan times, but there are good reasons to believe that some do. For example, at Sarnath the brick apsidal hall discovered west of the main shrine and noticed above, not far from the Asokan pillar, was excavated in the earlier part of this century (Fig. 11.15). Although no real evidence of its date was obtained, we think it highly probable that it belongs to the Mauryan period. Again, the two apsidal halls at Sanchi (known as temples 18 and 40, respectively), carefully excavated by Marshall, are both ascribed by him to the time of Asoka, and we can only say that we accept his argument (Marshall 1936, 112–22). Both buildings passed through several stages of reconstruction. In the case of the former the earliest construction is contemporary with the initial levelling of that part of the hilltop, and part of the same process as the construction of the great stupa (Fig. 11.16). Marshall, with his usual keen sense of enquiry, noted that among the debris from the destruction of the earliest structural stage were many terracotta roof tiles, which he inferred to have come from that building, as well as a fine stone bowl of Chunar sandstone, which may lend further support to his views. Marshall's dating of temple 40 is equally cautious and well argued: principally he believes that as the stone pillars employed in the rebuilding of the hall after its initial destruction by fire bear inscriptions in Brahmi script of around the second century BC, therefore the original construction may well date back to Asokan times.

The circular caitya hall

A number of circular halls are known, principally from surviving rock-cut examples. However, near the Asokan inscriptions at Bairat remains of a

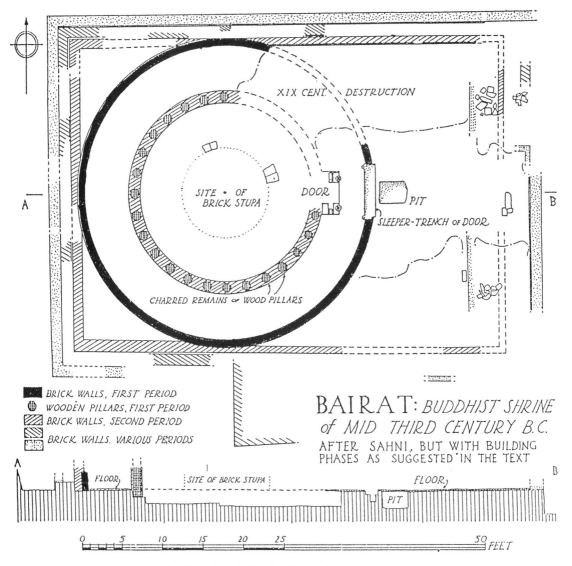

Fig. 11.18.   Bairat, circular caitya hall (after Piggott).

substantial circular shrine were excavated by Sahni (1937). The structure was in essence a circular domed hall supported on wooden octagonal pillars with plaster infilling, and surrounded by a circumambulation path with brick walls (Fig. 11.18). Fragments of Chunar sandstone pillars and a stone umbrella of the same material were also found in the excavations. The nature of the roof with central dome and surrounding semivault can be clearly understood from a study of the number of rock-cut and early relief examples (see Fig. 12.18). Although there is no firm date for this circular hall, its proximity to the Asokan edicts and to monastic remains in

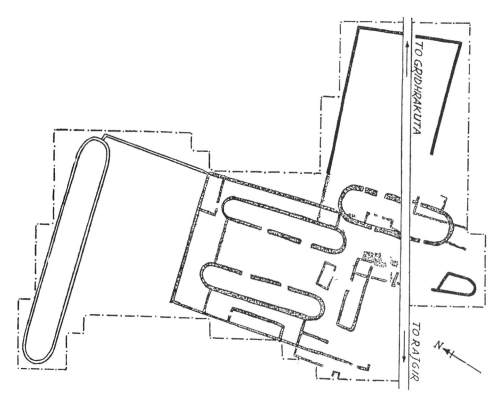

Fig. 11.19. Plan of Jivakarama monastery, Rajgir (courtesy Archaeological Survey of India).

a comparatively isolated spot, and its association with fragments of polished Chunar sandstone pillars, certainly argue for its Mauryan date.

Monasteries (viharas)

As far as one can say no examples of the familiar square courtyard monasteries, which become so familiar a feature of Buddhist architecture from the beginning of the first century AD, can be dated to the Mauryan period. It is generally believed that most of the early monastic residences were small individual structures of temporary materials. It is commonly accepted that the site traditionally known as the Jivikarama monastery at Rajgir may represent an early monastery, but there is no way this can be proved and it has so far not been dated (Fig. 11.19). Certainly some of the depictions of early Buddhist sites on reliefs of the first to second centuries BC at Bharhut and Amaravati suggest that the long narrow buildings with rounded ends, reminiscent of those found in the Jivikarama, may represent a local folk building type of that time.

Rock-cut architecture

The tradition of rock-cut architecture, which from the second century BC on to the end of the first millennium AD was to become so characteristic a feature of Indian architecture, has its roots in the Mauryan period. Perhaps the first example is the small cave known as Son Bhandar at Rajgir. This traditionally marks the site of the first Buddhist council, and therefore may belong to pre-Mauryan times. It consists of an oblong chamber with a crudely vaulted roof and square undecorated doorway. The fact that the cave contains a later Brahmi inscription is in our view not significant: many other early and well-dated caves also contain later inscriptions.

In the neighbouring Barabar hills is another important group of caves, several bearing inscriptions recording Asoka's benefaction to the Ajivika sect. These caves show several forms. One set have oblong vaulted rooms, while others contain circular domed shrines, with elements of timber structure represented in stone. The interiors of several of the caves bear the high polish which is commonly referred to as 'Mauryan polish'. Architecturally the cave known as Lomas Rishi is the most important (Figs. 11.20(1) and 11.21). It has a carved rock facade of a timber *caitya* arch on the rock face around its entrance, and a circular room at the end of the oblong vault. This cave has been closely studied by Huntington (1974–75) and Gupta (1980) and the reader is referred to their work for further details. Similar features occur inside the Sudama cave, where there is again an inscription of Asoka (Fig. 11.20(2)). A third group of caves is in the nearby Nagarjuni hills, and these bear inscriptions of king Dasaratha, the grandson of Asoka. Like the Barabar caves these appear to have been dedicated to the Ajivika sect. In our view all these examples may be safely ascribed to the later Mauryan period. No other rock-cut caves in any part of India can claim equal antiquity, and those of the succeeding centuries witness to the steady growth of technical skill and design on the part of their craftsmen. For this reason we conclude that the caves of the Bihar group represent the beginnings of the tradition of rock-cut architecture in India.

The beginnings of Vaisnava and Saiva architecture

So far we have been considering religious architecture which can all be assigned to the unorthodox sects, Buddhists and Ajivikas. We must now make a very brief reference to the beginnings of orthodox Brahmanical monuments, particularly those associated with the cults of Visnu and Siva. A number of reliable studies of the origins of these cults is available, but discussion of their archaeology and art history is less easily available. Although much new data has appeared since the publication of the late J. N. Banerjea's study of *Religion in Art and Archaeology* (1968), this is still a useful source.

The cult of Visnu, with its special emphasis on *bhakti*, devotion, can be traced

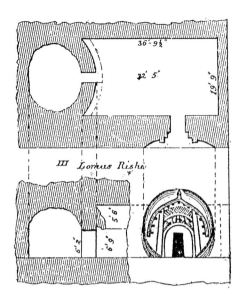

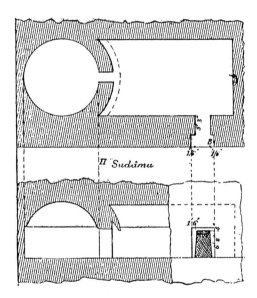

Fig. 11.20. (1) Barabar hills, plan and section of Lomasrishi cave; (2) plan and section of Sudama cave (after Cunningham).

from Vedic times, but it appears particularly to have developed between the time of Panini (c. BC 400) and the end of the Mauryan period. Most of the early archaeological and art historical indications are not before the second to third centuries BC. Indeed we should have been inclined to leave this topic for consideration in chapter 12, were it not for the important excavation of the site at Vidisa, long famed for its inscribed pillar of Heliodorus, the Greek ambassador

Fig. 11.21. Lomasrishi cave, facade (courtesy S. P. Gupta).

from king Antialcidas of Taxila, datable to c. BC 125. Excavations by the late M. D. Khare in 1963–64 revealed that the pillar was the sole survivor of an original row of eight which were contemporary with the later period of construction of what was evidently a shrine of Vasudeva (Bhandarkar 1914; Irwin 1978; Khare, 1978) (Fig. 11.22). Below were the remains of an earlier stage of the building, represented by the foundation trenches of an elliptical structure, some 8 × 3 m in extent. This little building produced sherds of NBP and punchmarked coins from its floor deposit, and should probably be dated to the third century BC. Its importance is that it represents a style of structure occasionally depicted on reliefs of the following centuries, being a timber and brick structure with twin apsidal ends and a vaulted roof with a semi-vaulted circumambulation path running around it. The inner section was clearly the sanctuary or *garbha griha*. Although the published photograph does not show it, the excavator assured me that the building had a projecting porch in the centre of one side of its long axis.

Fig. 11.22. Vidisa, excavation of Bhagavata shrine (courtesy Archaeological Survey of India).

There can be no reason to doubt that the earlier structure, like its immediate successor, was a temple of the Bhagavata cult.

A closely related building was discovered by R. D. Bhandarkar in 1920 at Nagari, north of Chitor in Rajasthan. Here a massive stone railing bore several copies of an inscription of a king who names himself a Bhagavata, claiming to have made a stone wall around the Narayana (Visnu) enclosure, dedicated to Vasudeva and Sankarsana (Krishna and his brother Balarama) (Banerjea 1968, 87; Bhandarkar 1920). The inscription probably belongs to the late second century BC. In the centre of this enclosure Bhandarkar discovered the foundation walls of an elliptical structure some 13 × 7 m in size. This description suggests that the enclosure, or *Narayana vatika*, contained a building closely similar to the Vidisa temple, and also dedicated to the Bhagavata cult. There is unfortunately no indication of its age, but it may well pre-date the stone enclosure.

There is as yet no evidence of the structures of any cult sites associated with the worship of Siva from so early a date: the earliest example so far reported is that of the celebrated Gudimallam *linga* and its shrine near Renigunta in Andhra

Pradesh. Excavations here by I. K. Sarma have indicated that the first construction of the temple which houses the *linga* took place in c. the 2nd century BC. No radiocarbon dating was obtained and the estimated date is somewhat lacking in precision, although in no way implausible (Sarma 1982).

3. Sculpture and the other arts

By way of introduction to this section it may be remarked that in identifying a sculpture or other work of art as Mauryan, unless by virtue of its association with an inscription or a dated excavated context, we are frequently faced with the problem of identifying its age by other means. As a general rule the principal method is art historical, to have recourse to consideration of its stylistic aspects. For the early materials we are now discussing, where the number of comparative pieces is often so small, an element of subjectivity must be accepted.

The Mauryan columns

Halfway between architecture and sculpture, the sandstone columns with their finely carved capitals and their characteristically polished surface, are one of the special features of Mauryan art. It has long been accepted that almost every one of these columns, whether found complete or in fragmentary form, had originated from Chunar, an area of sandstone hills some 25 km west of Banaras on the south bank of the Ganga river. Recently, apparently for the first time, a group of archaeologists from Banaras Hindu University visited the area of the quarries and was rewarded by the discovery of many roughly shaped blocks of stone, some cylindrical and some partly rounded in section. They found also on the rocks a number of short Kharosthi inscriptions, and realized that this must be the actual site of the long-famed Chunar quarries (Pant and Jayaswal, 1990, 49–52). The ancient quarries are not now worked and are easily distinguished from the more recent. Quarrying of sandstone still goes on in the neighbourhood, and querns and grindstones are widely distributed in the local markets.

The archaeologists were able to reconstruct much of the ancient technology. Rectangular blocks of stone were first removed from the parent rock and then chiselled to cylindrical shape in the vicinity of the quarry. They were then rolled down the gentle hillslopes to level ground in valleys from where they were prepared to be transported to the Ganges bank for transshipment. It is probable that the blocks for carving the capitals were similarly detached and roughly prepared at the quarry and were only carved into their final forms when they had reached the required site.

This discovery is of considerable importance. It has long been apparent that the successful transportation of Chunar sandstone pillars to sites as remote as Lumbini and Sanchi, let alone Taxila, involved distances of hundreds of miles and called for a remarkable logistical base. Taken in conjunction with the radiocarbon dating of extensive copper and zinc mining activity in other parts of India noticed in the previous chapter, it reinforces the long-held view that the technological and economic resources for quarrying and transporting the Chunar sandstone were present and being exploited during Asokan, if not even earlier, times. This discovery serves as an example of how major problem-oriented research can be carried out using methods largely, if not entirely, stopping short of excavation. It also lends support to our view that the pillars are unlikely to be substantially earlier than the Mauryan period. The presence of Kharosthi inscriptions is also most suggestive. There has long been a suggestion that a guild of stone-working sculptors and masons operating in the Ganges valley may have originated in the northwest, and followed the demands of the market down to the metropolitan area in Magadha. It has been noticed that the masons' marks employed at Bharhut on the stupa gateway take the form of Kharosthi letters, and the recent discovery of numbers of sherds inscribed in the same script from the Bengal area suggests a further extension in that direction (Mukherjee 1990).

There is an extensive literature on the Asokan pillars and their capitals: we may cite, as important references, Fergusson's *History of Architecture* (1910, 56–61); V. S. Agrawala's *Indian Art* (1965, 93–110); John Irwin's 'Asokan pillars, a reassessment of the evidence' (*Burlington Magazine* 1973–76); and S. P. Gupta's *Roots of Indian Art* (1980, 19–51, etc). We do not propose to involve ourselves in the controversies which have arisen regarding the age, symbolism or other aspects of the pillars and their capitals. Instead we shall aim to present a succinct conspectus of the subject, as it appears to us.

The first external notice of the pillars is in the writings of the Chinese Buddhist pilgrims Fa-hsien (c. AD 400) and Xuan-zang (Yuan-tsang) (c. AD 630–45) who in the accounts of their travels in India refer respectively to six and fifteen stone pillars as the work of Asoka. Modern research has recorded at least fifteen pillars, possibly more, as well as a number of sites where excavations have revealed portions of capitals or pillars, or fragments of polished sandstone which both by their character and archaeological contexts may be assigned approximately to the same period. Ten of the pillars bear Asokan inscriptions.

The pillars share a number of salient features, with a number of variants, whose significance has been variously interpreted. They are all monolithic shafts, most of them tapered, of between 12 and 14 m in height and 1–1.25 m in diameter at the base. The base was buried in the ground, to a depth of c. 3 m, and the lower part of the shaft was left untrimmed, while the remainder was given a fine polish. In some cases the base was surrounded by a brick or stone enclosure, with rock packing, resting on bare rock, in other cases, where the soil was alluvial, it stood on a square stone slab.

The capital, too, consisted of a number of elements, some with further variations. In the one adequately recorded case, the capital was attached to the shaft by a finely made biconical copper bolt, 62 cm in length, which fitted equally into the shaft and capital. The capital consists of several elements (Fig. 11.23):

Fig. 11.23. Asokan column from Lauriya Nandangarh. The most perfect standing column with its capital still in place (courtesy S. P. Gupta).

1. The lowest part, immediately above the shaft, is bell-shaped, resembling an inverted lotus bud. This element offers distant resemblances to the bells of Achaemenid columns, although there is no reason to think that they were its main source. The bells of the Vaisali and Lauriya Nandangarh capitals are comparatively squat, perhaps indicating their relative earliness. On some capitals the bell rests on a moulding in the form of a rope, above which is a second bead and reel moulding. On top of the bell a further moulding is found, sometimes as a plain torus, sometimes rope-like.

2. Above the bell is a rounded drum or abacus, which is variously decorated with acanthus and/or honeysuckle-like designs, with lines of feeding geese, and in one case (Sarnath) with four *Dharma-cakras* interspersed by the four noble beasts (the lion, bull, elephant and horse) representing the four directions (Figs. 11.25); on the Vaisali capital, the abacus takes the form of a plain square platform.

3. The most common main emblem of the capital is a seated lion, but in two instances there are four addorsed, seated lions (Fig. 11.24), and in others a bull (Fig. 11.26), an elephant, or in an example known from a relief of the second century BC, a horse. These main emblems constitute the most important body of Mauryan sculpture. In all cases the work was finished with a fine polish;

4. One additional element is found at Sarnath, where the main emblem of the capital, four addorsed lions, is appropriately crowned by a polished stone *Dharma-cakra* (Fig. 11.23).

The symbolism of the pillars is in most cases established as being Buddhist, by their being found or at least recorded in proximity to the great places of pilgrimage (that is at Lumbini, Bodh Gaya, Sarnath and Sravasti), or beside other major Buddhist stupas or shrines. In the case of the Sarnath capital an interpretation of its symbolism may be offered as follows: the pillar was erected by Asoka adjoining the main shrine in the Deer Park at Sarnath which marked the spot where the Buddha preached his first sermon, thereby setting in motion the wheel of the Dharma (*Dharma-cakra pravartana*). The abacus depicts four *Dharma-cakras* facing the four quarters, interspersed by four noble beasts, who in early Buddhist texts represent the four quarters. We are inclined to read the main symbol of the four lions seated, addorsed above the four *Dharma-cakras*, as symbolizing the proclamation of the Dharma in all four directions. But there may well be other meanings in the symbolism of the lions. The Chakkavatti Simhanada Sutta of the Digha Nikaya emphasizes the world-conquering aspect of the Dharma and the Dharma-cakra (Agrawala, 1964); while the Chula Simhanada Sutta (or shorter lion's roar Sutta) of the Majjhima Nikaya suggests a different emphasis, in that in this passage the Buddha gives a warning against schism and heresy. That Asoka may have had in mind this meaning is indicated by the

Fig. 11.24. Sarnath capital, the four lions (courtesy Archaeological Survey of India).

Fig. 11.25. Sarnath capital, the four noble beasts on the abacus (courtesy S. P. Gupta).

Fig. 11.26.   Rampurva bull capital (courtesy Archaeological Survey of India).

minor pillar edict he had carved on the shaft, which expressly addresses itself to the suppression of schism and heresy.

Other sculptures

S. P. Gupta (1980, 80–5) gives an exhaustive list of the principal pieces of early stone sculpture which may be assigned either to the Mauryan, Late Mauryan or even post-Mauryan periods, but which are stylistically in the same tradition. They include:

(a) A large group of important pieces, mainly fragments, found at Sarnath, in excavations west of the main shrine;

(b) The famous Didarganj Yaksi, found in a village near Pataliputra (Patna), and hotly disputed in regard to its age (we are prepared to accept it as a work of the 3rd–2nd century BC, but persuasive arguments can be offered for a later date, perhaps even second century AD) (c.f. Harle 1986, 31, etc.): whatever its date may be, it is a fine piece of polished Chunar sandstone (Fig. 11.27);

(c) A pair of almost lifesized nude male torsos from Lohanipur, Patna, generally believed to be Jaina images (Fig. 11.28);

(d) A splendidly lively elephant carved from the living rock, in front of the Asokan edict at Dhauli, Orissa (Fig. 11.29);

(e) Two addorsed, recumbent bull capitals from Kumrahar and Lohanipur, Patna;

(f) Two strange capitals in a kind of oriental Ionic style, one from Bulandibagh, Patna, and the other from Sarnath (Fig. 11.30, a and b); and

(g) A number of other important pieces, mainly fragmentary, from other sites at Patna, Chirand, Hajipur and Masarh.

We do not pretend that all these pieces can be certainly dated to the Mauryan period, but we believe that the majority should be, and that the remainder may be dated in the second century BC.

To conclude this section a few comments may be made on the style and character of the sculptures listed above. Fergusson (1910, 58), discussing the honeysuckle motif on the Asokan capitals, remarked:

> In this instance, however, it is hardly probable that it was introduced directly by the Greeks, but is more likely to have been borrowed through Persia, from Assyria, whence the Greeks also originally obtained it.

In some respects scholarship has not advanced much farther towards understanding the question of origins and influences of the stone sculpture

Fig. 11.27. Didarganj, Patna, sandstone Yaksi, height 2.06 m (courtesy S. P. Gupta).

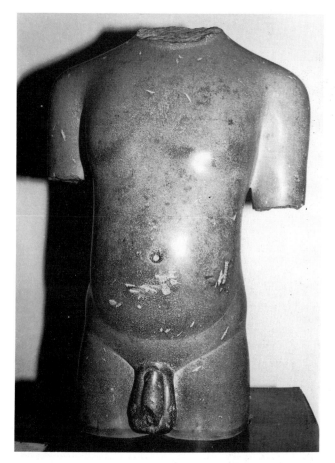

Fig. 11.28.   Lohanipur, sandstone torso (? Jaina), height 66 cm (courtesy Patna Museum).

of the Mauryans. To us it appears that three strands are interwoven in the style:

(a) Undoubtedly there is a major Achaemenid, Persian, influence which expresses itself in the design of the pillared hall at Pataliputra and in the rather stiff depiction of the animals on the capitals. The treatment of the Rampurva bull for example is reminiscent of the Assyrian winged lions who were taken up and adapted by the Achaemenids: they are designed to be seen from two or three separate viewpoints, but not fully conceived as sculpture in the round. The testicles of the bull are shown separately on each side (Fig. 11.26). Perhaps another aspect of this strand may be called Scythian, to be seen in such features as the prancing horse on the Sarnath abacus (Fig. 11.25, b).

Fig. 11.29.   Dhauli, elephant (photograph Allchin).

a

b

Fig. 11.30.   Stone brackets or capitals suggestive of the Ionic order: (a) Sarnath
(courtesy S. P. Gupta); (b) Pataliputra, Bulandibagh (photograph Allchin).

(b) The second strand is Greek or Hellenistic, and is mainly noticeable in the mouldings and decorative details, acanthus, honeysuckle, etc. This therefore appears to be a relatively minor influence.

(c) The third strand is that which is most obvious in the depiction of the elephants at Dhauli or Sankissa, where a much freer, indigenous Indian style takes over, and the sculptors emancipate themselves from the earlier stiffness. This assertion of what has been taken to be an Indian folk tradition seems to us to be the most significant element, since it will become increasingly dominant in the art of the following centuries.

The Ringstones

Another class of small carved stone objects which are generally agreed to be associated with the Mauryan period are those commonly referred to as ringstones (Fig. 11.31). This name is somewhat misleading as it includes several rather different types of stone discs, and a number of other pieces of finely carved stonework which give the impression that they were designed for use by goldsmiths, either as forms or as moulds. In most cases the stone employed seems to be a soapstone or metamorphosed schist. The size of the discs varies between c. 10 cm in diameter for the larger varieties, which often have a pierced central hole, and 5–6 cm for a smaller, unpierced variety. The larger, pierced ringstones have a hole cut in the centre, having a convex profile, being wider at the top and smaller at the bottom. This inward-curving surface is included in the design; the outer face of the disc is uncarved, as is the underside. The carving on all the pieces of this group is in low relief and shares a distinctly individual style and iconography. The two most comprehensive studies of the ringstones to date are by Gupta (1980, 53–77) and Pramod Chandra (1971).

The dating of the ringstones and allied pieces remains somewhat problematic. The evidence of stratigraphy, from the excavations at the Bhir mound, Taxila, suggests that they belong to the late fourth to mid-second centuries BC, possibly continuing into the opening of the Christian era. Another clue to dating is provided by two specimens, one from Patna and the other from Kausambi, bearing inscriptions in early Brahmi. Of these the first contains a name, presumably of the owner; the second is mainly legible, being roughly scratched on the outer edge, but it has so far defied all attempts at translation. Both inscriptions may be dated palaeographically to the third or second centuries BC. The distribution of the discs and ringstones is as follows: Patna (21 examples), Kausambi (12), Taxila (7), Banaras (6), Mathura (6), and single finds from Vaisali, Chirand, Bhita, Sohgaura, Jhusi, Sankissa, Rupar, Haryana, and Purana Qila, Delhi. There are some regional varieties discernible, but the central features are in the main common throughout.

Fig. 11.31.   Ringstones: 1. from Taxila; and 2–5. from Patna, (Murtaziganj),
(courtesy National Museum, New Delhi, and Patna Museum).

The subject matter of the reliefs on some of the ringstones is mysterious and problematic. Two recurrent features are the presence of alternating naked females and trees, carved around the curved inner face of the ringstones and on the upper register of the discs. Between these two motifs on the latter is an infilling of prancing elephants, horses, rams, hares, lions and winged lions, humped bulls, stags, rhinoceroses, lizards and various birds, animals and mythical creatures. Occasionally human beings or dwarves are depicted. The males wear short tunics with some sort of headdress or binding. One holds up what is evidently a torch (or perhaps cornucopia), another is seated in front of a leaf hut and holds a spherical object, perhaps a fruit, in his hands: he is approached by a heavily draped female with a long plaited pigtail.

The recurrent naked females have been generally regarded as a goddess. She invariably stands frontally, with her arms loosely hanging and hands extended. she has often a prominent coiffure and in numerous instances can be seen to wear heavy circular earrings. In one instance, from Rajghat, she is shown wearing a sari (Gupta 1980, Pl. 36 h). The trees occur particularly in the Patna group, and all appear to be palm trees, one variety resembling the treatment of palms in Assyrian reliefs. Outside the Patna group, the naked female alternates not with palm trees but with the honeysuckle motif.

Some parts of the same iconography appear on a number of equally small, related pieces of stone carving. One may note in particular a small piece from Rajgir, divided into three panels (Fig. 11.32): the upper panel shows a harpist, wearing a dhoti, playing before a dancing female, who wears a lower garment but has a head identical to that of the naked female, with large earrings; the middle panel shows a similarly clad male holding up a wine cup to a similarly dressed and pigtailed female, a wine jar stands on the floor between them; and the third panel shows a naked male, holding up a cup to a naked female, who here assumes the identical posture of the goddess of the ringstones. There is a closely related fragment in the Victoria and Albert Museum, believed to have come from the NWFP, with a winged lion in the upper panel and the upper parts only of the naked male and female, the latter holding up a wine cup in her hand. A third piece is a small cup form of soapstone from Kausambi, now in Allahabad City Museum (Fig. 11.33). This shows a row of heavily draped dancing females with bird heads (or masks), and a seated harpist (male) before a dancing female with large earrings and arms adorned with bangles. This piece unfortunately is broken and part is missing, but it is remarkable for the Greek elements which are present in the otherwise typically Indian treatment of the carving as a whole. The Greek character is emphasized by a vine scroll which runs around the lower part of the form, by the garments of the draped females and by their gestures. A fourth piece is a tiny sphere of stone in the Eilenberg collection of the Metropolitan Museum of Art, New York (Lerner and Kossak 1991, 52–3). This shows three scenes, divided by lush vegetation: first a draped couple advance towards the left, the woman has a small flask in her hand, the man an unidentified object; in the

Fig. 11.32.   Rajgir, stone relief (courtesy Archaeological Survey of India)
(c. 1.5:1).

Fig. 11.33. Kausambi, stone cup-form with relief figures, two views (courtesy G. R. Sharma).

Fig. 11.34. Vaisali, stone relief (after Deva and Mishra) (3:4).

second the man and woman face each other, the woman wearing a sari, the man a dhoti, and holding a musical instrument (?); in the third the man stands playing on a harp, while the woman, still clad, dances. A goose (?) stands between them with upturned beak. A grapevine runs round the upper register of the sphere. On its top sits a winged *yaksa* figure with splayed legs, playing twin horns. A fifth piece is a small jasper goldsmith's form, found at Vaisali, with a closely related female with sari, in relief, having large earrings and bangles (Fig. 11.34) (Deva and Mishra 1961).

We come finally to the vexed question of the significance of these stone rings, discs and other pieces. Almost the only thing on which all agree is that the naked female must be a goddess. But there have been widely diverging views as to who she may be, some seeing her as the Earth Mother (Bhumi), others as Sri (Fortune), and others again as the Great Mother. Gupta (1980, 70) percipiently remarks that

> The ringstones seem to have some esoteric meaning and the rituals connected with them appear to have been of a somewhat special kind.

We cannot explore this problem fully here, but some further points may be made. No one so far has commented in this connection on the discovery in excavations at Prabhas Patan in Saurashtra of a 'jasper' ear disc with a gold repoussé lotus formed decoration. This piece dates from the period of the NBP, and appears to be a hitherto unrecognized example of the ringstone series. We suggested above that the extremely delicate relief carving of the whole series might indicate some association with the goldsmith's craft. We may now advance one step farther and suggest that either the ringstones and discs may have been used as forms for the manufacture of repoussé gold plates which could later be filled with lac, to give the impression of solid gold earrings, conveniently without the weight that would involve; or that they may have been covered with gold plate and employed in some esoteric manner connected with a cult, as suggested by Gupta. The gold repoussé naked females from stupa deposits at Piprahawa and Lauriya Nandangarh may add some support to this idea, the suggestion being that they may originally have been parts of such cult objects which were later cut up and given an entirely different function, when they were deposited as relics in stupas.

We noticed above that the naked goddess and several features of dress and iconography, as well as the raw material employed, are shared between the ringstones and discs on the one hand, and the 'secular' pieces on the other. This leads us to wonder whether the two series may not be linked in other ways. For instance, might they be the product of a closely knit craft group, involved in making goldsmiths' forms, and perhaps engaged in producing golden wares and trading them over an area extending from Taxila in the northwest to Patna in the east? Their products may well have included narrowly secular as well as religious objects: particularly they might be expected to have included items of jewelry.

This leads us to a second, intriguing aspect of the problem, suggested by the way in which the naked goddess is approached and apparently worshipped by men, with rites which include the consumption of almost certainly intoxicating liquor, and orgiastic dancing. This prompts us to enquire whether the esoteric cult of the naked goddess may not have been associated in particular with the class of Devadasis, the female 'slaves' of a god. That Devadasis already existed in the immediately post-Mauryan period is indicated by a unique, early inscription found in a partly natural cave at Ramgarh in Madhya Pradesh. The cave has been cut so as to provide a series of benchlike seats, and may even have been intended as an arena for dancing or play acting. Here, a young sculptor or painter, named Devadinna, records his love for a Devadasi Sutanuka by name (*Annual Reports of the Archaeological Survey of India* 1903–4, 122). Palaeographically this inscription probably dates from the third or second century BC. Putting these various elements together, we are led to a strange and unexpected conclusion, that the ringstone series may have formed part of a religio-sexual cult, and that the discs and rings were used for making the large earrings which were one of the elements of the cult, either for votive purposes or for actual wear.

Terracottas

After the tremendous burst of terracotta art in the Indus valley and Baluchistan through the fourth and third millennia BC, throughout South Asia the evidence for terracottas during the second millennium is at best meagre, and remains so for the opening centuries of the first millennium BC. This does not mean that terracottas were not made in many parts of the subcontinent during that period, but that finds are comparatively few. The first millennium witnesses a new beginning in the Ganges valley, and from Mauryan times onwards terracottas once more become a major feature of the popular art. The discussion of the terracottas of the early historic period has hitherto been largely conducted on the basis of style, and for that reason lacked precision. S. P. Gupta recently made a brave and welcome attempt to correct the picture by discussing the growing volume of excavated sequences, dated by radiocarbon, which provide evidence of the development of types and styles during this period (Gupta 1980, 137–82). This useful approach is hampered by the imprecision of much radiocarbon-based dating. This effectively limits the usefulness of the archaeological approach for studying the stylistic development of many categories of objects, terracottas among them. Erdosy has argued in chapter 7 above, on the basis of a fresh examination of the radiocarbon dates, that the period of NBP may be divided into three stages: Early, from BC 550–400; Middle, BC 400–205; and Late, BC 250–100. Helpful as this may be, until more precise dating is achieved, archaeological dating can be of only limited assistance in such contexts. This being the case we shall discuss the terracottas assignable to the Mauryan period

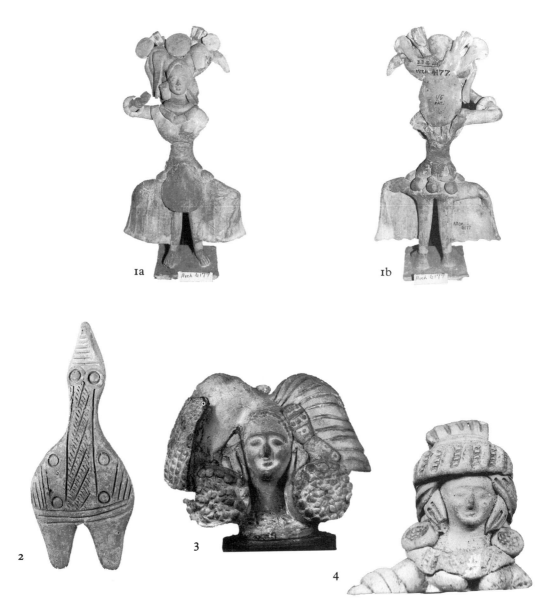

Fig. 11.35.   Mauryan terracottas from Patna and Buxar.
1. Patna, Bulandibagh, buff-grey clay figure of a dancing girl with elaborate headdress and clothing, height 27 cm, Mauryan (Patna Museum, Arch. 4177);
2. Patna, terracotta figure of a serpent, height 12 cm, Mauryan (Patna Museum, Arch. 8722);
3. Buxar, head of a girl with characteristically broad, flattened face, and florid earrings, Mauryan;
4. Buxar, head of a smiling girl, with distinctive headdress and concave earrings.

Fig. 11.36.   Mauryan terracottas from Mathura.
1. Mathura, grey clay, hand-modelled figure of a mother goddess with elaborate headdress and adornments, stylistically 'Mauryan', height 17 cm (from the Archaeological Survey excavations, 1974–75, period I, 'Middle NBP' (i.e. c. BC 400–250));
2. Mathura, terracotta elephant with raised trunk, in grey clay with traces of NBP type dressing on surface, stylistically Mauryan, Mathura Museum (photograph Allchin).

primarily in terms of the art historical and stylistic data (Figs 11.35 and 11.36). For further reading on this aspect we recommend the useful synthesis by Poster (1986).

Following Poster our discussion will be in two parts: the first will briefly review the question of pre-Mauryan terracottas, and the second will survey the Mauryan. For the first period Poster identifies a number of subjects, *naginis* (snake goddesses), birds, animals, and human female figurines. Of the latter there are three main types, all of them hand-modelled:

(a) a wide-eyed female with round face, punched earlobes with large circular earplugs, prominent breasts, and perforations on the crown of the head for decoration. This type is seen at Buxar, Pataliputra and Kausambi;

(b) animal-faced, hand-made figurines from Pataliputra; and

(c) a thick-necked female type, looking upward, found at Vaisali, Kausambi and Mathura.

Poster concludes that the first and third types survive into the Mauryan period, 'gradually acquiring embellishment'. We are not convinced that any of this early group can date from before the fourth century; but whatever their dates may be it is certain that they represent the beginnings of the Ganges valley terracotta tradition.

The second period of this classification is Mauryan. Once again we are closely following Poster. Certain types, such as the snake goddesses and the simple mother goddesses, continue from the preceding period and show, as we noted above, a continuing elaboration of their embellishment. This is particularly clear in the austere hand-modelled mother goddesses from Mathura, who are now adorned with appliqué headgear, dress and jewelry. Also there is evidence of growing popularity of animal figurines, elephants, some made of NBP including examples of the red and black painted variety, horses, bulls, rams and birds. But the most important innovation of this period is found particularly at Pataliputra and other sites in Magadha: this consists of a small but unique series of female figures. An important group was found at Bulandibagh, Patna (Fig. 11.35, 1), and others at Kumrahar and Buxar. These figures appear to be largely hand-modelled, except for the head which was made in a double mould, and they stand on small terracotta stands or pedestals. They are notable for the way in which items of clothing, drapery and headgear are added appliqué, and for the fact that many of the subjects appear to be dancing girls. They have a sophistication quite unlike the general run of terracottas and this suggests that they were even then rare, luxury items, the products of specialist urban craftsmen. They have been studied in detail by Desai (1985), who agrees with Poster in recognizing in them the strong influence of Greek terracotta art of the fourth to third centuries BC. We too had quite independently arrived at this view. When we remember that, according to Megasthenes, at this time Pataliputra was thronged with foreigners, including Greeks, the source of a Greek terracotta influence is not hard to imagine. The same influence may be seen in the terracotta monkey mask from Chirand period III (i.e. to the Mauryan period), which strongly recalls the comedy masks of the contemporary Greek drama (IAR 1970–71, Pl. 9a).

4. Conclusion

This chapter indicates that, despite the unsatisfactory nature of so much of the archaeological evidence, there is a considerable body of material, both architectural and artistic, which can reasonably be ascribed to the Mauryan period. By comparison, there is very little, if any, firmly dated material from the preceding period. By Mauryan times, however, both architecture and art show a substratum of an indigenous tradition, continuing from earlier times and permitting us to postulate its prior existence as the basis upon which innovation took place. Both architecture and art show evidence of powerful external influences in the creation of an appropriate 'urban' style. In the case of the architecture and stone sculpture one may cite the beginning of stone working, stone construction, and stone carving as offering strong hints of at least an awareness of the already centuries-old Achaemenid tradition. In the case of the ringstones and terracotta art, and of the use of details on stone sculpture, there appears to have been a different external stimulus deriving from Greek sources.

CHAPTER 12

POST-MAURYAN STATES OF MAINLAND SOUTH ASIA (c. BC 185–AD 320)

D. K. CHAKRABARTI

The focus of this chapter is on the growth of settlements in general and cities in particular in northern India and Pakistan between the end of the Mauryas (c. BC 185) and the beginning of the Guptas (c. AD 320), a period of about five hundred years in all. In Indian historical studies the term post-Mauryan generally denotes this period. Northern India has rather looser geographical connotations, sometimes meaning something as narrow as the Gangetic plain and the area north of the Vindhyas, but here we shall take it to mean all those parts of the subcontinent which had been at one time or another within the Mauryan sphere.

I. The political framework

The political history of this period was enacted in the following geo-political orbits (Figs 12.1 and 12.2):

1. The area between the north of Hindukush and the Indus including both Punjab and Sind. This as a whole witnesses, during the first phase of this period, the Indo-Greek and Indo-Parthian dynasties between c. BC 250, the date of the revolt of the Bactrians and Parthians against their Seleucid overlords, and roughly the beginning or the middle of the first century AD when the Kusana kings carved out an empire far outstripping the extent of this zone.

2. Western India, comprising basically the whole of Gujarat but including at times both Sind and parts of Rajasthan and the central Indian Malwa plain. The political history of this age after the Mauryas is somewhat uncertain but from the early centuries AD onwards this was dominated by a group of kings called the Western Satraps.

3. The Gangetic valley and the Malwa plateau. The period after the Mauryan is dominated first by the Sungas and Kanvas and later by the Kusanas but interspersed in between are some miscellaneous local kingdoms of the region, each having their distinctive coin-types. The upper part of the *Doab*,

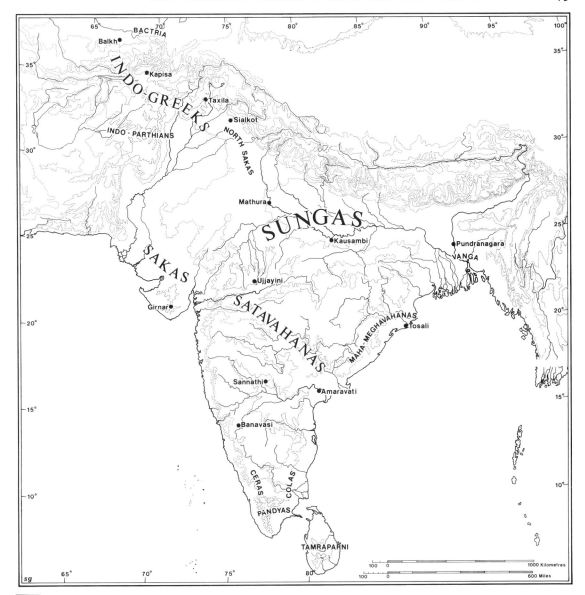

Fig. 12.1.   Map of cities and principal states of South Asia (c. BC 200–1).

particularly the area from Mathura upwards, also saw the rule of some virtually independent provincial governors or satraps who claimed descent from the Indo-Scythians or Sakas.

4. Coastal Orissa. This region which emerged into the historical light only with the Mauryans, politically consolidated itself under a king called Kharavela in the first century BC. Apart from these four major geo-political orbits of north India, there were at least four others in the south.

Fig. 12.2.   Map of cities and principal states of South Asia (c. AD 1–250).

5. The Deccan plateau, including the Krishna-Godavari delta. The area was
   under the dynastic rule of the Satavahanas between the first century BC and
   at least the middle of the third century AD but later on their successors
   established smaller principalities in different parts of the region.

6. The Kaveri delta. The nucleus of the Chola kingdom which in its origin goes
   back to the Mauryan period.

7. South India west coast. The locale of the ancient Chera kingdom as early as the Mauryan period.

8. The extreme south. The centre of the Pandyan rule, also dating from the Mauryan period.

From the point of view of the present chapter the regions numbered 6, 7 and 8 can be almost totally ignored, but as far as the course of political history is concerned, the Deccan plateau (the region numbered 6) interacted both with Gujarat and Malwa. Before outlining the basic course of political events (mainly in the region numbered 1–4), it may be worthwhile to draw attention to two general points.

First, the dynastic lines in all these regions do not really mark solid individual columns which, if placed side by side, cover the whole of the country. The details are missing in most cases. For instance, if one thinks of coastal Orissa during this period, the only fixed point is the presence of the Mauryan Asoka in the third century BC. The other details are, to say the least, shadowy. Or, to take up the case of Bengal, the only fixed point before the Gupta period is the probable presence of the Mauryans at Mahasthangarh. Even in the case of the middle and upper Gangetic valleys and Malwa the details of political history are mostly incomplete. The Sungas and the Kanvas who represent more than 150 years of political history in this region have left behind very little concrete information about themselves. Even in western India and the region between the Oxus and the Indus where there are great quantities of coins and a fair number of inscriptions, the political history still remains uncharted beyond a few fixed points.

Secondly, as the knowledge of political events is so sketchy, it is difficult to assess the extent to which the individual components of these geo-political units were related to the thread of central authority or hegemony. This is an important point to consider and one may illustrate this with reference to the Gangetic valley where the Sungas ruled for 112 years (BC 185–73) and the Kanvas for 45 years (BC 73–28). However the Sunga–Kanva rule in the Gangetic valley is also precisely the period when one notes the spread of small, apparently independent (because they were coin-issuing) principalities at Ahicchatra, Kausambi, Ayodhya, etc., which were located throughout the length and breadth of the valley. This is true not merely of the Gangetic valley but also of Malwa and Punjab. One, in fact, does not really know the extent to which the Sunga–Kanva hegemony was pervasive throughout the Gangetic valley. However, despite these two limitations, the political history of the period in these regions shows the following outline.

Pushyamitra Sunga usurped the throne of Magadha killing the last of the Mauryan kings, Brihadratha, in BC 185. Malwa also was within his control. His son Agnimitra was stationed at Vidisa in Malwa. With the Gangetic valley and Malwa as his home-base he fought against the Orissan king Kharavela on the one hand and against the Indo-Greek kings of the northwest (and beyond) on the other. His son Agnimitra fought a war against Vidarbha or Berar, a part of Maharashtra (roughly the area around Nagpur). The nature of political interaction of the succeeding Kanvas is not known but the last of the Kanva kings died in BC 27 or 28 at the hands of a Satavahana king of the Deccan. This shows that Maharashtra must have had close links with the Gangetic valley during this period. This is also suggested by Agnimitra's war with Berar. There is not much to note about the Orissan king Kharavela except that he carried his inroads into Magadha or the middle Gangetic valley and tried his might further in the direction of Andhra along the coast.

This is the period when the region between the Oxus and the Indus assumed a crucial geo-political role in Indian political history. The process began with the shaking off of the Seleucid suzerainty by Diodotus I of Bactria (c. BC 250) and the Parthians who had their territory to the southeast of the Caspian. The focus falls first on the Bactrians. The history of the Indo-Greek Bactrian kings falls into two geographical segments, one lying to the north of the Hindukush and the other lying to its south, including the Indian borderlands and Punjab. After Diodotus I, the important king of the Bactrian kingdom to the north of the Hindukush was Euthydemos who fought a war against Antiochus the Great of Syria. This culminated in a treaty (c. BC 208) accepting the independence of the Bactrian kingdom. In about BC 206 Antiochus forced a tribute from an Indian king Subhagasena who probably ruled in the Kabul valley. The first major inroad into India by a Bactrian king was undertaken by Demetrius (c. BC 190) who came to control Kabul, Punjab and Sind. His expedition was to parts of Rajasthan and the Gangetic valley. In Bactria the power of Demetrius was usurped by Eukratides who was followed by Apollodotus (c. the middle of the second century BC). Roughly from this period onwards the history of the Bactrian kings is essentially a motley of names known principally from their coins, of which a great many survive. The Indo-Afghan borderlands and Punjab were parcelled out among many Indo-Greek princes. The name of Menander who had his capital at Sialkot in Punjab and prominently figured in the Buddhist text *The Question of Milinda* stands out among them.

Towards the end of the second or the beginning of the first century BC the Indo-Parthian kings appear firmly in the Indian political horizon. The first Parthian king to exert influence in Indian political affairs was however Mithridates I (c. BC 171–36) who reputedly annexed the territory between the Indus and the Jhelum. Maues in about BC 95 seems to be the first Indo-Parthian (or Indo-Saka) king to have been firmly established in the region of Taxila in Punjab. At about the same time one notes the presence of apparently a different line of Parthian kings with their base in Arachosia and Sistan. The names of Vonones, Azes I and Azes II appear in the records, and by the beginning of the first century AD Punjab, Sind and the region up to Mathura were in the possession of the Parthian kings. The Christian apostle St Thomas supposedly paid a visit to the court of the Indo-Parthian king Gondophares.

In the opening centuries of the Christian era the Indo-Greek and Indo-Parthian powers were swept aside by the rise of the Kushans (Kusanas). From the northwestern part of China they moved first into the Jaxartes valley and thence to the north of the Hindukush. This provided their base of expansion further south. Under Kadphises I they annexed India up to Benares. Kashmir was annexed by his successor Kaniska (c. AD ?78–c. AD ?142) who is said to have moved into Magadha as well. The Central Asian possessions were not, however, given up by the Kusanas and Kaniska's territory in that direction was in fact increased by his conquest of Kashgar, Yarkand and Khotan. The empire was more or less intact under Kaniska's three successors, Vasiska, Huviska and Vasudeva, but its end was precipitated by the invasion of the Sassanian Shapur I between AD 250 and 271. The smaller Kusana principalities, however, survived for a longer period in the borderlands.

The history of the Western Satraps, kings of Saka origin and professing viceroyalty to a Saka overlord (hence the term satrap), is an interesting one. They are different from the satraps of Mathura and Taxila and appear in the historical records in the first century AD. Bhumaka, the earliest one known to us, belonged to the Kshaharata dynasty and reigned over Malwa, Gujarat and possibly parts of Rajasthan and Sind. The next satrap, Nahapana, was more powerful and ruled over a territory from Ajmer in Rajasthan to Nasik and Pune in Maharashtra. His ambition in the Deccan brought him into conflict with the Satavahana king Gautamiputra Satakarni who defeated him. The Kshaharata dynasty gave way to the Kardamakas, another Western Satrap dynasty. Castana, its founder, regained control of the region north of the Vindhyas and ruled from Ujjayini. He is mentioned as Tiastenes of Ozene in Ptolemy's *Geography*. The struggle between the Satavahanas and the satraps continued till Castana's grandson Rudradaman I (roughly the middle of the second century AD) drove out the Satavanas from Gujarat, Malwa and Sind. The fortune of the satraps generally waned after him but their power partly lasted till the beginning of the Gupta period.

The Satavahana heartland in the Krishna-Godavari delta in general and Godavari valley in particular was certainly included in the Mauryan empire, and the independent states arose in this region only in the second to first centuries BC after the demise of this empire. From this point of view it is somewhat unlikely that Vincent Smith's chronology for the early Satavahanas which places kings like Simuka and Krishna around the middle of the third century BC can be accepted. We here accept the chronology offered by H. C. Raychaudhuri (1972 (1953)), according to whom the first major king of the dynasty, Simuka, ruled from BC 60 to 37. He delivered the final blow to the Sunga–Kanva power. He was followed by his brother Kanha/Krishna described in a Nasik inscription as a 'raja of the Sadavahana-kula' (BC 37–27). Krishna was succeeded by Satakarni (BC 27–17) who, according to the Nanaghat inscription of Nayanika/Naganika, became sovereign of the whole of Dakshinapatha. He also annexed eastern Malwa, and a Sanchi inscription records the gift of a certain Anamda, the son of

Vasithi, the foreman of the artisans of Rajan Siri Satakarni. The principal capital was Pratisthana and after his death Nayanika was proclaimed regent. The glory of the later Satavahanas began with Gautamiputra Satakarni (end of the reign c. AD 130) who according to the inscription of his mother Gautami Balasri was the slayer of the Sakras, Yavanas and Pahlavas (Parthians). Apart from Maharashtra his power extended to an extensive area in both central and west India, from Malwa and Kathiawar on the one hand to north Kanara on the other. He is also known as a Brahman reformer, a preserver of the Varna system. He was followed by Vasisthiputra Svami Sri Pulamavi of inscriptions and coins, and his reign, successful in all directions, came to an end around the middle of the second century AD.

The last great Satavahana king was Yajnasri Satakarni who ruled over both Maharashtra (including Konkan) and the Andhra country. His coins bearing the figure of a ship suggest that the king's power extended over the sea. The later Satavahana rulers ruled in Berar, the eastern Deccan and the Kanarese country.

The general implications of the political framework

Even a cursory outline of the political events such as the preceding one makes clear that there was a close interaction between the different geo-political units in the post-Mauryan period. The major foci emerged. On the one hand one notes that the Kusana might extended from the Gangetic valley to the area north of the Hindukush as well as the Himalayas, and on the other, one notes the firmly established control of the Western Satraps and the Satavahanas over the seaboard of Sind, Gujarat and the Deccan. Both these developments were important.

The first one made possible the commercial and cultural interaction between the geographically disparate units of the Kusana empire on a scale which could not be visualized before. The region between the Oxus and the Indus has had close interaction from the beginning of settled agriculture in the region and this trend continued through its Achaemenid and Greek occupations. The continuity of the tradition is reflected also during the Seleucid, Mauryan and subsequent Indo-Greek and Indo-Parthian phase of the regional history. What however the Kusana rule achieved for this region was to expand considerably the scope and depth of this interaction, first by establishing a political control which extended right up to the middle Gangetic valley and secondly by securing Chinese Turkestan which brought about an organized traffic to China across the Pamirs and the Karakorum. This was also the period when the Silk Route between China and Rome was in its heyday, and the Kusana empire not merely directly participated in it by virtue of its control of Central Asia and Chinese Turkestan but also by making the entire stretch of northwestern India participate in it through the Hindukush, Pamir and the Karakorum passes. It is not without reason that one finds a proliferation of settlements and Buddhist monasteries and stupas (some of them, like Begram near Kabul, were very rich trade-marts) all over Central Asia, Afghanistan, Chinese Turkestan and the Indian borderlands including the mountain valleys from Swat to Chitral in the early centuries AD.

The second aspect of the political development to which we have drawn attention here, i.e. the establishment of firm political controls over the western seaboard (up to Maharashtra) under the Western Satraps and Satavahanas, resulted in a smooth and uninterrupted commercial traffic with the Mediterranean, bringing into its orbit the Persian Gulf, Arabian, Egyptian and east African littoral. This traffic affected not merely the seaboard but also the hinterland which supplied various commodities. One of the results was the consolidation of various internal trade routes in these regions. The outline of the route to the Deccan from the Gangetic valley is now more clearly traceable by the location of such Buddhist stupas as those at Bharhut and Sanchi, both of which belong generally to the post-Mauryan period. The routes in the Deccan are now more clearly indicated by the numerous rock-cut caves which are similarly dated.

As far as the internal archaeological sequence in different parts of India during this period is concerned, we would like to draw attention to a point which is not always emphasized in Indian archaeology. By c. BC 200 there is considerable uniformity in various categories of simple material remains throughout the length and breadth of northern India. At present this is manifest mainly in pottery but one can easily trace it in other items, especially urban terracottas and various art-styles. The post-Mauryan period in Indian history is not a period which can be visualized primarily in regional terms. The Mauryans brought about the end of protohistory in many parts of the subcontinent (cf. Bengal, Orissa, Andhra, Tamilnadu, Karnataka, Kerala, among others) and ushered in their transition to the historical limelight. The interaction between the different historical units of the country was much strengthened during the post-Mauryan period. This was the time when early historic India assumed a clear and mature shape.

One can isolate the basic components of this shape. The sheer abundance of inscriptions in the post-Mauryan period comes readily to mind. These inscriptions cover a wide spectrum of the contemporary life and politics. The same is true of coins. Punchmarked and cast copper coins no doubt antedate c. BC 200 but there is a noticeable increase in the coin types only after this period. Again, in contrast to the rigorously upheld court art of the Mauryan period, we get, from the second century BC onwards, an exuberance of art forms concerned with a close depiction of popular life. The pattern of political events also suggests that the different geo-political orbits of the subcontinent find their first clear historical expression during this period. All these concomitants of Indian urbanism will be considered in greater detail in section III below.

II. The cities

While discussing the cities of this period it must be remembered that this marks only the third phase of early historic urban growth. The first phase (chapters 6 and 7) goes back to the 7th–6th centuries BC and was confined initially to a limited area in the middle Gangetic valley and Malwa on the one hand and the northwestern region including west Punjab on the other. The urban growth in the Indo-Gangetic divide (cf. Mathura) may also date from this period. The second phase falls in the Mauryan period (chapters 10 and 11) and one now detects the growth of urban settlements in a large number of areas, covering virtually the whole of the subcontinent except perhaps the deep south. The post-Mauryan period constitutes a distinctive third phase. We shall examine the evidence, region-wise.

1. Northwest

The geographical environment of the northwest region has been discussed in chapter 2, although the relative aridity of some parts of the region must be recalled. What it lacks in agricultural productivity has been made up by another vitally important factor, i.e. its position at the mouth of one of India's most important openings to the west. The Khyber is famous, but besides there were other important routes, one of which ran along the Kabul river, for instance. The coming of the Achaemenids brought this entire area into the orbit of contemporary West Asia and made the whole system of passage markedly significant. The successive early stages are: the coming of the Achaemenids and Alexander, the establishment of the Mauryan hegemony, the close contact of the Mauryans with the Hellenistic courts, the dominance of the Indo-Greeks till finally with the Scytho-Parthians and Kusanas the entire area teemed with traffic with the West. Another important route branched off from around Taxila to Kashmir and thence to central Asia. In the submontane Indus region it is these trade routes which brought about the existence of urban settlements. Very aptly Mortimer Wheeler (1962, 4) describes both Charsada and Taxila, the two most notable urban centres, as 'caravan cities'.

Charsada

The early Indian sources (cf. Law 1950, 14) refer to modern Charsada as Puskalavati while in the classical sources (cf. Majumdar 1960) it is known as Peucelaotis and Proclais. As a specific coin-type bearing the city-goddess (Rapson 1962, 530, pl. VI, 10) suggests, the city was considerably important during the Indo-Greek period. Its importance is likely to have declined with the growth of modern Peshawar or ancient Purushapura under the Kusanas. But if the evidence of the *Periplus* is to be believed, it still retained its share in the extra-Indian trade of this period – goods from the Kabul valley, Kashmir, sub-Hindukush area and those imported from Scythia, were sent to Proclais, to Barygaza or modern Broach on the Narmada (Majumdar 1960, 303–4).

Of its four mounds spread over an area of four square miles, only those known as Bala Hisar (Marshall and Vogel 1902–3, 141–84; Wheeler 1962) and Shaikhan Dheri (Dani 1965–66, 17–214) have revealed something by way of planning. The mound of Shaikhan, about 600 m to the north-northwest and between the arms of two rivulets, Sambor and Zinde, was more important during our period. Air photography revealed here a city in the negative, in that what appeared to be the walls of houses were actually the trenches of robbers who had dug out any available building materials (Fig. 12.3). Wheeler described it as:

> A series of parallel streets – not less than five can be identified – 40 yards apart divide the site into blocks in which coherent house-plans can be isolated. One street-interval, slightly larger (50 yards), included the precinct of a massive circular structure which can only have been a stupa or Buddhist (less probably Jaina) shrine. The stupa stood on a slight rise and both by situation and by plan dominated the scene ... It can be said that the whole site was laid out upon a single co-ordinated rectangular plan with the temple in its midst. (Wheeler 1962, 16–17)

A. H. Dani's excavations in 1963–64 (Dani 1965–66, 17–214) have shown that the city was in all probability founded by Menander in about the middle of the second century BC and that its occupation continued up to the reign of the Kusana king Vasudeva in the close of the second century or the middle of the third century AD. Dani's excavation area was limited, and unearthed for the most part structures of the Kusana period. The civic plan laid down by the Indo-Greeks, however, continued unchanged. The excavations identified three parallel streets and a side street crossing at right angles. The drains, refuse pits and cess pools of a wide street all belonged to the Kusana period. The houses of this period were of mudbrick while those of the earlier ones were of diaper-masonry. A Kusana-period room contained a fireplace which was 38 cm square and 'placed in the middle just in the same fashion as we see in modern Pathan houses' (Dani 1965–66, 27). A house of the same period is associated with a Buddhist teacher, Naradakha, (identified from a record at the base of a pedestal of a relic-case) and consisted of a central open courtyard with rooms on three sides, the fourth side being closed by a high dividing wall (Fig. 12.4). In the courtyard of the house was a bathing place connected by a stone drain with the street outside. The house underwent a number of reconstructions, towards the end of which a shrine with a Buddha figure was installed.

To the west of the Indus, Charsada happens to be the only well-known and excavated urban centre. As the stupa at Shah-ji-ki-dheri (Spooner 1908–9, 38–59) suggests, Peshawar or ancient Purushapura must have been considerably important under the Kusanas but its precise features are still uninvestigated archaeologically. In about the same period there was a considerable number of Buddhist settlements, stupas and monasteries in the Swat valley and the adjacent areas, all possibly subsisting on the religious generosity of the princes and merchants rich from the Central Asian traffic. The wealth resulting from the same

Fig. 12.3. Shaikhan Dheri, aerial photograph (after Wheeler).

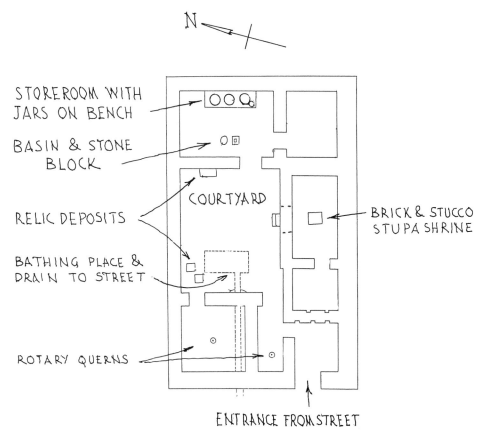

Fig. 12.4. Shaikhan Dheri, house of Naradakha (after Javed Husain).

traffic again is likely to have caused some increase in the number of urban centres in the area but of their number and character we know very little.

Taxila

To the east of the Indus, Taxila, ancient Taksasila, in the Potwar plateau, was a trade centre par excellence, owing its importance to its position on the route converging upon Bactria in Afghanistan. A second route moved up from Taxila to Central Asia by way of Kashmir. It may also be emphasized that Taxila gave an easy access to the Indus system and thus to the Arabian sea and thence alternatively to the Red Sea and the Persian Gulf.

The importance of Taxila is reflected in all categories of Indian literature (cf. Sukthankar 1914–15, 36–41; Law 1954, 129–31) – Hindu, Buddhist and Jaina – and also in the writings of the Graeco-Roman historians (Majumdar 1960, 113, etc.). Archaeologically Taxila is the most extensively excavated city site of the subcontinent. Lured by both its Greek association and 'something appealingly

Greek', (Marshall 1951, preface to Vol. I) in its countryside, John Marshall excavated there between 1913 and 1945 while a season's work was added by Wheeler in 1944–45. Work at the site since then has been somewhat sporadic in nature. The geographical setting of Taxila has been described in Chapter 2.

The three successive urban settlements of Taxila, the Bhir mound, Sirkap and Sirsukh, grew in the western part of the northern valley within three and a half miles of one another: for this chapter the evidence from Sirkap and Sirsukh is important. The earliest settlement has been discussed in chapter 8 and that of the Bhir mound in chapters 10 and 11.

In the beginning of the second century BC, a new city was laid out in the valley of Taxila, somewhat to the northeast of the Bhir mound. The local name of the site is Sirkap. Unlike the earlier city at the Bhir mound (see pp. 131–32) the new one is characterized by full grid-planning (Fig. 12.5).

The site of Sirkap offered certain natural advantages. It included in the south a portion of the Hathial ridge and thus the background of the low defensive hill and an isolated knoll, the last spur of the Hathial, suitable for an acropolis. Besides, the level space in the north provided a town planner with a suitable site for planning. The Tamra Nala skirting its western side could provide an effective source of water.

According to Marshall (1951, Vol. I, 118) there are seven occupational strata in Sirkap spanning three or four centuries of occupation. The earliest (stratum VII) is pre-Indo-Greek; the sixth and fifth date from the Indo-Greek period and the rest belong to the Saka and Parthian domination. The excavated remains of Sirkap are mostly of the second stratum and thus of the Saka-Parthian period.

Marshall, after some questioning, concluded that the stone city walls, whenever they were last rebuilt, followed closely the line of the original Indo-Greek fortifications. A different view was advanced by Wheeler who believed that the earthen rampart known as Kaccha Kot marked the northern boundary of the Indo-Greek city, and that the present line of the city wall dated only from the first century BC; and others have followed this view. However, Allchin has argued that field observation reveals no traces of occupation in the area enclosed by the Kaccha Kot, and that Marshall's view is further supported by the street layout of the Indo-Greek structures excavated in Sirkap itself (Allchin 1993). We are inclined to accept this view.

The periphery of the Saka-Parthian Sirkap was more than 4.8 km long, the entire length being protected by a stone wall. This did not form any rectangle or parallelogram but followed closely the lie of the land. Except in the north and east the wall was never straight. Its thickness varied between 6 m and 9 m. On the northern side it was strengthened by a raised berm about 7.5 m wide and it had a series of rectangular bastions, possibly more than one-storeyed, set at regular intervals along its face. The curtain wall between the bastions had also a berm on the inside for the use of the defenders and was loopholed above.

Of the gateways only the northern one has been excavated. In all probability

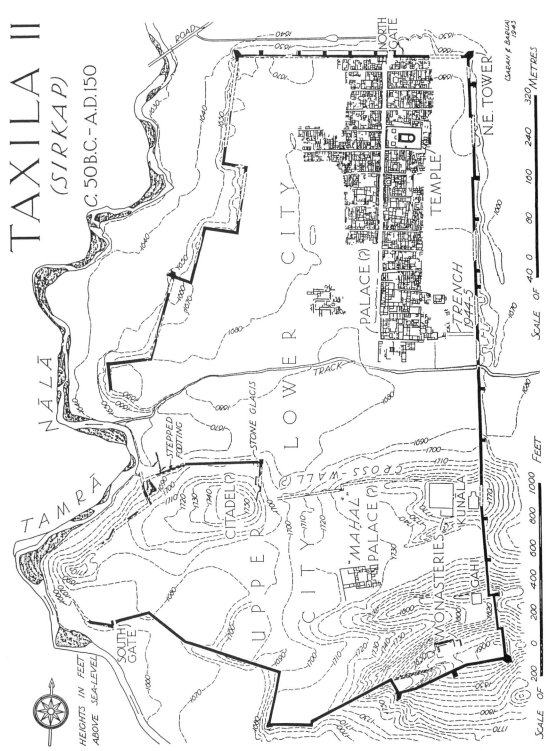

Fig. 12.5. Taxila, Sirkap, plan of defenses (after Wheeler).

there were gateways on the other three sides also. The northern gateway was set slightly to the east of the main street. Marshall (1951, Vol. I, 114) suggests two reasons for this particular arrangement: no invader could rush the gateway and the street at the same time and secondly, the rainwater coming down the street would meet the city wall before sliding down the culvert below the gateway. The gateway, a large hall (inside measurement: 19 m × 10.6 m) projected about 6 m on both sides of the wall. The outer projection was of a more solid construction, possibly a later addition. The four guardrooms were set against the outer face of the wall. There were two wells here, meant possibly for both sentries and wayfarers. The solidity of the construction of the gateway suggests that it had at least one upper storey.

An inner defence separated the acropolis on the Hathial spur from the lower city. Marshall (1951, Vol. I, 117) could only hypothesize its existence; but the 1944–45 excavations identified 'the actual remains of the western part of the cross-wall. At one point it is based upon a stone-revetted glacis and at another on a high-stepped foundation' (Ghosh 1948, 32).

The excavated portions of Sirkap are limited to a broad strip which begins at the northern wall and continues along the main street for about 600 m. Besides, some work was carried out at a site called *Mahal* and two stupas (known as Kunala and G respectively), all within the fortification but situated on the Hathial ridge. Little is known about Sirkap earlier than the Saka-Parthian period. It has however been established that the alignment of the main and side streets and consequently the alignment of the outer walls of the houses remained unchanged throughout (Fig. 12.6). The rubble masonry of the sixth stratum (the first Indo-Greek phase) was coarser than that of the fifth (the second Indo-Greek phase) and Marshall infers on this basis that in the building of the original city of Sirkap the Greeks were compelled to work in haste but that a generation or more later they were well settled, and thus improved upon their initial efforts (Marshall 1951, Vol. I, 123). A few Indo-Greek structures were also revealed in the 1944–45 excavations.

The Saka-Parthian Sirkap is a compact specimen of grid-planning (Fig. 12.5). The main street is remarkably straight. The side streets which branch off from it are narrower but seldom less straight (the 12th street however has a distinct bend). The blocks of houses between them are mostly clusters of private dwellings but a few small stupas (cf. the stupa between the second and third street) and at least two temples (an apsidal temple between the fifth and sixth streets and the shrine of the double-headed eagle in block F) are found among them.

Except a few under the city wall which are poor and shoddy, the houses in this part of Sirkap are commodious, each having on average an area of some c. 1,400 m², and represent in all probability the wealthiest part of the city, an inference which may be supported by the magnificence of some of the antiquities here – the hoards of jewellery, silverware, etc. The house-plan centred around a courtyard or more than one courtyard with rooms on all sides. A particularly big

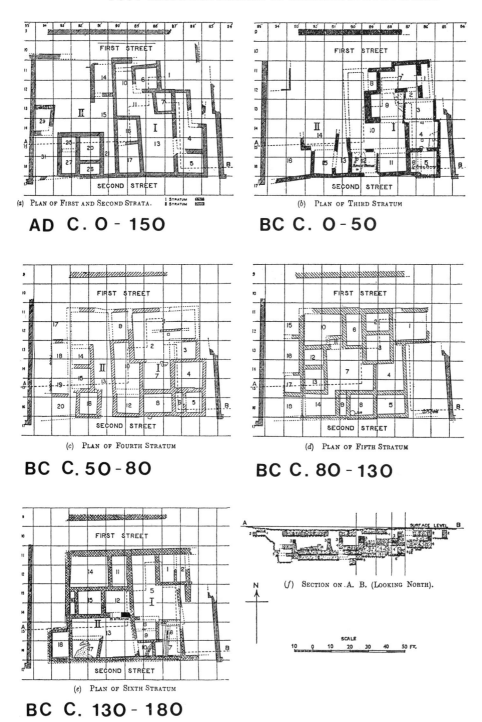

(a) Plan of First and Second Strata. I Stratum II Stratum

AD C. 0 - 150

(b) Plan of Third Stratum

BC C. 0 - 50

(c) Plan of Fourth Stratum

BC C. 50 - 80

(d) Plan of Fifth Stratum

BC C. 80 - 130

(e) Plan of Sixth Stratum

BC C. 130 - 180

(f) Section on A. B. (Looking North).

SCALE
10   0   10   20   30   40   50 FT.

Fig. 12.6. Taxila, Sirkap, successive plans of house 2, block 1, indicating continuity of the street and block plan (after Marshall).

house is that marked 1G on the plan, which with its four courts and more than thirty rooms on the ground floor covers an area of about 2,200 m². The rooms opening onto the main street may have served in most cases as shops (Marshall 1951, Vol. I, 167). Built of rubble masonry, the house walls were mud plastered both inside and outside. Occasionally colour was applied to the plaster.

A structural complex in the southeastern extremity of the excavated part has been called a palace by Marshall (1951, Vol. I, 171–6). Its overall area was 105 × 127 m, and besides the main street on the west it was surrounded by the 12th and 13th streets. The entrance from the main street led to a court with a raised hall on its south, supposed to be the 'court of private audience' with an adjunct, something like the Mughal *Diwan-i-Khas*. The entrance from the 13th street led to two other courts, 'court of the guard' and 'court of Public Audience'. From the 'court of Public Audience' one could go through a door in the north to a few rooms supposedly meant for the state guests while further north lay the zenana or ladies' quarter where a small stupa and a few votive terracotta tanks were meant for the religious rites of the ladies.

Marshall's description of this structural complex as a palace rests on three grounds: (1) its similarity with the Khorsabad palace of Sargon ('There is the same great court surrounded by chambers and one side of it the same court of retainers; on the other, the apartments of the zenana. There also, the other half of the palace is occupied just as it is at Taxila, by reception and public rooms.'); (2) its size, far more massive than that of the private houses; and (3) the comment of Philostratus based on Apollonius that there was no great display of buildings in the palace of Taxila and that the men's quarters, the portico and the court were all of a modest, subdued character (Marshall 1951, Vol. I, 176).

The high ground on the ridge at the extreme western end of the Hathial spur, known as the *mahal* (signifying royal residence), has revealed a complex of buildings which cover an area of 93 m by 73 m. The basic unit consists of a number of open courts which measure between 15 m and 18 m each way and the principal rooms around them compare favourably with those in the 'palace'. Its regulated planning is also noteworthy and in marked contrast with the rest of the houses in the lower city. Constructed originally earlier, the excavated remains of this complex belong to the first century AD (Marshall 1951, Vol. I, chapter 7).

In the closing years of the first century AD the Kusanas laid out a new city at the site of Sirsukh, about a mile north-northeast of Sirkap across the rivulet of Lundi (Fig. 12.7). What we know about Sirsukh is confined essentially to the fortification wall and a limited area inside. An interesting but unexplored feature of Sirsukh may be the chain of mounds to its northwest. Somewhat like an irregular rectangle on plan, the Kusana Sirsukh measures some 1,375 m along its northern and southern sides and 1,000 m along its eastern and western ones. An idea of the fortification wall comes from the exposure made near its southeastern corner. It was constructed of rough rubble faced with neatly fitting limestone masonry of the heavy diaper type. On the outer face it had an added roll plinth for the

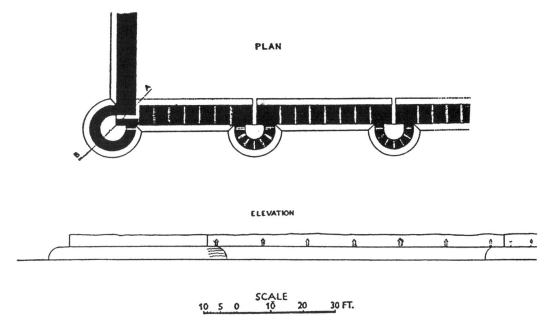

Fig. 12.7.   Taxila, Sirsukh, view of part of defenses (after Marshall).

strengthening of the foundation and the prevention of undermining. There were bastions, semi-circular in plan, at regular intervals. Inside the fortification wall the excavations near what is known as the Pindora mounds have revealed two open courts with attached chambers, apparently part of a big building.

2. Kashmir

Archaeologically it is still difficult to determine when the valley of Kashmir, essentially a narrow mountain-girt strip, about 84 miles long and up to 15 miles wide, passed into the light of history. It could have been within the Achaemenid orbit. The NBP, the hallmark of the early historic period in northern India up to c. BC 200, has been reported from the site of Semthan (Buth, Bisht and Gaur 1982) but little else besides. Aurel Stein's analysis of the historical geography of the valley suggests that the Kusana period was perhaps the most significant occupational phase in the early history of the valley (for a detailed bibliography see Chakrabarti 1984). The three successors of Kaniska, Huviska, Juska (Vasiska) and Vasudeva, reputedly established cities in the valley but no archaeological evidence survives; no systematic attempt has in any case been made to find them. Kashmir was very much a subcontinental gateway to Central Asia, both across the Gilgit–Hunza–Pamir axis and the Ladakh line through Karakorum. Thus, an intense occupation of the valley in the early centuries AD is probable.

3. The Punjab plains

The Punjab plains proper lie between the Salt Range and the Sutlej. One is not quite sure when the early historic period began in this area but an investigation of the route of Alexander's campaign and the associated places should provide a convenient starting point. Alexander Cunningham (1963, 130–209), who first investigated this area, located a number of settlements but his work has not been followed up by excavations except at one place, Tulamba in the valley of the Ravi (Mughal, 1967). This is a big mound (c. 500 × 370 m) with traces of a citadel, and according to the excavator it could be a city of the Malloi taken, not by Alexander himself but by one of his generals. One particular site in the Punjab plains needs close attention, though only on the basis of the literary sources. Sakala or Sagala, the capital of the Indo-Greek king Menander, has been described as a rich and prosperous city laid out on the typical chess-board pattern in a contemporary text, *The Questions of Milinda* (Law 1969). In the *Mahabharata* this was the capital of the Madras, the land of the Madras corresponding to the modern district of Sialkot 'between the Chenab and the Ravi or between the Jhelam and the Ravi' (Law 1969). The literary sources further indicate that Sakala was an important early historical trade centre with connections with both the west and the Gangetic valley (for this aspect of Sakala, see Chakraborti 1966, 167–9). Sakala has been identified with modern Sialkot (for the controversy, see Law 1969). A proper archaeological investigation of the site remains a desideratum, a thing which may be said about the other contemporary Punjab plains sites as well.

S. M. Ali (1966, 127) has pointed out that before the irrigation canals came into existence, the population distribution in the Punjab Doabs was always concentrated in the northern belt, i.e. the piedmont zone of the mountains. It would also be interesting to know on the basis of a proper archaeological survey of the Punjab plains how far the location of ancient sites corresponded to this distribution pattern.

4. Sind

The early historical archaeology of Sind also remains largely a terra incognita, though the occurrence of the word *Sindhu*, ancient name for the modern province of Sind, should be quite early in Indian literature (Law 1954, 127). The chronology of the classical references is more or less precisely fixed. In BC 510 there was a Persian-inspired voyage under Scylax to explore the course of the Indus beginning from the region of modern Attock (cf. Majumdar 1960, 4). In BC 326 Alexander, while sailing down the Indus, encountered a number of independent tribes and there is a reference to the kingdom of Mousikanos whose capital, according to Vincent Smith (1914 (1904), 100–1) may be located at modern Alor or Aror in the Sukkur district. Alexander's chroniclers also refer to a port called Patala in the delta where Nearchus embarked for his coastward journey to the Euphrates-Tigris mouth. Despite a suggestion for its identification with the modern Bahmanabad (Smith 1924, 107) the place has not been positively identified, nor is there any proof of any settlement of comparable antiquity in the entire province. Archaeological proof is also lacking for the suggestion that in the second century BC the merchants from the Indus delta were travelling as far as the island of Socotra, and that Sind during that period was commercially significant enough to find mention in a Chinese source (Mukherjee 1970). Sind became unmistakably significant in the early centuries AD when it came perhaps within the Kushan empire and acquired a role catering to the Indo-Roman trade (Mukherjee 1970). Archaeologically even this fact remains largely uncorroborated though the many Buddhist stupas which were built in Sind in the early years of the Christian era (Cousens 1929, 168) point to its increased importance. There have been some investigations at the site of Bahmanabad (Cousens 1929, 51; also *Pakistan Archaeology*, 1, 1964, 49–55) which, though later an Arab capital Mansurah, seems to have had a considerably earlier beginning. One detects unmistakable early historic terracotta ringwells and beads at the site.

5. Indo-Gangetic divide

The Indo-Gangetic divide, dividing the two great river systems of India, lies between the Sutlej and the Yamuna and has as its other limits the Siwaliks on the north, the dried-up course of the Ghaggar in the Rajasthan desert in the south and the Aravalli ridge reaching out to Delhi in the southeast. Spate (1967 (1954)) emphasizes the significance of this area as a physiological unit and calls it a transitional area both physically and culturally.

> Commercially and culturally it is the great marchland between Islam and Hindustan: Muslim culture today probably finds its highest expression in Lahore, while on the other side of the region Muttra is rich in Hindu tradition; between them Delhi is (or was until recently) a Muslim outpost, yet with deep roots in the remoter Hindi Past. (Spate 1967 (1954), 534)

This analysis based on latter-day Indian history seems to find a significant correspondence with the earlier archaeological aspects of the region. The early archaeological stages are: the Indus-based Harappans whose influence spread over the entire area from Rupar at the foot of the Siwaliks to the sites on the Ghaggar; the ochre-coloured pottery which occurs in both the divide and the upper Gangetic valley; the painted grey ware which possesses a similar distribution, and finally the NBP which heralds the beginning of the historic period in a broad sweep from the lower Gangetic valley to the divide. From then on to AD 300 the entire area was a ferment point of both Indian and extra-Indian impulses; the growth of the tribal republics of the

Yaudheyas and others; the advent of the Indo-Greeks, Parthians, Scythians and Kusanas – all are archaeologically reflected in the distribution of their coins and other traits. The Indo-Gangetic divide was in fact an indisputable area of cultural transition where influences from inner India and the west mingled together.

The specific archaeological evidence of the beginning of history in the region is, however, still meagre. The archaeological investigations have been inadequate, though there is no lack of promising mounds: Khokra Kot near Rohtak and Sunet near Ludhiana, both associated with the tribal republic of the Yaudheyas of the early Christian period; a series of mounds in the Kurukshetra area two of which, when excavated, yielded Indo-Greek and other coins; Agroha near Hissar which showed elaborate structural remains, though of a later period; Sirsa, also near Hissar but unexcavated; Jalandhar in the Beas-Sutlej Doab; and many others which are neither listed nor explored in a proper way (see Y. D. Sharma, 1953, 123–31).

Rupar, Sugh, Kuruksetra, Rangmahal

Towards the east there are several major sites, but none has as yet been fully studied. At the foot of the Sivaliks, Rupar is important but little has been published regarding its post-Mauryan occupation. Sugh, identified with ancient *Srughna* (Law 1954, 8–19), has, according to Cunningham (1963, 291), a fortification with a circuit of about four miles. Another fortification reportedly of the Kusana Period has been discovered at Kuruksetra by the Archaeological Survey of India, but details are not published. In the Ghaggar valley, on the southern fringe of the divide, the available evidence suggests that the area became historically significant under the Kusanas. The early historical sites discovered so far in the region all belong to the Kusana period. It is reasonable to infer that in the early centuries AD there was a direct route from Sind to the Sutlej-Yamuna area along the course of the Hakra and the Ghaggar. The contemporary sites in the area grew up along this route. A season's excavation at Rangmahal (Rydh 1959) yielded little by way of planning but its importance has been demonstrated by a large collection of terracottas, mostly of the Gupta period.

6. Upper Gangetic valley

The downward limit of the upper Gangetic valley has been suggested by Spate to be a line running roughly from the Ganges-Yamuna confluence at Allahabad across the northnorthwest–southsoutheast section of the Ghagra (Spate 1967 (1954), 546). In terms of modern political units this conforms broadly to the western two-thirds of Uttar Pradesh excluding the montane districts of the north and the districts of Jhansi, Banda and Hamirpur lying on the peninsular foreland.

As in the Indo-Gangetic divide, there is no dearth of early historical sites in this area. But only a few of them have been properly excavated or have yielded any co-ordinated data regarding urban growth and town planning. Besides, numerous sites with unmistakable urban significance in the contemporary literary records have so far not been excavated:

Hastinapur

Hastinapur is identified with a place of the same name in the Mawana tehsil of Mirath (Meerat), on an old course of the Ganges, five miles west of the modern course, and had distinct epic, Puranic and Jaina associations. It was excavated by B. B. Lal in 1950–52 (Lal 1955). He points out that:

> the settlement seems to have developed more along the bank which runs north–south, than at right-angles to it. This is suggested by the extent of ancient ruins which cover over half a mile from north to south, but hardly a quarter of a mile from east. (Lal 1955, 9)

Period IV has been dated between the early second century BC and the late third century AD. In this period there were seven structural sub-periods. Houses were invariably of burnt bricks and squarish bricks were used for flooring. There is also evidence of a regular house planning, the orientation being roughly along cardinal directions. Indraprastha in the Purana Qila area of modern Delhi was the Pandava capital in the *Mahabharata*. The Archaeological Survey of India excavations at the site in the early seventies remain unpublished (cf. IAR 1970–71 for a brief report). Burnt bricks and terracotta ringwells were noted in the early historic level.

Mathura

During the Indo-Greek period, *The Questions of Milinda* refers to Mathura as one of the chief cities of India. The numerous inscriptions and *ayagapatas* recovered from the Kankali Tila mound testify that from about BC 200 onwards it was an important centre of Jainism. The Jaina image inscriptions are also significant for the fact that they refer to various local persons and their professions – caravan leader, perfumer, banker, metalworker, treasurer, etc. Mathura was also a noted centre of the Bhagavata and the Naga cults. In the second century BC Patanjali speaks of its kettledrums, garments and coins or *karsapanas*. Megasthenes refers to Methora in the country of the Surasenoi. Subsequently it is also mentioned by Pliny and Ptolemy (for the literary and epigraphic references to Mathura, Law 1954, 106–10; Dey 1927, 127–8; Chakraborti 1966, 169–73). These literary sources amply testify that Mathura was both a religious centre and an important entrepot of trade and commerce. The commercial significance obviously sprang from the fact that it lay at the junction of two important Indian trade-routes: one which travelled from the Gangetic valley to the northwest and the other branching off to west India from Mathura itself. On the political level Mathura was the southern capital of the Kusanas. This inclusion in a political unit which had its epicentre in the northwest and extension up to the west coast must have made Mathura one of the most important commercial centres of the period. Despite intermittent explorations spread over more than a century, primarily aimed at recovering antiquities, Mathura remains one of the most inadequately excavated important early historical sites of the subcontinent, one of the reasons being the location of the modern built-up area over much of the ancient settlement.

A co-ordinated picture of the layout of the ancient settlement is hard to come by. In 1862 Cunningham (1966, 1–4) recorded nine separate mounds among which he gave some prominence to the Katra and Kankali Tila mounds because of their wealth of stone sculptural and architectural pieces and inscriptions. None of the subsequent explorations and excavations aimed at giving a comprehensive idea of the site as a whole till Stuart Piggott (1945, 45) in the early forties, whose fieldwork results have been embodied in his brief essay on Mathura, detected the alignment of a mud-brick fortification wall. His observation on the fortification is relevant:

> Today the walls are a string of irregular mounds of clay and earth, but it is possible to see in sections put through them that they originally consisted of a mud brick wall probably twenty feet thick and fifty or more feet high backed by a substantial earthen rampart. The square Katra area is enclosed with similar walls, with indications of towers at the angles, and may have constituted a citadel within the main city walls. (Piggott 1945, 45)

Regarding the date of the fortification he suggests that 'it is to the Kushana period that we should attribute the great city-walls that enclose an elongated horseshoe shaped area based on the right bank of the Jumna'. Evidence of the fortification has also been confirmed by a subsequent exploration, during which a limited area of the Katra mound was also excavated, exposing the stratification at the spot. 'Exploratory survey revealed the existence of two rings of mud ramparts, the first elliptical in shape and the second quadrangular and comprised within the first, as if signifying a citadel' (IAR 1954–55, 15). The more recent Archaeological Survey of India excavations at the locality called Dhulkot showed two phases of mud fortification, the earlier of which belonged to c. third century BC and the second to the Saka–Kusana times (IAR 1973–74, 31–32; 1974–75, 48–50). In fact this important work which remains unpublished has demonstrated that Mathura was a broadly crescent-shaped city on the bank of the Yamuna, and this corroborates a reference in the *Ramayana* to Mathura describing it as such.

Sankisa (Sankissa)

Modern Sankisa, about 23 miles west of Farrukhabad, finds mention as Samkasya in the epics. This was the capital of Kusadhvaja, the younger brother of Janaka-Videha, the father of Sita. According to the *Ramayana* it was on the banks of the Ikshumati, surrounded by ramparts. In the *Jatakas* it has been referred to as Samkassa. The literary sources leave no doubt that it was an important city (Dey 1927, 177; Law 1954, 120). While exploring the ruins of Sankisa in 1843 and later, Cunningham (1963, 311–14) noted a rampart upward of three and a half miles in circuit. Visual observation of the ruins suggested that the gates were on the northeast, southeast and east sides. Hiranand Shastri (1927) unearthed an assortment of structures. Among the antiquities there were many clay seals, the earliest of which has been palaeographically dated to BC 200.

Ahicchatra

Ahicchatra, the capital of north Panchala, in Bareilly district, UP, is referred to in the Pabhosa cave inscription of Ashadhasena, dated about the beginning of the Christian era. The *Satapatha Brahmana* refers to it as *Paricakra* while Ptolemy knows this as Adisadra. By the eleventh century AD the position of Ahicchatra as the capital of north Pancala was usurped by modern Budaon (for details, Law 1948). A systematic investigation of the site was initiated in 1940–44, to be renewed in 1963–65.

According to Ghosh, the ruins consist of:

> a brick fortification of the shape of a rough isosceles triangle with a perimeter of about three miles and a half, enclosing a series of rolling mounds, the highest of which, representing the site of a temple, stands to a height of 5 feet above the level of the cultivated field outside. (Ghosh and Panigrahi 1946, 37–8)

The defence wall was built in the early centuries AD and underwent four phases of construction. In the first phase it was built of mud and in the second the mud wall was topped by one of burnt brick. In the third phase this brick wall was given the protection of a mud cover, with another addition in the fourth phase. The structures inside the fortification are not fully reported but it was pointed out in the report on the 1940–44 work that 'each stratum [of Ahicchatra] had its own plan and alignment of houses radically different from those of the next stratum' (Ghosh and Pahigrahi 1946, 39). This point has been contradicted by the subsequent report (cf. IAR 1963–64) which says that the houses 'followed the same cardinal alignments throughout the successive levels'.

Saketa-Ayodhya

According to A. N. Bose (1961, 205–6), Saketa and Ayodhya, both celebrated in the Buddhist sources and the Ramayana, were the same city. The excavations conducted at the site in 1975–77 showed a burnt-brick fortification wall with a ditch outside dating possibly from c. BC 200 (IAR, 1975–76, 1976–77).

Kausambi

The references to Kausambi in early literature and epigraphical records have been collated by N. N. Ghosh (1935), B. C. Law (1939) and G. R. Sharma (1969). The earlier history and archaeology of the city have been discussed in chapters 6, 7 and 10.

Periods 3–5 of the fortification wall belong to the time-span of this chapter. Period 3 was dated by Sharma to the period of the Mitra kings of Kausambi who, on grounds of palaeography and other historical considerations, have been assigned to the period from the 2nd to the 1st century BC (Sharma 1960). Again, 'on numismatic grounds', Sharma states, 'rampart 5 seems to have been built by the Maghas, who made Kausambi their capital in the second half of the 2nd century AD' (Sharma 1960). This numismatic argument has also been supplemented by the evidence of inscribed terracotta seals, terracotta figurines and iron arrowheads. The rampart wall rises even now to an average height of 1.5 m from the level of the surrounding plain, with its towers touching the 21–23 m level (Fig. 11.4). There were eleven gateways in all, of which five, two each on the east and north and one on the west, have been considered to be the principal ones. The road leading to each gate was flanked by two mounds, obviously watchtowers, which lay across the moat encircling the rampart (except, of course, on the river side). About a mile away from this complex, there is another ring of mounds which once might have encircled the city. The rampart (of mud and burnt-brick revetment) was extended in the third stage and an interesting discovery was that of an altar outside the eastern gate at the foot of the rampart. This altar is supposedly shaped like an eagle flying to the southeast and associated with a fireplace, animal and human bones including a human skull. Sharma (1960, chapters 8–10) has adduced a mass of literary material to suggest that certain details of its construction correspond to the fire altar prescribed for *purushamedha* or human sacrifice in ancient Indian ritualistic texts. The excavations inside the fortification brought out only a limited area of the general residential quarter of the city. Whatever evidence there is suggests that the houses conformed to the usual pattern of having a courtyard as the central focus. An important discovery is a road, originally 2.44 m wide but subsequently widened to 4.88 m, having a compact surface with regular rut-marks. The drainage system depended on both soak pits and regular burnt-brick drains. There were also terracotta ringwells. The other details of the Kausambi excavations do not belong to our period, except that the Ghoshitarama monastery still flourished during the period. This monastery lay inside the fortification between the eastern gateway and the northern bend of the rampart. The identification has been possible due to the find of a terracotta sealing belonging to the monastic order of Ghoshitarama. The central plan of the monastery with several building phases comprised a central courtyard with rooms arranged around it.

Bhita

The ruins at Bhita with the traces of an oblong fortification pierced by gateways lie south of the Yamuna, about 5 miles downstream of Kausambi (Marshall 1911–12, 29–94). The rampart was built in the early Mauryan or pre-Mauryan period and the major excavated house-remains too belong to the Mauryan period and have been discussed in chapters 7, 10 and 11 (Fig. 11.9). However, the earlier plan continued in our period and the excavated structures and antiquities (quite a few of the seals bear the names of merchants) both suggest that Bhita (ancient *Vichhi* or *Vichchigrama*) was a prosperous trade centre. One of the excavated houses had twelve rooms arranged around a courtyard and probably possessed an upper storey. In most cases the houses were fronted on the roadside by a row of rooms which had in front of them a raised platform or verandah, a feature which may still be seen in the Indian bazaars.

7. Middle Gangetic valley (Eastern UP and Bihar)

Varanasi (Banaras)

On the basis of a terracotta sealing bearing the legend 'the seal of the city administration of *Varanasi*' in Gupta characters, ancient Varanasi, a city with extensive early literary references, may be identified with modern Rajghat, 'an extensive table-land rising about 60 ft above the surrounding ground-level', in the northeastern outskirts of modern Benares (Narain and Roy 1976; 1977; Narain and Singh 1977; Narain and Agrawal 1978). The site lay between the river Varuna on the north and northeast and the Ganges on the southeast. The literary sources, especially the *Jatakas*, are unequivocal about its importance as a trade-mart and commercial centre and its connection with such distant places as Taxila. It was, in fact, the meeting point of at least three trade-routes. On the one hand it was connected by the river with all important centres further downstream and on the other a route travelled from here to the northwest. A land route also went to Vaisali and if a reference in the *Jatakas* is correct, there was also a route down the river to the sea and then to Burma (for details see Chakraborti 1966, 178–81).

Period II of the site, which has been dated between c. BC 200 and the beginning of the Christian era, had two structural phases, in the earlier of which was found a house with two rooms, a vestibule, a bath and a well. In the upper levels of this period there were the remains of a brick foundation and a terracotta ringwell. On the basis of some 'impressive' structures Period III, dated 2nd to 4th century AD, has been suggested to represent the most prosperous phase of the site.

Sravasti (Saheth-Maheth)

Cunningham (1963, 343) identified the site of Saheth-Maheth on the border of Gonda and Bahraich districts of UP with an ancient Sravasti on the basis of a locally found dedicatory inscription on a Buddha statue. The literary data on Sravasti (Law 1935) suggest that it was a nerve centre of commerce and a number of routes emerged from here, which connected several cities of northern as well as western India. It had routes for Saketa, Rajagriha, Kausambi, Varanasi, Alavi, Samkasya and Taksasila. It had direct trade routes for Ujjayini, Mahishmati, Pratisthana, Bharukaccha and Surparaka (Srivastava 1968, 76). The local name of the ancient fortified city-state is Maheth while Saheth, about a quarter of a mile to the west, represents the ancient monastery site of Jetavana, celebrated in the Buddhist literature as a gift of the merchant Anathapindaka to the Buddha. The city-site of Maheth is 'an almost semi-circular crescent with a diameter of one mile and a third in length, curved inward and facing the north-east along the old bank of the Rapti river' (Vogel 1907–8, 83). The total circuit of the enclosing rampart, occasionally rising to 12 m above the surrounding ground level, is slightly more than 4.8 km. The city wall, excavated at the point of the eastern gateway, is about 2.75 m wide and built on the top of an earthen rampart. On both sides of the gate the city walls 'curve inwards so as to form two bastions leaving a space of 60 m in width between' (Vogel 1907–8, 111). Immediately south of this there are two rooms which might have acted as guardrooms. Recent excavations (Sinha 1967) have shown that the fortification had five constructional phases and was first constructed c. 250–200 BC. However, in the absence of radiocarbon or other absolute dating this must be treated with caution. Evidence regarding the habitational remains inside the rampart is very limited. What has been called *Kachchi Kuti* in J. Vogel's report on the eastern sector near the rampart is perhaps a temple-site while his *Pakki Kuti* may be a stupa. There was a stupa, called Stupa A, on the eastern edge of the rampart. Saheth, the site of ancient Jetavana, is a usual monastery site, comprising shrines, monasteries and stupas.

Sites in the Nepalese Terai

The most significant work in this area has been at the sites of Piprahwa and Ganwaria in the Basti district of UP, establishing the location of ancient Kapilavastu on the basis of a monastic seal impression which mentions the guild of the monks at Kapilavastu (IAR, 1970–71 to 1976–77 for brief reports). On the Nepalese side of the area Tilaura-Kot, a large fortified settlement, is a major site, with its fortification apparently coming up around BC 200 (IAR 1961–62, 73–74), although the settlement itself is clearly much older.

Balirajgarh, Katgragarh, Vaisali

All these sites are in north Bihar. Katragarh (IAR 1975–76 to 1978–79) showed a fortification wall built in the post-Mauryan period and so did Balirajgarh (IAR 1962–63). The habitational and fortified mound of Vaisali, the capital of the ancient Licchavis, is locally known as Raja-Visal-Ka-Garh. In period I there was a burnt-brick defence wall, about 6 m thick and ascribed to the second century BC. In period II which was not much later there was a massive earthen rampart, 20.7 m wide at the base, 6.4 m wide at the extant top and 4 m in the extant height. The moat was dug during this period. In period III, dated late-Kushan–early-Gupta (3rd–4th centuries AD) the brick defensive wall was rebuilt, being 2.75 m wide and described as having military 'barracks' attached. Inside the fortification a network of structures was revealed, leading up to hardly anything significant. The other excavations in the Vaisali area were conducted mostly on religious establishments (for Vaisali, Deva and Misra, 1962; Bloch, 1903–4; Spooner, 1913–14; IAR 1957–59).

Pataliputra and Rajagriha

As far as Pataliputra is concerned (Patil 1963; Altekar and Misra 1959), virtually no excavated remains can be ascribed to our period except perhaps those of a monastery called Arogyavihara which falls in the Gupta period or slightly earlier. This does not mean that the city was not important in post-Mauryan times; rather it simply shows how little we still know about Pataliputra. The fortifications of 'New Rajagriha' possibly belong to our period or may be somewhat earlier. Its outer fortification is an irregular pentagon in shape (total circuit of about 3 miles) and associated with a ditch. The mud rampart around the habitation was not found to go back earlier than the third century BC (for details see Chakrabarti 1976).

8. Lower Gangetic valley (Bengal)

The following early historic sites are noteworthy: Kotasur in the Birbhum district, West Bengal, with a rectangular fortification going back possibly to the second century BC (Chakrabarti, Nag and Chakrabarti 1978–79, for the plan of this site on the bank of the Mayurakshi); Tamluk or ancient Tamralipti on the bank of the Rupnarayan in the Midnapur district, West Bengal, where no significant work has been done; modern Pokharna or ancient Pushkarana on the bank of the

Damodar in the Bankura district, West Bengal, an extended site whose antiquity can be traced back to c. BC 200; Chandraketugarh, a fortified site in the Vidyadhari delta not far from Calcutta, which shows a fascinating range of Sunga terracottas; Mahasthangarh on the bank of the Karatoya in the Bagura district of modern Bangladesh, a fortified site of about three and a half miles in circumference with corner towers and bastions still rising to a height of about 10.67 m from the surrounding level; and finally, Wari-Bateshwar in a stretch of old alluvium near the Meghna in the Dhaka/Narsinghdi region of Bangladesh, where *in situ* punchmarked coins have been known since the thirties without the early historic significance of the site being noticed. Tamluk, Pokharna and Wari-Bateshwar are not fortified settlements. Tamluk figures in many early literary sources including Ptolemy (Chakraborti 1966 for a comprehensive survey) and was no doubt the most important early historic port in east India. A limited excavation in 1954–55 (IAR 1954–55, 19–20) showed that Period II dated 3rd to 2nd centuries BC, while Period III was placed in the first two centuries AD. The only structural evidence of these two periods was a brick-built tank and some terracotta ringwells. A rampart wall is clearly visible at Chandraketugarh and the total fortified area should be more than one square mile (i.e. c. 250 hectares). The mud-built rampart wall has not yet been satisfactorily excavated but a limited cutting traces its beginning to c. 2nd century BC (IAR 1956–57 to 1964–65, for brief reports). Very little is known of the early levels at Mahasthangarh (*Pakistan Archaeology*, 1968, 101–15). As far as the present author could determine, Wari-Bateshwar, a site which does not show any mound in a formal sense, has yielded a large number of silver punchmarked coins, a very large number of typical early historic beads of semi-precious stone, a Sunga in-curved bowl, the pointed bottom of what possibly was an amphora, a stone seal in early historic style and miscellaneous metal objects. This was possibly a settlement catering to both the southeast Asiatic and the Indo-Roman trade contacts of the period, and possibly the imports from Assam were funnelled through it. An old course of the Brahmaputra can be related to the site.

In addition to the above-mentioned sites one must mention Champa near Bhagalpur in Bihar and Bangarh, or ancient Kotivarsha, in the Dinajpur district, West Bengal. Although Champa is in Bihar, geographically it can be appreciated more in relation to such Bengal sites as Bangarh and Tamluk. The mud rampart wall at Champa dates from the third–second centuries BC while the burnt-brick defence wall at Bangarh also belongs roughly to the Sunga period (for Champa, IAR 1969–70 to 1971–72; for Bangarh, Goswami 1948).

9. Orissa

The two early historic cities of coastal Orissa, Sisupalgarh and Jaugada, have already been noticed in chapter 8. There is comparatively little that can be added regarding the later occupation which may belong to the period under

Fig. 12.8. Sisupalgarh, houses built of laterite blocks (? c. 1st century BC–AD) (courtesy Archaeological Survey of India).

review (Fig. 12.8). The presence of Rouletted ware and other objects elsewhere associated with the periods of Hellenistic–Roman trade contact, and of copper and lead coins, including a number of Kusana coins, is reported particularly in periods IIB and III.

10. Eastern Rajasthan and Madhya Pradesh

The excavated early historic sites which are important in eastern Rajasthan are Bairat (ancient Viratanagara, the capital of the Matsyas in the *Mahabharata*), Rairh, Sambhar and Nagari (Sahni 1937 and 1938; Puri n.d.; Bhandarkar, 1920). All these sites seem to be Mauryan in core, having substantial post-Mauryan deposits. The details of these deposits are however not at all clear.

Among the excavated cities in Madhya Pradesh Vidisa was the western capital of the Sungas. It has also been suggested as the capital of east Malwa, and of the Dasarnas being a tribe in the *Mahabharata*. Its political importance has been further emphasized by a stone pillar at the site set up by a certain Heliodorus who was the envoy of the Indo-Greek king Antalkidas of Taxila to the court of the king Kasiputra Bhagabhadra of Vidisa. Secondly, Vidisa was an important break-point on the route linking north India, Deccan and west India. Its economic prosperity may be generally deduced from the references to its labourers, bankers and artisan guilds in some early dedicatory inscriptions in such stupas as Bharut and Sanchi. It may also be emphasized that Vidisa seems to have been an important craft centre, particularly noted for ivory, weaving and sharp swords. Finally, on the religious level, Vidisa was, as the Heliodorus pillar testifies, an important early centre of the Bhagavata cult (Dey 1927, 35; Law 1954, 336–40; for the economic data, Chakraborti 1966, 192–5). The ruins at the site primarily lie in the fork between the converging rivers Betwa and Beas but they also extend 'for at least two-thirds of a mile north of the river Bes' (Bhandarkar 1913–14, 186). Excavations have been concentrated mainly around the Heliodorus pillar inscription which lay outside the habitational area of the city. The comparatively recent excavations at the town site (IAR 1963–65) have shown nothing more than the bare sequence.

Pawaya or ancient Padmavati lies in the fork formed by the confluence of the Sindh and the Parbati and covers about two square miles. The site has not been excavated but 'the brick remains and fragments of sculpture scattered among them attest the existence here of an ancient city from at least the first or second century AD down to the late Gupta period' (Garde 1915–16).

Ujjain or ancient Ujjayini should rank in importance with Rajagriha, Kausambi, Taksasila and such other cities of ancient India. We have already discussed its early history in chapters 7, 8 and 9. After the Mauryas its important political masters were the Satavahanas of the Deccan and the Saka Ksatrapas of western India and finally, under Candragupta II of the Guptas in the 4th century AD it came to acquire fame for culture and beauty, which has been adequately reflected in many places in ancient Indian literature (Law 1944).

This political and cultural fame of Ujjayini must have been conditioned to a great extent by its economic and commercial significance. The route from the Gangetic valley bifurcated here for the Deccan and west India: 'Ujjain gathered up and forwarded the trade between the Northwest India, the Ganges valley, the southern and western India' (Chakraborti 1966, 195). Its importance in this field has been unequivocally emphasized by the classical sources, particularly the *Periplus* and Ptolemy (Chakraborti 1966, 195–8).

Modern Ujjain stands on the bank of the Sipra, a tributary of the Chambal. Period III spans the time between the Sungas in the second century BC and the Paramara in the 9th–10th centuries AD. The site plan is shown in Fig. 8.6, with a rampart with eight gateways. The river flanks the site on the west and north. On the east and the south there was a moat. Very little specific information is given about Period III. All that we know is that the moat was reduced to the width of 39.4 m during this period. The building tradition of Period II (mud and burnt-brick houses on a plinth of rubble and clay and roofed by oblong tiles with double perforations) continued in Period III (for a brief report on the Ujjain excavations see IAR 1955–58).

11. Gujarat

With its inclusion in the Mauryan empire Gujarat emerges into the full light of Indian history and since that time, particularly with the development of India's Mediterranean trade, the Gujarat coastline attained a new stage of economic prosperity which must have been the most important single factor in the growth of its early historic cities.

The most important early historic city in Gujarat was ancient Bharukaccha or Bhrigukaccha of the Indian and Barygaza of the classical sources. Identified with modern Broach on the Narmada estuary this was a port par excellence. Not only was its immediate hinterland fertile, producing wheat, rice and cotton, but its connection stretched to Ujjayini in central India and Pratisthana in the Deccan, thus touching the arterial routes of inner India. The evidence of the *Periplus* is most explicit, and gives an elaborate list of the imports and exports through this port (Majumdar 1960, 304). It did not, however, cater only to the Mediterranean trade; in some *Jatakas* it is said to have had connections also with Sri Lanka and Southeast Asia (Chakraborti, 1966, 92), a likely enough phenomenon considering the importance of the Gujarat coast in India's Southeast Asian trade over a long period, continuing even up to modern times.

The results of excavations at Broach (IAR 1959–60, 19) have been extremely limited. A mud rampart associated with a moat possibly dates from the third century BC. In the subsequent period there was a red polished ware, possibly of Mediterranean origin. The rampart was provided with heavy brick revetments during this period.

The archaeological data from the other relevant sites of Gujarat are related only to the vertical sequence. Only at Shamlaji in northeastern Gujarat (Sabarkantha district) has some semblance of early historic planning been found. The site possesses an oblong brick-built fortification measuring 670.5 m by 304.8 m. The bastions are visible and in places intact up to a height of 7.62 m, from the present ground level. Period II with two phases in the construction of the defence was dated AD 100–500, the first phase falling in AD 100–300 (IAR 1961–62, 12–14).

12. Deccan: Maharashtra, Karnataka and Andhra

The following early historic urban sites may be noted, among others, in this region: Bhokardan, Paithan, Tagara, Brahmapuri, Adam and Kaundinyapur in Maharashtra; Banavasi, Isila and Sannati in Karnataka; and Nagarjunakonda, Satanikota, Dhanyakataka, Kondapur and Peddavegi in Andhra. Ancient

Bhogavardhana (Bhokardan) in Aurangabad district had in its Satavahana phase burnt-brick houses with tiled roofs and stone foundations and a large number of antiquities including amphora fragments, Satavahana and Ksatrapa coins and an ivory mirror handle showing a bejewelled woman standing undraped with two female attendants. Covering about 4 km² on the bank of the Godavari, ancient Pratisthana (Paithan) in the Aurangabad district originated as a Chalcolithic settlement but later developed into the southern terminus of the route between the Deccan and the Ganga valley. It must have been one of the largest cities of its time. In 1936–37 G. Yazdani unearthed brick structures, terracottas, coins and beads there. No major work has been done since then. Tagara, mentioned in the *Periplus* and by Ptolemy (Ter), was a great inland mart. Its sequence began with the NBP and it had in the 2nd century AD a spoked wheel-shaped Buddhist stupa of 26 m diameter. Brahmapuri (Kolhapur) better known as the find spot of a number of Roman bronze images and vessels, was a Satavahana city with burnt-brick houses, numerous glass beads and coins. Near Nagpur Adam shows a pre-Mauryan–Mauryan fortified settlement with a rampart with a ditch. An ancient capital of Vidarbha, Kaundinyapur on the bank of the Wardha was a flourishing city of the Mauryan-Satavahana period. In Karnataka Isila, the Mauryan provincial capital in the Chitaldrug district, lies basically unexcavated. Banavasi in North Kanara, an ancient capital city of the region measuring 1 km², goes back at least to the Satavahana period and shows a burnt-brick fortification on rubble foundations and a moat. Sannati in Gulbarga on the bank of the Bhima has a stone rampart and covers some 200 ha within a 4 m wide and 2–3 m high mound and may represent a citadel dating from the Mauryan period. Now submerged in the Nagarjunasagar dam across the Krishna, Nagarjunakonda (Fig. 12.9), or ancient Vijayapur, a capital city of the Iksvakus in the 3rd and 4th centuries AD with an earlier antecedence, revealed an urban settlement with a fortified citadel complex and an extensive residential area embellished by, among other things, a large number of both Buddhist and Hindu religious structures, bathing ghats, pavilions and a Roman-type amphitheatre. Satanikota on the bank of the Tungabhadra was a fortified Satavahana place with a ditch cut into the natural bedrock (Fig. 12.10). The Satavahana capital at Kondapur remains almost wholly unexcavated whereas ancient Vengi (Peddavegi) had its earliest excavated phase in the 4th–5th centuries AD, the extent of its fortified enclosure covering 6 km² Dhanyakataka was the urban adjunct of the famous stupa of Amaravati. Its urban antecedence goes back to the third–fourth centuries BC.

III. Aspects of post-Mauryan culture

Having reviewed the political history of the period covered by this chapter in section I, and having made a broad survey of the massive, if uneven, evidence provided by the vast number of sites which during this period qualify to be

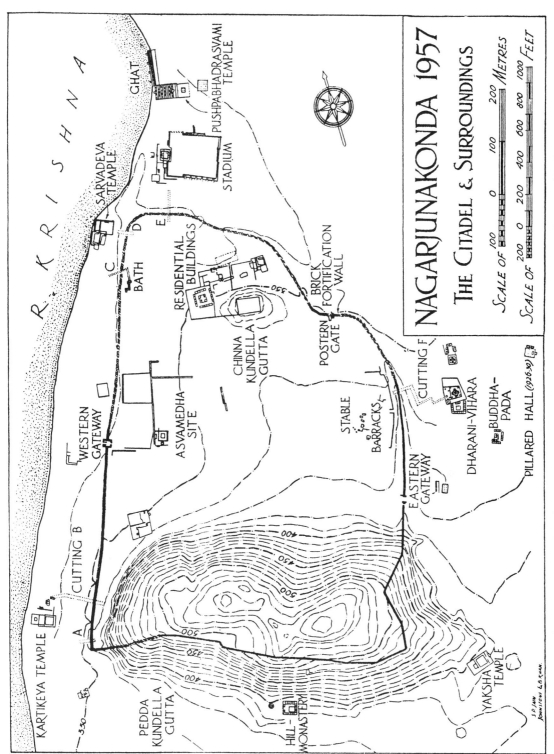

Fig. 12.9. Nagarjunakonda, city plan (c. 2–4th centuries AD) (courtesy Archaeological Survey of India).

The following labels appear on the map:

NAGARJUNAKONDA 1957
THE CITADEL & SURROUNDINGS

SCALE OF METRES
SCALE OF FEET

R. KRISHNA

KARTIKEYA TEMPLE
SARVADEVA TEMPLE
GHAT
PUSHPABHADRASVAMI TEMPLE
STADIUM
BATH
RESIDENTIAL BUILDINGS
CUTTING B
WESTERN GATEWAY
ASVAMEDHA SITE
CHINNA KUNDELLA GUTTA
BRICK FORTIFICATION WALL
POSTERN GATE
CUTTING F
DHARANI-VIHARA
BUDDHA-PADA
PILLARED HALL (1926-7)
STABLE
BARRACKS
EASTERN GATEWAY
YAKSHA TEMPLE
HILL-MONASTERY
PEDDA KUNDELLA GUTTA

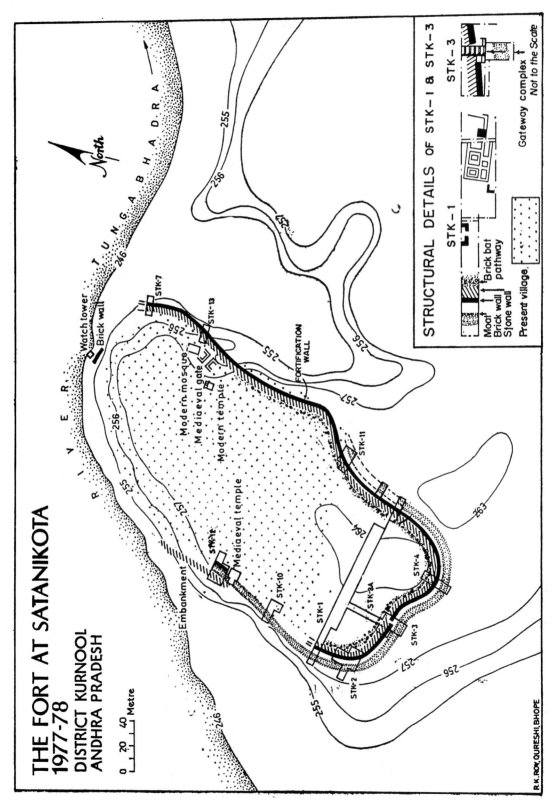

Fig. 12.10. Satanikota, plan of fortified settlement (c. 2–3rd centuries AD) (courtesy Archaeological Survey of India).

regarded as cities in section II, we shall now briefly review certain continuing themes of urban culture which were raised in earlier chapters.

The use of writing

We discussed in chapters 7, 9 and 10 the earlier history of the Brahmi and Kharosthi scripts and the evidence for the growth of the use of writing. From the second century BC onwards writing becomes more widespread and diversified. It has been suggested that the first signs of regional variations of script may already occur during the Mauryan period, but certainly by the first centuries BC and AD several clearly defined regional patterns of script begin to emerge. These are in some cases ancestral to the later development of the modern regional scripts.

The Brahmi script continued to occupy a dominant position. We find its increasing use in the records of pious donations to Buddhist monumental constructions, by Buddhist monks and laymen, many of them merchants or craftsmen, by guilds of craftsmen and by royalty. Such inscriptions occur, often in large numbers, at Bharhut, Sanchi, Amaravati, Bodh Gaya and elsewhere. Few if any are amenable to precise or accurate dating, but in terms of their contexts and the accompanying evidence of architecture and palaeography a substantial number may be assigned to the second and first centuries BC. Throughout Sri Lanka large numbers of early Brahmi inscriptions occur on rocks and natural caves, and later on monuments. Almost all refer in some way or another to Buddhist monastic foundations. In north India inscriptions in Brahmi also begin to occur on monuments or occasionally in caves associated with the rising cult of the Bhagavata Vasudeva and his brother Sankarsana during the second to first centuries BC. A small number of Jaina inscriptions also occur, in widely scattered parts of India. From the early second century BC Brahmi inscriptions are found on coins. Among the earliest examples are the copper *panca nigama* (or *negama*) coins from Taxila (Fig. 10.13). When the Indo-Greeks first extended their rule south of the Hindu Kush, they issued bilingual coins in Greek and Brahmi (see below), from c. BC 180. In the southern coastal regions a remarkable development of Brahmi, adapting it to the special phonetic requirements of Tamil, is found from the second–first centuries BC, often in coastal contexts. These Tamil inscriptions occur on pottery (Fig. 8.15) and occasionally in caves. Royal inscriptions became more varied during the first century BC. The Kharavela inscription from Orissa (probably mid-first century BC) is written in Prakrit in a characteristically poetic, eulogistic style, which later becomes standard usage for royal eulogies (*prasastis*) in Sanskrit. One of the first inscriptions to employ Sanskrit, or at least Prakrit showing Sanskrit influences, appears on the Heliodorus pillar inscription at Vidisa, dating to c. BC 120. Here a couplet is quoted which closely paraphrases a verse from the Sanatsujatiya section of the Udyoga Parvan of the Mahabharata (Banerjea 1968, 8–9). The Ghosundi inscription of a king Sarvatata of the following century (mid-first

Fig. 12.11.   South Asian coinage (BC 200–AD 200):

Indo-Greek: 1. silver tetradrachm of Demetrius I, c. BC 200–190; 2. bronze coin of Agathocles, c. BC 190–180.

Saka: 3. bronze coin of Azes, c. BC 57–10; 4. silver tetradrachm of Azes.

Kusana: 5. bronze tetradrachm of Kaniska, c. AD 100–126; 6. gold stater of Huviska, c. AD 126–163.

Western Saka (Ksatrapa): 7. silver hemidrachm of Nahapana, c. AD 119–125; 8. silver hemidrachm of Rudradaman Simha I, c. AD 191–197.

Satavahana: 9. lead coin of Siri Sata (Siri Satakani), c. BC 30–20; 10. potin coin of a king (?Satakani), c. BC 30; 11. lead coin of Gautamiputra Vilivayakura (Satakani), c. AD 106–130. (1:1) century BC) is already in Sanskrit, still showing slight influence of Prakrit (Sircar 1965, 90). With the northwestern invasions of the Saka-Ksatrapas and Kusanas, in the first centuries BC–AD, inscriptional Sanskrit began to make rapid progress, and the scripts of the northwestern region and Mathura in particular developed an individual character of their own.

In the northwest Kharosthi continued to flourish and most of the known inscriptions in that area were written in this script between c. BC 200 and AD 200 (Fig. 10.7). Kharosthi gained wide currency for coin inscriptions in the same region. That its use spread at an early date into the Ganges valley can be inferred from the fact that at Bharhut the masons used Kharosthi letters for their masonry marks. Recently a number of Kharosthi inscriptions have been discovered on potsherds from sites in Bengal.

Coinage

Around the opening of the second century BC the establishment of an Indo-Greek kingdom in Gandhara introduced into the northwest a major new currency system, with a predominantly silver and bronze coinage (Fig. 12.11, 1 and 2). At an early stage the Greeks employed bilingual inscriptions in Greek and in Prakrit in Brahmi or Kharosthi script, and their coins provided a model which later rulers in the region were to imitate. The Greeks were followed into India by a series of foreign groups, first the Sakas (Fig. 12.11, 3 and 4), and later the Kusanas who were among those to emulate the Greek patterns of coin (Fig. 12.11, 5 and 6). From the early first century AD the Kusanas created a distinctive currency of their own. Following the new vogue of the Roman aureus they issued a golden dinar, along with their own copper coinage. On the coins of Kaniska and his successors in the second century AD a wide variety of deities was depicted, including, beside the mainly Iranian pantheon, the Buddha and Siva, as well as Greek and Egyptian deities.

In parallel to this development of essentially exotic coinage, the old silver punchmarked currency continued for some time in circulation, while a local copper currency arose which derived one part of its inspiration from the later Mauryan copper currency and another from the Indo-Greek. This copper coinage has been called 'Tribal', and extended series are found in many parts of northern India and Pakistan. The earliest are mainly uninscribed, an exception being the Taxila *panca nigama* coins, and thereafter the coin legends generally bear the names of kings, in Brahmi or Kharosthi, in some series showing progressive development of their script, and dating between extremes of c. BC 200 to c. AD 300. This coinage may be assigned to the independent states which emerged after the end of the Mauryan period. For example, the early 'local' coins from Taxila probably belong to the short period of independence prior to the Greek takeover; and the local coinage from Mathura may be assigned to the Surasena *janapada*. Here, the earliest inscribed coins are those of a king called Gomitra, who was succeeded by around twelve further kings. Likewise, the coinage of Pancala yields the names of no fewer than twenty one rulers; the coins of the Vatsa *janapada*, with its capital at Kausambi, yield the names of eighteen rulers, etc. As might be expected this local currency must cover a considerable period, sometimes existing independently and sometimes co-existing with more widely diffused imperial coinage, such as that of the Kusanas.

In the Deccan other dynasties arose and produced their own coins. In Gujarat and western India the Western Ksatrapas ruled from Ujjain, for several centuries from around the first century AD, producing a predominantly silver currency, with inscriptions in Brahmi and in Kharosthi (a relic of their northern origin) (Fig. 12.11, 7 and 8). Throughout much of the Deccan the Satavahana dynasty and their feudatories ruled from c. BC 50 onwards. Their coins were predominantly in copper, lead or potin (an alloy of lead and copper) (Fig. 12.11, 9–11). Thus the picture emerges of the widespread employment of money throughout most of the areas in which the Mauryan empire had formerly flourished.

Architecture

In architecture, as in coinage, there are two main lines of development, the first of the indigenous styles which we have already encountered during the Mauryan period; the other of the specifically foreign, Greek and Central Asian influences which are in evidence particularly in the northwest. As the first of these tendencies is by far the more widespread and influential we shall consider it first.

We have already discussed some of the principal examples of secular architecture in the body of this chapter, and shall not repeat them here (Figs 12.3–10). In general the mainstream of secular architecture follows closely on that of the Mauryan period, except insofar as there is an extraordinary change in the quality of domestic architecture in almost all parts of South Asia, manifested in the much greater use of burnt brick and tile, and consequently greater permanence of the structures. It is in the field of religious architecture that most new activity is recorded. It is often stated that the post-Mauryan, Sunga period was one of Brahmanical reaction against Buddhism, and this might be expected to be reflected in a reduction of Buddhist structural activities, but the archaeological evidence scarcely supports this view. The same styles and structures seen in embryo in the late Mauryan period continue to flourish. At Sanchi, Bharhut, Bodh Gaya, Sarnath, Amaravati, Pauni and Bairat, there are important developments. At Sanchi and Bharhut the main stupas, doubtless Asokan in origin, were enlarged and in the course of a series of reconstructions had stone railings and gateways added to them, both soon to be adorned with many inscriptions and relief carvings (Fig. 12.12). At Bodh Gaya, the

Fig. 12.12.   Sanchi, the great stupa (photograph Allchin).

Mahabodhi shrine was probably rebuilt more than once. Its earlier form can be recognized in relief depictions at Bharhut and Sanchi. Around BC 100 it was surrounded by an elaborate and beautifully carved railing, dated by a Sunga period inscription, and it was probably completely rebuilt in the first or second century AD, when it assumed the form of a tower temple, represented on a terracotta relief plaque from Patna. At Amaravati, the great stupa, also we believe an Asokan foundation, was several times enlarged and during the first two centuries AD was given a distinctive railing and gateway complex, notably different from those of the north Indian stupas, but resembling contemporary work in Sri Lanka in some respects (Fig. 12.13). At Pauni a great stupa was adorned with stone relief carvings and inscriptions in the 2nd century BC. The earliest phase of all this work seems to have been fairly closely synchronized, as

Fig. 12.13. Amaravati, drum slab relief of the great stupa, 3rd century AD (courtesy British Museum).

almost identical inscriptions and labels referring to the subjects of the reliefs are found at Bharhut, Amaravati and Pauni. It is difficult to date this development, but it was probably in the second half of the second century BC. At Bairat the splendid circular *caitya* hall with a dome, referred to in chapter 11 (Fig. 11.18), compares closely with structures illustrated on reliefs at Bharhut and elsewhere, which therefore provide a clue to what its original architectural form may have been.

The paucity of monumental stone structures dating from the first two centuries

Fig. 12.14. Bhaja, rock-cut caitya (photograph Allchin).

BC is compensated for to some extent by the rapid growth of rock-cut architecture. Starting from the small beginnings mentioned in the previous chapter, we find two main groups of such work: the first is on some of the main routes through the western Ghats, between Bombay and such centres as Pune and Nasik; and the other is in eastern India, in Orissa and Andhra. The date at which this burst of activity begins is not firmly established, but it appears to be around the end of the second century BC. From that time forward there was intermittent, but continuing construction of rock-cut monumental architecture for many centuries. The earliest caves in the west, for example at Bhaja (Fig. 12.14), are all Buddhist and include Caitya halls, some containing stupas, and monastic complexes. Their importance is that they reflect closely the style and construction of timber buildings, and indeed some have actual timber beams attached to the face of the rock. From this it is possible to reconstruct the superstructures of some of those buildings known otherwise only from their ground plans, etc. The height of the early rock-cut architecture may be seen in the halls at Karle and Kanheri (c. AD 75–150) (Fig. 12.15). The less ambitious

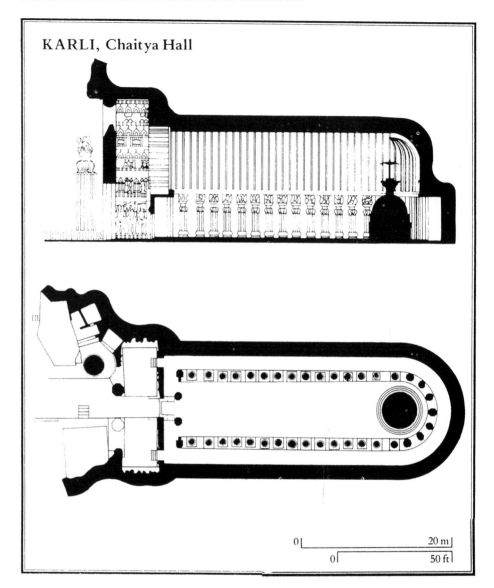

KARLI, Chaitya Hall

Fig. 12.15.   Karle, rock-cut caitya, plan and section (courtesy G. Michell).

caves of the eastern coastal regions, in Orissa and in Andhra, are both Jaina and Buddhist.

There is also a small but significant body of evidence for the development of monumental architecture belonging to the Vaisnava and Saiva movements. We noticed the early shrine at Vidisa in chapter 11. As mentioned above, this was reconstructed during the second century BC, probably as a domed circular shrine standing on a raised platform. The inscriptions at Nagari indicate that a similar shrine existed there. At Mathura during the first centuries AD there are

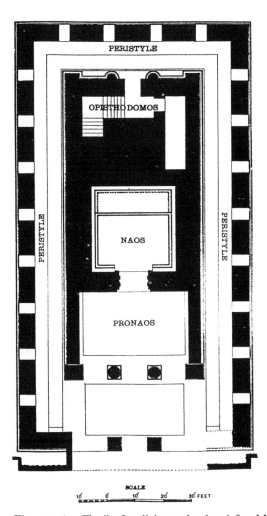

PLAN OF JANDIAL TEMPLE

PERISTYLE

OPISTHODOMOS

PERISTYLE

PERISTYLE

NAOS

PRONAOS

SCALE

10 0 10 20 30 FEET

Fig. 12.16. Taxila, Jandial temple plan (after Marshall).

numbers of Brahmanical icons, indicating the existence of temples which have so far not been discovered. In South India the shrine at Gudimallam was probably built during the second–first centuries BC, and provides the earliest evidence to date for an actual Saiva shrine: its important stone *linga* probably belongs to this period. Rich evidence of both Saiva and Vaisnava shrines has been discovered from the second to third century AD at Nagarjunakonda, where inscriptions and ashlar masonry foundations reveal some of the earliest such shrines known to date.

We have treated the northwest of India-Pakistan as a distinct province, architecturally, because here the Indo-Greeks and their successors left an indelible mark on the stylistic development. The rise of the Gandhara style in architecture and sculpture is a clear indication of our meaning. The great

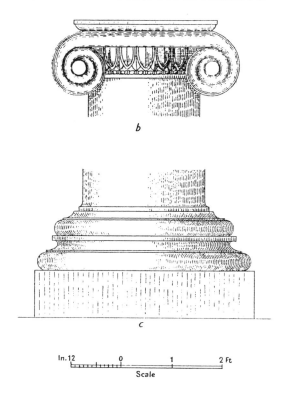

Fig. 12.17.   Taxila: Jandial, detail of capital and base of pillar (after Marshall).

Dharmarajika stupa at Taxila is without doubt an Asokan foundation. But from the first century BC its development takes a distinctive form differing from that of Buddhist stupas elsewhere in South Asia. The first change was to build a circle of small votive stupas around the circumambulatory *pradaksina patha* and, soon after, these stupas were absorbed in a ring of small chapels, facing in towards the main stupa. Equally clearly the small shrines from the first century AD Sirkap show a synthesis of Indian and Greek elements not found in other regions of South Asia. The temple at Jandial, outside the north gate of Sirkap, Taxila, is even more firmly Greek in character, with its characteristically Greek peristyle and Ionic order of columns and pilasters (Figs 12.16 and 12.17). Its date is not firmly fixed, but we may follow Marshall in placing it in the Indo-Greek period, i.e. the second to first centuries BC.

Sculpture, painting and other arts

The main branches of the arts whose earliest examples we noticed in the previous chapter show a continuing development similar to that of architecture. The relief sculptures which adorn the early Buddhist railings at Bharhut and Sanchi show a

Fig. 12.18. Bharhut, relief sculpture, with inscribed label identifying the scene as the worship of the Buddha's hair-knot in a circular caitya hall in the palace of Indra (Cunningham 1879).

liveliness and earthy quality which moves away from the rather stiff character of much Mauryan sculpture. We noticed above that the earliest examples of such sculpture at Bharhut and Amaravati share the practice of labelling narrative scenes with short inscriptions (Fig. 12.18). This usage soon disappears, never to return in Indian Buddhist sculpture, and its presence suggests the novelty of the medium at that time. By the first centuries AD the style of relief carving at Amaravati has moved some distance from its earlier stage and entitles it to be regarded as a distinct Amaravati style (Fig. 12.19). Equally clearly the styles of Mathura and Gandhara, in the first two centuries AD, both influenced by the Greek and Kusana presence, show a distinct divergence from that of the previous century (Figs 12.20–22). There is a growing variety of sculpture, almost all of it religious in character, including Buddhist, Jaina, Brahmanical and other.

From this period we find evidence of the development of wall painting. At Ajanta, where the main body of mural art belongs to the 4th–5th centuries AD,

Fig. 12.19. Amaravati relief sculpture from drum of great stupa showing scenes of the miraculous conception and birth of the Buddha, 2nd century AD (courtesy Trustees of the British Museum).

Fig. 12.20.   Gandhara relief sculpture of phyllite, the Buddha goes to school, late 1st–early 2nd century AD (courtesy Victoria and Albert Museum).

there are several early caves, dating to the first century BC–AD, with paintings in a recognizably early style. These panels are not only datable stylistically by comparison to the reliefs on the gateways of stupa I at Sanchi, but include several fragmentary inscriptions dating palaeographically to the same period.

The flowering of the popular terracotta art of the Ganges valley is one of the special features of the Post-Mauryan period. The typical 'Sunga' terracottas were

Fig. 12.21.   Mathura, Katra Keshava Deva, seated Buddha (Bodhisatva) with undated inscription, c. late 1st century AD (courtesy Mathura Museum).

Fig. 12.22. Gandhara Buddha figure, Loriyan Tangai, c. 2nd–3rd centuries
AD (courtesy Calcutta Museum).

made from single moulds, and probably such moulds were carried and dispersed widely between the Ganges delta in the east and the Northwest Frontier province (Fig. 12.23). Here too in the northwest some typical Greek features occur, with the introduction of double moulding and several typical Hellenistic types. The majority of the terracottas appear to have had religious functions, the goddess Sri and other goddesses were popular themes. Some of the figures also appear to have been purely secular, probably toys. Finally, the period witnesses the beginning of the tradition of ivory working, and the first appearance of religious icons cast in bronze.

We may conclude that the art of these centuries enjoyed a lively and creative period of great vigour, open to absorb and adapt influences from many quarters, including Greek and Roman, and experimenting with a wide variety of media. Along with the architecture it represents the flowering of early Indian urban culture, and the extension of the much more restricted art and architecture which we saw in the Mauryan period. At the same time the period provides a clear bridge between the early beginnings of the Mauryan period and the classical art of India, as it developed from Gupta times onwards.

IV. Conclusion

The present chapter has outlined the massive evidence that is to hand relating to the spread of cities and states throughout South Asia during the post-Mauryan period. As we have remarked more than once in the preceding pages one of the contributory factors in this proliferation was the ongoing process of expansion already witnessed during the Mauryan period; another factor, which cannot but strike an archaeologist working on the Early Historic period in any part of South Asia, is the impact of Rome and the Mediterranean world, which during the first century BC and the first two centuries AD provided a stimulus to all types of economic activity.

It was remarked in chapter 1 that the archaeology of the Early Historic period has been strangely neglected in South Asia, and particularly so during the past half century. This has led to the situation where sites which were already identified over a century ago have still been left unexcavated, sometimes at the cost of their decay or even disappearance. A prime target for a rejuvenated archaeology of South Asia must be to apply modern methods of research to the study of some of the great neglected cities (for example, Pataliputra and Pratisthana). We know nothing of the house plans or city plans of either of these great sites. Hitherto, beyond the sectioning of ramparts, some of the religious complexes and establishments have constituted almost the only other target for archaeological research. The present condition is not a happy one, and its contemplation serves once again to emphasize the enormity of the archaeological tasks awaiting attention in the subcontinent.

Another area of neglect arises from the fact that even within the Early Historic

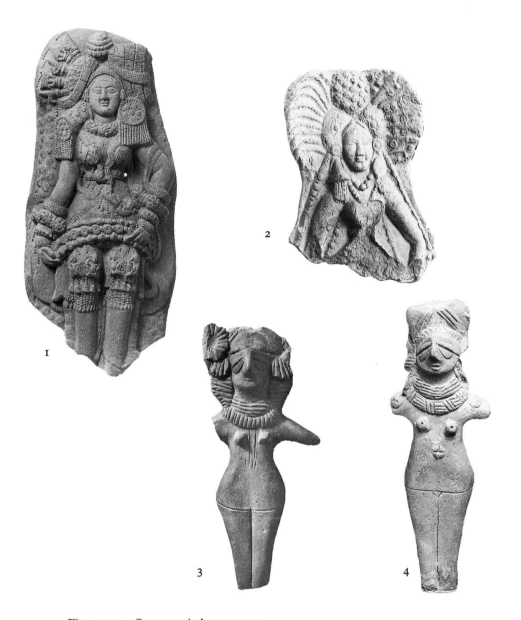

Fig. 12.23. Sunga period terracottas:

1. Tamluk, Bengal, figure of a Yaksi or mother goddess, typical of single-moulded terracotta of 2nd century BC, height 21 cm (courtesy Ashmolean Museum, Oxford);

2. Mathura, a figure of similar type, technique and date found at Mathura, height c. 9 cm (courtesy Mathura Museum);

3. Northwest Frontier Province, Pakistan, figure of a mother goddess, type prevalent from 2nd century BC to 2nd century AD (courtesy Ashmolean Museum, Oxford).

4. Charsada, Balar Hisar, figure of a mother goddess from excavation (Wheeler 1962, Pl. XXA) c. 3rd–2nd century BC.

period attention has been disproportionately focussed on the very beginning of the historical phase. In north India it is the NBP level which forms the staple of a not-inconsiderable literature. By the time the Mauryas leave the scene, historic India has developed deep roots, and this makes the archaeologists take a merely routine interest in the subsequent levels. Taxila and Charsada form a category by themselves, but then, it is the post-Mauryan period which is most significant at these sites.

Without striking a note of despair, however, one can point out, with some pride, the fact that archaeological research has at least been successful in establishing the detailed ramifications of the spread of historic settlements in all parts of the subcontinent and that at least some of the major cities mentioned in literature have been subjected to archaeological scrutiny.

PART IV

CONCLUSION

CHAPTER 13

THE EMERGENCE OF CITIES AND STATES: CONCLUDING SYNTHESIS

F. R. ALLCHIN

In this final chapter we draw together some of the topics discussed in the book and present a short interdisciplinary summary of some selected aspects of Early Historic South Asian civilization. It is obvious that many matters which have been raised and discussed in greater or lesser detail cannot be included in this section. For example, in chapters 3, 4 and 6 we touched on the possible causes of the end of the Indus civilization and some attendant problems. We also dwelt on such vexed questions as the use of the terms 'Aryan' and 'Indo-Aryan', and whether we should speak of acculturation or 'ethnicity' in this connection. However important these things may be they are subsidiary to the main thrust of our book, and therefore we shall not discuss them further. Our conclusion will mainly dwell on two topics: some major aspects of the social and political genesis of the cities and states of Early Historic South Asia; and a brief survey of the character of the civilization which flourished alongside the rise of cities and states. In writing this section we would like to acknowledge the very real debt we feel towards a number of scholars, some of whom we regard as our teachers, others as our contemporaries and friends. Among the first category should be the late D. D. Kosambi whose *Introduction to the Study of Indian History* (1959) inspired a whole generation of students of early Indian history; also the late Debiprasad Chattopadhyaya whose *Lokayata* (1959) and subsequent works, particularly the two volumes of *History of Science and Technology in Ancient India* (1986 and 1991), demonstrated their author's profundity and extraordinary originality of thinking about ancient Indian society; we never met F. J. Richards, who combined with his career as a magistrate in South India an amateur interest in archaeology and its relationship to geography, but his writing left its impression on students of Indian archaeology of our generation (Richards 1930, 1932, 1933). In the next category should come our contemporaries and among many others Professors Romila Thapar and Ram Sharan Sharma whose numerous works and, respectively, their *From Lineage to State* (1984) and *Material Culture and Social Formations in Ancient India* (1983), have each provided us with many new insights on the subject of this book. Among many members of the younger generation we would like to mention Dr Ranabir

Chakravarti whose short essay 'Early historical India' (1991) remarkably coincides with many of the points we have made in this concluding chapter.

Social and political development

1. Post-Harappan north India and the Rigveda (c. BC 2000–1000)

In chapters 3 and 4 we have presented an archaeological overview of the post-Harappan period in north India and Pakistan, and suggested a model for the arrival and spread of Indo-Aryan-speaking people in the same area. We put forward a view of the formation of a multi-ethnic society in which Indo-Aryans at first represented a numerically small but increasingly powerful minority; and the earlier population, whose language or languages have not as yet been firmly established, formed the majority. With the passage of time the majority population became bilingual, and finally abandoned their own languages in favour of Indo-Aryan speech. From the archaeological point of view, settlement sequences are recorded in many regions, but to determine their ethnic components with any confidence is not as yet possible. Wherever there is evidence it indicates that the basic economy was characterized by mixed agriculture and pastoralism, and in many respects shows a direct continuation from that of rural areas during the Indus civilization. It is difficult to relate this model to that offered by the Rigveda, where Romila Thapar (1984, 22–7) and Ram Sharan Sharma (1983, 22–32) agree in finding the subsistence base of Rigvedic society and economy to have been 'essentially pastoral'. Our knowledge and understanding of the second millennium BC still leaves much to be desired, and this indicates the importance of further focussed, problem-orientated research on these and similar topics.

2. Settlement and expansion of the Late Vedic period

In chapter 6 Erdosy examined the changes which took place during the Late Vedic period (c. BC 1200–600). These developments had already been anticipated in the final sections of the previous chapters. They involved an eastern spread of a new settlement pattern accompanied by a slow but steady increase in the manufacture and use of iron tools. What, in archaeological terms, were the main causes of these changes may still be the subject of discussion: initially, a period of desertification in the Indus valley, possibly linked to river change and capture, may have provided a powerful pressure towards the eastern shift of population and settlements; while the availability of iron tools opened up the possibility of forest clearance on the rich alluvial plains of the eastern Punjab, Haryana and Uttar Pradesh. This in turn promoted the production of subsistence crops, and particularly of rice, and created the conditions needed for a rapid growth of population. By this time there appears to be a clear correspondence between the settlements and culture referred to in Late Vedic literature and those known to archaeology. The period must have witnessed the further development of a multi-ethnic society in which Indo-Aryans or their descendants, and self-styled Indo-Aryans of various origins, formed elite groups, claiming dominance and power over a mixed population of whom an increasing proportion were what we referred to as 'acculturated Aryans', that is to say descendants of the earlier population of any region who had acquired Indo-Aryan speech and perhaps other traits. Something of the character of this rule and of the role of tribal chiefdoms and kings can be found in the literature of the period. It is this newly emerging elite and its claims to cultural superiority which are seen by Erdosy (above, p. 91) as offering the final stimulus to the rapid expansion of 'Indo-Aryan' cultural dominance.

3. The emergence of cities and states (c. BC 600–300)

It is possible to sense a certain inevitability about the onward march of the social and economic developments of this and the succeeding centuries. The period from BC 600 onwards has been charted in chapter 7, where the factors involved in the rise of cities in the Ganges system are discussed. It must be borne in mind that by comparison the evidence from other regions of South Asia, particularly the northwest and the peninsula (discussed in chapter 8), is less full and hence less well defined. In the Ganges valley the archaeological evidence of the growing number and size of settlements points towards a substantial and continuing increase in population (further discussed by Coningham in chapter 5). A significant outcome of the extending clearance of the fertile land of the Ganges-Yamuna alluvium, has been pointed out by R. S. Sharma (1983, 96–7). It amounted to a virtual 'Green Revolution' in the production of rice, brought about by the development of new varieties, including the *sastika* (sixty day) rice, and the introduction of new techniques of transplanting paddy. This, Sharma suggests, extended its scope from being an exclusively monsoon crop to being also a winter, and hence two or three season, crop. This change was almost certainly the principal factor in the rapid increase of population which appears to have accompanied it. Here again, we recall Richards who as early as 1933 saw population density as a 'common multiple' among the variable factors affecting human existence (Richards 1933, 236). In this environment the first great cities came into being, frequently marked by massive fortification walls and controlling a hinterland of smaller agricultural settlements. These cities, in conjunction with their peripheral settlements constituted the newly emerging city states or *janapadas*. This is the period of the sixteen great states or *Mahajanapadas*, which during these centuries are referred to in textual sources as major settled areas. From this point on a coherent developmental process was set in train, whose main themes recur or endure for centuries to come. It may be helpful in understanding this process to consider what some of these themes were.

4. Features of early Indian urbanism

Perhaps the first point which demands notice is the aggressive and expansive character of early Indian urbanism. This stands in marked contrast to the commonly stressed, and equally present, promulgation of doctrines of non-violence, *ahimsa*, which arose in the Ganges valley, among Buddhists, Jainas and orthodox Brahmanical sects alike, perhaps as a reaction to the violent times. Aggression took the form of internecine fighting between the cities and states, leading to the gradual elimination of the smaller and weaker by the stronger. In a way this is a parallel development to the doctrine of *matsya-nyaya* (*Arthasastra* 1.4.13), the maxim of the fish, through the analogy of fish eating smaller fish, and in turn being eaten by still bigger fish. Such a situation was seen as producing an undesirable breakdown of law and order, and hence a state of anarchy. The cure generally recommended for such anarchy was the strong rule of a king, and the general desire to establish the rule of law was a major factor leading to the formation of states. For a further study of *matsya-nyaya* see Spellman 1964, 4–8, 20–21, etc.

The aggressive character of the early city states was not only internal, directed at the fellow states of the Ganges valley; it was also external, directed more widely at the capture and control of further tracts of territory, either already settled for agriculture or still awaiting clearance and settlement, probably mainly forest lands, in some cases inhabited by agricultural communities, in others by forest tribes. This expansionist aspect of early Gangetic urbanism was to provide a vehicle for the spread of a unifying 'Indian' ideology throughout South Asia. In such situations it took the form of the colonization of land, and the colonization or creation of new cities with their own surrounding territories. Such colonization has been mentioned in chapters 8 and 9, as one of the factors in the rapid spread of cities outside the central Ganges regions, particularly in central India, peninsular India and Sri Lanka. It has been further considered in chapter 10, as a factor in the Mauryan imperial expansion.

A second enduring feature of early historic urbanism was the formation of states and the formulation of an early Indian theory of the state. For this, as we have seen in chapter 10, we are fortunate to have a splendid source in Kautilya's *Arthasastra*, a source which may with considerable confidence be assigned to the early Mauryan period. One is repeatedly struck by the clarity and force of Kautilya's language, and by the consistence of his viewpoint. The state is defined in terms of its seven constituent elements; it is the dynamic relationship of these elements which symbolizes the state itself. The first element is the ruler or king, hence a state may also be spoken of as a *rajya*, a realm or kingdom. A king is powerless without his council of ministers and administrators, hence the second element, defined in a single word, is the ministers. The third element is *janapada*, the occupied territory, beautifully defined by Kautilya, in another context, as 'the earth endowed with population' (*manusyavati-bhumi*) (*Arthasastra* 15. 1,1), and it is this combination of land and population which in the view of Kautilya provides the potentials for the creation of wealth. The fourth element in the structure is the fortified settlement: this includes therefore the fortified city, both as capital and as regional administrative centre, as well as forts, as parts of a military and defensive network. In this way the fortified city is one of the basic elements of a state. One of the functions of the city is to provide a safe location for the fifth element, the treasury in which the king conserves and protects his wealth. The sixth element *danda*, the 'big stick' or 'rod', includes several means by which force may be exerted to maintain the state. Among these are the administration of justice, the infliction of punishments and the role of the army. Finally the seventh element, the ally, includes a whole network of political relationships with neighbouring states, both friends and foes, and leads to the formation of a supporting system of foreign policy.

The concept of the state, which we believe was already clearly formulated by c. BC 300, forms the basis for almost all later attempts to define the state in early South Asia. It poses the question 'which came first, the city or the state?', to which the answer seems to be somewhat similar to the conundrum of the chicken and egg. Both cities and states emerged as part of a complex process and their interdependence in this light is recognized by the *Arthasastra*.

A further feature of the emergence of cities and states was the breaking down of tribal societies throughout north India, and the corresponding extension of a new set of urban and sub-urban social relations. There is ample evidence in early Indian literature of the widespread distribution of tribal groups throughout the Ganges system and beyond. These tribes are variously referred to as *ganas* and *sanghas*. Panini in his great grammar uses both terms, and contrasts them with states having a single ruler (Agrawala 1953, 434–66). He cites many examples by name. Such names of tribal groups are often given in the plural, the Vrijis, Yaudheyas, Malavas, etc., suggesting that their corporate character was still regarded as important. Panini also refers to some *sanghas* as living by the use of weapons, suggesting their warlike propensities. Perhaps the most penetrating discussion of these tribal groups and their significance is by Debiprasad Chattopadhyaya (1959, 153–80). Chattopadhyaya contests K. P. Jayaswal's earlier view that the *sanghas* were 'Republican states' as opposed to monarchies, and argues convincingly that they were tribal groups who had not as yet become absorbed into the expanding urban society, and therefore had not reached the stage of state formation. He points to the unevenness of development of Indian society as a characteristic feature through successive ages, even down to the present time. He cites references in the early Buddhist texts to the Magadhan king Ajatasatru's decision to attack and destroy the confederacy of the Vajjis (Vrijis), and to the contrasting view of the Buddha that such *sanghas* might only be disposed of by diplomacy or by breaking their alliances. This very point is discussed as a matter of state policy by Kautilya who argued that such tribal groups had peculiar strengths which meant that they were virtually impossible to conquer by war, and must be tackled by other means. One way he proposed was to break up the tribal groups by resettling them in small agricultural communities, thus providing a means of absorbing them into the wider urban and sub-urban society, at the same time helping to promote the expansion of the state into surrounding territories which were still beyond its frontiers.

5. The emergence of empire

The logical climax of the internecine process is reached when the sixteen major states are progressively reduced to four, then to two, and finally to one. Theoretically this point coincides with the establishment of a single uniform rule, and therefore to the complete control of the warring factions. At this stage the state takes on an altogether different complexion and becomes an empire. We do not mean to imply that such a supreme power actually ruled uniformly over all the states it had 'conquered' or had admitted allegiance to it. The reality was almost certainly more complex and more fluid. This climactic process took place during the second half of the fourth and early third centuries BC. It was first achieved when the kingdom of Magadha, under the Nanda rulers established Magadhan supremacy and began the policy of imperial expansion which was to be followed by their immediate successors the Mauryas. We do not know exactly when the Nandas began their rule, but it was evidently still extant in BC 327–325 when Alexander the Great invaded the northwestern parts of South Asia. The subsequent conquests of the Mauryans not only subdued the territories of the Gangetic *janapadas*, but carried their rule over the greater part of South Asia, from Kandahar in the west to east Bengal in the east, and to the southern borders of modern Karnataka and Andhra Pradesh in the south. Pataliputra became what Thapar calls the Metropolis of this empire, and must have been at that time a splendid city, if we are to judge by the account of the Greek emissary Megasthenes and by the meagre finds of sporadic and unsystematic archaeological research. The *Arthasastra*, which as we have seen provides the main historical evidence for this period, claims to be the composition of the minister of Candragupta Maurya, who helped his master to drive out the Nandas, and to defeat the armies of Alexander, and more importantly succeeded for a few decades in uniting most of South Asia into a single, loosely knit empire.

Turning again to archaeology, we have attempted in chapters 9 and 10 to put together the somewhat uneven evidence it provides in support of this discussion. The political expansion we have been reviewing must have involved a quite unprecedented proliferation of urban settlements, and of an urban settlement pattern throughout all parts of the empire, and furthermore must have had reciprocal repercussions in the territories which lay beyond its frontiers. Therefore we may detect, in the still often fragmentary evidence, what for want of a better term we can call a 'Mauryan' influence affecting the style of a range of very diverse local cultures. That this was the period of the establishment of a quite new kind of 'all-India' culture seems certain. In one sense the promulgation of Asoka's edicts in a mainly uniform script or scripts, throughout his empire, symbolizes another aspect of this development, in that it was responsible for taking Buddhism, together with many other aspects of what had hitherto been a mainly Magadhan, or Gangetic, culture to every corner of South Asia.

6. The breakdown of the empire and its aftermath

Throughout the subsequent course of Indian history there is a recurrent pattern in the formation of political powers each of which for a time, often only a short time, held sway over a greater or smaller area, and then fell apart. It seems probable that the inadequacy of means of communications and transport contributed to the inevitability of such a process. The Mauryan empire began to disintegrate shortly after the death of Asoka and its final disappearance took place within half a century of this event. But this period of political decay in no way implied a return to earlier structures and forms. What is striking is the way in which in one region of South Asia after another smaller new regional groupings arose, or re-emerged, frequently based upon cities which had been provincial Mauryan capitals, or even capitals of earlier *janapadas* (chapter 12). The new states had often a markedly regional character. In the Ganges valley the Sunga dynasty held sway; in Orissa the Mahameghavahanas; and elsewhere in Maharashtra the Satavahana dynasty emerged. In the northwest a similar pattern seems to have developed, but here it was soon submerged by the invasions of the Indo-Greeks, driven out of their kingdoms in Bactria and Kapisa; and shortly after followed into India by the Saka-Ksatrapas who established their rule in Mathura, Ujjain and Saurashtra. Our own view of the social and political implications of these newly emerging states coincides closely with those of Ranabir Chakravarti (1991, 330–5).

The pattern of the post-Mauryan period was soon to be influenced by a far greater external force than any hitherto experienced; this was the economic strength of the Roman empire. From the first century BC Roman trade with all parts of South Asia, and particularly with the coastal states, becomes increasingly evident, providing a greater external stimulus to trade than any previously experienced (Thapar 1992, 1–27). It is in this context that the relatively greater wealth of cities of the early centuries AD should be envisaged.

The character of early Indian civilization

1. Writing and coinage

In the foregoing chapters we have attempted to map out, chapter by chapter and period by period, some of the more important features of the civilization which accompanied the rise of cities and states. We may now cast a retrospective glance over these special aspects in the wider context of the whole period.

Foremost among these is the introduction of the use of writing, which as we saw appears in Sri Lanka by BC 450, if not earlier. The inscriptions found there are in the Brahmi script, which is ancestral to all later Indian scripts, with the exception of Kharosthi. In its earliest manifestations Brahmi shows some variations from the Brahmi script of the Mauryan period, not least in the comparative irregularity, not to say ungainliness, of some of its letters. The language of these early inscriptions is, perhaps unexpectedly in this setting, a typical north Indian Prakrit, and so far there is no dated evidence for so early an occurrence of Tamil. The discovery of inscriptions dated by such objective means permits us, incidentally, to place greater reliance than had hitherto been possible on some of the textual references to writing in early literature, and to the resolution of such longstanding debates as that concerning the feasibility of the composition of a text such as the *Astadhyayi* of Panini without the aid of a developed form of Brahmi script. In chapter 9 we have discussed the important contributions to the subject made by Buhler and Winternitz, and found ourselves substantially in agreement with their conclusions regarding the origins of the script and the stages by which its use was extended.

We expressed the view that there is not as yet enough evidence to prove exactly where or when the first development of the Brahmi script took place, nor whether it was in the north or south, or on the east or west coasts of South Asia; and indeed we do not see this as a matter of very great moment. What we see as more important is the indication (already hinted at by Buhler) that the earliest use of the script arose in a mercantile context. We expect that when systematic excavation and dating is carried out in other parts of South Asia, further dated occurrences will come to light, and that through such additional evidence a fuller picture may be found of the introduction and early use of both the Brahmi and Kharosthi scripts. There is not the same difficulty in establishing the source of the Kharosthi script, in that it is patently an adaptation of the Aramaic script which was employed as the administrative script and language of the Achaemenid rulers of the northwest between the sixth to fourth centuries BC. Great interest must attach to discovering datable evidence for its first introduction and for its chronology relative to that of Brahmi. It seems probable that the introduction of the two scripts was quite independent, and that Brahmi was developed at an earlier date than Kharosthi.

We further commented briefly upon the growth of the scope of writing as we inferred it from the admittedly limited evidence available. The first introduction of the script was in the course of mercantile exchanges, and only at a somewhat later date was the script refined by north Indian grammarians so as to make it an adequate vehicle for writing Sanskrit as well as Prakrit, for scholarly use as well as for governmental and administrative uses. We suppose this development began in late pre-Mauryan times and that the scope and use of writing expanded rapidly under the stimulus of the Mauryan empire. It was probably only in post-Mauryan times that writing began to be used on coins. Finally we agreed with the views expressed by Winternitz regarding the relative reluctance to introduce writing of sacred texts, although we supposed that the non-orthodox sects, such as the Buddhists, had probably begun this practice already by Mauryan times. We would expect that the writing and copying of texts advanced by progressively greater strides in the Sunga and Kusana periods.

In chapter 10 we noticed that a grammatical example, quoted around the seventh century AD, commenting on a *sutra* of Panini, attributed the regulation of weights and measures to the Nanda dynasty. This subject has not as yet been researched in a systematic manner by early historic archaeologists in South Asia, although some attention was paid to its numismatic aspects, by the late D. D. Kosambi. We have still therefore to rely on early textual references for much of our knowledge of early weights and measures. It seems probable that there was already some degree of standardization and that the Nandas systematized the divergent weight standards between certain different regions or states of the time. It has often been suggested that there are links between both the Early Historic metrical systems and actual weight standards on the one hand, and those known from the long-passed Indus civilization on the other. Interesting as such questions are, the evidence certainly demands more study of a carefully controlled and precise kind before they can be answered. An important aspect of the problem is the access of new research data from intelligently planned and executed excavations.

We remarked on the foregoing chapters that the introduction of coinage into South Asia appears to have taken place during the late fifth or early part of the fourth century BC, and that it is generally agreed to have done so in the context of Achaemenid imperial contacts with the northwestern regions. Be this as it may, a distinctly Indian coinage soon developed, showing a silver and later a copper currency, and providing the basis for the monetary system which played so central a role in the Mauryan state. It seems too that the earliest currency in South Asia developed in the northwest, and soon spread to the *janapadas* of the Ganges valley. From there it further spread to almost all regions of South Asia during the Mauryan period. In the post-Mauryan period regional styles of coinage developed, that of the north being greatly influenced by the Indo-Greek and later Roman currency. Thus writing, the standardization of weights and measures, and coinage were all comparatively recent developments in the cities and states of the Mauryan period, but nonetheless all are present in a distinctive form which we regard as a characteristic Indian style.

2. Early South Asian art and architecture

During the centuries of state and city formation in the Ganges valley a new style was emerging in both architecture and the arts which was finally disseminated during the Mauryan period throughout almost all parts of South Asia. This involved the use of stone sculpture and other architectural stonework, often carved to resemble wooden members, for construction of certain types of monument. As yet, in the absence of adequately dated excavations or other means of dating surviving monuments, we know very little about the pre-Mauryan history of the development of stoneworking of all kinds, and it is only during and after the Mauryan period that more or less solid evidence is available for it. However, by the Mauryan period, it is evident that what had hitherto been a regional, Gangetic style of both architecture and sculpture became an all-India style, establishing for the first time since the decline of the Indus civilization, some fifteen hundred years earlier, an inter-provincial urban style. Accepting that the evidence for this development belongs almost exclusively to the Mauryan and Sunga periods, and not earlier, in chapters 11 and 12 we have attempted to indicate some of the main achievements and monuments of this style. Viewed from the hindsight of history, we may say that the Mauryan inter-provincial style in both architecture and stone sculpture formed the basis of the stylistic development for many centuries thereafter. Only later did there begin to develop a whole series of specifically regional styles which were further modified and enhanced by new, often external, influences. In chapter 12 we have seen how Hellenistic or Roman influence on sculpture and architecture appears, and how it was particularly strong in Gandhara, in the northwest, where a sculptural style developed to which such names as 'Indo-Roman' have been applied.

The beginnings of the tradition of wall painting, which finds its early climax in the Ajanta caves, are also traceable during this period, but the available evidence is extremely limited. There is a well-established tradition of prehistoric cave painting throughout the hilly regions of Central India, but most of this painting is, strictly speaking, undateable. In a few instances, as Wakankar noted (Wakankar and Brooks 1976, 33), Early Historic Brahmi inscriptions have been found superimposed on the earlier paintings. We have recently however seen an instance whose full significance was not noted by Wakankar. Here there is a palimpsest of three distinct periods of work: prehistoric paintings; a small group of early Vaisnava icons, clearly identifiable as Vasudeva-Sankarsana, dated by an attached inscription to c. the first century BC; and a much more recent sectarian inscription. We noted also in chapter 11 the occurrence of early paintings in a partly man-made cave, dated by another Early Historic inscription to approximately the same date. The third stage of this process is represented by the early paintings in cave X at Ajanta, which Dehejia dates through their contemporary inscriptions, one of which is actually painted on the surface, to the early part of the first century BC (Dehejia 1972, 157–8). There is a vast difference between the early Vaisnava painting, whose style combines an obvious familiarity with the iconography of the second century BC with a typically 'folk' style, and the early Ajanta paintings which show clear affinities with the reliefs of the Sanchi stupa gateways, and thus suggest a slightly later date.

Among minor arts terracottas reveal a similarly interesting admixture of styles. We noted the evidence of a group of figures from Patna and its vicinity which are believed to belong to the Mauryan period and which show distinctive traits suggesting the influence of contemporary Hellenistic terracottas. A similar tendency is noticeable, though at a later date, in terracottas from the northwest. But beside these influences there is a clearly defined development of an indigenous Gangetic style of terracottas, which for one reason or another spread to the cities of the northwest, but scarcely spread either to the Deccan or to Sri Lanka in the south.

3. The emergence of new religions and sects

The rise of cities and states between c. BC 600–300 was accompanied by a number of other notable developments which deserve mention in that they contributed to the make-up of the distinctive character of Indian civilization. Perhaps none of these is more striking than the flowering during these centuries of religious speculation and the appearance of a series of new religious movements. These were disseminated within South Asia along with the urban culture, and some of them were to spread far beyond its frontiers. Not the least reason for their interest to us is that these movements played a leading role in the development of religious architecture and sculpture, and that these categories represent almost the total known repertoire of monuments and sculptures for most of the period. Thus some understanding of the religions themselves is helpful to an understanding of the art and architecture.

- In late Vedic literature and in the early Upanisads there is a consistent image of Brahmanical sages living in forest retreats (*asramas*), instructing their pupils (*sisyas*) in the role of *gurus* and from time to time visiting the local kings for religious disputations and discourses. It is evident that such sages could not have existed in an Arcadian vacuum, but must represent one of the attendant aspects of the emerging urban society. That is to say, such forest retreats must have been in close and constant contact with a neighbouring city, and their occupants almost certainly relied on the generosity of city dwellers and merchants for a part of their subsistence. The chronology of the early Upanisads has been discussed by Ruben (1954), and by Belvalkar and Ranade (1927), and we may accept a broad framework of between c. BC 600 and c. BC 300 for the period they embrace. Teachers such as Yajnavalkya or Uddalaka Aruni were as much powerful and original thinkers as were the great teachers of the unorthodox sects. Their teaching on *atman, karma* and *brahman* presents us with a fundamental basis for the great wave of creative thought which produced the Buddha and Mahavira.

By the same light, the 'new' or unorthodox sects and religions which arose during these centuries may be understood as products of the same broad social development towards the formation of cities and states. Max Weber recognized this in respect of Buddhism, and gave it clear expression in his study of *The Religion of India* (1958, 205). The early literature refers to these new sects and religions in various ways: the Brahmans regarded them as heretics, *Nastikas*, in that they denied the revelation of the Vedas and the existence of the *atman*. It is perhaps significant that many of the new teachers were not Brahmans, but belonged to the Ksatriya caste; thus emphasizing their links with the ruling group and with kings. The most widely spread and therefore best known were the Buddhists, followers of Gautama, the Buddha, whose teaching that 'all things are without atman' and silence regarding God or the 'gods' sets the tone for his unorthodoxy. Equally unorthodox was the slightly earlier Mahavira, the founder of the Jaina or Nirgrantha sect, who according to doubtful tradition died in BC 527. Mahavira taught that a man's salvation can be achieved by rigorous asceticism and by non-violence towards all beings. Another of the early sects was founded by Makkali Gosala, a contemporary of Mahavira, whose followers were known as the Ajivikas. He taught a fatalistic doctrine that destiny (*niyati*) ordains man's *karma*, and that consequently human endeavours were unavailing. A fourth sect was the Lokayata, founded by Ajita Kesakambali (Ajita of the hairy blanket). This sect adopted an uncompromisingly materialist position, denying the existence of the *atman* and arguing that death was the total annihilation of a person.

The foregoing sketch suggests that there was a broad distinction between the orthodox Brahmanical religion with its emphasis on the sacredness of the Vedas, the importance of sacrifices for the maintenance of world order, and holding a variety of fundamentally theistic world views; and the various unorthodox sects who were largely drawn from the ranks of non-Brahman castes, and who promoted a variety of views, all challenging the divine revelation of the Vedas, the importance of sacrifice, and therefore the supremacy which was claimed by the Brahmans, and all to some degree or another positively maintaining atheistic or non-theistic positions. As we have remarked, this conflict arose in the context of the rising urban society, and merchants and princes were sought out as the supporters of both the Brahmanical and the new religions alike. The patronage offered by the wealthy is an indication of their affluence and ability to play such roles. It has also been observed that the great majority of the supporters of Buddhism came from cities rather than from rural backgrounds (Sarao 1989, 41–7). With the rise of urban states and their expansionist policies, the new religions adopted a similarly expansive missionary stance. We have seen in chapter 9 (pp. 158–59) how, in the case of Buddhism, the conversion of Asoka led to a South Asia-wide missionary programme, carrying Buddhist teaching to countries as far apart as Burma, Sri Lanka and Gandhara, and also to countries of the western world.

In the aftermath of Alexander's campaigns in India, cultural interaction between the Mediterranean world and South Asia increased, influences travelling in both directions. These contacts may have contributed new elements to the rise of Brahmanical sects, such as the cult of saviour deities, during the centuries following the break-up of the Mauryan empire. It is generally agreed that in the second century BC, during the rule of the Sungas, something of a Brahmanical reaction set in in the Ganges valley, and that it was in this context that Saivism and more particularly Vaisnavism gained new prominence. This is most clear in the case of the latter, which finds such full expression in the Mahabharata. These new movements, with their foundations of devotionalism, and their Brahmanical institution of *ahimsa*, non-violence, even to the extent of discouraging animal sacrifice, set trends which were to be followed for many centuries to come.

Conclusions

This final chapter has attempted to present a brief picture of the Early Historic civilization of South Asia, as it appears to an archaeologist, and undoubtedly it has neglected many important things. Most of all, we have been unable to offer more than passing references to a few of the vast number of texts which were composed during these centuries, or to their contents and special characters. The literature of a literate age offers insights which are likely to elude the archaeologist who disregards it; while at the same time his more earthbound view may provide a useful and necessary corrective in interpreting these often enigmatic and frequently undateable texts. We have long believed that the early history of India suffered from being too 'text-bound' and that an archaeological perspective was needed to provide a more balanced view. In writing and editing this book the importance and relevance of the textual data have been constantly in our mind. We have also come to believe that too sceptical an approach to the texts may lead to the exclusion of much valuable material that deserves inclusion. An outstanding example of this is the reluctance to accept the *Arthasastra* as a source book for the Mauryan period because doubt exists regarding the extent to which the text as we have it is the work of one author, whether it contains later additions, and so on. Our reading of the *Arthasastra* suggests that, whatever later additions there may be, its main thrust is the work of the period it purports to represent.

Finally, and in conclusion, we express the hope that this book will succeed in offering the reader a clearer and in some ways new perspective on the early historic civilization of South Asia as a whole; while at the same time suggesting ways in which archaeology can be employed to make a more effective contribution to the advancement of knowledge of the subject. Perhaps, in retrospect, we should moderate our earlier strictures on the neglect of Early Historic archaeology in South Asia. The volume of relevant data is certainly enormous, but the quality of so much is poor. There is an almost universal need for more problem oriented research; for a more innovative approach to theoretical problems and interpretation; and for much wider applications of scientific analysis.

BIBLIOGRAPHY

Adams, R. McC. 1981. *Heartland of Cities*. Chicago: University of Chicago Press.

Agrawal, D. P. 1971. *The Copper–Bronze Age in India*. New Delhi: Munshiram Manoharlal.

— 1982. *The Archaeology of India*. Scandinavian Institute of Asian Studies Monograph Series, No. 46. London: Curzon Press.

Agrawala, V. S. 1953. *India as known to Panini*. Lucknow: University of Lucknow.

— 1964. *Chakra-dhvaja, the Wheel Flag of India*. Varanasi: Prithivi Prakashan.

— 1965. *Indian Art*. Varanasi: Prithivi Prakashan.

Ali, S. M. 1966. *The Geography of the Puranas*. Delhi.

Allan, J. 1936. *Catalogue of the Coins of Ancient India*. London: The British Museum.

Allchin, B. and Allchin, (F.) R. 1968 (reprinted 1993). *The Birth of Indian Civilization*. Harmondsworth: Penguin Books.

— 1982 (reprinted 1986). *The Rise of Civilization in India and Pakistan*. Cambridge World Archaeology. Cambridge: Cambridge University Press.

Allchin, B., Goudie, A. S. and Hegde, K. T. M. 1978. *The Prehistory and Palaeogeography of the Great Indian Desert*. London: Academic Press.

Allchin, F. R. 1968. Archaeology and the date of Kaniska: the Taxila evidence. In *Papers on the Date of Kaniska*, ed. A. L. Basham, Symposium, 4–34. Leiden: Brill.

— 1980. Archaeological and language historical evidence for the movement of Indo-Aryan speaking people into India and Pakistan. *Journal of the K. R. Cama Research Institute* 48:68–102.

— 1981. Archaeological and language-historical evidence for the movement of Indo-Aryan speaking peoples into South Asia. In *Ethnic problems in the History of Central Asia in the early Second Millennium BC*, ed. B. A. Litvinsky, M. S. Asimov, *et al.*, 336–49. Moscow.

— 1982a. How old is the city of Taxila? *Antiquity* 56:8–14.

— 1982b. The legacy of the Indus civilization. In *Harappan Civilization*, ed. G. L. Possehl, 325–33. New Delhi: Oxford and IBH.

— 1985. The interpretation of a seal from Chanhu-daro. In *South Asian Archaeology 1983*, ed. J. Schotsmans and M. Taddei, 369–84. Naples: Istituto Universitario Orientale.

— 1989. City and state formation in Early Historic South Asia. *South Asian Studies* 5:1–16.

— 1990. Patterns of city formation in Early Historic South Asia. *South Asian Studies* 6:163–73.

1993. The urban position of Taxila and its place in Northwest India–Pakistan. In *Urban Form and Meaning in South Asia: the Shaping of Cities from Prehistoric to Precolonial Times*, ed. H. Spodek and D. M. Srinivasan, 69–81. Studies in the History of Art, 31. Center for Advanced Study in the Visual Arts, Symposium Papers XV. Washington: National Gallery of Art.

Allchin, F. R. and Norman, K. R. 1985. Guide to the Asokan inscriptions. *South Asian Studies* 1:43–50.

Altekar, A. S. 1949. *State and Government in Ancient India*. Delhi: Motilal Banarasidass.

Altekar, A. S. and Mishra, V. K. 1959. *Report on Kumrahar excavations (1951–1953)*. Patna: K. P. Jayaswal Research Institute.

Ardika, I. W. and Bellwood, P. 1991. Sembiran: the beginnings of Indian contact with Bali. *Antiquity* 65:221–32.

Auboyer, J. 1969 (1965). *Everyday Life in Ancient India*. London: Weidenfeld & Nicolson.

Ball, V. 1881. *A Manual of Geology in India*. London: Trubner & Co.

Bandaranayake, S. 1992. The settlement patterns of the Protohistoric–Early Historic interface in Sri Lanka. In *South Asian Archaeology 1989*. 15–24, ed. C. Jarrige. Madison Wisconsin: Prehistory Press.

Banerjea, J. N. 1968. *Religion in Art and Archaeology (Vaishnavism and Saivism)*. Dr Radha Kumud Mookerji Endowment Lectures, 1961–62. Lucknow: University of Lucknow.

Banerjee, N. R. 1960. The excavations at Ujjain. In *Indologen Tagung 1959*, ed. E. Waldschmidt, 74–96. Gottingen: Vandenhoeck-Ruprecht.

1965. *The Iron Age in India*. 1–264. Delhi: Munshiram Manoharlal.

1968. *Nagda*. Memoirs of the ASI, 85, 1–290. New Delhi: Archaeological Survey of India.

Barth, F. 1969. Introduction. In *Ethnic Groups and Boundaries*, ed. F. Barth, 9–38. Boston: Little, Brown.

Beal, S. 1884. *Si-Yu-Ki, Buddhist Records of the Western Worlds*. London: Trubner & Co.

Bechert, H. 1982. The date of the Buddha reconsidered. *Indologia Taurinensia* 10:29–36.

1991. *The Date of the Historical Buddha*. Symposium zur Buddhismus forschung, 2 vols. 4. Gottingen: Vandenhoek & Ruprecht.

Begley, V. 1983. Arikamedu reconsidered. *American Journal of Archaeology* 87:461–81.

1986. From Iron Age to Early Historic in South Indian archaeology. In *Studies in the Archaeology of India and Pakistan*, ed. J. Jacobson, 297–319. New Delhi: Oxford and IBH.

Begley, V., Lukacs, J. R. and Kennedy, K. A. R. 1981. Excavations of Iron Age Burials at Pomparippu, 1970. *Ancient Ceylon* 4:49–132.

Belvalkar, S. K. and Ranade, R. D. 1927. *History of Indian Philosophy, The Creative Period*. vol II. Poona: Bilva-Kunja Publishing House.

Bhan, S. and Shaffer, J. G. 1978. New discoveries in Northern Haryana. *Man and Environment* 2:59–68.

Bhan, Suraj. 1975. *Excavation at Mitathal (1968)*. Kurukshetra: Kurukshetra University.

Bhandarkar, D. R. 1914. Excavations at Besnagar. *Annual Report of the Archaeological Survey of India*. Calcutta: Archaeological Survey of India.

1920. *The Archaeological Remains at Nagari*. Memoirs of the Archaeological Survey of India, vol. 4. Delhi: Archaeological Survey of India.

Binford, L. R. 1964. A consideration of archaeological research design. *American Antiquity* 31:203–11.

Bisht, R. S. 1982. Excavations at Banawali: 1974–77. In *Harappan Civilization a Contemporary Perspective*, ed. G. L. Possehl, 113–24. New Delhi: Oxford & IBH Publishing Co.

Bisht, R. S. and Asthana, S. 1979. Banawali and some recently excavated sites. In *South Asian Archaeology 1977*, ed. M. Taddei, 223–40. Naples: Istituto Universitario Orientale.

Bloch, T. E. 1903–4. Caves and inscriptions in the Ramgarh hill. *Annual Report of the Archaeological Survey of India*: 123–31.

1913–14. Excavations at Basarh. *Annual Report of the Archaeological Survey of India*. Calcutta: Archaeological Survey of India.

Bose, A. N. 1961. *Social and Rural Economy of Northern India circa 600 BC–200 AD*. Calcutta.

Brohier, R. L. 1934. *Ancient Irrigation Works in Ceylon*. Colombo: Government Press.

Brown, Percy. n.d. *Indian Architecture (Buddhist and Hindu Periods)*. Bombay: D. B. Taraporewala Sons.

Buchignani, N. 1987. Ethnic phenomena and social theory. In *Ethnicity and Culture*, ed. L. Auger, 15–24. Archaeological Association. University of Calgary.

Buhler, G. 1904. *Indian Paleography*. J. F. Fleet trans. *The Indian Antiquary*.

1962. *Indian Palaeography*. 2nd edn. Calcutta: K. L. Mukhopadhyaya.

Burrow, T. 1973. The Proto-Indoaryans. *Journal of the Royal Asiatic Society* (2):123–40.

Buth, G. M., Bisht, R. S. and Gaur, G. S. 1982. Investigation of palaeolithic remains from Semthan, Kashmir. *Man and Environment* 6:41–45.

Carneiro, R. L. 1970. A theory of the origin of the state. *Science* 169.

1981. The chiefdom: precursor of the state. In *The Transition to Statehood in the New World*, ed. G. D. Jones and R. R. Kautz, 37–79. Cambridge: University Press.

Carswell, J. and Prickett, M. 1984. Mantai 1980. *Ancient Ceylon* 5:3–80.

Casal, J. M. 1949. *Fouilles de Virampatnam-Arikamedu*. Paris: Imprimerie Nationale.

1956. *Site urbain et sites funéraires*. Paris: Presses Universitaires.

Chakrabarti, D. K. 1968. 'Aryan hypothesis' in Indian archaeology. *Indian Studies Past and Present* 4:333–58.

1972. Early urban centres in India: an archaeological perspective, c. 2500 BC–c. 300 AD. Calcutta: unpublished monograph.

1973a. Concept of urban revolution and the Indian context. *Puratattva* 6:27–32.

1973b. Beginning or iron and social change in India. *Indian Studies Past and Present* 14:329–38.

1974. Some theoretical aspects of Indian urban growth. *Puratattva* 7:87–9.

1976. Rajagriha: An early historical site in eastern India. *World Archaeology* 7:261–8.

1977. Distribution of iron ores and the archaeological evidence for early iron in India. *Journal of the Economic and Social History of the Orient* 20:166–84.

1979. Size of the Harappan Settlements. In *Essays in Indian Protohistory*, ed. D. P. Agrawal and D. K. Chakrabarti, 205–15. Delhi: B. R. Publishing Corporation.

1984. The archaeology of the iron age and the early historical period of Kashmir. *Man and Environment* 8:109–16.

1988. *Theoretical Issues in Indian Archaeology*. New Delhi: Munshiram Manoharlal.

1992a. *Ancient Bangladesh*. Delhi: Oxford University Press.

1992b. *The Early Use of Iron on India*. Delhi: Oxford University Press.

Chakrabarti, D. K., Nag, A. K. and Chakrabarti, S. 1978–79. An archaeological reconnaissance in Birbhum. *Puratattva* 10:25–32.

Chakraborti, H. 1966. *Trade and Commerce in Ancient India*. Calcutta.

Chakravarti, Ranabir. 1991. Early historical India: a study in its material milieu (c. 600 BC–300 AD). Appendix I. In *History of science and technology in ancient India, II*, author and ed. D. P. Chattopadhyaya, 305–50. Calcutta: Firma KLM Pvt Ltd.

Chandra, Pramod. 1971. The cult of Laksmi and four carved discs in Bharat Kala Bhavan. *Chhavi: Golden Jubilee Number, 1920–1970*: 139–48.

Chattopadhyaya, D. P. 1959. *Lokayata. A study in Ancient Indian Materialism*. Delhi: People's Publishing House.

1986, 1991. *History of Science and Technology in Ancient India*. vol. I and II. Calcutta: Firma KLM.

Childe, V. G. 1929. *The Danube in Prehistory*. Oxford: Clarendon Press.

1979 (1950). The urban revolution. In *Ancient Cities of the Indus*, ed. G. L. Possehl, 12–18. Delhi: Vikas Publishing House.

Claessen, H. J. M. 1978. The early state: A structural approach. In *The Early State*, ed. H. J. M. Claessen and P. Skalnik, 533–96. The Hague: Mouton.

Claessen, H. J. M. and Skalnik, P. 1978. The early state: models and reality. In *The Early State*, ed. H. J. M. Claessen, and P. Skalnik, 637–50. The Hague: Mouton.

1981. The study of the state conference in retrospect. In *The Study of the State*, ed. H. J. M. Claessen and P. Skalnik, 469–510. The Hague: Mouton.

Codrington, H. W. 1924. *Ceylon Coins and Currency*. Colombo.

Cohen, R. 1978. State origins: a reappraisal. In *The Early State*, ed. H. J. M. Claessen and P. M. Skalnik, 31–76. The Hague: Mouton.

Coningham, R. A. E. 1990. Anuradhapura Citadel archaeological project, British sub-project, Anuradhapura Salgaha Watta preliminary report 1989–1990. *Ancient Ceylon* 9.

1991. Preliminary report on the second season of Sri Lankan–British excavations at Salgaha Watta June–August 1990. *South Asian Studies* 7:167–75.

1993. Anuradhapura Citadel Project: preliminary results of the excavation of the southwest rampart. *South Asian Studies*, 8:111–22.

In press. Anuradhapura Citadel Archaeological Project: preliminary results of the first three years of Sri Lankan–British excavations at Salgaha Watta, 1989–1992. *Ancient Ceylon*, 13.

Coningham, R. A. E. and Allchin, F. R. 1992. Preliminary report on the third season of Sri Lankan–British excavations at Salgaha Watta, July–September 1991. *South Asian Studies* 8:157–67.

Connah, G. 1987. *African Civilization: Precolonial Cities and States in Tropical Africa: an Archaeological Perspective*. Cambridge: Cambridge University Press.

Cousens, H. 1929. *The Antiquities of Sind*. Calcutta: Government of India, Central Publication Branch.

Craddock, P. T., Freestone, I. C., Gurjar, L. K., Middleton, A. and Willies, L. 1989. The production of lead, silver and zinc in early India. In *Archaometallurgie der alten Welt*, ed. A. Hauptmann, E. Pernicka and G. A. Wagner, Symposium, 51–69. Bochum: Deutschen Bergbau-Museums.

Cribb, J. 1985. Dating India's earliest coins. In *South Asian Archaeology 1983*, ed. M. Taddei, 535–54. Naples: Istituto Universitario Orientale.

Cunningham A. 1963. (1871). *The Ancient Geography of India*. Delhi (London): Motilal Banarasidass (Trubner & Co).

1966 (1871–72). *Report for the year 1871–72*. Varanasi: Archaeological Survey of India.

Dalal, L. A. 1989. The historical geography of the Mathura region. In *Mathura: The Cultural Heritage*, ed. D. M. Srinivasan, 3–11. Delhi: American Institute of Indian Studies.

Dales, G. F. 1965. Civilization and floods in the Indus Valley. *Expedition* 7(2):10–19.

Dani, A. H. 1965–66. Shaikhan Dheri excavations. *Ancient Pakistan* 2:17–124.

Dehejia, V. 1972. *Early Buddhist Rock Temples*. London: Thames & Hudson.

Deraniyagala, S. U. 1972. The Citadel of Anuradhapura 1969: excavations in the Gedige area. *Ancient Ceylon* 2:49–169.

1986. Excavations in the Citadel of Anuradhapura: Gedige 1984, a preliminary report. *Ancient Ceylon* 6:39–47.

1990a. The prehistoric chronology of Sri Lanka. *Ancient Ceylon* 12:211–50.

1990b. The proto and early historic radiocarbon chronology of Sri Lanka. *Ancient Ceylon* 12:251–92.

1990c. Radiocarbon dating of early Brahmi script in Sri Lanka. *Ancient Ceylon* 11:149–68.

1992. *The Prehistory of Sri Lanka*. Colombo: Department of Archaeological Survey, Government of Sri Lanka.

Desai, Devangana, 1985. Terracotta dancing girls. *Marg* 37:72–4.

Despres, L. A., ed. 1975. *Ethnicity and Resource Competition in Plural Societies*. The Hague: Mouton.

Deva, Krishna and Mishra, V. K. 1961. *Vaisali Excavations 1950*. Vaisali: Vaisali Sangh.

Dey, N. L. 1927. *The Geographical Dictionary of Ancient and Medieval India*. London.

Dhavalikar, M. K. 1975. The beginnings of coinage in India. *World Archaeology* 6:330–8.

1988. *The First Farmers of the Deccan*. Pune: Ravish Publishers.

Dhavalikar, M. K. and Possehl, G. L. 1974. Subsistence pattern of an early farming community of western India. *Puratattva* 7:39–46.

Dhavalikar, M. K., Sankalia, H. D. and Ansari, Z. D. 1988. *Excavations at Inamgaon*. Pune: Deccan College.

Diakonov, I. M. 1969. The rise of the despotic state in ancient Mesopotamia. In *Ancient Mesopotamia: Socio-economic history*, ed. I. M. Diakonoff. Moscow: Akademia Nauka.

Dikshit, K. N. 1981. The excavations at Hulas and further exploration in the upper Ganga-Yamunā Doab. *Man and Environment* 5, 70–6.

1982. Hulas and the Late Harappan complex in Western Uttar Pradesh. In *Harappan Civilization, A Contemporary Perspective*, ed. G. L. Possehl, 339–52. New Delhi: Oxford & IBH Publishing Co.

1984. Late Harappa in Northern India. In *Frontiers of the Indus Civilization*, ed. B. B. Lal and S. P. Gupta, 253–70. New Delhi: Books & Books.

Earle, T. 1991. *Chiefdoms: Power, Economy and Ideology*. Cambridge: Cambridge University Press.

Elwin, V. 1942. *The Agaria*. Calcutta: Oxford University Press.

Erdosy, G. 1987. Early historic cities of Northern India. *South Asian Studies* 3:1–23.

1988. *Urbanisation in Early Historic India*. British Archaeological Reports: International Series. Oxford: British Archaeological Reports.

1989. Ethnicity in the Rigveda and its bearing on the question of Indo-European origins. *South Asian Studies* 5:35–47.

1993. The archaeology of early Buddhism. In *Studies in Buddhism in Honour of A. K. Warder*, ed. N. K. Wagle and F. Watanabe. Toronto.

1995. Language, Material culture and ethnicity: theoretical perspectives. In *Language, Material Culture and Ethnicity*: the Indo-Aryans of Ancient South Asia, ed. G. Erdosy, 1–31. Berlin: W. de Gruyter.

Feinman, G. 1991. Demography, surplus and ideology: early political formations in highland Mesoamerica. In *Chiefdoms: Power, Economy and Ideology*, ed. T. Earle, 229–62. Cambridge: Cambridge University Press.

Fergusson, J. 1910 (1876). *History of Indian and Eastern Architecture*. Revised and ed. J. Burgess. London: John Murray.

Flannery, K. V. 1968. Archaeological systems-theory and early Mesoamerica. In *Anthropological Archaeology in the Americas*, ed. B. J. Meggars. Washington: Anthropological Society of Washington.

1972. The cultural evolution of civilisations. *Annual Review of Ecology and Systematics*, 3:399–426.

Friedman, J. and Rowlands, M. J. 1978. Notes towards an epigenetic model of the evolution of civilisation. In *The Evolution of Social Systems*, ed. J. Friedman and M. J. Rowlands, 201–76. London: Duckworth.

Garde, M. B. 1915–16. The site of Padmavati. In *Annual Report of the Archaeological Survey of India*. Calcutta: Government Press.

Gaur, R. C. 1983. *The Excavations at Atranjikhera: Early Civilisation in the Ganga Basin*. Delhi: Motilal Banarasidas.

1989. The rise of urbanism in the upper Ganga-Yamuna Doab. Unpublished Paper read at a conference on *Old Problems and New Perspectives in the Archaeology of South Asia*. Madison, Wisconsin: Department of Anthropology.

Geiger, W., trans. 1950 (1912). *The Mahavamsa or Great Chronicle of Ceylon*. Assisted by M. H. Bode, with an Addendum by G. C. Mendis. Colombo: Ceylon Government Information Department.

Ghosh, A. 1948. Taxila (Sirkap) 1944–45. *Ancient India* 4:66–78.

1973a. *The City in Early Historical India*. Simla: Indian Institute of Advanced Study.

1973b. Concept of urban revolution and the Indian context. *Puratattva* 6:34–5.

ed. 1991. *An Encyclopaedia of Ancient India*. Leiden: E. J. Brill.

Ghosh, A. and Panigrahi, K. M. 1946. The pottery of Ahicchatra (UP). *Ancient India* 1:37–59.

Ghosh, N. C. 1986. *Excavations at Satanikota 1977–78*. Memoirs of the Archaeological Survey of India, No. 82. New Delhi: Archaeological Survey of India.

Ghosh, N. N. 1935. *Early History of Kaushambi*. Allahabad.

Gillespie, R. 1984. *Radiocarbon User's Handbook*. Oxford: University Committee for Archaeology.

Gonda, J. 1975. *Vedic Literature*. Wiesbaden: Otto Harrassowitz.

Goswami, K. G. 1948. *Excavations at Bangarh (1938–41)*. Calcutta: University Press.

Gunasekara, B., trans. 1900. *Rajavaliya, A Historical Narrative of Sinhalese Kings.* Colombo: Government Printer.

Gupta, P. L. 1969. *Coins. India – The Land and People.* New Delhi: National Book Trust.

Gupta, S. P. 1980. *The Roots of Indian Art.* Delhi: B. R. Publishing Corporation.

Guruge, A., trans. and ed. 1989. *Mahavamsa, the Great Chronicle of Sri Lanka.* Colombo: Associated Newspapers of Ceylon.

Harle, J. C. 1986. *The Art and Architecture of the Indian Subcontinent.* Harmondsworth: Penguin Books.

Harmatta, J. 1981. Proto-Iranians and Proto-Indians in Central Asia in the 2nd millennium BC. In *Ethnic Problems in the History of Central Asia in the Early Period,* ed. B. A. Litvinsky, M. S. Asimov, *et al.,* 75–83. Moscow: Nauk.

1992. The emergence of the Indo-Iranians: The Indo-Iranian languages. In *History of Civilizations of Central Asia,* ed. A. H. Dani and V. M. Masson, 357–78. Paris: UNESCO.

Härtel, H. 1976. Some results of the excavations at Sonkh. In *German Scholars on India,* 2, 69–90. Bombay: Nachiketa Publications.

1993a. Die Kusana-Horizonte im Hugel von Sonkh (Mathura). In *Excavations at Sonkh,* ed. H. Hartel and V. Moeller. Monographien zur Indischen Archaologie, Kunst und Philologie, vol. 9, 1–24. Berlin: Dietrich Reimer Verlag.

1993b. Pottery of Mathura. In *Mathura: The Cultural Heritage,* ed. D. M. Srinivasan, 181–92. Delhi: American Institute of Indian Studies.

Hartley, C. 1913. *Spolia Zeylanica.* Vol. 9. *The Stone Implements of Ceylon.* Colombo: Government Printing.

Hasan, S. J. 1982. The distribution of beads in the Ganges Valley. *Puratattva* 11:131–40.

Hegde, K. T. M. 1975. The painted grey ware of India. *Antiquity* 49:187–90.

Helms, S. W. 1979. Old Kandahar Excavations 1976: Preliminary report. *Afghan Studies* 2:1–8.

Hodder, I. 1978. The spatial structure of material cultures. In *The Spatial Organisation of Culture,* ed. I. Hodder, 93–111. London: Duckworth.

1979. Economy and social stress and material culture patterning. *American Antiquity* 44:446–54.

1986. *Reading the Past.* Cambridge: University Press.

Holst, W. 1970. India's self sufficiency in food grains. In *Agricultural Policy and Self-Sufficiency,* ed. S. C. Mathur. New Delhi: Associated Publishing House.

Huntingford, G. W. B., ed. and trans. 1980. *The Periplus of the Erythraean Sea.* London: The Hakluyt Society.

Huntington, J. C. 1974–75. The Lomas Rishi: another look. *Archives of Asian Art* 28:34–56.

Indian Archaeology – a Review, 1953–54 – 1988–89 [abbreviated IAR (year) in text]. New Delhi: Archaeological Survey of India.

Irwin, J. 1973, 1974, 1975, 1976. 'Asokan' pillars: a reassessment of the evidence. *The Burlington Magazine* 115, 116, 117, 118:706–20, 712–27, 631–43, 734–53.

1978. The Heliodorus pillar at Besnagar. *Puratattva,* 8:166–76.

Jarrige, J-F. 1985. Continuity and change in the North Kachi Plain (Baluchistan, Pakistan) at the beginning of the second millennium BC. In *South Asian Archaeology 1983,* ed. J. Schotsmans and M. Taddei, 35–68. Naples: Istituto Universitario Orientale.

Jarrige, J-F. and Santoni, M. 1979. *Fouilles de Pirak*. Publications de la Commission des Fouilles Archeologiques: Fouilles du Pakistan No. 2. Paris: Diffusion de Boccard.

Jarrige, J-F. and Usman Hassan, M. 1989. Funerary complexes in Baluchistan at the end of the third millennium. In *South Asian Archaeology 1985*, ed. K. Frifelt and P. Sorenson, 150–66. London: The Curzon Press.

Johnson, G. A. 1973. *Local Exchange and Early State Formation in Southwestern Iran*. Anthropological papers of the University of Michigan No. 51, Michigan.

1987. The changing organisation of Uruk administration on the Susiana Plain. In *The Archaeology of Western Iran*, ed. F. Hole, 107–39. Washington: Smithsonian Institution.

Joshi, J. P. 1972. Explorations in Kutch and excavations at Surkotada. *Journal of the Oriental Institute, Baroda*, 21:89–144.

1991. Mathura. In *An Encyclopaedia of Indian Archaeology*, Vol. II, *Gazetteer of Sites*, ed. A. Ghosh, 263–6. Leiden: Brill.

Joshi, J. P. *et al.* 1990. *Excavation at Surkotada 1971–72 and Exploration in Kutch*. In *Memoirs of the Archaeological Survey of India, No. 87*. New Delhi: Archaeological Survey of India.

Joshi, J. P. *et al.* 1993. Excavations at Bhagwanpura, 1975–76. *Memoirs of the ASI*, 89:1–263. New Delhi: Archaeological Survey of India.

Joshi, J. P., Madhu Bala and Jassu Ram. 1984. The Indus Civilisation on the basis of distribution maps. In *Frontiers of the Indus Civilization*, ed. B. B. Lal and S. P. Gupta, 511–30. Delhi: Archaeological Survey of India.

Joshi, M. C. 1973. Concept of urban revolution and the Indian context: comments (on Chakrabarti 1972). *Puratattva* 6:36B.

1974. Early historic urban growth in India: some observations. *Puratattva* 7:91–2.

Joshi, M. C. and Sinha A. K. 1981. Chronology of Mathura – an assessment. *Puratattva* 10:39–44.

Juleff, G. 1990. The Samanala-wewa archaeological survey. *Ancient Ceylon* 9:75–106.

Kangle, R. P., ed. and trans. vol. I, 1960; vol. II, 1963; vol. III, 1965. *The Kautilya Arthasastra: University of Bombay Studies: Sanskrit, Prakrit and Pali*. Bombay: University of Bombay.

Keesing, R. M. 1981. *Cultural Anthropology, a Contemporary Perspective*. New York: Holt, Rinehart and Winston.

Keith, A. B. 1914a. *Harvard Oriental Series 25*. 2 vols. *The Rigveda Brahmanas*. Cambridge, Mass.: Harvard.

1914b. *The Vedas of the Black Yajus School entitled Taittiriya Samhita*. Cambridge, Mass.: Harvard.

1920. *Rigveda Brahmanas*. Cambridge, Mass.: Harvard University Press.

1925. *Religion and Philosophy of the Veda and Upanisads*. Cambridge, Mass.: Harvard.

Kenoyer, J. M. 1991a. The Indus tradition of Pakistan and West India. *Journal of World Prehistory*, 5(4):331–85.

1991b. Urban process in the Indus tradition: a preliminary model from Harappa. In *Harappa Excavations 1986–1990. Monographs in World Archaeology No. 3*, ed. R. H. Meadow. Prehistory Press: Madison, Wisconsin. 29–60.

Khare, M. D. 1969. Discovery of a Vishnu temple near the Heliodorus pillar. *Lalit Kala*, 1967–69:13–14, 21–7.

1978. Comments (on Irwin's paper). *Puratattva*, 8:176–8.

Kluckhohn, C. 1960. The moral order in the expanding society. In *City Invincible: A Symposium of Urbanization and Cultural Development in the Ancient Near East*, ed. C. H. Kraeling and R. M. Adams. Chicago: Chicago University Press.

Kosambi, D. D. 1950. The origin of Brahmin Gotras. *Journal of the Bombay Branch of the Royal Asiatic Society* 26:21–80.

1956. *An Introduction to the Study of Indian History*. Bombay: Popular Book Depot.

1963. The beginning of the iron age in India. *Journal of the Economic and Social History of the Orient* 6:309–18.

1965. *The Culture and Civilization of Ancient India in Historical Outline*. London: Routledge and Kegan Paul.

Kramrisch, S. 1933. *Indian Sculpture*. Calcutta.

Kristiansen, K. 1991. Chiefdoms, states and systems of social evolution. In *Chiefdoms: Power, Economy and Ideology*, ed. T. Earle, 16–43. Cambridge: Cambridge University Press.

Kumar, L. S. S. 1963. *Agriculture in India*. Bombay, London: Asia Publishing House.

Kumar, M. 1987. Archaeological investigation in Kurukshetra. In *Vajapeya: Essays on the Evolution of Indian Art and Culture*, ed. A. M. Shastri *et al.*, 53–62. Agam Kala Prakashan.

Lal, B. B. 1949. Sisupalgarh 1948: an early historical fort in Eastern India. *Ancient India* 5:62–105.

1951. Further copper hoards from the Gangetic basin and a review of the problem. *Ancient India*, 7:20–39.

1955. Excavations at Hastinapura and other explorations in the Upper Ganga and Sutlej Basins. *Ancient India* 11:5–151.

1960. From the Megalithic to the Harappan: tracing back the graffiti on the pottery. *Ancient India* 16:4–24.

1982. Are the defences of Kausambi really as old as 1025 BC? *Puratattva* 11:89–94.

1985. The so-called 'Syenaciti' at Kausambi: a fallen brick mass. *Puratattva* 15:94–104.

Lal, B. B. and Dikshit, K. N. 1981. Sringaverpur: a key site for the protohistory and early history of the central Ganga valley. *Puratattva* 10:3–7.

Lal, Makkhan. 1984a. *Settlement History and Rise of Civilization in the Ganga-Yamuna Doab from 1500 BC–300 AD*. Delhi: B. R. Publishing Corporation.

1984b. Summary of four seasons of explorations in the Kanpur District. *Man and Environment* 8:61–80.

1987. The stages of human colonisation in the Ganga-Yamuna Doab: archaeological evidence. *South Asian Studies*. 3:25–32.

Larick, R. 1987. Men of iron and social boundaries in Northern Kenya. In *Ethnicity and Culture*, ed. L. Auger, 67–75. Calgary: University of Calgary Archaeological Association.

Law, B. C. 1935. *Sravasti in Ancient Literature*. Memoirs of the Archaeological Survey of India. Delhi.

1939. *Kausambi in Ancient Literature*. Memoirs of the Archaeological Survey of India. Delhi.

1944. *Ujjayini in Ancient Literature*. Gwalior.

1948. *Panchalas and their Capital Ahichchhatra*. Delhi.

1950. *Collected Papers*. Calcutta.

1954. *Historical Geography of Ancient India*. Paris.

1969. Sakala: an ancient Indian city. *East and West* 19:401 ff.

ed. 1959. *The Dipavamsa*. Maharagama, Ceylon: The Ceylon Historical Journal.

Lerner, M. and Kossak, S. 1991. *The Lotus Transcendent: Indian and Southeast Asian Art from the Eilenberg Collection*. New York: Metropolitan Museum of Art.

McCrindle, J. W. 1926 (1877). *Ancient India as described by Megasthenes and Arrian*. Calcutta.

Macdonnell, A. A. and Keith, A. B. 1912. *Vedic Index of Names and Subjects*. London: John Murray.

Mackay, E. J. H. 1943. *Chanhu-daro Excavations, 1935–46*. American Oriental Series, vol. 20. Boston: Museum of Fine Arts.

Majumdar, R. C. 1960. *The Classical Accounts of India*. Calcutta: 1960.

Mallory, J. P. 1989. *In Search of the Indo-Europeans*. London: Thames and Hudson.

Marshall, J. 1936. *A Guide to Sanchi*. Delhi: Manager of Publications.

Marshall, J. H. 1912. Excavations at Bhita. *Annual Report of the Archaeological Survey of India 1911–12*:29–94.

1951. *Taxila, an Illustrated Account of Archaeological Excavations*. Cambridge: University Press.

Marshall, J. H. and Vogel, J. P. 1903. Excavations at Charsada. *Annual Report of the Archaeological Survey of India 1902–03*:141–84.

Mehta, R. N. 1968. Sudarsana lake. *Journal of the Oriental Institute, Baroda* 18:18–28.

Misra, V. D. 1977. The excavations at Koldihwa. In *Some Aspects of Indian Archaeology*, ed. V. D. Misra, 107–19. Allahabad: Abinash Prakashan.

Misra, Y. *An Early History of Vaisali*. Delhi: 1962.

Mitchiner, M. 1973. *The Origin of Coinage*. London: Hawkins.

Mitra, D. 1958. Bhubaneswar. New Dehli: Archaeological Survey of India.

1971. *Buddhist Monuments*. Calcutta: Sahitya Samsad.

Mookerji, R. K. 1953 (1951). Chandragupta and the Mauryan Empire, etc. In *History and Culture of the Indian People: The Age of Imperial Unity*, ed. R. C. Majumdar and A. D. Pusalkar, 54–100. Bombay: Bharatiya Vidya Bhavan.

Mughal, M. R. 1967. Excavations at Tulamba. *Pakistan Archaeology* 4:11–152.

1982. Recent archaeological research in the Cholistan desert. In *Harappan Civilization, a Contemporary Perspective*, ed. G. L. Possehl, 85–96. New Delhi: Oxford & IBH Publishing Co.

1984. The Post-Harappan phase in Bahawalpur district, Pakistan. In *Frontiers of the Indus Civilization*, ed. B. B. Lal and S. P. Gupta, 499–503. New Delhi: Books & Books.

1990a. The Harappan 'twin capitals' and reality. *Journal of Central Asia* 13(1):155–62.

1990b. The protohistoric settlement patterns in the Cholistan desert. In *South Asian Archaeology 1987*, ed. M. Taddei and P. Callieri, 143–56. Rome: ISMEO.

1992. The consequences of river changes for the Harappan settlements in Cholistan. *The Eastern Anthropologist* 45:105–16.

Mukherjee, B. N. 1970. *The Economic Factor in Kushana History*. Calcutta.

1990. *Kharoshti and Kharoshti-Brahmi Inscriptions in West Bengal.* Calcutta: Indian Musuem.

Nanavati, J. M. and Mehta, R. N. 1971. *Somnath 1956.* Baroda: M. S. University.

Narain, A. K. and Agrawala, P. K. 1978. *Excavations at Rajghat (1957–58; 1960–65).* IVA and IVB, Terracotta Human Figurines. Varanasi: Banaras Hindu University.

Narain, A. K. and Roy, T. N. 1967. *Excavations at Prahladpur.* Varanasi: Banares Hindu University.

Narain, A. K. and Singh, P. 1977. *Excavations at Rajghat (1957–58; 1960–65).* III, Small Finds. Varanasi: Banaras Hindu University.

1976–78. *Excavations at Rajghat.* Varanasi: Benares Hindu University.

Orton, N. in press. The early ceramics of Kantarodai. *Ancient Ceylon* 13.

Pant, P. C. and Jayaswal, V. 1990. Ancient stone quarries of Chunar: an appraisal. *Pragdhara: Journal of the UP State Archaeological Organisation* 1(1):49–52.

Parker, H. 1909. *Ancient Ceylon.* London: Luzac.

Parpola, A. 1974. On the protohistory of the Indian languages in the light of archaeological, linguistic and religious evidence. In *South Asian Archaeology 1973,* ed. J. E. van Lohuizen-de-Leeuw and J. J. M. Ubaghs, 90–100. Leiden: E. J. Brill.

1988. The coming of the Aryans to Iran and India. *Studia Orientalia* 64:195–302.

Patil, D. R. 1963. *The Antiquarian Remains in Bihar.* Patna.

Pearson, G. W. and Stuiver, M. 1986. High precision calibration of the radiocarbon time-scale 500–2,500 ^{bc}. *Radiocarbon* 28:839–62.

Piggott, S. 1943. The earliest Buddhist shrines. *Antiquity* 17:2–6.

1945. *Some Cities of Ancient India.* Oxford: Oxford University Press.

1950. *Prehistoric India.* Harmondsworth: Penguin Books.

Pleiner, R. 1971. The problem of the beginning of the Iron Age in India. *Acta Praehistorica et Archaeologica,* 2:5–36.

Possehl, G. L. 1977. The end of a state and the continuity of a tradition. In *Realm and Region in Traditional India,* ed. R. Fox, 235–54. Durham: Carolina Academic Press.

1980. *Indus Civilization in Saurashtra.* Delhi: B. R. Publishing Corporation.

1986. African millets in South Asian Prehistory. In *Studies in the Archaeology of India and Pakistan,* ed. J. Jacobson, 237–56. New Delhi: Oxford & IBH Publishing Co.

ed. 1989, 1994. *Radiocarbon Dates for South Asian Archaeology.* Occasional Paper. Philadelphia: University Museum, University of Pennsylvania.

1990. Revolution in the urban revolution: the emergence of Harappan urbanism. *The Annual Review of Anthropology,* 19:261–82.

Possehl, G. L. and Raval, M. H. 1989. *Harappan Civilization and Rojdi.* New Delhi: Oxford and IBH.

Poster, G. Amy. 1986. *From Indian Earth – 4000 Years of Terracotta Art.* New York: The Brooklyn Museum.

Puri, K. N. n.d. *Excavations at Rairh.* Jaipur.

Ragupathy, Ponnampalam. 1987. *Early Settlements in Jaffna, an Archaeological Survey.* Madras: Mrs T. Ragupathy.

Raikes, R. L. 1965. The Mohenjo-daro floods. *Antiquity* 39:196–203.

1967a. The Mohenjo-daro floods – further notes. *Antiquity* 41:64–6.

1967b. *Water, Weather and Prehistory.* New York: Humanities Press.

Randsborg, K. 1982. Rank, rights and resources: An archaeological perspective from

Denmark. In *Ranking, Resource and Exchange.* ed. A. C. Renfrew and S. Shennan. Cambridge: Cambridge University Press.

Rangarajan, L. N., trans. 1992. *The Arthashastra.* New Delhi: Penguin Books.

Rao, S. R. 1965. Excavation at Rangpur and other explorations in Gujarat. *Ancient India* 18 & 19:1–207.

1979, 1985. *Lothal: A Harappan Port Town, 1955–62.* Memoirs of the Archaeological Survey of India, vol. 78. Delhi: Archaeological Survey of India.

Rapson, E. J., ed. 1962 (1922). *The Cambridge History of India,* vol. I. Delhi (Cambridge): Cambridge University Press.

Ray, N. 1976. Technology and social change: A note posing a theoretical question. *Puratattva* 8:132–8.

Ray, S. C. 1959. Stratigraphic evidence of coins in Indian excavations and some allied issues. *Numismatic Notes and Monographs,* 1–41. Varanasi: The Numismatic Society of India.

Raychaudhari, H. C. 1972 (1953), 7th edn. (1932). *Political History of Ancient India.* Calcutta.

Renfrew, A. C. and Level, E. 1979. Transformations: Mathematical Models of Culture Change. In *Exploring Dominance: Predicting Polities from Centres,* ed. A. C. Renfrew, and K. Cooke, 145–67. New York: Academic Press.

Renfrew, C. 1978. Space, time and polity. In *The Evolution of Social Systems,* ed. J. Friedman and M. J. Rowlands, 89–112. London: Duckworth.

1979. Systems collapse as social transformation. In *Transformations: Mathematical Approaches to Culture Change,* ed. A. C. Renfrew and K. L. Cooke. New York: Academic Press.

1986. Peer polity interaction and socio-political change. In *Peer Polity Interaction and Socio-Political Change,* ed. A. C. Renfrew and J. F. Cherry, 1–18. Cambridge: University Press.

Renfrew, C. and Bahn, P. 1991. *Archaeology, Theories, Methods and Practice.* London: Thames and Hudson.

Renfrew, Colin. 1987. *Archaeology and Language: The Puzzle of Indo-European Origins.* London: Jonathan Cape.

Rennell, J. 1783. *Memoir of a Map of Hindoostan.*

Richards, F. J. 1930. Periods in Indian History. *Indian Antiquary* 59:33–7, 61–4, 84–7.

1932. Cultural geography of the Wynad. *Indian Antiquary* 61:170–74, 195–97.

1933. Geographic factors in Indian archaeology. *Indian Antiquary* 62:235–43.

Roy, S. R. 1969. The Northern Black polished ware in Bihar. In *Potteries in Ancient India,* ed. B. P. Sinha, 167–73. Patna: Bihar Government Department of Antiquities.

Roy, T. N. 1983. *The Ganges Civilization.* New Delhi: Ramanand Vidya Bhawan.

Ruben, W. 1954. *Geschichte der Indischen Philosophie.* Berlin.

Rydh, H. 1959. *Rang Mahal.* Lund: C. W. K. Gleerup Publishers.

Sahi, M. D. N. 1974. Stratigraphic position of the NBP Ware in the Upper Ganga basin and its date. *Puratattva* 7:91–4.

1977. New light on the Painted Grey Ware People. *Man and Environment* 2:101–3.

Sahni, D. R. 1937. *Archaeological Remains and Excavations at Bairat.* Jaipur: Jaipur State.

1938. *Archaeological Remains and Excavations at Sambhar.* Jaipur: Jaipur State.

Sankalia, H. D., Deo, S. B. and Ansari, Z. 1969. *Excavations at Ahar (Tambavati).* Poona: Deccan College.

1971. *Chalcolithic Navdatoli,* 459 pp. Poona: Deccan College.

Santoni, M. 1984. Sibri and the South Cemetery of Mehrgarh. In *South Asian Archaeology 1981,* ed. B. Allchin, 52–60. Cambridge: Cambridge University Press.

Sarao, K. T. S. 1989. *The Origin and Nature of Ancient Indian Buddhism.* Delhi: Eastern Book Linkers.

1990. *Urban Centres and Urbanisation as Reflected in the Pali Vinaya and Sutta Pitakas.* Delhi: Vidyanidhi.

Sarasin, P. and Sarasin, F. 1908. *Ergebnisse Naturwissenschaftlicher Forschungen auf Ceylon.* Vol. 3–4. *Die Veddas von Ceylon: Die Steinzeit auf Ceylon.* Wiesbaden.

Saraswat, K. S. 1983. Plant economy of ancient Sringaverpur. *Puratattva* 12:79–89.

Sarma, I. K. 1982. *The Development of Early Saiva Art and Architecture (with special reference to Andhradesa).* Delhi.

1985. Early sculptures and epigraphs from south-east India: The evidence of Amaravati. In *Indian Epigraphy, its Bearing on the History of Art,* ed. M. F. Asher and G. S. Gai, 15–24. New Delhi: Oxford and IBH.

Schortman, E. 1989. Interregional interaction in prehistory. *American Antiquity* 54:52–65.

Seneviratne, Sudarshan, 1984. The archaeology of the Megalithic–Black and red ware complex in Sri Lanka. *Ancient Ceylon* 5:237–307.

Service, E. R. 1975. *Origins of the State and Civilisation.* New York: Norton.

Shaffer, J. G. 1978. *Prehistoric Baluchistan: A Systematic Approach.* Delhi: B R Publishing House.

1982. Harappan culture: A reconsideration. In *Harappan Civilisation,* ed. G. L. Possehl, 41–50. Delhi: Oxford and IBH Publishing.

1984. The Indo-Aryan invasions: cultural myth and archaeological reality. In *The People of South Asia,* ed. J. R. Lukacs, 77–90. New York & London: Plenum Press.

1986. Cultural development in the Eastern Punjab. In *Studies in the Archaeology of India and Pakistan,* ed. J. Jacobson, 195–235. New Delhi: Oxford & IBH Publishing Co.

1993. Reurbanisation: the eastern Punjab and beyond. In *Urban Form and Meaning in South Asia: The Shaping of Cities from Prehistoric to Precolonial times,* ed. H. Spodek and D. M. Srinivasan, 53–67. National Gallery of Art Washington. Hanover & London: University Press of New England.

Sharma, G. R. 1960. *The Excavations at Kausambi (1957–59).* Allahabad: Department of Ancient History Culture and Archaeology, University of Allahabad.

1969. *Excavations at Kausambi (1949–50).* Memoirs of the Archaeological Survey of India. Delhi: Manager of Publications.

1973a. Stone Age Vindhyas and the Ganges valley. In *Radiocarbon and Indian Archaeology,* ed. D. P. Agrawal and A. Ghosh, 106–8. Bombay: Tata Institute of Fundamental Research.

1973b. Mesolithic lake cultures of the Ganga valley, India. *Proceedings of the Prehistoric Society,* 39:129–46.

1980. *Beginnings of Agriculture.* Studies in History and Archaeology, 4. Allahabad: Department of Ancient Indian History, University of Allahabad.

Sharma, J. P. 1968. *Republics in Ancient India.* Leiden: E. J. Brill.

Sharma, R. S. 1974. Iron and urbanization in the Ganga Basin. *Indian Historical Review* 1(1).

1981. *Light on Early Indian Economy and Society*. Delhi: Manaktalas.

1983. *Material Culture and Social Formations in Ancient India*. New Delhi: Macmillan.

Sharma, Y. D. 1953. Exploration of historical sites. *Ancient India* 9:118–69.

1982. Harappan complex on the Sutlej (India). In *Harappan Civilization, a Contemporary Perspective*, ed. G. L. Possehl, 141–66. New Delhi: Oxford & IBH Publishing Co.

Shastri, H. 1927. Excavations at Sankisa. *Journal of the U P Historical Society* 3:99–118.

Shennan, S. J. 1978. Archaeological 'cultures': an empirical investigation. In *The Spatial Organisation of Culture*, ed. I. Hodder, 113–41. London: Duckworth.

1989. Archaeological approaches to cultural identity. In *Archaeological Approaches to Cultural Identity*, ed. S. J. Shennan, 1–39. London: Hyman.

Shrimali, K. M. 1983. *History of Pancala to 550 AD*. Delhi: Munshiram Manoharlal.

Silva, R. 1988. Religious architecture in early and medieval Sri Lanka. Ph.D. Diss. (Amsterdam): Krips Repro Meppel.

Singh, P. and Lal, M. 1985. Narhan 1983–85: a preliminary report of archaeological excavations. *Bharati (NS)* 3:113–44.

Singh, S. B. 1981. *Archaeology of the Pancala Region*. Delhi: Agam Kala Prakashan.

Sinha, B. P., ed. 1969. *Potteries in Ancient India*. Patna: Directorate of Archaeology and Museums, Bihar.

1979. *Archaeology and Art of India*. Delhi: Sundeep Prakashan.

Sinha, B. P. and Narain, L. A. 1970. *Pataliputra Excavation: 1955–56*. Patna: Directorate of Archaeology and Museums.

Sinha, B. P. and Roy, S. R. 1969. *Vaisali Excavations (1958–62)*. Patna: Directorate of Archaeology and Museums.

Sinha, K. K. 1966. Sun-symbol on punchmarked coins and terracotta discs. In *Seminar Papers on the Chronology of Punchmarked Coins*, ed. A. K. Narain and L. Gopal, 54–55. Benares: Department of Ancient History, Culture and Archaeology.

1967. *Excavations at Sravasti: 1959*. Varanasi: Benares Hindu University.

1969. The Northern Black Polished Ware – fresh hypotheses in the light of the Sravasti excavations. In *Potteries in Ancient India*, ed. B. P. Sinha, 174–84. Patna: Bihar Government Department of Antiquities.

1973. Stratigraphy and chronology of early Kausambi. In *Radiocarbon and Indian Archaeology*, ed. D. P. Agrawal and A. Ghosh, 231–38. Bombay: Tata Institute of Fundamental Research.

Sircar, D. C. 1965. *Select Inscriptions bearing on Indian History and Civilization*. Calcutta: University of Calcutta.

Smith, R. M. 1957. On the ancient chronology of India (II). *Journal of the American Oriental Society* 77(4):267–80.

1973. *Dates and Dynasties of Early India*. Delhi: Motilal Banarasidass.

Smith, V. A. 1909. *Asoka, the Buddhist Emperor of India*. Oxford: Clarendon Press.

1914 (1904). *The Early History of India*. 3rd edn. Oxford: Clarendon Press.

Spate, O. H. K. 1967 (1954). *India and Pakistan – a Regional Geography*. London: Methuen.

Spellman, J. W. 1964. *Political Theory of Ancient India, A Study of Kingship from the Earliest Times to circa AD 300*. Oxford: Clarendon Press.

Spooner, D. B. 1909. Excavation at Shaji-ki-dheri. *Annual Report of the Archaeological Survey of India 1908–09*:38–59. Calcutta.

　　1913. Mr Ratan Tata's excavations at Pataliputra. In *Annual Report of the Archaeological Survey of India 1912–13*:53–86.

　　1914. Excavations at Basarh. *Annual Report of the Archaeological Survey of India 1913–14*:98–185. Calcutta.

Srinivas, M. N. 1966. *Social Change in Modern India*. Berkeley: University of California Press.

Srivastava, B. 1968. *Trade and Commerce in Ancient India*. Varanasi.

Sterner, J. 1989. Who is signalling whom? Ceramic style, ethnicity and taphonomy among the Sirak Bulahay. *Antiquity* 63, 451–9.

Stuiver, M. and Becker, B. 1986. High-precision decadal calibration of the radiocarbon time-scale. A.D. 1950–2500 B.C. *Radiocarbon* 28, 863–910.

Sukthankar, S. 1915. Selection of literary references to Taxila gleaned from Indian sources. In *Annual Report of the Archaeological Survey of India 1914–15*. Calcutta.

Sundara, A. 1981. Vadgaon-Madhavapur (Belgaum) in Karnataka. In *Madhu Recent researches in Indian Archaeology and Art History*, ed. M. S. Nagaraja Rao, 87–98. Delhi: Agam Kala Prakashan.

Tainter, J. 1978. Mortuary practices and the study of prehistoric social systems. In *Advances in Archaeological Method and Theory*, vol. I, ed. M. Schiffer. London: Academic Press.

Taylor, W. W. 1948. *A Study of Archaeology*. American Anthropological Association Memoir, vol. 24.

Thapar, B. K. *et al.* 1967. Prakash 1955. *Ancient India*. 20–21: 5–167. New Delhi: Archaeological Survey of India.

Thapar, R. 1961. *Asoka and the Decline of the Mauryas*. Oxford: Oxford University Press.

　　1984. *From Lineage to State: Social Formations in the Mid-first Millennium BC in the Ganga Valley*. Delhi: Oxford University Press.

　　1987. The Mauryas revisited. *The S. G. Deuskar Lectures on Indian History, 1984*, 60 pp. Centre for Studies in Social Sciences. Calcutta: K. P. Bagchi.

　　1992. Black gold: South Asia and the Roman maritime trade. *South Asia*. NS. 15. 1–27.

Trautman, T. T. 1971. *Kautilya and the Arthasastra*. Leiden: E. J. Brill.

Vavilov, N. J. 1951. The origin, variation, immunity and breeding of cultivated plants. Trans. K. S. Chester. *Chronica Botanica* 13(1–6). Waltham, Mass.

Verma, V. S. 1970. Excavations at Chirand: new light on the Indian Neolithic culture complex. *Puratattva*, 4, 19–23.

Vishnu-Mittre. 1974. Palaeobotanical evidence from India. In *Evolutionary Studies in World Crops*, ed. J. B. Hutchinson, 3–30. Cambridge: Cambridge University Press.

Vogel, J. P. 1908. Excavations at Saheth-Maheth. *Annual Report of the Archaeological Survey of India 1907–08*:81–131. Calcutta.

Waddell, L. A. 1903. *Report on the Excavations at Pataliputra (Patna)*. Calcutta; Bengal Secretariat Press.

Wagle, N. 1966. *Society at the Time of the Buddha*. Bombay: Popular Prakashan.

Wakankar, V. S. and Brooks, R. R. R. 1976. *Stone Age Painting in India*. New Haven & London: Yale University Press.

Ward, G. K. and Wilson, S. R. 1978. Procedures for comparing radiocarbon age determinations: a critique. *Archaeometry* 20:19–32.

Weber, Max. 1958. *The Religion of India: The Sociology of Hinduism and Buddhism.* ed. and trans. Hans H. Gerth and Don Martindale. New York: Free Press.

Wenke, R. J. 1984. *Patterns in Prehistory.* New York: Oxford University Press.

Wheatley, P. 1971. *The Pivot of the Four Quarters.* Chicago: University of Chicago Press.

Wheeler, R. E. M. 1946. Arikamedu: a Roman trading-station on the east coast of India. *Ancient India* 2:17–124.

　1948. Introduction to Ghosh, A. Sirkap excavations. *Ancient India* 4:84.

　1956. The first towns. *Antiquity* 30.

　1959. *Early India and Pakistan.* London: Thames & Hudson.

　1962. *Charsada, A Metropolis of the North-West Frontier.* Oxford: Oxford University Press.

　1968 (1953). *The Indus Civilization.* Cambridge: Cambridge University Press.

Wiessner, P. 1983. Style and social information in Kalahari San projectile points. *American Antiquity* 48:253–76.

　1989. Archaeological approaches to cultural identity. In *Archaeological Approaches to Cultural Identity,* ed. S. J. Shennan, 1–39. London: Hyman.

Winternitz, M. 1927, 1933 (1909, 1920). *A History of Indian Literature.* Calcutta: University of Calcutta.

Wittfogel, K. A. 1957. *Oriental Despotism: A Comparative Study of Total Power.* New Haven: Yale University Press.

Witzel, M. 1980. Early Eastern Iran and the Atharvaveda. *Persica* 9:81–127.

　1987. On the location of Vedic schools and texts. In *India and the Ancient World,* ed. G. Pollet, 173–213. Leuven: Department Orientalistik.

　1989. Tracing the Vedic dialects. In *Dialectes dans les litteratures Indo-Aryennes,* ed. C. Caillat, 97–265. Paris: Diffusion de Boccard.

　1995. Rgvedic history: poets, chieftains and polities. In *Language, Material Culture and Ethnicity: The Indo-Aryans of Ancient South Asia,* ed. G. Erdosy, 173–213. Berlin: de Gruyter.

Yash Pal *et al.* 1984. Remote sensing of the 'lost' Sarasvati river. In *Frontiers of the Indus Civilisation,* ed. B. B. Lal and S. P. Gupta, 491–97. Delhi: Archaeological Survey of India.

INDEX

Page numbers in *italics* refer to illustrations